STAGES

by *Albert Poland*

with a Foreword by *Michael Riedel*

D0711337

STAGES

For information about this title or to order other books and/or electronic media, contact *Author@STAGESbook.com*

Publisher's Cataloging-In-Publication Data
(Prepared by The Donohue Group, Inc.)

Names: Poland, Albert, author. | Riedel, Michael (Theater critic), writer of supplementary textual content.
Title: Stages : [a theater memoir] / by Albert Poland, with a foreword by Michael Riedel.
Description: [Wappingers Falls, New York] : [Albert Poland], [2019] | Subtitle from cover. | Includes bibliographical references and index.
Identifiers: ISBN 9781733934503 (softcover) | ISBN 9781733934510 (ebook)
Subjects: LCSH: Poland, Albert--Career in theater. | Theatrical producers and directors--New York (State)--New York--Biography. | Theater--New York (State)--New York--History--20th century. | Actors--New York (State)--New York--History--20th century. | LCGFT: Autobiographies.
Classification: LCC PN2287.P5712 A3 2019 (print) | LCC PN2287.P5712 (ebook) | DDC 792.092--dc23

Library of Congress Preassigned Control Number: 2019908890

ISBNs
Softcover: 978-1-7339345-0-3
eBook: 978-1-7339345-1-0

Cover illustration by Paul Silva, Paul Silva Design.

Printed in the United States of America

for good friends here and gone

Contents

Preface

I sat on the tarmac of the Grand Rapids airport. I was about to embark on my first plane ride—to New York—where I hoped to have a career in show business. On the observation deck, I saw my mother and father and my younger brother. Through the warped plane window, they looked like a faded kinescope, devoid of color, the essential image of this sea change in my 19-year-old life.

Reflecting on the moment, my thoughts went to the person who first let me know such journeys were possible, without even telling me. She was once and forever the heart and soul of show business, and, because I loved her so much, she was at the center of my first-ever venture into that magical world.

Her name was Judy Garland.

Foreword

By Michael Riedel

*L*ike many people in the theater, I owe Albert Poland a huge debt of gratitude. In 2011, I landed a contract with Simon & Schuster to write a book about Broadway and its most powerful player—the Shubert Organization—in the 1960s, '70s, and '80s. After the glow of getting a book deal wore off, I panicked. I'd never written anything longer than a thousand-word column for the *New York Post*. Now I had to write a book. That would require more than a thousand words.

I called a friend who'd written fifteen books and asked him for advice. "Calm down," he said. "Take your time. Don't even think about writing. Do the research, interview everybody you can, and then you'll find your story. And remember—you're only as good as your sources."

I took a deep breath and called Albert. I hope he won't mind my writing this, but he'd been around for a while—a "veteran producer," as we say in the newspapers—and he knew his way around the theater business. He also had been close to Bernard B. Jacobs and Gerald Schoenfeld, the lawyers who saved the Shuberts from bankruptcy in the '70s and helped turn Broadway into the multibillion-dollar empire it is today.

I went up to Dutchess County and met Albert at his elegant French manor country house. We were only ninety minutes from Manhattan, but it felt so much like Normandy I could practically smell the escargot. We settled down on the sun porch, sipped cranberry juice, and began to talk. Within ten minutes, I knew I could write my book. If you're only as good as your sources, I had found one hell of a source. Albert told hilarious stories—and he did so with flair. He also had insight into the key people who would become my cast of characters.

I left Dutchess County eager to "do the research, interview everybody . . . and find my story." My chat with Albert gave me the confidence to tackle a book. If *Razzle Dazzle: The Battle for Broadway* is any good, it's because of sources like Albert.

I spent about three hours with him that afternoon. The joy of reading *Stages* is that you get to spend a lot more time with him. He is a delightful companion. He's a terrific writer because he instinctively understands that good writing is like having a chat with someone fun and interesting. Albert invites you to pull up a chair and listen to tales of larger-than-life theatrical characters, many long gone but brought back to life in these pages.

Ever heard of Helen Menken? Probably not, but Albert's depiction of her will send you to Google to find out more about this "faded but moneyed grand dame" of the theater, as Albert calls her.

"Put down your luggage and make an entrance, darling," Menken tells young Albert, who's just gotten off the plane from Grand Rapids to audition for the American Theater Wing School.

"Project, darling," she adds. "Project, dear. We can't hear you."

After the audition, Menken tells Albert, "It's a tough business, darling. But it can be good to you."

Thus begins Albert's rollicking ride through the American theater.

Albert is there for the beginnings of Off Off Broadway in Greenwich Village. You need a movie star's income to live in the

Village today. But Albert evokes a neighborhood of struggling actors, writers, musicians, and painters who hang out at the San Remo Cafe (gone) and talk about Lotte Lenya and Kurt Weill or the latest play at La MaMa.

He meets Sam Shepard: "He was wearing Levis and no shirt. He looked like an American god. Sensing I was a little tense, he put a soft black leather vest on over his skin. I transitioned from not being able to breathe to mild hyperventilation."

And, while only in his twenties, Albert becomes the producer of a touring company of *The Fantasticks,* Tom Jones and Harvey Schmidt's long-running Off Broadway musical. Every aspiring producer should read Albert's chronicle of that tour. They will learn that, to make it in this rough-and-tumble (and often absurd) business, you'd better have chutzpah. Albert did, and his outwitting of the powerful musicians' union is David Merrick-like in its cunning and hilarity.

At the height of the battle, Albert met Schoenfeld and Jacobs, then toiling in relative obscurity as lawyers for the mothballed Shubert Organization. They staged a boardroom coup in 1972 and would eventually rise to the top of the American theater. Albert had a ringside seat at the Shubert circus, and he became one of Bernie and Jerry's closest confidants. Back then Albert, always one for the grand theatrical gesture, took to wearing a cape. Schoenfeld called him "David Belasco."

They didn't always see eye to eye, however. Bernie and Jerry were fighting for their turf—Broadway. Albert's heart was with Off Broadway. In the '70s he produced or general managed such seminal—and sometimes controversial—shows as *Futz, Peace, The Unseen Hand*, and *The Dirtiest Show in Town*.

Some are probably dated now, but back then, as the country was being torn apart by the Vietnam War, they had so much potency they'd leave mainstream critics such as Walter Kerr foaming at the mouth. Albert's chapters on these shows remind us of how vital, in a time of social upheaval, theater can be.

From their perch in their offices above the Shubert Theater, Bernie and Jerry looked down at Off Broadway with disdain.

"How are things in the sewer?" Jerry once asked Albert, a remark that infuriated the young producer.

Eventually, Albert would lure Bernie and Jerry into " the sewer." He did so with a musical by Alan Menken and Howard Ashman called *Little Shop of Horrors*. Albert helped broker a deal that made the Shuberts co-producers of the show with Cameron Mackintosh, another one of Albert's friends who has some delicious cameos in this book. When *Little Shop* became a big hit at the Orpheum Theater in 1982, the Shuberts started calling it "our little slot machine."

When they wanted to raise ticket prices, Albert fought back, fearing high prices would drive Off Broadway theatergoers away. He lost the battle, but his objection to higher prices resonates today. Tickets to *Hamilton* are $800, which means that, on any given night, the theater is full of kids with trust funds. Broadway, like so much of New York City, is increasingly for the one percent.

The theater Albert was most passionate about was for everyone.

Albert brought that passion to Broadway, producing or general managing such acclaimed plays as *The Grapes of Wrath*, *The Song of Jacob Zulu*, *The Last Night of Ballyhoo*, and *Dirty Blonde*.

But he's no snob and enjoys a bit of fluff such as *The Boy from Oz,* starring Hugh Jackman. That show was the only time there was ever a rift between Albert and myself. He tells the story in these pages, and I have no quarrel with the way it unfolds. I didn't care for the show and, trying a bit too hard to be a contrarian, made fun of the hype surrounding Jackman's performance as Peter Allen. Albert was having none of it, chastising me for failing to appreciate Jackman' s remarkable talents.

Judging from the way things have turned out for Hugh, I think Albert may have had a point.

As much fun as *Stages* is, there's some sadness here, too. Albert did not have an easy relationship with his father, coming to any understanding (of sorts) with him only toward the end of his father's life. And Albert does not shy away from his battle with alcohol, which he overcame three decades ago after some harrowing nights described in *Stages*.

Most poignant of all, though, is his decision to leave a world he loved so much. Theater in New York, especially Broadway, has changed in profound ways since Albert auditioned for Helen Menken back in 1960. Most of the experimental theaters that dotted the Village are long gone, replaced by high-end restaurants or wine bars where a glass of sauvignon blanc costs twenty dollars.

Production costs have skyrocketed. Where once it took a handful of people to produce a show, it now takes a committee of heiresses—or a corporation such as Disney. Hours are spent deciding what color the poster should be. I know of one instance where a rich lady investor insisted the color should be powder blue so it would match the shoes she was planning to wear on opening night.

Producers from Albert's era have no patience for such nonsense.

Audiences have changed, too. Albert worked in a theater that attracted New Yorkers with an appetite for vigorous, provocative plays. Today more than 65 percent of the Broadway audience is from out of town. Most want to see something that goes down easy with the wine in their sippy cups.

While Albert does not say so in this book, I suspect someone who worked on *As Is, Modigliani*, and *Orphans* just can't get all that excited about *Anastasia, Charlie and the Chocolate Factory*, or *Frozen*.

The columnist Hedda Hopper always said, "Never be the last one to leave the party."

Albert followed her advice. He's living, quite happily, in that French manor house in Dutchess County, where he wrote *Stages*. It evokes an exciting time in the American theater, reminding us of how much we had—and how much we've lost.

STAGES

CHAPTER 1

Stop the Midwest, I Want to Get Off

A well-known Hoosier author once wrote that those of us who grew up in Indiana in the 1950s felt like we were being suffocated by someone holding a pillow over our faces.

It was the pillow of conservatism.

Indiana at that time was under the sway of McCarthyism, and my parents were conservative Republicans. Daddy was a college professor, a self-made man who had been raised in a poor family of thirteen in Fairland, Indiana. Both my parents had gone through the Great Depression, and it had left them fear-ridden.

Almost from babyhood, they were obsessed with raising me in what they believed was the ideal mold for American sons. At the top of the list were playing sports and spending hours each day "building a body." Otherwise, as my father lectured me every night at dinner, "You're going to be a weakling and die before you're thirty."

My DNA had something quite different in mind. I played with dolls.

Until I was five.

I was running across the backyard when my mother approached me and pulled them from my hands.

"You're almost six now," she said, "and six-year-old boys don't play with dolls."

I felt a deep sense of despair. *There must be something wrong with me.*

In search of companionship, I began going around the neighborhood, visiting with the older ladies who were home while their husbands were at work. I would knock at the door and say, "Do you have time to chat?" We would talk, and they would give me toast or a piece of chocolate. By the time I was seven, the visits had evolved into performances of little magic shows.

An attempt to direct my friends in a play was a fiasco. We rehearsed in an alley. I couldn't control them, and cars kept driving through the rehearsal. I turned to marionettes, putting on shows in the basement, at school, and in children's polio wards. I got supporting roles in plays at the Indianapolis Civic Theatre, and my fourth-grade teacher gave me an hour every Friday to put on shows during class time.

My frequent collaborators on the puppets and school shows were my two friends Dennis Leibowitz and Victor Rosenbaum. I had other friends, but Denny and Victor were a much-needed lifeline to things that were real and meaningful.

Denny and I were best friends and competitors and thus spurred each other on to be better than we would have been. He started a newspaper in his block, I started a small radio station in mine. We campaigned together for Adlai Stevenson in 1952.

Victor, playing his own compositions for student assemblies at the age of eight, was a classicist to be sure, but he saw the world through the lens of show business, and it was from him that I got a rich sense of what show business was—it was vaudeville, it was the great early television comedians, it was rich Jewish humor, and it was getting a bad break and making it into a song.

When the Civic Theatre offered me the leading role of Hans Brinker in *Hans Brinker and the Silver Skates*, my parents refused to allow me to do it. Instead, my father suggested I play basketball in the court he had built for me in the backyard.

My father did teach me honesty. And by saying "No" to every request I made, he taught me how to negotiate. After several hours of making my case in every possible way, his "No" often became a "Yes." When I was a grown man, he was to tell me that he loved that process with me. As a child, I just viewed him as an enemy that had to be dealt with.

More and more, I retreated into the world of show business. I lived in the movie magazines. I watched the great entertainers who had migrated from vaudeville to television: Milton Berle, Bob Hope, Sophie Tucker, Jack Benny, George Burns and Gracie Allen, Eddie Cantor, Jimmy Durante. I marveled at the enormous "heart" of the entertainment industry and identified with what I perceived as the need of these performers to be loved. The for-the-people style they had evolved in vaudeville was perfect for our living rooms and gave television its first golden age.

Sometime in 1953, I began reading about Judy Garland and the excitement about her return to the screen in *A Star Is Born*. She, too, had begun in vaudeville, and the tumultuous events of her life and career reached out to me in a way that was compelling. As the October 1954 engagement of *A Star Is Born* at the Indiana Theatre drew near, I campaigned for it to be the first movie I could see by myself. It was a long bus ride from our house near Butler University, but I was determined and won my parents' consent.

The day finally came. Almost prophetically, I arrived in the middle of "Someone at Last" and was instantly captivated by the seeming spontaneity of the gamine figure cavorting across the enormous CinemaScope screen. As the picture went on, I was mesmerized by the sheer vocal power of one so vulnerable and then electrified when those two qualities came together in "The Man That Got Away." I sat through the picture two and a half times, and, since it was the uncut version, that came to about eight hours, during which time I was transformed.

I felt more love for Judy than I had ever felt for anyone. I thought she was the most talented person I had ever seen, and I thought she needed my help.

As I left the theater, I rushed to the newsstand next door and bought my first copy of *Variety*. The show-business bible was now in my own thirteen-year-old hands. Everything I wanted seemed within reach.

When I got home, my parents had called the police.

But it was too late.

I had escaped.

CHAPTER 2

Judy

*L*ife changed.

Judy dominated my thoughts twenty-four hours a day. I was energized. Her talent had awakened my passion. And I wanted to convert the world.

I searched for a fan club to join and was amazed to find there were none. I now had a mission. I would start one myself.

I sent away for a book about fan clubbing. I had always thought of fan clubs as bobby soxers traveling in swarms and screaming. But the serious ones were strong, political organizations that wielded powerful support for their star. The clubs held contests to see who could write the most letters to the movie magazines.

I was up for all of it. But there was an obstacle. The movie magazines wouldn't print the club address unless a letter from the star was provided indicating that the club was "official." Every letter I sent to Judy was returned or went unanswered.

After three months of existence, we had only three members. The club faced its first crisis. I called a summit at my house with the other two members on December 31, 1955. We were about to give up the ghost when one of them suggested we call her on the phone. My parents weren't home. The timing was perfect.

Excited—and terrified beyond measure—I typed up a script and we got the operator on the line. A long-distance call in 1955 was an event. A family might have one or two a year.

When we told the operator we wanted to call Judy Garland, she was as excited as we were. And not having a phone number wouldn't stop us. I had a list of places in Hollywood I thought might have it, and she was willing to try them all. After trying Ciro's, Romanoff's, and The Brown Derby, we got the phone number from Warner Bros., and soon it was ringing. I wrote "HELP" on the now-moist script and waved it in the air. A woman answered and the operator announced the call. "Just a moment, please."

And a low musical voice said, "Hello."

"Miss Garland, my name is Al Poland, and I'm the president of a fan club for you."

"A fan club for me? How wonderful!"

"Oh, Judy, I love you so much!" I said as the script fell to the floor.

I told her I wanted a career in show business and that she was my inspiration. I told her we needed a letter from her giving us permission so the movie magazines would list us. She immediately asked me for my address. *My God*, I thought, *Judy Garland asked me for my address*.

"And, may I have yours?"

We chatted for a few more minutes, and I started to say, "Goodbye."

"Oh, and Al," she said, "I want to wish you a Happy New Year."

"Oh, Happy New Year to you, Judy!"

The entire membership of the Judy Garland Fan Club hugged each other and jumped up and down.

Looking back, it felt as if someone had taken my hand and pulled me into the world I had been creating—a world in which I would come to know and work with the people I thought were the best and most talented. I was fourteen, and this was my entry into show business.

I sent Judy a long letter and our first *Garland Gazette*. Two weeks later, her letter arrived, and the magazines began publishing our address. In no time, I was getting thirty letters a day, and I enlisted two neighbor girls to help answer them. Soon our membership was several hundred, and we even had a British chapter that exists to this day.

The club was rapidly becoming a force in the fan-club world. It was an awakening for me and gave my life purpose and, in my eyes, importance. But by the end of the first year, I realized that several thousand members and sixty letters a day were beyond what a high school sophomore could handle.

Our star member was Pat McMath, a woman who had tried to start a club for Judy in 1949 but was turned down by Judy's management who felt her "hold on the public" at that time was such that one was not needed. I proposed to Pat that she take over the club. I don't think it would be an exaggeration to say that, on her watch, it became the biggest and best of all the American fan clubs.

In the spring of 1957, months after my family moved from Indianapolis to a small Michigan town called Big Rapids, the *Detroit Free Press* announced that "the Nederlanders" were bringing Judy to the Riviera Theatre. I thought, *Why are prehistoric men bringing Judy to Detroit?* Actually, they are a distinguished family who own theaters on Broadway and across the United States.

Pat McMath was organizing a convention for the engagement. What an opportunity. We would see three performances and have at least one backstage visit. I told my mother to make me a special shirt, "something people would wear in Hollywood." She came up with a lime-green fabric imprinted with black jungle vines.

We sat in a block of seats reserved for the fan club members. The three thousand-seat Riviera was packed to the rafters. There were older people, who had grown up with her in the movies and on the radio, and young people like me, who had fallen in love with her in *A Star Is Born*. The anticipation was electric. The first half featured Sid Krofft and his marionettes, the Amin Brothers acrobats, the fabulous dancing Szonys, and closed with the comedian Alan King.

The overture began, and soon "Judy's Eight Boy Friends" were doing their routine, which used placards with the letters in her name to spell out words describing her. Suddenly, Judy materialized behind the boys in a black dress and a glittering, long black-sequined coat. Amid our rousing welcome, she launched into "We're Having a Party."

She was transcendent. Her voice was astonishing. The overtone, the richness, the sheer power whenever she wanted it. That was the first thing that just knocked me out. Solid tone whether at pianissimo or full fortissimo. It was perfection, exceeding her best vocal work on recordings. As for her performance itself—she took us into "WOW" territory, and we stayed there, ending with her classic rendition of "Over the Rainbow," in tramp costume, feet dangling into the orchestra pit—and no mic, her dreamy legato effortlessly filling the hall.

We were shown backstage and immediately encountered an inebriated but very welcoming Sid Luft, who took us to her dressing room. He opened the door, and there was Judy, still in her fright wig. She chatted with us as she scraped the black off her teeth and drank Gilby's gin accompanied by a Miller High Life chaser.

She was wonderfully warm and good-humored. I had the good taste to present her with a bootleg of her soundtrack of *Annie Get Your Gun*. Looking back, I can't imagine what I was thinking. But Judy looked at it and said, "Oh! *Annie Get Your Gun*. I wasn't 'available' for that picture." And, with a raised eyebrow, "Available? I was fired!"

I told her how magnificently she was singing, and she said, "Did you hear 'Come Rain or Come Shine?' That was no goddam good." She had somehow come in on the wrong last note but she smiled through it like a good vaudevillian.

Just at that moment, Alan King stuck his head in the door, and Judy introduced us as her club members. He took a liking to us and would try to find us in the audience and play to us.

She signed our programs, and we asked about having a picture with her. At first, she said yes, but then she said, "Why don't we do it tomorrow before the matinee when I'm all purty?" We were delighted with that.

We were seeing show business glamour at its pinnacle. At lunch on Saturday, we got a little taste of the darker side. Sitting in an enormous circular booth at a restaurant near the theater, we overheard two men talking intensely in the booth next to us. "Sid Luft hasn't paid us in four weeks, and I'm goddam sick of it," one of them said. We turned discreetly and discovered Sid Krofft and his brother Marty.

We posted ourselves at the stage door an hour before the matinee. Judy was taking singing lessons at the time from Gene Byram, New York's top voice teacher, and he was traveling with her. He spoke of the greatness of her instrument and said she could have done grand opera. He loved hanging out at the stage door and chatting with us.

In the meantime, we waited and waited, and there was no Judy. The show began. The vaudeville acts. Alan King. Intermission. Still no Judy.

Alan King joined us outside, chain smoking and pacing. I realized that if an announcement had to be made, it would be by him. We told Alan that Judy had promised we could have a photo with her.

In a flash, the limo pulled up. Judy got out, signed a couple of autographs, said, "I've got to do my show" and rushed in. We were crestfallen that now maybe our photo wasn't going to happen.

Alan King followed her in, then returned, grabbed us, and said, "Come on, we'll get you your picture."

We could hear the overture as Judy emerged from her dressing room in her black dress and long sequined coat. She saw all of us and said, "Oh yes, let's do your picture." There was no one around to take it. As the orchestra launched into "The Man That Got Away," Judy yelled out, "Sid, you take it!"

In high school in Big Rapids, I had an active social life, wrote a gossip column for the school paper, and had my own radio show. I sang in the band shows and acted in the school plays, eager for every taste of show business I could get.

That was how things looked on the outside. On the inside, I was struggling with my desires for several of my handsome male friends, a daunting prospect that energized me but that I didn't dare pursue. Instead, I took that energy and sublimated it into all my activities.

To appease my parents, who were certain I'd fail at my chosen profession, I agreed to go to Western Michigan University to prepare for "something to fall back on."

Once there, my classes quickly became an intrusion on the time I spent rehearsing and performing in four shows in my freshman year. During the last one, I became best friends with my director, Anthony Tunick. We took to wearing each other's clothes, and people even said we had begun to talk alike.

After the closing performance, Anthony and I stayed up all night in my dorm talking about how we wanted to break out and go where we could just do shows. By the time the sun rose, we were hell-bent for New York. I called my father to tell him. "This is the damnedest thing you've done since you called Judy Garland long distance!" he bellowed. That little call, which cost $8.13, had become the family measuring stick for outrage. As a face-saving measure for the family, I agreed to finish out the semester at Western and enroll in the fall semester at the American Theatre Wing School in New York to at least maintain the appearance of continuing a formal education.

That summer, Anthony married his girlfriend Mary, and they flew to New York to begin their new life. I was in Big Rapids doing a season of summer stock with actors from the Goodman Theatre in Chicago. I had joined up as an apprentice but was shortly cast in major roles: Jules in *My Three Angels*, Desmonde in *The Happy Time*, and Teddy Brewster in *Arsenic and Old Lace*.

The summer primed me for my coming journey. It amazed me that, with all their training and experience, none of the Goodman actors planned to take their talents to New York, the only place I thought counted.

CHAPTER 3

"Make an Entrance"

As the muttering and cursing cab driver brought me closer and closer to the smoggy New York skyline, my childhood dream of the surging choruses of *Manhattan Tower* was overwhelmed by the powerful reality, the absoluteness, of the city itself. In no time, we were at the American Theatre Wing School on West Ninety-Third Street, where I was to have my audition for Helen Menken, the chairman of the board.

Miss Menken had starred in *Seventh Heaven* on Broadway in 1922, was once married to Humphrey Bogart, and had great wealth that she used beneficently. She was of a type the theater inevitably cast in a figurehead role: the faded but moneyed grande dame.

My name was called right away. Fearing my suitcase might be stolen, I carried it onstage. Miss Menken and her assistant rolled their eyes. I tried to smile. Miss Menken was an elderly but commanding figure who wore a wig that appeared to be spun out of pure gold. In the center was a large black bow.

"Put down your luggage and make an entrance, darling," Miss Menken said. She sounded like Tallulah Bankhead.

She indicated a door in a frame at center stage. "Come through the door," she said. "Close it and begin your monologue. Start with your Shakespeare."

I came through the door, which slammed unpoetically as I began my classical monologue.

"If music be the food of love—"

"Project, darling," Miss Menken interrupted. "Project, dear." I had no idea what this meant. So, I just stopped. "Go ahead, dear. Project."

Oh, I thought, *maybe my fly is open.* I looked down at it. "No, no, dear. Not that. We're not getting your words." They were totally exasperated. *This isn't going well,* I thought.

For my contemporary monologue, I launched into Teddy Brewster, which I had just performed successfully in stock. Miss Menken laughed.

I finished and felt a sudden surge of confidence as Miss Menken rose and came toward the stage. She took me in her gaze for a moment and then spoke to me in a very personal way. "It's a tough business, darling," she said. "But it can be good to you." The simplest, best words I have ever heard about it.

Feeling my first moment of comfort, I confided that I had no place to stay and wondered if the school had a list of recommended accommodations. "Go to the Y," her assistant twinkled. "The West Side YMCA on Sixty-Third Street."

The thrill of my first subway ride was another assurance that, yes, I was really in New York. I got off at Sixty-Sixth Street, and, after a short walk, I arrived in the lobby of the West Side YMCA. It was a revelation.

All of the fears I had felt these many years, the strong conviction that I might be alone in the world, the only one, were wiped away in an instant by a new and more immediate terror. Six or seven young men, handsome and otherwise, were coming at me from all sides like dive bombers. There was no denying their interest or intent. I had never experienced anything like it.

I got my key and ran to my room. I shut the door on this dangerous new world and didn't come out for twenty-four hours.

CHAPTER 4

Discovery

The next day, I called Anthony and Mary and raced to their apartment on West Sixty-Eighth Street. My heart pounded. We were seconds away from our first moment together in New York. The scene that greeted me did not match my expectations. There was a feeling of crisis in the air.

It was mid-afternoon, and Anthony was in his bathrobe. He had lost a lot of weight and had broken out in boils. He looked withdrawn and depressed. After a moment of stunned silence, Mary grabbed me and said, "Let's go to the grocery."

We were barely out the door when she held my arm tightly and began to cry. Anthony had shut her out. He wouldn't talk to her, couldn't even look at her. "And," she confided, "the marriage has never been consummated." Despite what I was seeing and hearing, I didn't grasp the severity. I figured they had just had a quarrel and she was exaggerating.

Anthony was energized by my arrival, and we convinced him to go for some dinner. We jumped on the subway and went to Greenwich Village. I loved it instantly. Walking down MacDougal Street, we came to a spot with a very special glow, the San Remo bar and restaurant with a sidewalk cafe on the corner of Bleecker. Tom

Ziegler, the owner of the Cafe Figaro across the street, introduced himself and joined us. It was a real Village welcome. The next night, we went to our first Broadway show: Ethel Merman in *Gypsy*. The inviting warmth of the lights as we made our way down Broadway to Forty-Fifth Street was magical.

Having grown up with the vast Broadway stages of the movies, I was amazed at how small the Imperial Theatre really was and how close we were to the great Merman, who walked through her performance and at times seemed to be counting the house. But Merman was Merman. Her cutting-edge savvy and that voice filling a Broadway theater were worth the ticket price.

Anthony was coming back to life, and Mary assured me it was all because of me. He began looking at her and talking to her, and, as I seemed to be the catalyst, they asked me to move in, which I did. Then things took a very bad turn. We had an evening at the San Remo, and Tom Ziegler joined us as he now regularly did. As we left, Mary was upset. While Anthony and I were in an intense conversation, Ziegler had made a pass at her. And further, he told her Anthony and I were two homosexuals who were very much in love with each other.

I wanted to go across the street and punch him out, but the damage was done. Tom Ziegler had articulated an emerging truth that was about to overtake us. Within days, Mary packed up and went home to Tennessee. In a moment that will haunt me forever, she looked down at me in my bed that October morning and said, "I don't know why I'm leaving and you get to stay."

That night, I told Anthony I was a homosexual. The next night he responded by reading me some poems by Walt Whitman and, trembling, we began a tumultuous two-year relationship in which all the good qualities we had together were decimated by our own homophobia and our conflicts of conscience.

Once again, my outside life provided an escape hatch from life at home. Starting school at the Wing was a relief, and I threw myself into my classes. There was a full musical theater curriculum. The standout among the teachers was Phoebe Brand of the Group Theatre. She taught Shakespeare and was the wife of Morris Carnovsky.

Among my new friends, the most special was Gilbert Price. Whenever he performed, whether it was "Lost in the Stars" or a soliloquy under the direction of Miss Brand, we leaned forward in anticipation of something exciting and unique. In addition to his unassuming physical charisma, he had imagination, brilliant instincts, and a voice like Paul Robeson.

At nighttime our little group ran to coffee houses and piano bars all over Manhattan, anyplace where we could get up and sing. The Cafe Wha? on MacDougal was a favorite spot, though it had no piano. And we sang and danced, improvised and playacted, in each other's apartments. These were our salad days. Life in Manhattan was simple, and at that time, we could live it to the hilt with very little money.

The Wing arranged passes to the top Broadway shows. We saw Tammy Grimes in *The Unsinkable Molly Brown*, Angela Lansbury and Joan Plowright in *A Taste of Honey*, and Carol Channing in *Show Girl*, among many others. We felt inspired and welcomed by these great theater artists.

The highlight of the school year came on April 16, 1961, when we sat in boxes at the Waldorf Astoria for the American Theatre Wing Tony Awards. We watched as Miss Menken made the traditional Theatre Wing speech in a manner which the *Journal-American* critic described as "Medea playing Hamlet."

The room was full of glittering stars, but I wanted to meet Freddie Fields, the agent who had resurrected Judy Garland's career. I didn't know what he looked like, so I approached his client Phil Silvers to ask if he would introduce me. I wanted to thank Mr. Fields and tell him how excited I was to be going to her Carnegie Hall concert, which was only a week away. Fields was surprised to be sought out and was very gracious.

I saw Judy many times, but her Carnegie Hall performance remains, to this day, the most exciting night I have spent in a theater. Anthony and I watched as Richard Burton, Julie Andrews, Rock Hudson, Tammy Grimes, Anthony Perkins, Henry Fonda, Ethel Merman, Harold Arlen, Hedda Hopper, Louella Parsons, and others trooped down the aisles. Then came the spectacular overture, followed by Judy singing as she hadn't in years. Before the performance, some of the fan club members had told me, "Usually everybody runs down the aisle at the end, but that will never happen in staid Carnegie Hall." But it did. It has rightfully been called "the greatest night in show business history."

Following my year at the Wing, Anthony and I did a season of non-Equity summer stock in Beach Haven, New Jersey, for room and board and five dollars a week. We were young enough that it was great fun, until we had a fight and Anthony left in the middle of the season.

I did sporadic "club dates" with a group called the Winged Victory Chorus. We were promoted as veterans of the Korean War. Most of us, of course, had been disqualified for military service. My touring bookings with the Winged Victory Chorus brought things to a head with Anthony. He gave me an ultimatum. If I went out of town again, he would leave me, which, since I had become the sole breadwinner, made things very difficult.

When I got an early morning phone call from Winged Victory with an offer to play two weeks in Buffalo, after which I would be guaranteed six months at the Latin Quarter in New York, I asked them to give me fifteen minutes. I looked at Anthony asleep in his bed, called back, and said yes. I could count on my ability to do a day's work but count on him to be there? Never.

While we were in Buffalo, the leader said something I thought was insulting. I lipped-off at him and walked out of rehearsal. The phone in my room rang and rang and rang, and I would not answer. When I returned to the city, Anthony was gone, and so was my gig at the Latin Quarter. But I had made a life decision. I would ever after put my professional life first.

A new friend, Richard Lamparski, who would later do the series of *Whatever Became Of?* books and broadcasts, became a kind of mentor to me. He brought me into the world of Mabel Mercer, Max's Kansas City, the films of W.C. Fields, and the works of Noel Coward and Ruth Draper, revealing to me that being *gay*, as we now called it, was more than just a desire for sexual companionship with other men. It brought with it the privileges of a sublime sensibility.

That summer, I got an apprentice job in stock at the Sacandaga Summer Garden Theatre in Northville, New York, that would bring me my Equity card. After seeing my dancing in the opening production of *West Side Story*, I was offered the position of assistant press agent. Two weeks later, they fired the man I was working for and put me in full charge of the press. I found that I loved it, and I got my Equity card. *Variety* ran a squib, "Can He Act the Part?"

I took acting classes with Wynn Handman and Bob McAndrew, frequently getting applause from my fellow actors, who included Christopher Walken and Raul Julia. Wynn several times even called me a "comic genius."

So, I was not without talent, but I wasn't a professional. I went to auditions with an attitude—certain that the people on the other side were hostile or incompetent, and I generally auditioned badly, failing to find the spark I had in class.

In the fall, I was cast as an understudy on a bus-and-truck tour of *The Sound of Music* starring Jeannie Carson. We played one hundred cities in nine months. I was young enough to find adventure even in cities like Lima and Scranton.

In Houston, I called the Alley Theatre to ask if I could attend a rehearsal of *The Taming of the Shrew*. I went with a fellow cast member, and we were both astonished by the performance of Max Jacobs, the young actor playing Lucentio. In addition to his fine acting talent, he had handsome chiseled features and curly silvery-blond hair.

After the rehearsal, we rushed to meet him, and he immediately invited us to dinner, where we encountered his equally enchanting wife, Helen, she of gorgeous red hair and Hepburn-like cheekbones. The couple were newly married, and Helen supported his acting life as though it were a great adventure. They drove around in a Volkswagen camper, which Max described as "a Volkswagen with a swish!"

We were with them every night for the two weeks we were in Houston. Max loved Lenny Bruce and Jonathan Winters, and he eagerly played all of their recordings for us at least twice. We became real friends. I was sorry they didn't live in New York.

By the spring of 1964, Manhattan was in its last gasp as a newspaper and nightlife town, and Barbra Streisand, starring as Fanny Brice in *Funny Girl*, was giving the old Broadway glamour a nightcap. She was a transitional figure, perfect for that moment—a fusion of the old and the new, and her presence could be felt everywhere. In the columns of Dorothy Kilgallen, Earl Wilson, Winchell, Ed Sullivan, Leonard Lyons, Cindy Adams, and in the nightlife of Sardi's, El Morocco, 21, Toots Shor, the Stork Club, Lindy's, the Latin Quarter, the Copacabana, Arthur, the Peppermint Lounge—many of which were about to end their long runs as New York classics.

Sally Cooke, a voluptuous blonde Viking with whom I had become friends on *The Sound of Music* tour, was the mistress of the well-known concert impresario Felix Gerstman. She could turn on the flash with class, and on his opening nights, she stopped traffic in front of the concert halls. Felix was a distinguished-looking Viennese gentleman of about seventy and was second only to Sol Hurok as a presenter of top classical artists in New York. He had a raspy voice that seemed to emanate from his throat rubbing against his soft palate. He thought Sally and I were amusing together and loved taking the two of us out on the town.

Over lunch at Lindy's, Felix told us a hair-raising tale. Sammy Davis Jr. was currently starring on Broadway in *Golden Boy*, and on Sunday nights, Felix had booked him for a series of out-of-town concerts. The next was only days away in Detroit. Davis had just told Felix that there was a mob hit out on him there and if he played the date, Detroit would be his last gig.

"Tonight, there will be an accident at *Golden Boy* and Sammy will cancel," Felix said as we choked on our strudel. Sure enough, the front page of the next day's *Post* carried a photo and story of Davis being hit in the face with a chain on the stage of the Majestic.

Felix asked Sally and me to appear in a concert at Carnegie Hall with the legendary Lotte Lenya in January of 1965. The first half of the evening was to be Lenya solo with orchestra, and the second half a condensed concert version of *Die Dreigroschenoper* (*The Threepenny Opera*). Lenya was the widow of its composer, Kurt Weill.

I was to sing a duet of the "Kanonen Song" in German. Felix spent the better part of a Saturday afternoon coaching me in it, pounding out the notes on an old upright piano in his office and singing it to me in his inimitable rasp.

Threepenny was already my favorite musical, and I was completely riveted by Lenya during the week of rehearsal. The performance, before a sold-out house, was a triumph. Felix let me stand in the back for Lenya's solo turn, and I savored every moment, especially the songs from *Love Life*, an unsuccessful Broadway musical by Alan Jay Lerner and Kurt Weill. I visited her dressing room afterward to thank her, and she inscribed the deluxe Columbia box set of *Die Dreigroschenoper* to me.

The following Monday I was back at my temp job, typing names and addresses in an industrial-strength green, windowless office in the Garment District. Finally, I couldn't keep it inside any longer. I had to tell my story to the three matrons who were working with me in the airless room.

"I want to tell you about show business," I said. "On Saturday night I sang on the stage of Carnegie Hall with Lotte Lenya, and today I am here typing names and addresses." There was a stony silence.

The head matron looked at the others and said, "Send the temp fuh kawffee."

CHAPTER 5

Candy, Gum, and Destiny

*O*nly months after we met, Max and Helen Jacobs moved from Houston to New York. Max brought his remarkable talents to my acting class, and a life-changing friendship began.

While he looked for acting jobs, Max was working for his father, Louis M. Jacobs, and he invited me to join him. I had just landed a job at the Thompkins Square branch of the New York Public Library at $62.50 a week, and Max and his father were offering $125. From where I stood, that was a 100-percent increase.

L. M. Jacobs was among the poor Jewish immigrants whose families came to this country with nothing, shortly after the turn of the century, and who, remarkably, were to found major American industries, many of which had never before existed. Louis B. Mayer was one, and Mr Jacobs was another.

Years later I asked his widow, Genevieve Jacobs, what gave these men their drive. Without a moment's hesitation, she replied, "Their mothers. They told them they were going to be bums. It scared the hell out of them."

Soon after the family arrived on our shores, Mr. Jacobs lost a sister he cherished very deeply to tuberculosis, and it is felt that he submerged the pain of this loss into his unrelenting need to succeed in his new country. The family moved from New York to Buffalo, where his father found employment as a tailor.

At the age of fourteen, Louis M. Jacobs convinced a local banker that his customers would be made happy if they were offered the opportunity to buy a bag of peanuts as part of their morning banking. When the peanuts caught on, he added the option of a shoeshine. He began by doing this himself and then recruited his brothers and friends; in a short time, he had an exclusive franchise with all of the banks in Buffalo.

By the time I encountered Mr. Jacobs, he was nearing sixty-five, and his company owned eight hundred different operations in the United States, including the Cincinnati Gardens and the Cincinnati Royals, as well as racetracks, stadiums, and the food and beverage concessions at numerous arenas and airports throughout the country.

He was at his desk every morning at 6:00 a.m. and manning the phones by 8:00.

L.M. Jacobs was the most powerful man I have ever encountered. He treated me with respect, and, though he was very intimidating, I had a comfort level with him that I think grew out of my experience of standing up to my father.

Max and I were given the assignment of revamping the entire subway vending machine operation, which Mr. Jacobs had just acquired, and which had been losing money for years. We dove into it with enormous energy and enthusiasm. Mind you, we had no passion for vending machines, but the process was energizing, and I was learning the principles of business from a master. Max was not far behind him.

Within weeks, the vending machines were turning a profit, and I was raised to $140.

When I told Max I wanted more, he told me "the funds can't stand it," a line that made me laugh and stopped me cold at the same time. Over the years, I used it many times.

Now we wanted to apply our business skills to the theater. We decided to produce a play that Max would star in. I interviewed four producers and made a notebook about Off Broadway production. Theodore Mann and Paul Libin of Circle in the Square seemed to have the most consistent track record of success, and they produced the quality of American and European classics Max most wanted to act in.

We approached them about doing Eric Bentley's adaptation of Carl Sternheim's *The Underpants.* In the fall, Mann and Libin hired Max to appear in Dore Schary's Broadway production of *The Zulu and the Zayda* with the beloved Yiddish star Menasha Skulnik, and *The Underpants* sort of fell by the wayside.

But I was smitten, and with my newly acquired business acumen, I thought I had found a way back to my chosen profession.

CHAPTER 6

Rites of Passage

As the subway survey was ending, my good friends from summer stock, David and Gretchen Cryer, returned from the first season of William Ball's American Conservatory Theater (ACT) in Pittsburgh. They were full of excitement about the company and the dynamic and flamboyant Mr. Ball. The Carnegie Tech graduating class of 1955 had produced two gifted directors who were to make significant contributions to the American theater: Ball and Ellis Rabb. Rabb had started the Association of Producing Artists (APA) in 1959, which performed classical works in repertory for many years in New York.

I liked David and Gretchen enormously. They were talented, attractive, and had the air of people who were going to make it. Gretchen had a wonderful wit that fit her somewhat pessimistic life view. David was the model of personal integrity, a handsome young leading man with a glorious voice, and someone I looked up to. They noted my newly acquired self-assurance after my year with Max and his father and thought I should meet Bill Ball to see if there might be a place for me in the administration of ACT.

I went to meet with Ball and was startled to find that ACT's New York headquarters were in the American Theatre Wing building on West Ninety-Third Street, where I had gone to school only five years earlier. His office was in one of my classrooms.

We clicked. He was a small, bald man with intense, small features and an incisive intelligence. His ideas and enthusiasm were infectious. He wanted ACT to be the center of world theater and convinced you that he had the wherewithal to do it.

I had heard that, among his indulgences, Bill Ball was a patient of the notorious Dr. Max Jacobson, who numbered among his patients President John F. Kennedy and Alan Jay Lerner, and who injected his high-profile clients with an animal-gland extract laced with speed. The fame and power of Jacobson's patients not only afforded him a kind of legitimacy but put him in vogue, despite the widespread knowledge of what he was really doing. There was no indication of anything unusual with Ball at our first or second meetings.

The third meeting took place on his birthday. I wished him many happy returns, and we sat down. There was a long pause as he looked at me through glazed, slitty eyes. "It occurs to me," he said slowly, "that in our meetings together you have gained a great deal of information about this company." "Yes," I said, "I have."

He now stood up behind his desk. "It occurs to me that you may be a spy." "A spy?" I was incredulous. "Yes," he said, slinking dramatically around his desk and narrowing in for the kill. "A spy for the Arts Council."

The surprise of his accusation at first amused me, but I then realized he was serious. I tried for several minutes to convince him I was an information gatherer but no spy. He remained unconvinced. I became impatient and left. When he followed up with a call to discuss a position in the organization, I told him I enjoyed the complete trust of my present employer and wasn't interested.

It was the time of the Vietnam War, and Gretchen Cryer and her fellow DePauw alumna Nancy Ford had written an antiwar musical inspired by Gretchen's brother, Peter Kiger, who was a conscientious objector. I was already strongly opposed to the war and asked them to perform the score for David and me. I was very taken with their work. David suggested that we might team up to produce it Off Broadway. An exciting idea, but I thought we needed to get our feet wet.

The Fantasticks was a show we both loved. David had been one of the first and best El Gallos in the original Off Broadway production, and we hit on the idea of producing it as a college tour to try out our partnership. We approached our personal favorites from the New York cast to join us, and they were all up for it. *The Fantasticks* had been performed everywhere at least twice and booking agents wouldn't go near it. We decided to book it ourselves.

Securing extensive lists of deans and student activities coordinators, we typed, licked, and stamped every night for two weeks. Each mailing was blessed as we put it in the mailbox. We asked half our fee in advance, which we put into an escrow account to finance the tour once it was fully booked. There were no investors. The company would travel on a bus with half the seats removed to accommodate the sets, lights, and costumes. Our office was my fifteen-dollar-a-week room on West Eighty-Seventh Street.

Citing our address as being "outside of the theater district," one college dean questioned our legitimacy. We asked Tom Jones, the show's author, if he would write a letter vouching for us. He did, calling us "a wonderful company with just about the best of the talent from the New York production." As a result, the dean took three performances and touted us to other schools, who also took dates.

We put together an eight-week tour to begin September 26, 1966, at Xavier University in Cincinnati. Assured that the bookings were in place, I moved from my room to a luxury studio in Dorchester Towers on Broadway and Sixty-Eighth Street. As David and I signed our first booking contracts on my kitchen floor, he looked over at me and said, "This is FUN."

Everything was tightly organized. Our stage manager, Elissa Lane, created technical questionnaires for each college, and they were then sent lighting and tech plots to be set up by the student crew prior to our arrival. We sent press releases and photos every three weeks, staggering them in the hopes they would actually be used. Enthusiasm on all sides ran high. We had begun the groundwork in January, and, by April, everything was set.

One spring Sunday afternoon, Bill Ball called. "Can you meet David Balding and me at David's apartment at six?" I was breathless. Ivor David Balding was the most respected Off Broadway producer of the day. He had the beautiful New Theatre on East Fifty-Fourth Street and a string of hits that included *The Knack*, Mike Nichols' Off Broadway directorial debut, and *The Mad Show, Serjeant Musgrave's Dance,* and *Scuba Duba*. His productions set the gold standard for Off Broadway. "Yes," I responded, having no idea what the evening held in store.

From 6:00 p.m. until well after midnight, Bill Ball, David Balding, and I discussed plans for the future of the American Conservatory Theater, which would launch with a repertory season in June at the prestigious Westport Country Playhouse. The opening night would be a glittering gala of scenes from ACT staples that included *Charley's Aunt, Beyond the Fringe*, Ball's acclaimed Circle in the Square production of *Six Characters in Search of an Author,* and an extensively revised version of Albee's *Tiny Alice*. Gregory Peck was to be honorary chairman.

The Westport engagement was to be followed by a mainstage season at the famed Goodspeed Opera House in East Haddam, Connecticut, a season in Palo Alto, California, and spectacularly climaxed in August with four weeks at the Ravinia Festival in Chicago. These incredible plans and the dynamic presence of Ball and Balding stirred my imagination. Because there was no more work on *The Fantasticks* until we went into rehearsal in the fall, I told Ball that, subject to that time limitation, I was ready to join his organization in whatever capacity he deemed appropriate. My salary was to be five hundred dollars per week.

It was the last lucid conversation I ever had with him.

I became Ball's administrative assistant, which required me to be around him at all times. I would call it a "make-it-work" type of position. In Bill's office, I noticed many unopened registered letters from Edward Albee, both on his desk and on the floor, and assumed they were complaints about the changes and rearranging Bill had made in Albee's text, which resulted in his brilliant production of *Tiny Alice*. It had been a failure on Broadway.

On our first day in Westport, a portly gentleman named Noel Ferrand, to whom *Tiny Alice* was dedicated, arrived unannounced in the small reception area of the theater offices. Mr. Ferrand declared that he was there "on Edward's behalf" and would not be leaving until he had spoken with "Mr. Ball."

Bill did not wish to speak with Mr. Ferrand, but he was trapped in his office. The only way out was through the reception area where Mr. Ferrand was. "Take him next door to the inn, and I will flee while you are away," Bill advised.

Noel Ferrand, after an hour, was quite drunk. I was feeling pretty good myself and beginning to enjoy his company when his mood took a dark turn and he demanded we return to the offices. Thinking the coast must now be clear, I took him back, but Bill had not managed to leave.

My concerns were short-lived. As Noel Ferrand went to sit in the swivel chair, he hit it with such force that he and the chair fell over backwards. Hearing the crash, Bill opened his door, jumped over Ferrand, and flew through the reception area like a dervish. Humiliated and defeated, but feeling no pain, Noel Ferrand asked if I would be kind enough to put him on the next train back to New York.

On the second day, Henry Hewes, the well-respected drama critic of the *Saturday Review*, arrived for an afternoon visit. Bill, resplendent in toreador pants, cod piece, and sombrero with ball fringe, took me to his office window and pointed to a spot in the parking lot. "I am going now to walk with Henry Hewes. When we reach that spot, I want you to run out and tell me I have a long-distance call from London."

I noted the spot, and, at just the right moment, I ran up to them and delivered the news. "Bill, you have a long-distance call from London."

He turned. "Don't you EVER interrupt me when I'm talking to Henry Hewes!"

I started to speak, caught myself, and then put my head down. *Brilliant*, I thought as I put my tail between my legs and headed back to the office. *Nutty, but brilliant.*

On the third day, a stage manager rushed up to me. Everything at ACT seemed to be on *urgent*. "Bill wants you in the theater right away."

I ran to the playhouse where Bill was rehearsing his entrance as master of ceremonies for the benefit performance. It was pitch black, but I felt my way to a seat. As I sat, there was a penetrating bolt of organ music, and the door at the top of the *Tiny Alice* staircase opened slowly to reveal Bill, a tiny silhouette in a tux. As he came slowly down the staircase, the lights came up, and the organ chord reached a shattering crescendo. It stopped abruptly as he reached the edge of the stage.

He looked down at me and spoke. "Is it too much?" "It's everything," I answered.

That night was the gala, and Westport turned out in all of its evening finery. Gregory Peck, looking every inch the star, stood in front of the theater, watching the audience arrivals and greeting people he knew. Dr. Max Jacobson lurked about like a vulture, waiting with his black bag for the inevitable call from his patient.

Once again, a stage manager rushed toward me. "Bill wants you backstage." I went back and found Bill in his tux, looking not in a good way. "Get me Dr. Max," he said. I summoned Dr. Max and led him backstage to Bill.

Whatever he gave Bill that night, it was not speed. With the entire company seated onstage in folding chairs, Bill crept through his introductions *sotto voce*, his eyes glassy and vacant, his articulation uncertain. My patience and even my infatuation with his eccentricities evaporated that night. I felt contempt for what he did to his company, which included Rene Auberjonois, Austin Pendleton, and Cicely Tyson, all of whom did their best while being held hostage by their leader. The Westport engagement itself was a rousing success.

On our third day at the Goodspeed Opera House, Bill collared me for a chat in the parking lot. He informed me that, in my time with the company so far, I had proved to be "a lightweight." Then, without missing a beat, he told me he was sending me to Chicago to be in charge of the press, advertising, and advance work for the four-week engagement at the Ravinia Festival in August.

I was elated at the assignment. It was a real chance to spread my wings, learn, and work, with only the restrictions of a budget. There was no one supervising or overseeing me. There was no template.

The first thing I did was make the rounds of the Chicago theater community to rally their support and get a lay of the land vis-à-vis the press and theater climate. They were all tremendously helpful and willing to provide mailing lists and any information and support I needed. One of them steered me to Danny Newman, the country's leading authority on subscription brochure mailings who was right there in Chicago at the Lyric Opera. Danny designed a master brochure and a follow-up to be sent two weeks later, both of which he pushed through the post office at bulk rate—all at no charge. He was major to our success.

I began making the rounds of the Chicago press and found them equally supportive. Ed Hastings, the mild-mannered ACT general manager, called from Palo Alto to tell me the company was seriously considering becoming the resident company of Chicago if the reception warranted it. The excitement in Palo Alto was also causing a groundswell in San Francisco to offer the company a permanent home there.

I had become friendly with the city editor of the *Chicago Daily News*, and I went to see him after hours and leaked the resident company possibility to him. The following day, it was the lead story on the front page, "Chicago May Get Resident Theatre Company." The various aspects of the campaign were now in confluence, and we were selling some serious tickets. The Chicago sponsors were delighted.

The centerpiece of the campaign was to be the gala arrival of Bill Ball, followed by two days of tightly scheduled appearances that included everything from a press conference at Ravinia to one-on-one interviews with feature writers, luncheons and lawn parties with the very wealthy of the Chicago suburbs, hobnobs with gossip columnists, including the powerful Irv Kupcinet and Herb Lyon, and radio and TV interviews. I had planned it virtually to the minute.

As there was an air strike and no commercial flights to be had anywhere in the United States, we had arranged a private plane for Bill, courtesy of one of the Chicago benefactors. Days before all of this was to happen, I got a phone call from that sea-of-calm-amidst-the-chaos, Ed Hastings. "Bill has flipped out and gone to Greece," he said. "He won't be coming to Chicago for all of your stuff."

"I'll tell you what," I said. "I am going to get whoever I can to come in here and fill these appearances. And do whatever I have to do to get them here. This is a slap in the face to me and to a community that has bent over backwards for fucking Bill Ball and your fucking company. We have five days, so I suggest you get on the phone and see who you can get, too."

The only person I could land was Zsa Zsa Gabor, whose press rep assured, "Of course, she will need the poodles, the limos, the hotel suites." As much as this appealed to my darker nature, I just couldn't.

I made calls to the press to tell them Bill Ball could not make it, revengefully not explaining why, and told each one a different story about what we would do in his place. My favorite was ACT board member June Havoc landing in a hot air balloon on the lawn at Ravinia. Somehow, this tactic kept energy and excitement in the air.

After two days, Ed Hastings called and said that ACT company member Anthony "Scooter" Teague was willing to come. Teague, who had been a big hit in *110 in the Shade* on Broadway, had just completed filming a featured role in *How to Succeed in Business Without Really Trying*. The local sponsors were irate but agreed to go along with it. Ball's name was mud with them now. We chartered a plane, and Scooter was on his way.

I arranged to meet the plane and whisk him immediately to the Ravinia Festival, where all of the Chicago press, theater community, and local patrons of ACT awaited him. He emerged from the bumpy plane ride as sick as a dog. He was absolutely green and said he did not feel up to doing the press conference. At this point I identified him as part of ACT, which I had now designated as "the enemy." I told him firmly that there was no choice, he had to do it, and offered what comfort I could while totally sizzling inside.

As I took center stage at Ravinia, announcing that, as we all knew, William Ball was regrettably ill but had sent in his place a handsome and brilliant ambassador of good will, Scooter was in the wings puking his guts out. He could be heard from the audience. I thought it was simply the sound of the universe commenting on this entire sequence of events. To his credit, Scooter came out and charmed everyone, and for the next two days, he pulled off all of the scheduled appearances and press events effortlessly and flawlessly.

Chicago in the summer of 1966 was a city of demonstrations. Martin Luther King and civil rights were on the march, and I had taken time out to participate. I decided to stage a "demonstration" at Union Station for the company's arrival by train from San Francisco. The media loved the idea. I spent a sweaty weekend in my unairconditioned office above the Shubert Theatre painting the signs, interpolating the names of the shows and current phrases that were in the vernacular. I even exploited the notoriety of John Lennon's misunderstood remark that week that "the Beatles are now more popular than Jesus."

It was a grand success. Photos in all the papers and lots of TV coverage. And Richard Christiansen in the *Chicago Tribune* proclaimed the "ACT is now more popular than John Lennon" sign as "Sign of the Week."

By the time the company arrived, the first two weeks of the four-week engagement were completely sold out, and I knew that word of mouth would take care of the rest. I had no contact with Bill. I had nothing to say to him. I left for New York. Ed Hastings, in his understated way, thanked me. "You earned your keep," he said in the short note that accompanied my final paycheck.

On August 29, we went into rehearsal for our college tour of *The Fantasticks* at the Theatre at Riverside Church, a wonderfully intimate setting that David had secured rent free in exchange for inviting the parishioners to our dress rehearsal.

Buoyed by a big sendoff from the Riverside congregation and a boffo *Variety* story, spirits were high as we boarded the bus for our kickoff at Xavier University in Cincinnati. David and I sat in the two front seats. I was now twenty-four. It had been four years since I boarded the bus as an understudy in *The Sound of Music*.

We pulled up to the university theater, and David and I, without any prior discussion, opened the back of the bus and began unloading the set and lights. We took them to the auditorium, where the set would be assembled and the lights hung by a student crew under the strict supervision of Elissa Lane, our crack stage manager. This remained our custom for the duration of the tour.

We were greeted cheerfully by the dean of men, who told us our first performance was special because it would be the first shared experience of the freshman class. All three performances in the eight-hundred-seat theater were sold out, and we were about to find out how it would work in a larger theater. The tiny Sullivan Street Playhouse in New York had only 151 seats.

The freshmen warmed to the antics of the company during the overture, but when David began "Try to Remember," they melted. At the end of the performance, they stood cheering for several minutes. I sat in the rear of the balcony having the most gratifying moment of my life. At this performance at least, our plans had worked, and our work had been richly rewarded.

Our first real test came at our next stand, Marietta College, where we performed in a gymnasium. We carried in the set and I looked at Elissa. The otherwise iron lady was shaking. She said she would now really find out if her technical plot was going to work. The gym provided acoustical challenges as well as lighting ones. We would be playing to a sellout crowd of two thousand. The performance went off without a hitch, and we received our fourth standing ovation.

As we traveled over back roads and covered bridges, the feeling of being part of a pioneer effort permeated the tour, and that spirit was infectious among the company members, the students who worked with us, and the audiences who rooted for us. The show sold out in every situation and, without exception, finished to a standing ovation.

On November 6, 1966, the Off Broadway production of *The Fantasticks* passed the performance record held by *My Fair Lady* to become the longest-running musical in world theater history. That night we played the State University at Stony Brook, New York, and our guest of honor was Lore Noto, producer of the Off Broadway production who had struggled valiantly to keep his show running during its first year. When we called him to the stage, he was visibly moved to see an audience of three thousand standing and cheering his little dream.

We were contacted by a promoter about bringing the show to the Murat Theatre in Indianapolis at the end of the tour. My hometown. I had seen Blackstone the Magician and the Shrine Circus there as a child, and it was a perfect way to bring our happy venture to its end.

Most of all, it was my chance to publicly thank Helen Millikan, my fourth-grade teacher, for being the first person to encourage me in my show-business aspirations.

My parents came back to Indianapolis for the opening, and I had a magic show business moment with my father. As we crossed the street in front of the Murat Theatre, there on the marquee was "The David Cryer and Albert Poland Production of *The Fantasticks*." The look on my father's face said it all. His son was in show business, and his son was a success.

Word of our sold-out Indy performances reached New York, and we were contacted by Budd Filippo, a booking agent, about the possibility of a tour of first-class theaters in major cities. We arranged to have a union stamp put on our set, made a deal with the stagehands union to travel with only one man (an electrician), and for $13,000 we mounted the first national touring company of an Off Broadway show. We supplemented the customary piano and harp with bass and drums, using orchestrations created for the original cast album, which rounded out the sound nicely but kept the simplicity.

We would open January 9, 1967, at the Shubert Theatre in New Haven, the famed out-of-town tryout theater for shows coming in to Broadway. This was to be followed by a split week in Columbus, Ohio, and Louisville, Kentucky. That was it. A two-week tour. We risked losing everything, but our college success had filled us with blind enthusiasm. We went ahead.

We packed the bus and headed for New Haven. As had become our custom, David and I got off the bus to begin unloading the set. "Gentlemen," Elissa Lane said in her tone of stage-managerial authority, "you are producers now. Producers do not unload the set. Mr. Poland, I am sure you have business to do." And to David she added, "You I will see at rehearsal in exactly one-half hour."

Watching this, our affable bus driver pulled me aside. "I'm a Teamster," he said. "I'll load and unload you for an extra $75 a week." We started him on the spot, and I went to the theater lobby and watched the line at the box office, which was consistently about sixteen people.

Maurice Bailey, the distinguished operator of the Shubert, was beaming. "You're going to do just fine here. And don't worry, the rest of your tour will fall into place by the end of the week."

Bailey was right.

We were welcomed by a warmly enthusiastic opening night audience, followed by rave reviews and boffo box office.

Variety ran a big story headlined "*Fantasticks* on level of Title in Roadshow B.O." and called us "the surprise road hit of the season." By the end of the week, we were booked solid through April. The American in St. Louis, the Hanna in Cleveland, the Studebaker in Chicago, the Shubert in Boston, and the Forrest in Philadelphia were among the theaters that fell in line.

We were actually making a little history. And there were no stars. We maintained that the show was the star and we had the company to make it shine.

I was now the press agent and advance man, traveling three weeks ahead of the company and spending the same length of time in each city as the company would perform. Fresh from my Chicago experience with ACT, I loved doing press. I did double duty, billing myself as "Broadway's youngest producer" and booking myself on all the local talk shows. On the first one I thought I was overweight and went on a diet, which I kept track of by looking at myself in the monitors as the tour progressed.

We hired Jay Kingwill, a young, cultured Oscar Levant-ish person from the Sol Hurok office, to be our company manager. In the second week of the tour, we got a telegram from the Association of Theatrical Press Agents and Managers (ATPAM) informing us that we were required to have a union press agent and a union company manager. They told us they would throw up a picket in St. Louis if we did not comply.

I gathered up my press clippings, photos, and releases and went to the ATPAM offices in New York to appear before the board. I began by being diplomatic. I stated simply that Jay and I were both doing fine jobs and I saw no reason to replace us. I made them laugh. I cried, I screamed. They were unmoved. I showed them the considerable coverage I had been able to generate and said, "Are you telling me that simply having a union card would make me a better press agent?" "Yes," was the answer.

If I was happy with Jay and myself, they suggested we could continue doing the actual work but place a union press agent and manager under contract. "What would they do?" I inquired. "Whatever you want them to."

They told me I had two weeks to comply. I left shaken and depressed but determined to fight. A little research led me to the Condon-Wadlin Act, which entitles nonunion owners to employ themselves in a union position, and another act that states that a nonunion person can be employed if a union contract is filed, union regulations lived up to, and benefits are paid. We were prepared to follow that to keep Jay employed.

ATPAM's response was that I could stay on, but we had to replace Jay with a union member. I rejected this, and within forty-eight hours had a call from the manager of the American Theatre in St. Louis to inform me that his stagehands had thrown up a picket and we could not load in our set unless we met the ATPAM demand for a union manager. I was furious but knew this was the best we could get.

ATPAM arranged for me to meet their candidate for company manager, an older gentleman named Carl Abraham. I winced as he introduced himself as "The King of Bus and Trucks." We were a young company, and this was not what we had in mind. However, he seemed kindly and struck me as honest, so we hired him. I will always regret my treatment of this man. I wasn't mean; I just tolerated and ignored him. When he came to me with good news about our business, I responded coldly. I think his time with us was very lonely. His work was thoroughly professional, though unappreciated. He was usually to be found in the hotel lobby, sitting alone, wearing his hat.

During my summer in Chicago with ACT, I had gotten to know a young press agent named Aaron Gold. I watched him handle opening nights at the Ivanhoe Dinner Theater with dispatch and aplomb. He was witty and hip and knew Chicago the way great promoters know a town. I thought it would be prudent to supplement myself with him for our engagement at the Studebaker.

On my advance trip, he introduced me to Roger Dettmer, the theater and music critic of *Chicago's American*. Dettmer seemed responsive to me. The next day I had a drink with Aaron. "I'm just being a messenger," he said playfully. "What you do about this is up to you. Roger would like you to join him for dinner at his apartment." I raised my eyebrows. "It will mean a rave in the *American*," he added. I threw my head back, roared with laughter, and said, "No."

Opening night, I was surrounded by Chicago friends I knew from ACT. As he walked by, Dettmer cracked, "You seem to know the entire audience." His review the next day was scathing. In *Fantasticks* lore, it is thought of as the single worst review the show has ever gotten. Dettmer mainly attacked the text, which he said was "like the Bea Lillie song about Maud, rotten to the core like a lean roast of beef larded with dirty jokes and maggoty ideas." And so on.

I called the editor of the *American* and told him of the innuendo-laden dinner invitation and added that Dettmer had arrived at the theater "loaded for bear before the curtain even went up." I ended the tirade by canceling our advertising in the *American* for the remainder of the two-week engagement. The gang at Sullivan Street Playhouse, where *The Fantasticks* played in New York, was pretty much following all of our reviews. Reading Dettmer's notice, the box office treasurer quipped, "Somebody didn't put out."

Because I canceled our advertising in the *American*, there was no further coverage of *The Fantasticks* in any paper in Chicago. It was a joint policy created months earlier when Volkswagen pulled its advertising from the *Daily News* in an editorial dispute. A universal blackout, with one exception. Irv Kupcinet, probably the most powerful columnist outside of New York, ran an item on us every day in his column in the *Sun-Times*. He was the only one who dared to break rank. Business for the second week was even better than the first.

The musicians' unions in each city had to be dealt with. Most had minimum requirements for the number of musicians to be employed for musical shows, usually a number well in excess of the four we carried. For example, Boston required twelve, Milwaukee nine, and Philadelphia twenty. It was up to us to get this requirement waived or reduced or pay the required local musicians ourselves, though they would not play a note. These non-playing musicians were known as "walkers." In every city, the number was either totally waived or substantially reduced. We kept hearing that Boston and Philly were going to be the tough ones.

I appeared before the Boston union, and they agreed to a total waiver. Fresh from that triumph, we signed on with the Forrest in

Philadelphia, feeling that the union there would fall into line as had the others. *Variety* immediately began running speculative items about it, and the day came when the manager of the Forrest and I sat with the head of the Philadelphia local, who held fast to the requirement that we pay twenty local musicians, at a total cost of $6,000. The agreement we had signed with the Shuberts called for us to foot the entire bill.

I immediately went into fighting mode. I spoke with our lawyer who, to my annoyance, offered no support. Duly noted. I went off on my own. I canvassed the media in Philadelphia to apprise them of the situation and noted that they were sympathetic. Word got back to me that, in New York, the Shuberts were upset that I was in Philadelphia "making waves."

I had a call from a Shubert lawyer, Gerald Schoenfeld. He was amiable and chattily sympathetic to our plight and asked me to have lunch. I wasn't interested in lunch. Was there anything they could do? Would they be willing to pay them? Or get rid of them? I thought he imagined me as a harmless kid who would probably fade after an important phone call with the big boys. I began to build up a head of steam.

I prepared a press release stating that we would require the twenty musicians to sit onstage during the entire performance doing nothing "so the public can see twenty reasons why ticket prices are sky high and the American theater is headed for disaster." I also added facetiously that if any of our own musicians became ill during the performance, they could then be replaced without stopping the show. At every paper, I was directed to "cityside," which meant we were off the amusement page and into local hard news.

I also got a report that following our phone conversation, Gerald Schoenfeld had blown up at the national head of the American Federation of Musicians at a dinner in New York.

Maybe, I thought, *he's really on our side.*

The papers the next day were more than I could have dreamed of. Front-page coverage everywhere. We were even included in the local TV newscasts and on some stations in New York. *The Philadelphia Inquirer* headlined, "Twenty Musicians in Play Won't Toot a Note." The story went on to state that the minimum requirement had kept other small musicals out of Philadelphia and even noted that, for straight dramatic shows, seven musicians who did nothing had to be paid off.

I had hardly finished the papers when an angry Gerald Schoenfeld called. "You're ruining our relationship with the union," he said.

"How could it be worse?" I answered. "We're paying twenty people who are doing absolutely nothing."

"The men are ready, willing, and able to perform," he parried. "It's not our responsibility that you have nothing for them to play."

"I will certainly look into that," I fumed. I hung up and went off to G. Schirmer Music Publishers, where I purchased an orchestration of "The Star-Spangled Banner" for twenty pieces and headed to Philadelphia. I began to formulate my plan on the train.

On opening night, we would seat the musicians in folding chairs across the front of the stage for a half hour before the performance. At 8:30, they would rise and play "The Star-Spangled Banner" and then exit to their dressing rooms, where they would remain. The chairs would be struck, and the performance would begin.

For the remainder of the week, they would be required to be in their dressing rooms, but no more playing. We captured not only the sympathy but the imagination of the Philadelphia press, and within a few days, there was not a ticket to be had.

The coverage of the opening was tremendous. Page-one local coverage, the AP sent a wire photo of the musicians around the world, *The New York Times* ran an item, and, best of all, *The Wall Street Journal* ran an editorial that came down heavily on union featherbedding.

We had made our point and sold out the engagement. Weeks later, the union head was ousted, and the Philadelphia union changed its minimum requirement for small musicals from twenty to six. The theater manager called to thank me and said, "Come back to my theater anytime."

Fresh on the heels of this triumph and with the headiness of seeing our names in *Variety* every week, David and I were proceeding on two fronts. Gretchen and Nancy's show *Now Is the Time for All Good Men*, was now ready. As a first step, we showed it to Lore Noto and sought his advice. He thought it was a natural for Word Baker.

Baker had had an up-and-down career, but his direction of the Off Broadway production of *The Fantasticks* was magical. He had only one other notable success, a two-year run of Arthur Miller's *The Crucible*, produced by Paul Libin at his Martinique Theatre.

The four of us met with the formidable Mr. Baker. He and Gretchen and Nancy hit it off at once, and it was apparent that he wanted us and could bring energy, creativity, and prestige to our endeavor. Combined with our own fresh success with *The Fantasticks*, it made for a good package to present to investors.

We signed him up and went after the prestigious Theatre de Lys, a former movie house on Christopher Street in Greenwich Village, named for its previous owner Bill de Lys, and purchased for its present owner, Lucille Lortel, by her husband.

Lucille Lortel was a force of nature in the New York theater. She and Theodore Mann were the founding spirits of the modern Off Broadway movement. Miss Lortel had the money and the savvy to make things happen, and an appetite for self-aggrandizement that was unquenchable. She was someone I would love and fight with to the end of her days.

The de Lys had most notably been home to the seven-year run of the legendary *Threepenny Opera*, of which Lucille claimed to be a producer; it was the flagship theater of Off Broadway.

We were told that the key to the front door of the de Lys was to hire Paul Berkowsky, the theater's manager, to be the general manager of our show. It seemed like a conflict to us, but because we wanted the theater, we met with him.

"What does a general manager do?" I asked Paul Berkowsky. He was dumbfounded by the question. As the years went by and our history together unfolded, we laughed about it many times.

It seemed that he would negotiate and draft the agreements with the authors, director, designers, theater, actors, etc., on our behalf, prepare the production and weekly operating budgets, and, subject to our direction, be in charge of business operations for the run of the show. These were things David and I had done ourselves for *The Fantasticks* tour but, since *Now Is the Time* was an original production involving subsidiaries and future rights, the agreements would be more complex and far-reaching.

Our second project, coincidentally, was to be a touring company of *Threepenny Opera*, which I had loved ever since seeing David as the Street Singer and Gretchen as Jenny when we did it together in summer stock. Despite its de Lys success, *Threepenny* even at this writing has never had a national tour. There was an aborted one starring Gypsy Rose Lee as Jenny that folded in its opening stand in Toronto.

We hoped that our production would star Judy Garland as Jenny. Her career had been in a down cycle for more than a year, and we thought this could be a perfect situation for her. We would add "Mack the Knife" and "The Barbara Song" to Jenny's repertoire, and even with those additions, it wouldn't be as exhausting for her as her concert performances had been.

We went to Lotte Lenya, who was a great admirer of Garland, to ask if she would help us get a ninety-day free option from Tams-Witmark, the licensing agency for the rights. She immediately picked up the phone, and we had our ninety days.

Now the task was to track down Judy Garland and ascertain her health, availability, and interest. I began a telephone chase that took me to various lawyers and managers, all of whom had represented her briefly and referred me to their successors. "If you find her, tell her she owes me money." A picture had begun to emerge, and we became discouraged.

I loved going to Jilly's, Frank Sinatra's favorite hangout on Fifty-Second Street, run by his good friend Jilly Rizzo. One spring night I was there with a friend, and she leaned in to me and whispered, "You will never believe who just came in." It was Judy. Frail but seemingly in good spirits, she sat down with her current companion,

Tom Green, and they began heckling Bobby Cole, who was at the piano. "Trees!" she would yell out and clap her hands and laugh. It seemed strident.

I said to myself, "It's now or never," and walked over to her table. "Judy, I'm Al Poland from your fan club." She was immediately friendly, asked me to sit, and introduced me to Tom, who she said was a friend from Boston. At close range, she looked corpse-like, well beyond her forty-five years. It was disturbing, and although she was kind, she seemed affected and incoherent. Not the woman I had spent time with only ten years before.

I soon realized that I didn't want to even bring up *Threepenny*. My feeling was that it would be a nightmare, that I would be the babysitter, not the stage manager or the director, but me. It was not a role I wanted to play with Judy Garland. When I returned to my table, I sent them drinks, which the bill indicated were two large tumblers of straight vodka. The next day I thanked Lenya, and we dropped our free option.

In June, with industry buzz all around us, we held our first backer's audition for *Now Is the Time* in the Belasco Room at Sardi's. The most important guests were Lucille Lortel and Ted Brooks from Martin Erlichman's office. Erlichman was Barbra Streisand's manager, and there was a song in the show written with her in mind called "He Could Show Me." We were hopeful because she often included theater songs in her repertoire.

After everyone had one-and-a-half drinks, David and I launched into our presentation.

We talked about the show and about our success with *The Fantasticks*. When I modestly announced the profit figure for our tour, I directed it to Lucille Lortel, who blushed slightly and laughed. At that moment we became friends. Nancy and Gretchen, both wonderful performers, did about forty-five minutes of songs from the show, capped by David rendering the show-stopping ballad "Rain Your Love on Me."

At the end of what had been an exciting evening, we were rushed by people who wanted to invest. Lucille Lortel was charmed by all of us and by the show, which she praised as *"Our Town* set to music, dear." Not only could we have the de Lys, she invited us to present a backer's audition at the White Barn Theatre on her estate in Westport, Connecticut. Ted Brooks, too, was impressed and promised a favorable report to Barbra Streisand and Martin Erlichman.

Paul Berkowsky opened wide the door to Off Broadway. In early September, negotiations began for the new Off Broadway contract between Actors' Equity and the League of Off Broadway Theatres and Producers. Paul brought me into them and urged me to participate. I immediately loved everyone involved on both sides.

The League members were sleeves-rolled-up, emotionally invested, knowledgeable, and characters. Producer and general manager Lily Turner was a kind of Bronx dowager who had started the first Off Broadway theater company in 1947. Her opening salvo to me was to stand behind the chair I was sitting in and say, "Move." "Move?" I rejoined. I was the only one at the table. "Yes, I want that chair. I'm a lady." I was intimidated, so I moved. But I was also pissed, so I sat in the chair next to her. She was amused. The relationship went on like that for decades.

Dorothy Olim was a tall, imposing woman and the top Off Broadway general manager.

MacBird!, American Hurrah, and *Fortune and Men's Eyes* were her current running shows. She was the voice of experience, and when she cocked her jaw to one side and *started*, everybody listened.

William Hunt was a director and producer, not particularly successful but a necessary part of the mix. He was notable for having directed Lanford Wilson's first double bill, *Ludlow Fair* and *The Madness of Lady Bright*, which ran for fifteen performances in 1966. At a certain point in the negotiations, he could be counted on to nail Off Broadway to the cross in what he hoped would provide a dramatic turn of events in our fortunes. Being actors, the members of the opposing team had their own flair for drama, but Bill more than matched it.

Toward the end of the negotiations, a man with unkempt hair in a black leather jacket appeared. All of these people were rough riders, but he seemed to be the roughest of them all. He operated Shakespeare in the Park, and his influence and importance were immediately apparent.

He was the young Joe Papp.

Heading up the League side was Paul Libin, Ted Mann's partner at Circle in the Square. He was and is the best negotiator in the New York theater. Watching him was a joy. He involved all of us in the process, but things were clearly in his hands. He bullied, cajoled, and caressed, always with humor and always with a total working knowledge of Off Broadway at his fingertips.

After four weeks of intense negotiation, the weekly Off Broadway minimum went from $65 to $70, subject to a sliding scale, capping out at $145 when the weekly box office gross reached $9,500. As for me, I had found a home. These were my people; this was my community. Off Broadway had claimed my heart and owned it for several decades.

We set an opening date of September 26, 1967, and began to engage designers and arrangers, and to scout about for actors, press agents, and advertising agencies.

There were several theatrical advertising agencies, but the one Paul suggested was Brownstone Associates, geared strictly to Off Broadway. I looked at the posters of the shows they were handling and realized that these were all the titles that currently excited me. Arnold Wesker's *The Kitchen*, Barbara Garson's *MacBird!*, Norman Mailer's *The Deer Park*, Lanford Wilson's *The Rimers of Eldritch*, John Herbert's *Fortune and Men's Eyes*, Megan Terry's *Viet Rock*, Thornton Wilder's *Plays For Bleecker Street*, and Jean-Claude van Itallie's *American Hurrah* lit up the lobby walls with a beckoning energy.

Fred Segal ran Brownstone. He had a real passion for Off Broadway, and we hit it off immediately. After about an hour of talking, he said, "Do you have your press agent? Because there's only one press agent in this town for you. His name is Saul Richman."

Saul was cigar-smoking and fast-talking, the last of the ballyhoo press agents. And with a heart of gold. He had done the original *Hellzapoppin* and was currently handling his long-time accounts of Westbury Music Fair and Guy Lombardo, as well as Johnny Carson's clothing line and some kind of candy made with sugar and Rice Krispies.

Saul was a balding man who reminded me slightly of Sid Luft. His manner was thoroughly disarming as he sat with his feet propped up on his desk, puffing a Macanudo cigar. He listened to our spiel, took his cigar out of his mouth, and made a pronouncement. "Whether I get this show or not is unimportant. I just want you to know one thing. You have a friend in Saul Richman." I was knocked out by this guy.

With the money virtually in place, we began to audition actors. This was a revelation for me. When I was an actor, I always thought that the people doing the auditions were hostile and just waiting for me to screw up. Not the case at all. We sat hoping each person would be *it*—rooting for them.

Since we were actors, we went out of our way to be courteous and appreciative. Agents could be another matter. The agent for actor Clifford David said that his client would not audition. He suggested that if we wished to hear Mr. David sing, we could listen to him on the original cast album of *On a Clear Day You Can See Forever.* "Send the album at 2:10 on Tuesday," I answered, "and we will show a film of Word Baker conducting an audition."

Always in my mind's eye, I imagined David and Gretchen in the two leading roles in *Now Is the Time.* The tour had given David additional seasoning and stature, and Gretchen had the kind of presence that made audiences fall in love with her. But both felt it would be too much and make us look like a vanity production.

We found two actors who seemed well suited to the roles: a young actor who had made a couple of Western films and was ruggedly handsome with a good voice, and a very attractive and talented actress I had known in Wynn Handman's acting class who was strong in acting but slightly weak in the singing department.

Concurrently, we were arranging the second year of the *Fantasticks* tour, set to open at the Royal Alexandra in Toronto, October 2nd. I got an ominous call from Tom Jones.

"David isn't going out, is he, with *Now Is the Time* happening? Who will be doing El Gallo?" Tom asked.

"We haven't set El Gallo."

"Harvey and I are concerned. It was one thing with you and David there giving it the loving care you did, but we have a fear that *The Fantasticks* will become a stepchild while you're opening the show in New York," Tom added.

"Why don't you and Harvey come over next week and let's talk about this?" I suggested. I was sure we could address their concerns which, for the moment, we did.

We took the position with ATPAM that the show required only one union position, and for the second year, it would be the press agent. Jay Kingwill would be reinstated as the company manager. At the suggestion of Paul Berkowsky, we hired an old timer named Arthur Brillant in the press agent position.

Both shows swung into rehearsal, and the first day was everything you could hope for—everyone in high spirits, and all of us feeling like we had two winners. Word, Gretchen, and Nancy were bringing a wonderful energy to *Now Is the Time*.

We arrived at 10:00 a.m. for the second day of rehearsal at the de Lys to find a telegram waiting for us from the Society of Stage Directors and Choreographers (SSDC). "We are holding Word Baker in our offices until such time as you agree to sign SSDC Agreement as previously requested." It was signed by Mildred Traube, then head of the Society.

We had a signed contract with Word Baker that met union requirements, but at that time the SSDC was demanding that Off Broadway producers sign a second agreement committing them to use only SSDC members in perpetuity. Paul Berkowsky had advised us not to sign it, and we agreed, finding it coercive. This hardline tactic put it in a different perspective.

"We'd better sign it and get on with rehearsal," David said.

"David," I parried, "they didn't kidnap Word Baker and drag him up there. He went there willingly. Let him sit there. Let them bore each other to death until 6:00 p.m., and then we'll go up and sign it." David agreed, and rehearsal was canceled.

We went up at 6:00 and found Mildred Traube with a sheepish-looking but amused Word Baker and Gennaro Montanino, the director at the Sacandaga Summer Theatre, where David and I had met and who had threatened to blackball me from the New York theater when I quit the season early. He was now on the board of the SSDC.

How perfect, I thought. I signed the repugnant document, wadded it into a ball, and turned to Montanino. "Here, catch," I said, and walked out. An hour later, we were all laughing about it over dinner. "Ah knew exactly what y'all were doing," Word said in his best Texas drawl.

In the early weeks of rehearsal at the de Lys, it became apparent that the actress we had cast in the role of the young schoolteacher was under a severe handicap when it came to handling the songs, and her confidence seemed to diminish by the day. It was the perfect moment to turn to Gretchen. With a little gentle pressure, she agreed to do it, under the name of Sally Niven.

There was also growing dissension between Word Baker and the actor we had chosen to play the male lead, the new teacher who brings antiwar sentiment into the high school, creating a lynch mob mentality in the largely right-wing community. It shortly became clear that he, too, would have to leave, and we turned to David. I was jumping for joy. We now had the cast I had always wanted, and I was certain we would make it.

Through the good efforts of Martin Erlichman and Ted Brooks, Barbra Streisand committed her publishing company, Kiki Music, to produce and pay for an original cast album on Columbia Records, and there were strong indications we would have our dream of a Streisand single of "He Could Show Me."

Ted Brooks invited us into the studio to watch Roslyn Kind, Barbra's younger half-sister and a singer in her own right, record a demo of "He Could Show Me" they would then give to Barbra. The invitation to the session was a clear indication to us that the Streisand group was part of the family of our production.

We came to the first complete run-through of *Now Is the Time* under the work lights. No sets, no costumes, no special lighting, no musical arrangements. We invited a small group of friends and investors. It was electric. The performances were strong and the antiwar message against the backdrop of the conservative small town played powerfully.

Word Baker had a theory that shows should not preview. He felt that the most exciting performance of any show was the first one in front of an audience. I have seen this borne out many times. The concentration of the actors is never more intense than during that first performance, and the fear and nervous energy that make possible the leap from rehearsal to an audience can create stage magic.

The subsequent dress rehearsal, with full-tilt costumes, scenery, and lights wasn't as good as the work-light run-through. The orchestrations sounded thin and lightweight. In truth, the show had actually benefited from the starkness of the earlier run-through. But I was feeling young and inexperienced, and we had already made significant changes. I kept my mouth shut.

Suddenly we were all stressed, but we weren't talking about it. I felt permanently wired. Nancy was frequently making audible gasping sounds when she inhaled, and the normally placid David had punched out a man who jumped in front of him to get a cab. Gretchen and Word seemed to sail on relatively smoothly.

In 1967, there was a built-in Off Broadway audience for previews, and business was brisk. I began to feel that the show could go either way with the critics, but it now had a life of its own. By virtue of their performing in it, it had become more David and Gretchen's show than mine.

We were excited to hear that Clive Barnes, the new Dance and Drama critic of the *Times,* would be covering. In the past, the *Times* had generally sent a second-stringer to cover Off Broadway, but word was that Barnes was a real enthusiast.

Much has been written about opening nights. Suffice it to say, they are as natural as appearing on *The Tonight Show* and pretending you are in your living room.

Before the performance, David and I presented Paul Berkowsky and Saul Richman with letters awarding each of them 1 percent of our net profits for a job well done. Both were touched, as were we. The cheering audience of investors, family, and friends assured us we had a triumph.

We swept uptown for a swank opening night party at La Comedie, a French restaurant on the ground floor of Dorchester Towers. Saul came and got David and me and asked that we go upstairs to my apartment. He looked grim. The Barnes review was devastating. He wrote of "the story's general drift and the music's general drizzle," and concluded with "no one wants to go out onto the sidewalk humming the ticket stubs." The *Daily News* said, "What this show has is a long title" and seemed to take offense at its politics. Of course, it was the *Times* that counted.

Word spread quickly through the party, but David and I circulated and tried to keep a stiff upper lip. My mother did not take her eyes off of me for one second. The concern and love that came from her was unforgettable, as was the fact that Max Jacobs did not leave her side for the entire evening.

I went into that night a different person than I was when I came out of it. I realized I had no magic touch. I knew what it felt like to fail in front of a lot of people. The innocence of my youthful dream of myself dissolved into the bitter reality that I had been inadequate, not up to the task of producing a hit show in New York.

We woke the following morning ready to fight. We rallied our investors for more money, put up some of our own, and found that Edith Oliver in *The New Yorker* and Emory Lewis in *Cue* magazine liked the show very much, Oliver writing that "*Now Is the Time* towers over most uptown musical hits."

We got swarms of phone calls from people who attended previews who were outraged at the Barnes review. And Mr. Barnes got a flock of letters that suggested "usually in gently reasonable terms" that he had been "unfair" to the show. He returned for a reappraisal.

He didn't really like it much better the second time, but we ran with: "Clive Barnes has seen *Now Is the Time* twice! Have you seen it once?" In a *Newsweek* interview Barnes quipped that a company doing *Swan Lake* should say: "Clive Barnes has seen *Swan Lake* twelve hundred times."

We committed our newly raised funds to advertising, and Paul Berkowsky sent out a discount mailing to his enormous list of colleges and high schools, which seemed like a natural audience for the show.

Barbra Streisand and Columbia gave us the go-ahead for the cast album, and we were informed that she would record "He Could Show Me" as a single.

Ed Kleban, who had produced the superb *Jacque Brel Is Alive and Well and Living in Paris* cast album, among many others, was to be our producer. Our small orchestra was supplemented by an additional grand piano played by Nancy Ford, and Kleban was absolutely splendid, delivering a first-rate cast album. Columbia did a good ad campaign and, thanks to Paul Berkowsky's student ticket program, a large audience was seeing the show. The half-price tickets helped sustain a run but delivered no profit.

To add to our woes, *The Fantasticks* was sagging badly on the road, suffering from exactly the lack of attention that Tom and Harvey had feared.

Our press agent, whom we had renamed "Arthur Professional," was totally ineffectual and, despite my yelling and priming, his performance did not improve. Instead of a profit, as in the past, we found ourselves unable to pay our bills and $15,000 in debt. Things were unrelentingly tough all around.

David and I decided that David would jump back in as El Gallo and I would jump back in as the press agent for the three-week Baltimore engagement. We would close *Now Is the Time* on New Year's Eve, the same evening our fall tour would play its final performance. David's understudy, John Bennett Perry, would go on in New York.

It was do-or-die for *The Fantasticks* in Baltimore. and I pulled out all the stops, courting every journalist who could be found and appearing on every TV show and every college campus as "Broadway's youngest producer." With David back in the show, we captured raves from the critics and took in $100,000 in Baltimore, the highest three-week period we had ever had.

Exhausted and drained but out of the hole, we tried to cancel the spring leg of the tour that was five weeks of one-nighters in the south. The promoters wouldn't hear of it, so again David and I jumped in. We decided to keep the tour a secret from *Variety* and ATPAM so that we could continue with Jay Kingwill as company manager and me as the press agent. We called it *The Magical Mystery Tour* and it turned into a mini-triumph and was a lot of fun.

During our two years on the road, what became known as "the '60s" had begun, and we were all caught up in it. The winds of change had reached even the theater, and our tour ended in a different world than it had come into only two years before. A friend visited us when we were playing Birmingham and said he had just seen the Off Off Broadway tryout of a new play about "*it.*" "What is '*it?*'" I inquired. "Homosexuality," he whispered. The play was Mart Crowley's *The Boys in the Band*.

Everything had become more informal. People had become more open and loving. The things that had brought us together were civil rights, the Vietnam War, the music, and the drugs.

CHAPTER 7

Off Broadway—The Wild Years

Futz (1968)

As summer of 1968 approached, I realized that some distance had developed between David Cryer and me. The hurt of *Now Is the Time* not living up to everyone's hopes was probably the major cause, but our careers and lives were pulling us in different directions, too. He and Gretchen were on the verge of a divorce, and he was to marry Britt Swanson, a beautiful dancer he met in *Come Summer*, a short-lived Ray Bolger starrer that had moved David into the realm of Broadway leading man. "Mr. Cryer will return," wrote Clive Barnes in the *Times*.

Perhaps to fill the void, we decided to change lawyers. We sought Paul Berkowsky's advice and, to our great surprise, he suggested Gerald Schoenfeld and Bernard B. Jacobs, the Shubert attorneys. "They respect what you did in Philadelphia, and they represent a few select clients beyond the Shuberts," Paul told us.

We met with Gerald Schoenfeld, and I liked him straightaway. He was personable and had *gravitas*, a good sense of priorities, and looked faintly like my father's baby picture. He welcomed us. "You took the first round—let's see what we can do together."

Our first project together was something I never would have imagined. One noon in mid-May, I got a call from Paul Berkowsky. He was in selling mode. "I've got Harlan Kleiman," he said. "He's got a play in rehearsal here. Never seen anything like it. It's called *Futz.*" I liked the title. "Tom O'Horgan is directing. Random House is publishing. The La MaMa Troupe will do it for the first six weeks. There's a full page in *Newsweek.*"

Tom O'Horgan. That was enough. My ears were ringing. He had just galvanized Broadway with his production of *Hair.* I had seen it three times.

"It's capitalized at $22,000," Paul continued. "Harlan has raised twelve, but he's involved with rehearsals and doesn't have time to raise the other ten. Do you and David want to raise it and come in as associate producers?"

An opportunity to get in on a Tom O'Horgan show. It sounded too good to be true. "I'll call David and get right back to you." "Okay," Paul said, "but we have to move fast." David jumped at it and headed over to my apartment.

The agreement with Harlan, whom we had never met or talked to, arrived within the hour, with a copy sent to Schoenfeld and Jacobs, our new lawyers. We got on the phone with our investors. People arrived on English bikes waving checks, and by three o'clock we had the money in hand and had signed the agreements making us the associate producers of *Futz.*

"Now that we're the associate producers," I said to Paul, "can we read the script?" "Oh," he said, "you don't want to read it. Come down here tonight and see a run-through."

David couldn't go, so I went with our friend, Martin Herzer, who was beginning a good career as a stage manager, having started with us on *Now Is the Time.* Martin was bright, savvy, and had a wicked sense of humor.

The houselights went down, and we heard a barely perceptible human musical tone that was slowly joined by other harmonically discordant tones from the off- and backstage areas. The sound gradually increased in volume. It made the listener feel stoned.

The La MaMa Troupe then bounded onto the stage in farm clothes playing crude, handmade musical instruments like washboards and saws. The tones evolved into a wordless song that was at first gentle, then playfully confrontational, then maniacal, and finally unabashedly hostile. Suddenly it stopped. The play began.

"Let's give it a straaaaaaaaaaaaaaaaaaaaaaaange passion to a stooooooorrrreeeeeeeee," the Troupe said in unison as they ran about the stage whirling, swooping, and dipping. Paul Berkowsky was right. I had never seen anything like it. It was a nightmare. Actors running around the stage, screaming and licking each other, simulating sex acts, switching roles and genders, sometimes playing inanimate objects. This was not acting. These were not performers who wished to be loved.

The plot, such as it was, seemed to be about a farmer's sexual relationship with his sow, mercifully invisible, which, though in the privacy of his own barn, made his raunchy, incestuous neighbors so crazy they finally killed him.

No wonder they couldn't find the money, I thought. *This is insanity.*

Finally, it was over.

The slightly more than one-hour running time had seemed like forever. I was speechless but seething.

"Well, whatever it is, darling, you are the associate producer," said Martin, roaring with laughter. Paul Berkowsky was, wisely I thought, nowhere to be found. "Where is he? I'm going to kill him!"

We rushed out. Whether I was an associate producer or not, *Futz* incensed me. It was a violation of everything I knew about or expected from the theater. How would I ever explain it to my mother?

I went home and read the full-page review Jack Kroll had written in *Newsweek*. He spoke of an exciting new form and called the play "a parable for our time."

The next day I rampaged down to the Theatre de Lys and found myself alone in Paul Berkowsky's office with La MaMa herself, Ellen Stewart. There were two telephones on two desks, and she was on both of them, with Tom O'Horgan on one and Michael Butler, the producer of *Hair*, on the other. Every time she changed receivers, dozens of bracelets jangled percussively up and down her arms. She barely noticed me. For a producer, I was feeling very unimportant in my own theater.

Watching Ellen Stewart gave me perspective. I realized that she was the real producer. Whatever I thought of *Futz*, Ellen and Tom O'Horgan had performed the real alchemy that had created it. She didn't have to advertise it. It was all right there in her commanding presence. Our names might be the ones above the title, but we were, in fact, just checkbooks who, hopefully, might have something to say about the advertising. I felt like a phony, a poseur, involved with a show I didn't like or understand.

I introduced myself to Ellen Stewart. "Take good care of my babies," she said, and headed for the door. "How come the Troupe can only stay for six weeks?" I asked, trying to assert my producorial authority. "Oh, they have other things to do, Baby," Ellen said. "They've already done this show. Don't worry," she reassured. "We're already working on a second company, and they will be ready. We did the same thing with *Tom Paine*." *Tom Paine* was an O'Horgan and La MaMa success currently running at Stage 73. "The Troupe only does six weeks, then they move on, Baby." And with that, Ellen Stewart left.

Enter Paul Berkowsky. I had barely opened my mouth when he said, "Did you see it last night? Exciting, huh?" and slapped an advance copy of the Random House book in my hand.

Futz, and What Came After, with an introduction by the great theater statesman Harold Clurman. Clearly there was something going on here. I had to find out what in the hell it was.

At the first preview, I met the author Rochelle Owens in front of the theater. She was tall, Jewish, with beautiful long red hair and kind of eccentric, slightly exotic features. She spoke in a sometimes-shrill voice that seemed to be on permanent "anxious." I liked her, and she said she was glad I was involved with the show. At last I felt at least a little welcome.

"Have you done a lot of this kind of theater?" she asked. "I've never even seen this kind of theater," I responded. "Well, give it some time," she said, seeming to echo Harold Clurman's advisory in his introduction not to get to know her work too quickly. I certainly felt that particular danger had passed.

The hip-looking first preview audience arrived, and this time the play was preceded by a seven-minute color film clip from Ed Emshwiller's *Relativity*, which graphically showed the slaughtering of hogs, spurting blood, and convulsing to their deaths in the Chicago stockyards. The film repulsed and stunned the audience. The packed house seemed to be caught up in the play, and there were sustained cheers at the finish.

One night as I stood in front of the theater with Rochelle, she remarked, "There is something murderous in the air tonight." And she shuddered. Haunting—for only two hours later, Bobby Kennedy was shot as he wound up his primary campaign in Los Angeles.

Futz opened on June 13, 1968, and immediately became a reference point for the theater of the 1960s. Clive Barnes, an avowed O'Horgan fan, gave it a superlative review in the *Times*. "Bestiality— oh final horror—has come to Off Broadway. 'Futz' has beaten its controversial path into our ken. And I must say I am glad it did."[1] The other critics were either tantalized or outraged, or both.

Lucille Lortel carefully selected the productions that played her theater. Producers, actors, authors, and directors assembled in her suite at the Sherry Netherland Hotel on Fifty-Ninth and Fifth Avenue to read their plays aloud for her. In an unusual circumstance, she was away when *Futz* became a last-minute booking after another show closed abruptly. She had neither seen nor read it. And though a liberal thinker, there was much concern over what she might think. Harlan and Paul thought that, since she had become fond of me, I should accompany her to a performance.

Walter Kerr, on assignment for a Sunday *Times* piece, was seated directly in front of us, and kept his ears open for any pre-show chatter going on around him. Once the performance began, he cringed continuously and wrote feverishly. It was impossible not to notice. Lucille couldn't possibly be unaware of his response. I thought, *This is a disaster.* I feigned calm as the cast took its final bow. The house lights came up; Lucille patted me gently on the hand and said, "It's biblical, dear."

Kerr's scathing *Futz* review, adjoining a rave by the avant-garde critic, Eleanor Lester, dominated the front page of the *Times* "Arts and Leisure" for Sunday, June 30, adding the weight of the *Times* to the rapidly growing controversy.

I saw *Futz* many times in the next several weeks, at least twice stoned, and I finally got it. I could see why people hated it. I could see why I had hated it. Its minimalist form, its egoless performances, its anarchistic style, were the antithesis of what we had come to expect of the commercial theater. And yet it permanently influenced my aesthetic.

Rochelle's play was essentially a poem that was indeed biblical, capturing and using an essential part of rural America to illustrate the hypocrisy and hate of every society. The La MaMa Troupe did not "act" in the usual way, but, in service to Tom O'Horgan's masterful orchestration of the text, the actors offered a journey that explored and illuminated facets and possibilities of the characters, the situations, the rural society, the language, the imagery, and sometimes even the words themselves. The result was an anarchy in which everything was "freed."

One of my close friends later characterized my metamorphosis. "The first time Albert saw *Futz*, he ran out of the theater screaming. After it opened, he said it was a poem."

The initial weeks of *Futz* played to strong business. Producers and agents rushed to see it, to find out what it was. And as they got out of their cabs, most of them said the same thing: "Oh, I'm so stoned."

As the publicity subsided, *Futz* began to slow down. Word of mouth was horrendous. Harlan approached David and me about moving the play to the smaller Actors' Playhouse on Sheridan Square. The weekly operating costs would be trimmed by $3,000 and, if the present grosses held, our weekly shortfalls would hopefully be replaced by some profits.

Harlan and I stood on the sidewalk in front of the Theatre de Lys and told Paul Berkowsky of our plight. He was less than delighted. "I can't stop you from moving," he said, "but I'm not moving with you." "But, who will be our general manager?" I asked. Harlan and Paul both looked at me and said, "You." I was taken by surprise, but it didn't strike me as a half-bad idea. I said I would do it if Paul would give me a three-day crash course. He would.

And so, on the sidewalk in front of the Theatre de Lys, my real career in the theater began. As I took on more and more shows as a general manager, I realized that I had found my niche. I was a "second," the person behind the power, implementing, at their direction, what needed to be done and collaborating with them on decision-making. I was good at budgeting, negotiating, and promotion, and I lived to support people and projects I respected.

The move cut expenses, but the gross dropped even further, and *Futz* continued to operate at a small loss for most of the weeks of its run. But rather than close, we put our own money in each week to keep people employed and to achieve the longevity we hoped would enhance the subsidiary rights.

Some months after the closing on New Year's Eve of 1968, one of the actors called Gretchen Cryer to tell her that the La MaMa Troupe had met and determined that they were entitled to a portion of the profits from *Futz*. I told her to call him back and ask if they would like to share in the loss.

Peace (1969)

Early one November morning in 1968, the phone rang. It was the Paul Rudd of The New York Shakespeare Festival, and later the 1975 *Beacon Hill* miniseries. We didn't know each other, but he said he had been following my career, and he had seen a musical called *Peace* at the Judson Poets Theater the night before that he thought was for me. Located in the activist Judson Church on Washington Square South, Judson Poets was one of the three original giants of the Off Off Broadway movement, along with Caffe Cino and La MaMa.

Judson had its own style, a kind of sublimely mischievous version of camp, and its own set of superstars who were considered Off Off Broadway royalty. Headed up by the Reverend Al Carmines, its artistic director and composer-in-residence, and Lawrence Kornfeld, its director, the sensibility was silly, gay, and literate, with a sometimes-serious social conscience.

My only exposure to Judson had been Gertrude Stein's *In Circles*, which I saw in its long Off Broadway run at the Cherry Lane. Stein's words were given musical settings by Carmines, who sat at a piano looking very much like her. I hated it and left before it was over.

Rudd urged that I catch *Peace* and said the last performance was to be that evening. So, despite trepidations and a pouring rain, I went. I loved it.

Peace was a '60s East Village adaptation of the play by Aristophanes for which Carmines had provided a magical score. It was performed in minstrel style with the blackface characters of Liza and Rastus as slaves of the master, Trygaeus, who rode to heaven on a beetle with the foolhardy mission of asking the gods for peace on earth. The second act brought the gods to Earth, where they were presented with a minstrel show performed by most of the cast in blackface.

It was Judson high camp made earthy by the Carmines score and otherworldly by the fantastically hip Technicolor costumes by Nancy Christopherson. The second act was essentially the finale of every Garland-Rooney musical, as imagined by Jean Cocteau.

I ran to its director, Lawrence Kornfeld, after the show and told him I wanted to produce it Off Broadway. He said there were several interested producers but that he would lean in my direction because I had been one of the producers of *Futz*. He even knew of an investor who might put up all or most of the money, a man on Wall Street named Franklin de Boer, who had backed *In Circles*.

I met with de Boer in his office and, while he seemed to know his business, it was difficult to imagine why such a man would be interested in the Judson aesthetic. We sparred for an hour, and he agreed to put up the entire $20,000 needed to produce *Peace*. I had to ask him. "Why are you doing this?"

He called in his secretary and asked me if there would be a poster for the show. "Yes." Would his name be on it? "Yes." Next to mine, same size as mine? "Yes. Yes." "I'm going to hang it right over there," de Boer said, "and when I pinch her on the ass, she'll know she's being pinched by a producer." I ran all over Wall Street trying to find a working payphone to call Jerry Schoenfeld and tell him I had raised all the money in one meeting.

In the meantime, a producer named Beverly Landau called me and said she needed additional capital for her production of *Yes Yes, No No*, which was in rehearsal at the Astor Place Theatre. She described it as a female *Boys in the Band*. "You mean it's about lesbians?" I asked. "No," she said, "it's an all-female cast."

As I waited in the large Astor Place lobby, a small man in spectacles came sashaying through the silver doors carrying a drink. He looked faintly like Rex Reed. Beverly Landau introduced him as Bruce Mailman, the owner of the theater.

I was instantly and completely captivated. He had warmth, intelligence, great charm, and a little asthmatic laugh that seemed to happen in his chest. He seemed amused and slightly embarrassed by my interest but returned it.

As the rehearsal began, I audaciously plunked myself down right next to him, and he peered at me over his glasses. He said nothing but giggled softly, and we sat back like two small children to watch a play that was to run one performance at the Astor Place Theatre.

We immediately became front-and-center in each other's lives. He was a distinctly downtown person but also a crack businessman. In 1968, for the sum of $19,000, he had acquired the historic Astor mansion, which contained the Astor Place Theatre. The initial attraction under his auspices had been *The Indian Wants the Bronx*. More recently, he had acquired a theater on East Fourth Street that housed the long-running video hit Channel One and above it had built another theater called The Fortune.

He was witty, full of energy and ideas, and a great conceptualist. We drank and talked together every night for weeks. The attraction was so strong that we initially mistook as physical what was really the beginnings of a friendship for life. Bruce was deeply involved with John Sugg, a young and handsome doctor from Tennessee, who was his companion for life.

A big fan of Judson and of Al Carmines, Bruce began a relentless campaign for *Peace* to play the Astor Place. His mother turned her back on me at his Christmas party when I told her I didn't like the location—hilarious in light of my subsequent long history with the Astor Place that would begin with *Peace* playing there.

I was still living in West Side luxury in Dorchester Towers, but I felt myself being drawn more and more into a downtown lifestyle. John Long, an actor who had been in *Now Is the Time* and *The Fantasticks*, had moved in with me. With his elegantly adventurous spirit and his experience living in a commune, he became the backbone of the hedonistic '60s life of the apartment.

With the money for *Peace* in place and a February date set for the opening, I began thinking about the Christmas holidays. I decided on an acid Christmas. It was time to take LSD. On Christmas Eve John was away, but Arabella Colton, who was in Uta Hagen's acting class with him, was with me for the adventure. I had no idea what the drug had in store, but I was ready to give myself to whatever it was. After about forty-five minutes, I began to find out.

I first spoke in tongues and then started tonguing the air obscenely. I attempted to speak to God, but all I could get out was "Please God, please . . ." I couldn't finish it. I had a perception of love as an underground spring that had no beginning and no end, and that everything in the universe was a manifestation of that love and the beauty of it was in the attempt.

I looked at the table full of Christmas cards. All of them were animated. People were skating, rolling over the countryside in sleighs, the Baby Jesus lay quietly while Mary and Joseph and the animals looked on lovingly. The cattle, of course, were lowing.

Arabella asked what the Christmas tree was like. I said it was fine, but I was worried about its breathing.

The trip was full of wild fun, but I emerged from it with a strong urge to rid myself of my possessions, strip everything away, and find out who was there. As it happened, the events of the coming months took care of that without much help from me.

I was nervous about meeting Al Carmines, both because he was a formidable talent and because I was guilty about walking out of *In Circles*. I arranged to meet him at his apartment, which adjoined the rear of the church. I knocked on the door and introduced myself. He looked at me, smiled quickly, and loaded me up with two cases of soft drinks. "We're going to a party at John Herbert's loft," he said. I didn't think this was any way to treat a producer, and I had no idea who John Herbert was.

John Herbert was the composer John Herbert McDowell, a greatly revered artist of the avant-garde and a virtual saint of Off Off Broadway. When we entered his loft way east on Fourteenth Street, I saw everyone I had ever heard of or read about in the downtown theater. The wine and pot were plentiful, the laughter rang, and everyone was relaxed, joyous, stoned, and cozy on this cold winter night.

The work process with Al and Larry Kornfeld was wonderfully collaborative. I found them playful and fun and totally accessible to making the changes I thought would improve our chances for success.

I learned that blackface had been illegal in New York State for many years, but Jerry Schoenfeld did not think the law would be enforced.

We had an orchestra of two, with Al at the piano and young John Kaye from the *Fantasticks* tour on drums. There was a problem with Al not wanting to join the American Federation of Musicians Local 802, which at that time had a mandatory relationship with Off Broadway. He took the position that, as a member of the clergy, he should not have to belong to any organized union. The union demanded a meeting with Al and me. We walked in, and when they sat Al under a photo of Cardinal Cooke, I knew we were dead.

"Cardinal Cooke is a star member of Local 802," they said proudly. "Do you think you're better than Cardinal Cooke?" We all had a big laugh, and Al joined the union.

On opening night, the audience sat like a lump. At intermission Jerry Schoenfeld quipped to Paul Berkowsky, "*Promises, Promises* it's not."

We swept uptown for a party in my apartment, and to my amazement rave reviews began pouring in. Stewart Klein on Channel Five, followed by a man on the phone from the typesetting room of the *Times* who read us the enthusiastic *Times* review while pronouncing Aristophanes with a long "a."

The next day, Jerry Tallmer in the *Post* called Al "the greatest living American composer." That afternoon, as if to offer some perspective, *The Richard Rodgers Fact Book* was delivered to me by messenger, "With compliments of Mr. Rodgers." That evening, when Al came into the theater, I announced to the cast the arrival of "the greatest living American composer." David Vaughn, who played Hermes, added sardonically, "and several of the dead ones."

We were the darlings of the critics and the press, but our audiences were a mixed bag.

The show was loved by downtowners and hippies and despised by much of the theater establishment. Tom Jones wrote me a letter. "What is all this stuff about 'Peace'? Why do all of the critics love it? Why do all of our friends hate it?"

We billed *Peace* as "The Minstrel Musical," and it was not a surprise that few black people attended. One night, however, four black men and a black woman arrived to purchase tickets in the last row. There was a storm cloud over them, and I decided to stick around.

Toward the end of the first act, they began yelling things at the cast, and the cast members, who were political radicals, were very upset. I assured them during intermission that I would continue to monitor the performance. The blackface minstrel show in the second act brought things to a boiling point, and one of the group yelled, "Kill the actors!"

The cast was now visibly upset, but the show continued. The uncanny effect was that the actors, who were playing slaves, were now enslaved by the show. The "kill" threat was enough for me to call the Ninth Precinct police station, advise them of the situation, and ask them to come to the theater as a preventive, not confrontational, measure.

They arrived within minutes, and I sent them to the basement, where they would be safely out of sight of the audience. They agreed to stay there until and unless I called them, which I would do only in the event of trouble.

Seeing the police backstage further heightened the cast's concern. I assured them the police would stay out of sight unless there was real danger, but the police had no such intention. At the end of the performance, they emerged from the basement as the audience was leaving, making certain the black audience members knew they were there. This provocation further outraged the cast.

Al and I met with the company. We discovered that not only was the black group known to cast member Margot Lewitin, but that she had invited them because she and others in the company felt queasy about the blackface aspect of the show and wanted their take on it. She had a phone number where she thought we could reach them.

Al and I braced ourselves and took a cab to a small apartment on the Lower East Side to meet with the group. I can certainly say that we were frightened and had no idea what we would find, but we had an overriding desire to face up to the situation and see it through.

The group's view of the show was immoveable and ran deep. They found it objectionable and ignorant. They raged at us but respected that we had sought them out and come to them for a dialogue. There was extreme racial tension in the city at the time but, more than that, watching white people cavorting stereotypically around the stage as black slaves had unleashed real pain.

We, in turn, presented our view of the minstrel style, which I had loved as a performance style and years earlier had researched at length at the New York Public Library. The concept of joy rising up out of pain was not foreign to me. We left agreeing that both sides would invite people to attend the matinee the following Sunday, after which we would have a discussion and determine mutually how to address the matter. It was agreed that there would be no disruption during the performance.

Judson Church had many politically active black members in its congregation, and Al felt confident that they could be approached and would be supportive. I approached my good friends Dorothy Olim and Gerald Krone, the general managers of the Negro Ensemble Company. I told them there was a censorship issue at stake. Could they recruit some Ensemble members to see the show and participate in the discussion? They looked at me like I had lost my mind.

That Sunday began with a large feature about *Peace* on the front page of the *Times* "Arts and Leisure" section praising the show and celebrating Al Carmines' unique position in the theater as a minister and composer. I met with the cast before the matinee and promised them that, if there was any incident, I would stop the performance.

The large Astor Place lobby was jammed with invitees and with people who had read the *Times* and were eager to see the show. The theater was packed. All of our black friends were no-shows, which told me we had already lost the argument.

Although the tension was palpable, act one went reasonably well. It was our first performance ever before a sizable black audience. Halfway through the second act, a black woman who looked to be about ninety and had the look of an old slave stood up and screamed, "Stop this show!" Her heartbreaking cry broke the dam.

The black patrons began yelling and heckling, with the result that the white audience began cheering and applauding even harder. The audience had radicalized before our eyes, and the hate emanating from the whites was toxic. I was devastated. There was no going back.

As the audience became more and more confrontational, it was my judgment that, if we stopped the show, there would be a riot and people could be physically injured. Despite my promise to the cast, I let the performance continue.

When it was finally over, we attempted to have a discussion. Time after time, the black people made their points on solid ground, and, really, they were black, and we were not. The most lucid member of our team was Larry Kornfeld. The point that most hit home with him and with us all was when one of the black men asked him how he would like it if black people staged a satiric performance "dressed up as white people with hook noses singing and dancing in gas showers?"

That night, after *Peace* gave its last performance in blackface, Larry, Al, and I adjourned to Larry's apartment in Brooklyn to rewrite, or as we called it, to "bleach," the book and lyrics. We were joined by Howard Moody, the highly respected senior minister of Judson.

The blackface characters of Liza and Rastus became "Mama" and "Daddy," which changed their color and dialect but otherwise had little effect on script content or intent.

Bob Ganshaw, our press agent, sent out a book of wires to the press informing them of the changes, which soft-pedaled them as being made because the "blackface aspect of *Peace* had been found objectionable to black members of its audiences." It was, in fact, the convention of the time for New York television stations to edit out blackface routines from the old films of the '20s and '30s. Eddie Cantor's blackface routines were excised, and Al Jolson was nowhere to be found.

We were scorned in a few places for succumbing to "audience censorship," notably Marilyn Stasio in *Cue* magazine and one small radical paper that said we had "flushed *Peace* downs Mars's toilet." *The Daily Worker* was the only paper that covered the "discussion" performance, and it referenced the piece in the Sunday *Times*, which it memorably called "that fat dowager of a paper." The tumultuous events went largely unnoticed by press and public.

We recorded a cast album for Metromedia with Al on piano and won the Drama Desk Award for Best Musical Score, beating out *Promises, Promises*. Richard Schickel in *Life* magazine called it "one of the greatest scores in Off Broadway history."

As the box office sagged, I continued to pump money into the show every week, my own and whatever I could beg or borrow. By May of 1969, I was broke.

On the day I won the Producer of the Year award from *Show Business*, a casting newspaper for actors, I moved from Dorchester Towers to Avenue B and Sixth Street. Nancy Ford's husband, the actor Keith Charles, packed my belongings into his station wagon and helped with the move, while taunting me with, "Producer of the Year moves to Avenue B!" My post-acid wish to have no belongings was a rapidly emerging reality.

That summer, I divided my time between Avenue B and a time-share in the Fire Island Pines with Bruce Mailman and his circle of friends. To help pay bills, I became the chorus understudy in *Peace*.

One Sunday in June, when I happened to be in the City because I was performing, a call came in from one of my Fire Island house-mates. "Did you hear the news?" he asked. "Judy died." Honestly, I was relieved. Death had at last put an end to what I thought had become a torturous life.

After the curtain call of the *Peace* performances that day, Dallett Norris, who had replaced David Vaughn in the role of Hermes, stepped forward and said elegantly, "Ladies and gentlemen, if you please, we would like to pay tribute to a great artist, Judy Garland, who has died today." The audience gasped and joined us in singing "Over the Rainbow."

Six days later, on the day of her interment at Ferncliff Cemetery, members of the gay community in New York City erupted in what became known as The Stonewall Riots at the Stonewall Inn, a gay bar in Greenwich Village. Sick to death of Mafia and police oppression, they rose up and weren't going to take it anymore. In the struggle for universal civil rights, Gay Liberation had been born. Was there a relationship to Judy's death?

As the decades have gone by, Judy has endured. Her great body of work is there for all to see and hear. Her name is constantly in the press as a reference point, usually for great talent. My friend Bob Crewe put it so simply when he said, "She was the best conveyor of music."

My career is dedicated to her.

Days after Judy's passing, I came home to find my Avenue B roommates bound and gagged and my one possession, a camera, stolen. I got out of there the next day and began a period of several years of living on people's daybeds or in empty rooms with a foam-rubber slab and a desk. I had done it. I had stripped myself of everything and had only me.

I picked up a copy of the *Village Voice* and found myself listed in the cast of *Eye on New York*, Tom Eyen's new play coming to La MaMa. As a joke, I called Tom and demanded to really be in it. He told me to get down there, gave me a monologue, and threw me on the stage.

The Unseen Hand/Forensic and the Navigators (1970)

Seymour Peck, the well-respected liberal editor of the Sunday *Times* "Arts and Leisure" section, had a style of formatting headlines as questions. One Sunday I read a piece called "America's Great Hopes, White and Black?" It was about Sam Shepard and Ed Bullins. There was a sultry photo of Shepard that was just plain hot. He was the rage of the downtown scene at Theatre Genesis and La MaMa.

His agent, Toby Cole, gave me a pile of Sam's plays, which I read, and I began trooping around to see them at various Off Off Broadway haunts.

I went to the Old Reliable Theatre Tavern on East Third Street and Avenue C to see *Cowboys II*, directed by Bill Hart, an old Shepard crony, and after it was over, I was startled when most of the audience descended on me. They were all downtown playwrights, and word had got out that I would be there. After *Futz*, I was the great blond hope.

Once I got a handle on Sam's work, I selected two one-act plays that I thought could click on an Off Broadway double bill. *Back Bog*

Beast Bait was a voodoo-and-magic play set in a Louisiana bog. *Forensic and the Navigators* appealed to my sense of mischief. It was a paranoid speed trip that ended with the entire theater filling up with steam.

Conventional investors didn't get them, and the anarchistic nature of Sam's writing struck many as uncommercial, so I decided to skip traditional investors and go where it was warm.

My first stop was St. Adrian Company, the hip downtown restaurant in the Broadway Central Hotel at East Fourth Street and Broadway. I went in around 6:00 p.m. and introduced myself to the owner, Bruce Bethany. I told him what I was looking for and left with his investment and a friendship that continues to this day.

In a short time, the fund-raising took on a life of its own, and I soon had my choice of three investors who were willing to put up the entire remaining balance of capital. I chose Elliott Coulter, a savvy insurance executive, who was riding high on his investment in the current hit film of Philip Roth's *Goodbye, Columbus.*

Sam, at that moment, was away with Antonioni and the Open Theater shooting *Zabriskie Point*, and Lincoln Center had announced that, in the early spring of 1970, it would present Sam's first major full-length play, *Operation Sidewinder.* The play had been withdrawn from production at the Yale Repertory Theatre by Robert Brustein following violent opposition from black students, who objected to a Black Panther monologue, and from white students, who objected to the portrayal of radical whites in the play.

Toby Cole suggested I meet Jeff Bleckner, the student who had been slated to direct the ill-fated YRT production of *Sidewinder* and who had just graduated. We had a long and exhilarating dinner at the Five Oaks in Greenwich Village, and I thought Jeff would be the director for us. He had a wonderful creative mind, was rough-hewn, direct and honest, and had a great feeling for Sam's work.

It was now time to meet Sam Shepard. He was "busy with the Lincoln Center number" but he put aside some time for me.

When I arrived at his basement apartment on lower Sixth Avenue, Sam was wearing Levis and no shirt. He looked like an American god. Sensing that I was a little tense, he put a soft black leather vest on over his skin. I transitioned from not being able to breathe to mild hyperventilation.

In the beginning, he tried to categorize me, asking a series of questions to determine whether or not I was hip. "Are you into Dr. John?" he queried. "Naw, you wouldn't know who he is." I saw an album cover for Cat Mother and the All-Night Newsboys. I didn't know who they were, but I largely passed the tests, and we loosened up and really talked.

He was funny and straightforward. He showed me an image of his face smashed against the glass of a Xerox machine. It revealed crooked teeth and looked nothing like the handsome guy sitting across from me. "Is that really you?" I said. He replied, "It's me. I don't know if it's *really* me."

Then he surprised me. "I've had the awards and all that stuff. I want a hit. Do you think we can have a hit?" "I do," I swore, "and I'll put everything I've got into it."

Who would be in it? Enter a very pregnant Kewpie doll with big eyes and a deranged smile. Sam made an abrupt pointing gesture in her direction. She was O-lan Johnson, for whom he had written the part of Oolan in *Forensic and the Navigators*. They were shortly to be married. "And Lee," added a voice from above. "Yes, Lee Kissman," added Sam.

I looked up at what seemed to be a man impersonating a baboon, sitting high atop a bookcase, in the lotus position. "Greatest actor in America," piped up the baboon man, who then giggled and cocked his head. He was Bill Hart, and he punctuated the rest of the meeting with inarticulate remarks and giggles, providing a Dada ambience that I thought rounded out the afternoon very nicely.

We scheduled auditions for the following week at the Sheridan Square Playhouse. As the first round of actors, many of them Shepard vets, read from *Back Bog Beast Bait*, Sam became increasingly restless. On a break I asked if something was wrong.

"I don't know about this play, man," he said. "It sounds like bad Tennessee Williams."

He had another play at La MaMa that Jeff Bleckner was directing. Would I come to a rehearsal? The play was *The Unseen Hand*.

Ellen Stewart put us in a small room in the basement, and the actors were practically in my lap. It was overwhelming. It was an acid trip wrapped in a time warp of the old, Wild West, interrupted by the arrival of Lee Kissman as a space freak who represented a group of extra-terrestrials called "the silent ones." I thought it was a knockout.

I talked to Sam about doing some press. He was dead set against doing anything. Mel Gussow of the *Times* wanted to do a piece. With all the activity around him, Sam was news. Finally, Sam relented, and the interview went so well Sam invited Gussow to his wedding at St. Mark's Church-in-the-Bowery in the East Village. I was ecstatic.

I looked forward to attending the wedding, which was on a Sunday afternoon in spring. I planned to follow it with a small dinner party at the home of the actor Patrick Hines in Forest Hills. It had been generously arranged by my good friend Tom Jones, who thought Hines and some of his friends might be possible investors for us.

As I walked up the church steps, The Holy Modal Rounders, Sam's favorite rock group for which he sometimes played drums, were passing out purple tabs of acid. "Wonderful," I chuckled as I took one. "The reception will begin automatically."

The guests were turned out country style, with many of the ladies wearing white lace. The wedding party emerged, and I had never seen Sam so radiant. He was a beacon of light. It was a double wedding with playwright Walter Hadler and the actress Barbara Eda-Young. All of them were principals at Theatre Genesis, and the church was its home. The entire wedding party seemed to be speeding their butts off. Bill Hart was best man, and he stood next to Sam, his face bright red and dripping with sweat.

When the minister, Ralph Cook, asked, "Does anyone here present have anything to say?" Bill Hart yelped, "I wanna go OUTSIDE!"

Sam looked at Hart, smiled, and pulled him in for a hardy hug. The impact caused the entire wedding party to collide and fall backwards over the potted palms. Sam then picked up his pregnant bride, slung her over his shoulder, and marched up the aisle and out of the church. And not a moment too soon because, for me at least, the reception had begun. We adjourned to the church basement, where we drank a lot of wine and danced to shit-stomping music by The Rounders.

But enough of mirth. It was soon time for me to gather whatever poise I could muster and leave for my dinner party in Queens. It became clear on the subway ride that this would not be a normal visit. When the train came up out of the ground, I was certain we were flying through space. As I walked to the apartment, the sidewalk rippled under my feet.

Patrick Hines was a stout, elegant man. He sat me graciously in the parlor for a before-dinner cordial. On the wall to my right was an enormous oil painting of a ship caught in a storm on the high seas. As I looked at it, the ship tossed and turned violently, and, amidst loud claps of thunder and lighting, and people calling for help, Hines handed me my drink.

"THAT PAINTING!" I exclaimed in a manner that alarmed my host. "What about it?" he asked. "It's, like, amazing," I said. He watched me for a moment and asked, "Are you all right?" I confided that I was in the middle of an acid trip but was otherwise fine. "Do we need to call the police?" he inquired. "No, no. I will be fine."

We put it behind us for the moment and moved on to the dining room. I don't remember much about it, but it didn't seem likely that an investment would be forthcoming. The next day I made a discreet call to Tom Jones, who said he did not wish to discuss it.

We decided to open at the Astor Place Theatre on April 1, 1970, which would follow *Sidewinder*'s opening on March 12. Jules Irving, director of Lincoln Center Theater, and I decided it would be good to make acquaintance and become aware of each other's movements. A dinner was arranged with Sam at the Howard Johnson on Sixth Avenue and Eighth Street. After ice cream, Jules took us up to Lincoln Center. He unlocked the front door, switched on the lights, turned to us, and announced, "I've got to change the image of this fucking place." What made it funny was that he was wearing a floor-length fur.

The Astor Place has a very large lobby, and Sam wanted to make use of it. He asked me to find an esoteric rock band he liked called Lothar and the Hand People. The group used a theremin, which is an antenna connected to a box, played by waving the hands around the antenna. The sound is similar to someone playing a saw.

Paul Conly, their leader, whom I came to adore, told me about a brand-new electronic instrument called an ARP synthesizer, which electronically duplicated the sounds of other musical instruments as well as providing a multitude of sound effects.

It was decided that Lothar, with Sam on drums, would play for half an hour in the lobby before each performance. Paul Conly would then position himself in a small area in front of the stage and furnish incidental music for the plays, utilizing the synthesizer and theremin. He had very long hair and wore a tall pointed hat.

The other items in Sam's lobby fantasy were a carnival-style popcorn machine and a stand selling Moxie, a soft drink, and Abba-Zabba bars, which, very much like Mary Janes, were taffy bars stuffed with peanut butter.

Sam asked me to contact Joey Skaggs, a hip entrepreneurial prankster, whose accomplishments included organizing a bus load of hippies for a tour of Queens and floating a plastic iceberg in the Hudson. Sam said Joey had some paintings that would be interesting in the lobby.

Joey and I met for a drink at St. Adrian. He was handsome, macho, and an anarchist. He thought Sam's plays were conventional and told me I should produce a French Dada play in which shit rained down on the audience. His paintings were opaque swirls of color, and we hung them on the lobby walls. One lobby visitor said, "Have you ever seen these paintings on acid, man? *They make sounds.*"

We did some recasting, adding David Selby and David Clennon, and went into production, with Jeff's friend and classmate Santo Loquasto making his New York debut as our set designer, Roger Morgan doing the lights, and Judson's Nancy Christopherson the costumes.

When I decided to do *Peace*, I spoke to Larry Kornfeld about Nancy Christopherson. Her costumes, rich in color and surreal in style, were an essential part of the production. "She's supernatural," Larry said, and told me that people of fashion followed her work at Judson, and a few months later, you would see its influence in the magazines.

The first time I met her was in her large garret apartment on West 104th Street. I was totally captivated. I could see that she was fragile and vulnerable, an artist with an otherworldly sensibility who might tend to distrust people in my position. I wanted to reassure her. "I'll never lie to you," I said.

During the run of *Peace*, Nancy and I were together constantly. We both loved to dance and drink, and talking with her was fascinating. She was a recluse and had spent a great deal of her life reading the classics and studying the classical authors and composers.

She could discuss any period of world culture as though standing in the middle of it, and any historical figure of royalty or in the arts as though she had left them only moments before. She loved the gods and astrology. She would not take her next breath until she consulted the I Ching, which I found exasperating.

I began to realize that I was very much in love with her, and one night, sitting on a stoop on Grove Street in the Village, I told her. She felt the same. I moved in with her. It was a rich life. She made all of my clothes, mostly out of china silk, and she prepared sublime meals. We drank wine and talked and talked. We made enormous salads together. We made Alice B. Toklas brownies and accompanied them with the recommended mint tea. We were on the ceiling for three days.

She brought me into a universe of music and literature I had not previously encountered, and to the films of Cocteau, Dreyer,

Marcel Carné, Vittorio De Sica, and Jean Vigo. She found beauty in the cracks in the sidewalk.

One night, as an homage to Cocteau, we put on rubber gloves and tried to walk through a magnificent large antique mirror she had. Nancy attributed our failure to my lack of belief.

Ultimately, because I am a gay and earthbound Taurus, our life together became difficult and painful. Stopping to admire the cracks in the sidewalk became an exhaustion. My natural affinity was for worldly things. We separated, but our friendship endured for many years.

It was inevitable that when actors in a Christopherson show were first given their costumes, they went nuts. Her costumes always brought metaphysical and existential dimensions to the characters that were at first frightening to the actors. It had happened time after time at Judson. She was accustomed to it, and, although it took a toll on her, she dealt with it.

The night that *The Unseen Hand* and *Forensic* casts were first given their costumes, I had an angry late-night call from one of the principal actors. If he had to wear it, he said he would quit the show. He said a number of the other actors were equally upset. I was drunk at that late hour, and I called Nancy and fired her. It was a terrible decision. Nancy's costumes had promised a look of otherness and danger, and without them, I think a big chunk of the magic was lost from our production.

Sam, Jeff Bleckner, Roger, and Santo were dismayed by my decision. Ironically, I had been the one insisting that the worst thing we could do was to make Sam's plays safe. Nancy's replacement was adequate and not treated well by me. I was punitive out of guilt about Nancy and angry that the new designer could not possibly be her equal.

Nevertheless, the first preview was spectacular. Robert Ganshaw, our press agent, doubled his share of house seats, and we were off to St. Adrian to celebrate.

Joey Skaggs was increasingly eager to focus attention on his lobby paintings: What did I think about a plot to kidnap the noted gallery owner Leo Castelli and force him to come to the Astor Place on opening night to view them? Well, first of all, we were opening Sam's plays, not an art gallery. And I imagined that someone like Castelli might carry a small handgun or have some kind of protection nearby. Joey seemed assuaged.

Due to a full spring schedule, all of the critics attended *The Unseen Hand* and *Forensic* on opening night. Ellen Stewart danced around the lobby with Emery Lewis, the well-loved critic of *The Bergen Record*. While the rock band played on, I told Richard Watts of the *New York Post* that I was glad to see him. "Glad to see you, too," he said. "I wish I could hear you." I certainly looked forward to that review. Clive Barnes was a half hour late, and we held the curtain for him. By the time it began, the other critics were seething.

At the end of the evening, there was a brief moment of triumph as Sam, Jeff, and I stood in the rear of the theater and watched the critics disappearing as the wall of steam moved slowly to the back of the house. They looked at each other with slight alarm, but no one moved. We were jumping up and down and laughing. It was an outrageous sight.

We heard a noise and turned to see a group of sinister-looking men entering the lobby. They were wearing fedoras and double-breasted pin-striped suits and carrying violin cases. I identified two of them as Joey Skaggs and Tony Barsha, a Theatre Genesis director and former O-lan boyfriend. They had come to abduct Sam to the Port Authority Bus Terminal and put him on a bus to Azusa, California, where *The Unseen Hand* took place. They grabbed him and attempted to throw him to the floor.

Sam didn't take to it at all, and the critics emerged from the steam-filled theater to find themselves in the middle of a fistfight between Sam and his kidnappers. Disappointed that Sam could not take a joke, the kidnappers sulked out and sped into the night in the waiting getaway car. It happened so fast that it was hard to grasp what had really gone on.

The opening night party was at Silvers, the newest hip club, located on a high floor in a building on the west side of Union Square. I hired a rock band and contracted the club until 2:00

a.m. We had decided to allow reviews into the party. The television reviews, all scathing pans, rolled in, accompanied by loud booing noises and Bronx cheers from Sam.

In the *Times*, Clive Barnes said Sam wrote "good, disposable plays" but oddly went on to say that "you cannot be uninterested if you are at all interested in the American theater."

The most touching sight was Peter Maloney, one of the actors and a member of the Open Theatre Company. Peter was heartbroken and crying his eyes out about Sam's reviews. Once again, I was devastated by Mr. Barnes, who I thought would like these plays and who was not only late but didn't like them.

In the midst of all this, I was pulled away by a Silvers employee who told me that the boss wanted to see me. I was taken to a small room on another floor to face a sinister looking man in a double-breasted silk suit seated behind a desk.

"You're outta here by 12:30," he threatened. As if the bad reviews weren't enough, Silvers was now tossing us out an hour and a half early. "We have the place 'til two," I shot back, "and we're staying 'til two." He stood up, and underneath his suit jacket was the clear outline of a gun. "Get the fuck out of here."

The next morning the *Daily News* carried a front-page photo of the building. It was a pile of rubble. It had been occupied by the headquarters of the Black Panthers, and shortly after 3:00 a.m., it was blown off the face of the earth. As I write this, there is a McDonald's in that location, the only one-story building on Union Square.

Everyone involved had an emotional investment in Sam and his plays. We were devastated, and this was strike three for Sam following on the heels of the negative critical responses to *Sidewinder* and *Zabriskie Point*.

The day after opening, it was pouring rain. When I went to the box office, the treasurer sat in front of the silent phone with tears streaming down her face. There are few things more depressing than a silent box office. Sam came in, a poignant figure with rain dripping from his cowboy hat. "Guess we didn't make it, Al," he said.

By performance time that night, Sam was singing a different tune. As always, a lot of people had offered their opinions. "You're the producer, right?" he said. "So are you gonna find money to keep this running? That's what you're supposed to do, right?" Everybody was angry. Everybody was tense.

Peter Neufeld, the show's general manager, was always pink. This night, he rushed into the box office, and he was bright red. "Sam Shepard p-punched me!" he blurted. Every night Peter gave Sam a hand signal five minutes before the lobby band was to stop playing. That night Sam just didn't feel like stopping, and they kept playing until Peter insistently tapped Sam on the shoulder. Sam stopped for an instant and landed a solid punch to Peter's jaw.

Bruce Mailman called crying at 4:00 a.m. and said we could have the theater rent-free for as long as we could keep the plays running. The next night, the cast asked to talk to me and said they would take no salaries for as long as it took. They then presented me with a little over $2,500 that they had raised amongst themselves, in the form of checks, bills, and even coins. These were not people of wealth. The closing notice I had planned to post stayed in my pocket. Although I was convinced that business would not turn around, I felt that I must match the support and goodwill that were being shown. I had no means but took a personal loan from Elliott Coulter, and we ran an ad quoting Andy Warhol, Elia Kazan, Abbie Hoffman just days after his acquittal of conspiracy charges in the Chicago Seven trial, and the *East Village Other*, a *Village Voice* alternative. But as Sol Hurok famously said, "If they don't want to come, nothing will stop 'em." We closed after thirty-one performances.

Lee Kissman and Beeson Carroll won Obies. Sam began a couple of troubled years in New York that included work on a screenplay for Robert Redford, who had acquired a film option on *The Unseen Hand*. Sam lost interest in it before it was finished, and Redford dropped it.

Sam lived for a short, chaotic time with Patti Smith in the Chelsea Hotel, and O-lan, not to be outdone, took up with someone herself. "What's good for the goose," she told me. Sam and Patti costarred in Sam's play *Cowboy Mouth* at the American Place, but the run was aborted when Sam walked off during a performance. Ultimately, Sam and O-lan reconciled, spending the next several years living in Nova Scotia and London.

Shortly after *The Unseen Hand* opened, Tom Eyen invited me to the dress rehearsal of his new La MaMa production, *The Dirtiest Show in Town*. "I did this for you, darling," he said, "I want you to produce it Off Broadway." It had the Eyen wit, but it was a nude show. I thought it beneath me, and I really didn't feel like producing anything.

I fled to Buffalo to stay with my friends, Max and Helen Jacobs, who had moved there when the death of Max's father required that he return to an active role in the family business. I was emotionally and financially spent, and they were a great comfort. I pondered whether I would ever return to New York, let alone work in the theater.

The promise of an exciting spring for Sam had materialized into three failures. I felt that I had done Sam no good whatever, a feeling that was deepened by *Village Voice* ads for Murray Mednick's *The Deer Kill* that suggested people "See it at Theatre Genesis before some commercial producer moves it Off Broadway." For the moment, Max Jacobs and I were both theater expatriates. But, unlike me, he missed it. He missed the fulfillment of continuing his acting career, which had begun so auspiciously when Ted Mann and Paul Libin cast him in a featured role in their Broadway production of *The Zulu and the Zayda*.

The Dirtiest Show in Town (1970)

Bruce Mailman called to tell me that Tom Eyen's *The Dirtiest Show in Town* had opened at La MaMa and that he was going to produce it at the Astor Place. It had gotten a Barnes rave in the *Times* that included a quote of pure gold. "It makes *Oh! Calcutta!*

seem like *Little Women*." With onstage nudity all the rage at that time, such a quote could fill a theater for months.

He told me he couldn't do the show without me as his general manager. "I have no apartment in New York," I said. "You'll sleep in my living room." I laughed at the irony of the whole situation and thought it was a demotion I could accept.

As I was mulling it over, the massacres occurred at Kent State, where only four years earlier we had played *The Fantasticks*. When a demonstration was announced for Washington, DC, on May 9, I had to go, joining one hundred thousand others. Max generously offered me the family's private plane. When he told me that the cost of operating it was four hundred dollars an hour, I declined, thinking that it just wasn't the right way to go to a demonstration.

Back in New York, I immediately got caught up in the excitement of *Dirtiest Show*. Bruce had pulled me out of the doldrums for what looked to be a winner. He didn't think *Dirtiest Show* was a masterpiece, but he thought it would make money. As general manager, making money was a priority. My fatal flaw as a producer was choosing things I thought the public should see.

Tom had conceived it in a fragmented, nonlinear style that played like a series of sound bites and photo ops. It had the classic downtown style Eyen had first evolved at the Caffe Cino and was chock full of humor and erotica. The fragmented formats of his plays were a harbinger of what was to come in the media and pop culture.

Tom was a showman and savvy in every aspect of how to present his work. Sex was front and center, but he wanted it sold with class.

Ticket sales were brisk. As we approached the first performance at the Astor Place, Bruce suggested that we line the center aisle with folding chairs and sell them as "standing room." Seats were $10, the top Off Broadway price established by *The Boys in the Band*. Bruce felt the "standing room" could command $8.

"It's cheesy," I argued. "It will create a fire hazard." "Dear, it will still leave three feet of clearance, which is what is required." Beneath my dignity, I would not be party to it.

Ten minutes before curtain at the first preview, the lobby was mobbed with people on the waiting list, hoping for tickets. I had never seen anything like it. Their desperation to get in was palpable. I was energized. I rushed upstairs to Bruce's apartment. "What are you doing here?" he asked.

"I have come for the dinette set."

I grabbed the four chairs and took them into the house. I then went backstage and took all of the actors' chairs from the dressing room. In the excitement of the moment, they were happy to surrender them. As I whizzed by with chairs under each arm, Tom Eyen whispered, "Glamour, darling."

If anyone balked at the $8 standing room price, we told them they would actually be sitting. And we determined that they would only be sold on a day-of basis one half hour before curtain..

The preview audience went wild for the show, and I began to get my first taste of what a real New York hit could be. The celebrities, the clamor for tickets, people squashing fifty-dollar bills in my hand. True to my father's teaching, I would never take a penny that wasn't mine.

In addition to the folding chairs, once the show began, our three-hundred-pound stage manager, "Miss Bonnie, Friend to the Stars," occupied the center of the rear aisle with a home tape recorder that played "Let's Spend the Night Together" and other current hits throughout the show.

At the fourth preview, the house manager called me out of the box office. There was trouble inside. A patron who had purchased aisle seats was complaining loudly that with a folding chair next to him he was no longer on the aisle. He demanded that the chair be removed.

His was a party of four, and the first thing I did was move the discussion to the lobby. Since all eleven folding chairs had been sold, my only option was to offer him a full refund, which I did. In addition, he said, the folding chairs constituted a fire hazard. I told him that we had sufficient aisle clearance to meet fire department regulations. "I got something bigger than the fire department," he said, as his wife tried to restrain him. They left, and we resold their seats.

His words stuck with me, and I had a hunch. I determined that the following night we would sell no folding chairs. And I put Miss Bonnie on two theater seats holding the tape recorder on her knees—an act I could have booked on the Sullivan show. Sure enough, as I was doing the ticket count in the box office, we heard approaching sirens wailing louder and louder and coming to a stop in front of the Astor Place.

The district fire chief and sixteen firemen in raincoats and hats burst into the lobby and stormed toward the house. With great gusto, the chief threw open the house doors to peer down the aisle and see absolutely nothing.

He slammed them shut. I walked out into the lobby. "May I help you?" I said meekly.

"I WANT 'NO SMOKING' SIGNS IN THIS LOBBY!" he bellowed. And he and his sixteen firemen departed the theater. The following night, we resumed selling standing room, and Miss Bonnie returned to her position in the center of the aisle.

Tennessee Williams came and, seeing the lobby full of people, said to his friend, "We still have time to pee." I told Bruce it would make a good quote for the ad.

A well-tanned man asked for tickets in the name of Harburg. "And the initials?" I inquired. The man laughed and said "E.Y."

Butterfly McQueen arrived late, in sandals. She told us her Afro-Lesson had run overtime. She fled the theater ten minutes later. "They told me this was about pollution," she said.

Pearl Bailey looked at me as she was leaving and said, "What I need now, honey, is a stiff cup of black coffee."

Shortly before the opening of *Dirtiest Show*, Lester Nichols, a former fixture in the garment industry, opened a new bar and restaurant at the corner of Fourth Street and the Bowery. He named it Phebe's Place in honor of his pet bulldog. In no time, it became "the Sardi's of Off and Off Off Broadway." Every writer, director, and actor of Off Off and Off was there every night. All the people you had read about and all the people you knew. Table hopping was the order of the day. Every night was New Year's Eve. Plays were written there, shows were cast, dance companies and acting troupes were born. Everybody belonged. Robert Patrick's *Kennedy's Children* provides an insight into some of its people and the culture of the time. For a brief moment it was a scene with a beating heart, until Lester's untimely death of cancer in 1972, when it seemed to change overnight.

Bruce, heady with the success of *Dirtiest Show*, suggested that we do an anthology and history of Off Off Broadway. Through Sam Shepard, I had become friendly with Bob Amussen, editor-in-chief at Bobbs-Merrill, and with our relationships in the community, it seemed a natural. I resisted for a while because I knew that, while it was Bruce's concept, the bulk of the grunt work would fall on me.

We took a proposal to Amussen that involved printing thirty-seven of the seminal plays in Off Off Broadway's history to-date and front matter that would feature articles on the major Off Off Broadway theater companies, complete listings of their productions, and annotated bios of all of the playwrights based on interviews I would conduct. At a cost of $30,000, it was the most expensive project Bobbs-Merrill had undertaken, and I was especially thrilled because I had grown up on Bobbs-Merrill textbooks as a kid in Indianapolis.

Most playwrights were excited to have their plays included in what would be a definitive text on the first golden period of the Off Off Broadway movement. Some of the black playwrights, however, were in a militant period. The hardest play to secure was Imamu Amiri Baraka's masterpiece *Slave Ship*, which I had seen at the Washington Square Methodist Church with Sam and Jeff before rehearsals began for *The Unseen Hand*. We were blown away by the play and by the slave ship set by Eugene Lee. Afterwards, Baraka, in dark glasses and surrounded by bodyguards, looked right through Sam when he tried to say hello. They had been friends from the days when both had plays running on Second Avenue, and Sam was hurt by the snub.

Baraka's agent said "No" for the first three months. I went to his office and called upon his sympathies for my own experiences as a gay man, and he let us have the play. We got the rights to Ed Bullins' *Clara's Ole Man* from his publisher, but Bullins refused to be interviewed for his bio. "I don't want my play in no book," he muttered, and hung up on me.

It took a year to prepare the manuscript and another year to work over the galleys, and we loved every minute of it.

Toward the end of the summer of 1970, there were disquieting signs from Jerry Schoenfeld. Our press agent, Saul Richman, told me he was badmouthing *Dirtiest Show*. I called him about it and he said, "You tell Saul Richman that no press agent is going to put a muzzle on me."

Jerry, who had always been supportive of Off Broadway, now began referring to it as "the sewer." He called and asked how much weekly profit we were making. "About $6,000," I told him, on a capacity gross of $13,000.

"That's too much. You need some union stagehands down there."

"We have nothing for them to do," I shot back. I was troubled by the exchange. In another conversation, he spoke of getting me into ATPAM and asked if I thought I could "handle a house," by which he meant be the house manager of a Shubert theater. I told him I had no interest in house managing, that I loved what I was doing. Looking back, I realize that Jerry was offering me job security in a situation that was about to become very volatile for my home turf.

That fall brought negotiations for the Off Broadway actors, and we discovered that Equity was bringing in an outsider as its lead negotiator. Donald Grody was a former actor who had passed the Bar and had an extensive background at the Department of Labor and the National Labor Relations Board. Traditionally, the Off Broadway negotiations had been handled by the executive secretary of Equity for the actors and Paul Libin for the theater owners and producers, with both sides taking strong positions and an equitable outcome eventually achieved. At the end of the day, the union always realized that Off Broadway was primarily an investment in the future for its actors. Advance word was that Grody was tough and the negotiation was going to be brutal.

Equity opened with the staggering demand that the minimum salary for Off Broadway and Broadway be one and the same, one salary fits all. Off Broadway's size limitations at the time were 100 to 399 seats, while Broadway theaters ranged from 900 to 2,400 seats. We looked at that and their other demands and walked out.

Equity's approach had a new militancy, and as negotiations proceeded, attitudes hardened, and the relationship between the parties soon broke down. Equity called the first Off Broadway strike in its history, shutting down all seventeen running shows for thirty-one days. Some never returned.

Tom Eyen organized a street theatre piece called *The Death of Off Broadway (A Street Play)* that featured the cast of *Dirtiest Show*, his personal press agent Alan Eichler, and me, followed by assorted TV cameramen and news photographers. We started at the Astor Place and walked to every Off Broadway theater, burning dollar bills while William Duff Griffin yelled, "Heil, Money!" It concluded with a smart brunch at Sutters on Greenwich Avenue. Thanks to Alan, the stunt got extensive media coverage, but since there was no show running, there was no payoff.

In mid-December, both sides agreed to submit their proposals to binding arbitration. Past negotiations had resulted in a $5-per-week increase. The arbitrator now ruled for a $50 increase, from $75 to $125 plus an additional $75 for shows doing capacity business. The door of opportunity opened for the other unions, the theater owners, and our advertising vendors, and they walked through it.

Dirtiest Show managed another year but never again reached capacity, frequently operating at a loss. The audience had moved on in just thirty-one days. Off Broadway began a period of big-hit-or-die. The esoteric and quirky shows for discerning audiences, which had been its lifeblood, would now struggle.

It was no secret that while Off Broadway had been thriving in recent years, Broadway had been floundering. The strike and the new economics had certainly amounted to a reversal for Off Broadway, a place that Mr. Schoenfeld increasingly seemed to regard as a competitor that must be defeated.

I was convinced Jerry was behind the Off Broadway strike and told him so. He denied it, of course, but would frequently say, "I know you think I was behind the strike, Albert," and he continued to ask me, in front of whoever he was with, how things were in "the sewer." It was hurtful. It didn't prevent him, however, from once saying, "If you ever find a *Godspell,* Albert, we would be interested."

In June of 1972, I had a meeting with Jerry to discuss his preparing an agreement for me to produce Charles Ludlam's Ridiculous Theatrical Company in a "stoned" vaudeville show to be called *Bedlam Follies.* He was wound up so tight and was so uncharacteristically combative that I finally called the meeting to a halt and suggested we do it another day. He apologized and told me that he was, at that moment, under impossible pressure. Betty Spitz, his secretary for decades, looked like she was about to shatter.

Within days, all of these events reached astonishing confluence when I picked up the *Times* to see a story announcing that my lawyers, Gerald Schoenfeld and Bernard B. Jacobs, and a man named Irving Goldman, were now the Executive Directors of The Shubert Organization.

Shubert, which had long languished under the direction of the last living relative, the alcoholic Lawrence Shubert Lawrence, would now swing into high gear as its new leadership put forth a plan to revitalize the entire Broadway theater industry.

Shubert would reenter the producing arena for the first time in two decades and would make substantial investment available to other producers for desirable product for their theaters. Telecharge, an enormous telephone center, would be established to enable consumers to charge their tickets by phone and later by computer.

And so, while Off Broadway reeled from the effects of its strike, the Broadway theater entered a honeymoon period, an era of good feeling, between "the Shuberts," as Jerry and Bernie were now called, and all of the top Broadway producers.

Only months later—with the New York Attorney General's office investigating a possible Shubert role in an earlier "ice" scandal, daily headlines in the *New York Post* about the dubious alliances of Shubert partner Irving Goldman, and not every producer happy with the amount of Shubert interest in his or her projects—the honeymoon was over.

While these difficulties were raising their ugly heads, I had a conversation with Jerry. "I'm at the peak of my powers," he said. "With the theaters and the foundations, I have everything at my fingertips. But when I see someone who I think has as much as I do, I want to jump out the window."

The position Jerry Schoenfeld had reached had not placed him sufficiently above the throng to overcome a deep-seated personal insecurity or the years of insufferable treatment by J. J. Shubert. It saddened me. He was working hard and contributing much to the theater industry and to the city. It was evident that he and Bernie were bringing the Shubert Organization back to the forefront of world theater and expanding its profit sources in ways that its founders would have never thought possible.

The only response I could offer to him was a quote from "Desiderata," a 1927 Max Ehrmann prose poem: "If you compare yourself with others, you may become vain or bitter, for always there will be greater and lesser persons than yourself."

Jerry later revealed that, during this period, he had struggled through a nervous breakdown. While over time the severity of the situation diminished, these insecurities never disappeared and at times were to cause him to engage in cruel behavior, especially if he thought you were rising to a level of having more than he thought you should have.

In Mr. Schoenfeld's eyes, Off Broadway had reached that level.

Rain (1972)

Over the Christmas holidays in 1971, John Vaccaro approached me in Phebe's about appearing in his production of Leslie Lee's play, *Elegy for a Down Queen*, slated for La MaMa in February. John's Off Off Broadway company was The Play-House of the Ridiculous, and the productions were reflective of the name. Originally John and Charles Ludlam were a team, but a serious split had occurred, and they went their separate ways.

The role he offered me was The Family Parrot. Who could resist? The first day of rehearsal he put me on my perch and in his inimitable voice, part Mae West and part Italian mobster, he gave the only direction he was to give me. "Peaches, react."

The production was utterly mad. The show was produced on a grant that provided $50 per week for the black actors and $25 per week for the white actors. No one cared. We all loved each other. We cared about fun.

On opening night, I was sitting on my perch as the audience came in, and Jerry and Pat Schoenfeld arrived. They were seated down front, and I was startled when Jerry began talking to me. I answered back as the parrot. "Hi, Jerry (squawk, squawk). How are you, Jerry? (squawk)." The following day I got a phone call. "Albert, when we are alone you may call me Jerry. But in public you must call me Mr. Schoenfeld. And Albert, especially when you are a parrot, Albert."

There was a young man on the spotlight for *Elegy* who was getting quite a bit of attention from the audience as well as the actors. He was striking looking, unlike anyone we had ever seen. Like a divine *androgyne* from the imagination of Jean Cocteau. The other compelling thing about him was his concentration. It was as if operating that spotlight was the most important task in the universe.

He was fresh out of Purdue University, and his name was Peter Schneider. He seemed aloof from the rest of us, but I think he was just shy. I sought him out right away and found him to be as fascinating as he looked. We spent nearly every night together in Phebe's, and, while falling in love with him, I sought to mentor him and help him along in his career. He was mesmerizing, but underneath his seeming androgyny beat the heart of a heterosexual, which I made a less-than-perfect effort to accept and respect.

Madeleine le Roux was a tall blonde with a strong South African accent, frizzy hair, and a ski-jump nose that gave character to her overt sexuality. She was enjoying a vogue from the attention she garnered during *Dirtiest Show*. She was an archetypal Tom Eyen performer. Tom had a knack for peopling his plays with actors who were either very attractive and exotic-looking or bizarre, many of whom were high-strung neurotics. He wrote specifically for them, harnessing their neuroses in the service of his plays. He called his company Theatre of the Eye.

Madeleine lived in The Colonnades above the Astor Place Theater. It was the old John Jacob Astor mansion, now under Bruce's ownership. Caruso, Charles Dickens, and Harold Ross, founding editor of *The New Yorker*, were among the illustrious who had guested or lived there.

In the '50s it attained notoriety as the establishment that housed a call girl ring operated by the wealthy playboy Mickey Jelke. Now it was headquarters for actors, artists, and misfits, mostly from the realms of Off Off and Off Broadway, and Madeleine was one of its stars. She had a large apartment in which she lived with assorted boyfriends who came and went at her whim, and she held Bruce in great esteem.

Bruce unofficially became her manager, and his first move was to send her to a plastic surgeon who would "fix" her nose. He ruined it. It looked shapeless. One of her most distinguishing physical characteristics was utterly destroyed. His next mistake was to acquire the rights to that old John Colton property, *Rain*, as a star vehicle for her. *Rain*, based on a short story by Somerset Maugham, was a staple of stage and screen, having achieved success with such stars as Jeanne Eagels, Joan Crawford, Gloria Swanson, and Rita Hayworth. Bruce's obsession with *Rain* emanated totally from the fact that Marilyn Monroe had been frequently mentioned for a screen version, and he thought Madeleine could pick up where Marilyn left off. For Bruce, the link to Marilyn endowed the property with a mystique that, in the light of day, did not exist.

While I was recuperating from hepatitis, the production tried out at the Cleveland Playhouse under the direction of Michael Flanagan and was sufficiently successful that Bruce decided to bring it to the Astor Place. I was wary of it from the beginning, but Bruce wrote me in a two-page letter that he was going to do it with me or without me. Better with me.

Featured in the cast were James Cahill, Beeson Carroll, and John Travolta, making his New York debut in a tiny role. And, yes, I told his manager Bob LeMond that I thought he was going to be a star.

In preparation for what Bruce thought was going to be a heavy ticket demand, he set about to increase the Astor Place seating capacity from 199 to 299. People directly above the theater, whose apartments had filled with steam during *Forensic and the Navigators*, were now bought out as we began construction of a balcony.

The timing was unfortunate, coinciding as it did with the beginning of rehearsals for *Rain*, which were in the theater. But it did provide the particular brand of chaos that seemed indigenous to the Astor Place. Not only were the cold February winds blowing into the theater, it frequently snowed, too. Had the play been called *Wind* or *Snow*, the environment would have been perfect.

Actors' Equity had no rules governing weather, but after many complaints, an elaborate forced-air heating system was installed. When it was finally turned on, it blew cold air into the faces of the actors. After several days, it did emit heat, and the actors were utterly joyous until they went downstairs to their dressing rooms to discover that a sewage pipe had burst and their makeup and personal belongings were drenched in shit and piss. The stage manager and I were utterly exasperated.

We hired Peter Schneider to be the production assistant at a salary of $15 per week. At the end of his first week's work, I asked him what he had learned. He answered that he had learned how to live out of petty cash. Peter asked Bruce for an apartment in the building. "I know what I pay you," Bruce said. "You can't afford to live here." He adored Peter and gave him an apartment anyway. We also gave him a job in the box office. On his own, he joined the crew doing the theater renovations and building the set. Working the three jobs, he managed to eke out the rent.

Against my most strenuous warnings, Bruce asked his plumber to do the rain effect. This man was typical of the galaxy of eccentrics with whom Bruce surrounded himself. People who amused him, people who were capable, but people who could be erratic. There were constant plumbing problems in the building and, I am sure, Bruce viewed giving this man the creation of the rain effect as a kind of reward.

As the previews progressed, Madeleine's voice, never a resonant instrument, became ravaged from playing three acts eight times a week.

Opening night was unforgettable.

Bruce called me into his bedroom before the show (he conducted most business at that time from his bed) and handed me a letter assigning me five percent of the profits. "Oh, honey," I said, "make it *ten*."

We proceeded into the theater, and the performance began. Madeleine rasped through the creaky dialogue, and when it came time for the rain effect, an essential pipe had been jarred by the subway passing under the building, and the rain fell not on the actors but drenched the critics who were sitting in the first seven rows.

Early in the first act, Benjamin Benno, a deranged painter who had been written about by Henry Miller as "Benno, the wild man from Borneo" and was perhaps Bruce's most permanently angry tenant, began banging a chair on his floor directly above the stage. The banging continued, unabated, until the end of the act. At Bruce's urging, I called Benno at intermission and implored him to stop. I told him Bruce would meet with him the next day and address all of his grievances. As he had issued Bruce summonses by the dozens for years to no avail, he was incredulous that attention might now be paid. "Really?" he said. He stopped the banging.

We also had to make a decision about the rain effect. Despite the title and the constant references through the play, acts II and III were a drought.

Early in the second act, the house manager, who was Bruce's nephew, was fooling with the electrical panel and set off the emergency lighting system. The emergency lights careened wildly across the walls of the theater, in the words of one prominent critic, "as though they were searching for the nearest exit."

This was a total fiasco, and I was furious with Bruce. Brilliant as he was, each of these disasters, including the fact that we were even doing the production, could be attributed to his hasty judgment or his sloppiness.

We headed uptown for the opening night party at L'Etoile, which had been arranged through its press agent and for which we paid a flat $1,000. It was in keeping with the rest of the evening. After the two hundred guests passed by an intense man with a clicker, they were greeted by an open bar and one small tray of cold hors d'oeuvres. Several friends asked to borrow money to go across the street to Reuben's.

Peter Schneider hauled his small television set with its wire-hanger antenna to the party so that we could watch Stewart Klein's review on Channel Five. As we stared at the snowy, barely discernible picture, it became clear that there would be no review.

The reviews that did appear were, of course, awful.

The next morning, the phone rang in the otherwise quiet box office. It was a woman named Clemence Randolph, calling from Woodstock, and claiming to be the coauthor of *Rain*. Not only was she getting no billing, she said, no one had sent her any royalty money.

I called Sheldon Abend, the agent for the Colton estate, and he told me to tell her she was a whore, that she and Colton were never married, and that she didn't write one word of the play. I gave him her phone number and suggested he tell her.

And They Put Handcuffs on the Flowers (1972)

The Extension, in the former Episcopal Church of the Holy Communion on Nineteenth Street and Sixth Avenue, was an interesting physical space for Off Off Broadway work for many years, frequently used by Tom Eyen. It gained notoriety in the 1980s as The Limelight, the infamous disco owned and operated by Peter Gatien.

In the fall of 1971, I went to see a play there with the curious and poetic title of *And They Put Handcuffs on the Flowers.* It was written and directed by the Spanish playwright Fernando Arrabal. I was unprepared for the experience I had. The impassioned and powerful play, which had the sweep of a Goya painting, dealt with men imprisoned for political reasons and didn't spare us any of the brutal realities of their circumstances.

When Arrabal was four years old, his father, a Spanish army officer, was imprisoned for refusing to participate in General Franco's military coup. After six years in jail, he disappeared under suspicious circumstances. His son never saw him again. Arrabal exiled himself to Paris in 1955, and, though Spanish life and politics continued to dominate his work, he wrote and spoke only in French. He described himself as "*desterrado*," or "half-expatriate, half-exiled."

In 1967 on a return visit to Spain for a book-signing tour, he was arrested and imprisoned for twenty-four days for an inscription he wrote that the authorities considered blasphemous.

Only through an urgent international campaign, which included direct appeals from Arthur Miller, Samuel Beckett, and Eugene Ionesco, was his release secured.

And They Put Handcuffs on the Flowers is the culmination of these life experiences. I had earlier seen the historic Open Theatre production of *The Serpent* with a text by Jean-Claude van Itallie under the direction of Joseph Chaikin. Four of the *Handcuffs* actors had been in that production, and *Handcuffs* now joined *The Serpent* among my all-time great theater experiences.

I was elated when one of the actors in *Handcuffs* told me that she had recommended me to the producer, Ted Menten, who was moving it for a commercial run to one of the theaters at the Mercer Arts Center, a thriving Off Broadway theater complex fashioned from converted ballrooms behind St. Adrian Company in the Broadway Central Hotel on Mercer and East Fourth Street.

I first encountered the Mercer Arts when I was looking for spaces for Sam Shepard's plays. At that time, it was being renovated under the auspices of Art D'Lugoff, owner of the legendary Village Gate. When business slowed at the Gate and construction costs rose at the Mercer Arts, D'Lugoff found himself overextended. Sy Kaback, an air conditioning guru, came to the rescue with a large infusion of cash. As part of the deal, Kaback got the Mercer Arts.

It became such a popular destination that now, two years later, the *Village Voice* listed it among the top ten things it was sick of hearing about. *One Flew over the Cuckoo's Nest* and *The Effect of Gamma Rays on Man-in-the-Moon Marigolds* were having long runs there. The trendy cabaret room featured the New York Dolls with David Johansen as Buster Poindexter. Art D'Lugoff's vision for the Center had come to fruition, but he was not there to enjoy it.

Ted Menten was living in a modern East Side townhouse with Baruk Levi, the leading man of *Handcuffs*, who I had known for years as Bruce Levine. My job interview was delayed for about an hour while Ted and Bruce had a knockdown, drag-out fight, which I came to realize was the prevailing mode of the relationship.

Ted was about six-foot four-inches tall, solidly built, a devotee of the leather lifestyle, and a nightly attendee of the doings at the Eagle's Nest, New York's premiere S&M bar on West Twenty-First Street and the waterfront. He was also the author and illustrator of many successful children's books, a designer, and a noted authority on teddy bears.

My excitement at being hired was dampened when I arrived at the first rehearsal to find the cast sitting quietly as Duane Mazey, the stage manager, read a dramatic letter from Ted Menten informing them that he had resigned as their producer because Arrabal had flatly turned down his design for the set. Once the adrenalin of doom had had its effect, Ted dashed in, and with some prodding by Baruk, he reinstated himself, and saved the day from the crisis he had created.

Arrabal was gentle, mild-mannered, good-humored, and not at all what I expected. He had an attractive interpreter who was also his assistant and his mistress. He knew what he wanted and demanded it and could be sharp-tongued if the moment called for it.

I immediately clashed with Al Lewis, the Mercer Arts house manager, over the lackluster performance of the box office person assigned to me, and I arranged for Peter Schneider, who had learned box office at the Astor Place, to be our treasurer. Lewis walked around the Center like a penguin, with a pedometer in his pocket. He was permanently peeved at Peter and me. He was someone I neither liked nor took seriously.

Our theater had a long tunnel connecting it to the main lobby. Arrabal wanted it to be pitch black so that we could poke, pinch, and bite the audience as it came in. Everyone from the production was asked to participate. One of the critics ended up in a hammerlock. He wrote that the hammerlock was unnecessary as the play delivered that on its own.

Arrabal was majorly involved in the opening night seating chart, moving the *Times* critic, whom he called "Cleeve Barness," several times before he was satisfied. The reviews were largely superlatives, recognizing *Handcuffs* as an authentic piece of great theater.

The day after opening, my old friends at ATPAM called to tell me I couldn't manage the show because we were in a theater of more than 199 seats, thus requiring a union manager. I was still not in the union because I refused to apprentice for three years. They were prepared to strike. I told Ted, and he threw in for some beer and convinced the company to pitch in and move the show across the hall to a vacant 199-seat house.

One rainy Saturday, I got a phone call from the noted author, playwright, and male hustler, Dotson Rader, to tell me that he, Tennessee Williams, and the director Peter Glenville wanted to come that night. A photo of Arrabal and Williams would be a natural, and I called our press agent, Alan Eichler. We agreed that he would call Williams for permission and I would hunt down a photographer.

We had theater seats, but some of the audience sat on the floor in small cell-like cubicles, and Williams and Rader were quite boisterous in theirs, frequently tussling and rolling around.

As the performance ended, Alan had the photographer standing by, but Peter Glenville had that dazed, miffed look that dignitaries get when something has gone awry. Arrabal was not to be found. I asked Ted Menten where he was. "I will not allow the greatest playwright in the world to be insulted." "Did someone insult Tennessee Williams?" I asked.

Menten was referring to Arrabal. Menten had taken affront at the conduct of the Williams party and had locked "the world's greatest playwright" in a dressing room. When the offending parties finally left, he unlocked the door, and the unassuming Arrabal emerged, having no idea what had just happened.

Clive Barnes and Mel Gussow had both written eloquent raves for *Handcuffs* in the *Times*. Sy Peck now assigned Eric Bentley to write a Sunday *Times* piece. Since Bentley was a fellow playwright and sometime translator, I figured that I could get an advance sense of his notice by approaching him after the performance to ask if he would like to meet Arrabal.

When he declined and said, "I find myself in a certain situation," I correctly assumed it would be a negative review. It was an angry slaughter, written with the deliberate intent of killing the play. Bentley had previously incurred the wrath of Arthur Miller and Tennessee Williams with his reviews of their work, to such an extent that they threatened to sue him. We were only as good as our last *Times* review, and business began to drop sharply.

When the show eventually closed, I wrote the house manager Al Lewis a pretentiously polite letter that ended with, "And now, Mr. Lewis, go fuck yourself." A clause was subsequently added to the Mercer Arts lease agreement which, in effect, banned me from ever returning there as the employee of a show.

However, it all became moot on August 4, 1973, when the Mercer Arts Center literally collapsed. The Broadway Central Hotel imploded, taking all of the theaters and St. Adrian Company with it. Al Lewis, at last, moved on. He became the host at The Library, a restaurant on the Upper West Side.

The Bar that Never Closes (1972)

Bruce and I saw a revue at La MaMa called *Everything for Anybody*. It was directed by John Braswell, a professor at Sarah Lawrence, where it had been developed. The very talented score was by young Tom Mandel, who looked and acted like he could be the next rock idol.

Marco Vassi, a writer who had been acclaimed by Gore Vidal and Norman Mailer, provided a series of daring and provocative erotic sketches.

Braswell's students performed in an amateurish, camp style, and the overall androgynous look was polished off with a George Grosz surreality. Beneath the eroticism of the performance was the pure innocence of the performers. With Nixon just re-elected, Bruce and I thought it might shake things up a bit.

We changed the title to *The Bar that Never Closes* and moved it to the Astor Place.

Susan Haskins, who had done the high-style scenic drops for the play, provided the brilliant pen and ink artwork for the ad: a man in a bowler hat with a naked female breast hanging out of his jacket. A visit was required to the *Times* advertising censor, the aptly named Mr. Furie. This I left to Bruce. He placed the artwork in front of Mr. Furie, who gave it an immediate "No." "It's RELIGIOUS!" Bruce shrieked. The artwork was accepted.

We asked Bruce's new friend, Ina Meibach, to be our lawyer. Ina was partners with Nat Weiss in the powerful rock firm of Weiss & Meibach, whose clients included The Beatles, The Rolling Stones, The Who, Patti LaBelle, Janis Ian, and Patti Smith. Bruce said Ina was eager to add a theater practice to her portfolio and was excited about our show.

We met to discuss the authors agreement, and in the middle of it, Ina got a serious phone call from Toronto. The Who had destroyed their hotel room. She hung up and turned to us. "I can't do this now," she said. "Can you come back another time?" "No," I said, and I walked out with Bruce chasing me and Ina chasing both of us. "Come back. We'll do it now," Ina said. We spent the next several hours hammering out the agreement. This turnabout was a knockout and began a lifelong friendship between Ina and me.

A red flag was raised when I asked Charles Ludlam to sit through a rehearsal with me. During a sketch about a fat lesbian from Long Island named Butch Medusa, who conducts enema therapy sessions, he leaned over and whispered, "Albert, *this isn't commercial.*"

After a sketch about God coming back to Earth with a golden phallus to conjugate with a Queens housewife, my un-prudish friends Dorothy Olim and Betty Spitz told me they thought the theater was going to be struck by lightning.

As we went into the critics' weekend, Clive Barnes arrived an hour late for the 7:00 p.m. Saturday show. This time we didn't hold the curtain. A friend who was a student in his class at NYU took him to Phebe's, and he returned in time to see the 10:00 p.m. show. He wrote, "*The Bar that Never Closes* has a great deal to commend it . . . I liked it a lot."

Most of the critics were outraged. Four of them walked out. Martin Bookspan on WPIX said, "These people are a menace to the public welfare." The *Daily News* called it "excrescence" and the AP accused it of being "devised in a public lavatory." We closed on New Year's Eve.

There was one bright spot. On the Sunday afternoon of the critics' weekend, Dick Weaver, the executive secretary of ATPAM, stopped by. He was seeing a matinee across the street at the Public Theater and wanted a word with me.

"You have become an embarrassment to the union," he exclaimed. "How can I be an embarrassment? I'm not even in the union," I replied. "That's just it. You aren't in the union but you keep working, doing one show after another. It's an embarrassment to us. And every time I see Jerry Schoenfeld, he says, 'When are you going to let Albert Poland into the union?' Come and see me next week."

The upshot was that if Bruce would sign an agreement that the Astor Place would abide by the conditions that already existed for all 299-seat houses, the Astor Place would be considered "organized," and the union would admit me as a member without any apprenticeship. Bruce agreed and, at long last, I became a member of ATPAM.

In January of 1973, *The Off Off Broadway Book* was published, and we had the thrill of actual copies in our hands. I rushed the very first one over to Ellen Stewart out of respect for her and because I thought Bruce's piece on her was superb.

Later that night, Bruce and I were shocked to walk into Phebe's and find everyone abuzz that Ellen was going to sue us. She was said to have read Bruce's tribute and gone into a tirade. She said we made her sound like "Topsy rising up out of the cotton patch." She resented Bruce saying that she sometimes wore a bandanna, which she did, and that she was "magic," which she was. She found it racist.

The next day, I had a call from the La MaMa box office treasurer. "Ellen has asked me to tell you that you don't exist for her and that you can no longer have comps at La MaMa." "If I don't exist, how can I have comps?" I said.

I was upset and hurt. Bruce was not. "She'll need a favor," he said.

The San Francisco Mime Troupe in The Dragon Lady's Revenge (1973)

Nixon had broadened the Vietnam War to include massive bombings of Cambodia. In January, I went to see The San Francisco Mime Troupe in *The Dragon Lady's Revenge* at the Washington Square Methodist Church. It was based on ex-CIA agent Alfred

W. McCoy's astonishing book *The Politics of Heroin in Southeast Asia* that charted out clearly that the heroin trade in Southeast Asia and the CIA's involvement in it were among the primary reasons for the Vietnam War. He documented that heroin was flown into the United States on CIA Air America planes with the specific goal of keeping our poor black populations in place. McCoy also maintained that the government had been in bed with the Mafia since World War II, when it had cleared the way for our military campaigns through Italy.

The Mime Troupe was about as far left as you could get and not be in jail. Their performance style, evolved out of the necessity to reach their audiences in the parks of San Francisco, was agitprop cartoon-mime, with broad gestures and exaggerated props and costumes.

Dragon Lady opened with the troupe marching into the church, followed by Paul Binder and Michael Christensen doing some highly skilled juggling. Then the play began, depicting how the crimes of our own government and the CIA were defeating our ill-advised war effort. At the center of it was the Dragon Lady, with her drugs and whores. I loved the agitprop style and the use of humor as a lubricant for the message. The packed house was wild about it.

After the show, I spoke with the Troupe and was saddened to learn that they would have to close at the Church in two days because of a prior booking in the space. They had another three weeks of availability, so I offered them the Astor Place free of charge.

I enlisted all of the people who had worked with me over the years to donate their services, and with Bruce's generous cooperation, we booked the Mime Troupe into the Astor Place. With Saul Richman's invaluable help, the show was then reviewed by the mainstream critics and played to packed, cheering houses for the entire three weeks.

I developed a close personal relationship with the Troupe, and I was thrilled when Charles Ludlam and his company gave a party in their honor. "They are one of only two other companies I would even consider," he said.

The closing performance was a Sunday matinee, and, in an effort to pressure the Troupe into doing an unscheduled second show. I told the box office to take a waiting list for the matinee. The phone was ringing off the hook and, loving the excitement, I was taking a lot of the calls myself.

"You are number 394," I would say, and the person on the other end would say, "I will definitely be there." By the time we stopped taking names, there were well over four hundred people. And they all showed up.

When the Troupe came up the front stairs to do the marching band through the lobby, the door was blocked by people on the waiting list and could not be opened. I rushed backstage. "There are four hundred people on the waiting list," I pleaded, "and they are ALL here. You've got to do a second show."

The Troupe laughed. "We knew you would do this, Albert, but we can't do a second show." "Why not?" I asked anxiously. "Because we are taking you to dinner. And nothing is going to stop us." "Well," I smiled, "I guess you've got me." They made their entrance from backstage, leaving me to deal with the pandemonium I had created in the lobby.

The dinner was a blowout at Princess Pamela's Little Kitchen, a homey upstairs soul food place on First Avenue and East Tenth Street that was my current favorite. The Princess had no liquor license, so Lester Nichols sent over huge quantities of complimentary alcohol from Phebe's, which were replenished once or twice during the evening—a great time was had by all.

The engagement captured an Obie Award and became a special part of the legend of this extraordinary company. I worked with them on several subsequent engagements in New York, and it was always a labor of love.

After the closing of *Dragon Lady*, Michael Christensen and Paul Binder left the Troupe to go to clown school in Europe. *How curious*, I thought. Three years later, they returned to New York to start The Big Apple Circus.

The Faggot (1973)

Al Carmines asked me if I would produce a fundraiser to celebrate his tenth anniversary at Judson Church. With the financial assistance of Yoko Ono, we were able to secure The Downstairs at the Upstairs, the chic club where Julius Monk had presented his smart revues. Al arranged for Leonard Frey, the witty actor from *The Boys in the Band*, to emcee, and I put together a stellar group of theater names and Judson superstars.

Three days before the performance, Al called to say that Leonard Frey had to bow out. "Who will we get?" I asked.

"You," he said.

Although I felt I could never equal Leonard Frey, I agreed. The club was packed and I rose to the occasion. A few days after the event, I received a warm note from Al.

"My dear Polanda," he wrote. "Committee member par excellence, M.C. Extraordinaire, sultry-eyed dove of the Middle Village, your talents and your gifts are endless. Let appreciation from Carmines be added to the myriad tributes at your feet. In the midst of the tinsel and glitter is a fragile bloom called 'love for you.' It grows."

On the heels of this, I called Al and demanded a musical solo in his next Judson production. "I may have just the thing for you," he said, and told me he was preparing a musical called *The Faggot*.

I was cast as a college professor who was playing a john for a student doing a term paper on male hustling, and it was not a solo but a duet, sung in total darkness. His Worship was a playful one.

The Judson opening night was mobbed. and we had no idea what to expect. As we stood in the vestibule waiting to march in for the opening—a resounding choral round that got right to it with lyrics like "Faggot! Lesbian! Cocksucker! Homosexual! Dyke!"—we felt a little like Christians about to be thrown to possible lions.

Our fears further energized the night, and it was a triumph. At the opening night party, Bruce Mailman announced he would move *The Faggot* Off Broadway to his Truck and Warehouse Theater. I willingly gave up my role as the john to assume the role of the general manager.

Days before we began performances at the Truck and Warehouse, I was alone in the box office and a fat, tough-looking twelve-year-old visited me. "You the manager of this show?" he asked.

"Yes," I replied.

"My gang and I want drinking privileges from your water fountain," he said, indicating the fountain on the other side of the lobby. Then he added, "The last show, the lady wasn't nice with us so we torched the place, you know, the box office. And we set fire to the Orpheum, the one up the street, 'cause they weren't nice, either."

"How did you set the fire?" I asked.

He described in detail how it had been done. It matched exactly what had happened, and the fire had caused substantial damage to the theater.

"What do you have in the paper bag?" I asked. "Glue," he answered, taking a sniff.

"Are you a gentleman?" I asked.

"Am I a gentleman?" he repeated, somewhat incredulously.

"Yeah, I'd like to make a gentlemen's agreement with you," I offered.

I explained that this was a theater, a place of business, that needed to be respected. If he and his friends were prepared to do that, we would buzz them in for drinks of water. That seemed agreeable to him. Throughout the summer, in mid-afternoon, he and his friends made their visits.

One day, when I was away, they stole eight cans of soda from the cooler in the lobby. The following day when they began to arrive, I signaled that it was "no go." Soon the fat kid arrived, and I buzzed him in. "You haven't respected our deal," I said. "Your friends stole eight cans of soda, and I have to pay for them, twenty-five cents each. So our deal is off."

He said nothing, turned, and departed. Within fifteen minutes, eight young men came in, one at a time, and without comment, plunked a quarter down at the box office. Their privileges were restored.

The response from the large preview audiences was enthusiastic. There was a feeling that the show was being swept along by an energy larger than itself. It was four years after Stonewall. There was a growing public interest in the culture of gay life, and with the passing of time, people were more comfortable looking into it.

Tom Lehrer showed up at the box office, and I ran out to tell him that he had been "my introduction to hipness." He seemed both pleased and bemused. Richard Rodgers came. He had come to all of Al's shows since *Peace* and, as was his custom, arrived early and was by himself. I invited him to sit in the air-conditioned theater, and he was pleased to do so.

As we neared the opening, business was reaching a crescendo. One day when there were two lines on hold, I had a call from a man who told me he was having phone sex with people in the Off Broadway box offices. I said, "Call back when we have a flop!"

Opening night was euphoric. At intermission, Bill Raidy, the critic for *Newhouse Papers*, came up to Bruce and me and said, "This is heaven! Let's have a drink."

It looked like Al might have his first real commercial hit and Bruce might have a worthy successor to *The Dirtiest Show in Town*.

When the *Times* review came in, I got up on a table at Sardi's and read it in the manner of a town crier. It was a money review by Clive Barnes. He wrote that it was "really funny and at times touching" and that its purpose is "to reveal the similarities in the many faces of love." He went on to say, "Most homosexual shows are embarrassing for heterosexuals because they are either fiercely militant or atrociously maudlin. 'The Faggot' treats homosexuality as just a different kind of love . . . Vive la différence." He had opened a wide door and given a *Times* blessing for its readership to come and enjoy our show.

We quickly built to grosses of $17,000 a week, a high for Off Broadway at that time. Bruce's good friend rock lawyer Nat Weiss, partner of our attorney Ina Meibach, arranged for Ahmet Ertegun of Atlantic Records to see the show. Afterward, Bruce and Al went to supper with Nat and Ahmet.

When we met afterwards at Phebe's, Bruce and Al were feeling no pain. Ahmet had proposed to do *The Faggot* as the first original cast album ever on Atlantic Records. But there was other news. After a few drinks, Bruce had told Ahmet that he wanted to suck his cock.

Bruce was certain that Ertegun was flattered, but he politely declined.

Ahmet Ertegun's look had a tremendous impact on Bruce. A week after they met, Bruce had his hair weave removed and cultivated a dramatic shaved-head look that he kept for the rest of his life.

Under Al's superb direction, the cast went into the studio to record. A couple of nights later, Jerry Wexler, Ahmet's partner at Atlantic, came to see the show. I didn't know Wexler but thought his visit was important and wanted to get a bead on his response. I watched him emerge at the end of the performance. He looked grim. I called Bruce right away. "I think Jerry Wexler just left with your cast album," I told my dear friend.

There was an immediate cooling from Ahmet. Things got delayed, and amidst a flurry of excuses, the album was never released. Many years later, a pirated version found its way into Tower Records that was unmixed and not of good quality. Jerry Wexler was the harbinger of a change in our fortunes.

Saul Richman called to let me know that Sy Peck had requested tickets for Martin Duberman to cover the show for a Sunday *Times* piece. I found this curious because Duberman had already seen it. I suspected an agenda. And I remembered Eric Bentley's cold-blooded Sunday piece on *Handcuffs*. I watched as Duberman arrived at the box office, angry and hostile. Not a good sign.

Martin Duberman was the well-respected author of *In White America*, a long-running Off Broadway hit at the Sheridan Square Playhouse, and he was an early activist for gay and civil rights. Saul called me on Wednesday, moments after his advance copy of the Sunday *Times* "Arts and Leisure" arrived and read me the piece.

Duberman had written from a political point of view, and he thought us to be politically incorrect. We did not conform to his vision of Gay Liberation. He said of our show, "It's more than a failure. It's an affront." He found it to be a "cartoon" and compared its characters to "Stepin Fetchit, Charlie Chan, and the Bloody Injun." He summarized his argument as "with friends like *The Faggot* the gay movement needs no enemies." He went on to praise another more radical Off Off Broadway show called *Coming Out*. It was immediately clear that he had asked for the assignment to throw us overboard in favor of a show he already preferred.

I asked Saul to call Sy Peck and find out if the *Times* would run a response from Al the following Sunday and, if so, what was the deadline to get it to him. Saul called back. "End of the day, tomorrow."

Al was driving across Virginia. I got to work, obtained his license plate number, and called the State Police. I described the car and driver and told them it was a matter of life and death. Within two hours, Al called me back. I read him the piece. Shortly before midnight, he called me and dictated his response, which ran in the *Times* the Sunday after the Duberman piece.

Headlined "Politics Is Not Art," Al began by praising Duberman for his past work but correctly characterized his Sunday piece as a "broadside attack."

Al wrote that *The Faggot* is not "a political position paper" but rather "a personal, idiosyncratic, quirky, highly subjective theater piece. This is the crux of the disagreement between Mr. Duberman and myself. I do not believe politics is art, and I believe a confusion of those two human activities is a dangerous and ultimately catastrophic misunderstanding." About the cartoon aspect of *The Faggot*, Al wrote, "I would rather be Herblock than Max Lerner. And that, perhaps, is the real difference between Mr. Duberman and myself."

But the damage was done. Duberman had reached the sensitivities of the liberal *Times* readership, both gay and straight. His "review" was toxic. We dropped to a gross of $13,000 the following week, then $9,000, and so on. Our joyous journey into gay self-expression had the wind knocked out of it and ground slowly to a painful halt.

Sometime near the end of the run, a friend called to tell me that Martin Duberman *and* Eric Bentley were on WBAI signing off on a program that was supposed to be a discussion with Al Carmines about *The Faggot*. Al had not shown up. They were saying "Good night, Reverend Carmines, wherever you are." I called Saul Richman's chubby, barely-out-of-his-teens intern, Fred Nathan, who confessed that he had forgotten to tell Al about the broadcast. I gave him the lightest of reprimands, hung up, and said, "Tee-fucking-hee."

The 1973 fall season began with a spectacular party given by Tom Eyen in his West Ninth Street apartment. Everyone from Off and Off Off was there. When Bruce and I arrived, there was a sudden hush. Across the room was Ellen Stewart. It was the first time we had been in the same space since we had ceased to exist for her. She hadn't let up on her unhappiness with the book, continuing to sit newcomers down at La MaMa and reading sections aloud, followed by her own outraged commentary.

Within moments, Tom brought Ellen over to us. "Miss Stewart," he offered, "do you know Mr. Poland and Mr. Mailman?" "Why yes, I do!" "Mr. Poland and Mr. Mailman, do you know Miss Stewart?" "Yes, we do." "Baby," she blurted out, "I need the Truck and Warehouse." And the feud ended, just as Bruce had foretold.

The next day, the La MaMa box office treasurer called to inform me I existed and that my comp privileges had been restored. When I returned to La MaMa to see a show, Ellen's and my eyes met, and we both broke into big smiles. Then she chased me up the aisle and asked the audience, "Did you see what they wrote about me in that book?!" And that was the last of it. For a while.

By the fall of 1973, Bruce and I had reached a plateau. I was burned out in our working relationship, and we were both drinking too much. One late night at Phebe's, Bruce was discussing ideas for new projects, and I told him I thought it was time for us to work separately. He was hurt, but that's exactly what happened.

CHAPTER 8

A Gem

Jane Marla Robbins came to me just before Christmas. Jane was tall, statuesque, and had energy to burn. She had prepared a one-person play called *Dear Nobody*, based on the diaries of Fanny Burney, the patrician eighteenth-century British novelist and feminist. The financing was in place, and she sought a producer.

I liked her and said I would do it, provided I could have control of the physical production and the advertising. She could do as she wished with everything else. Noting the obscurity of her subject, I joked that the pre-opening ad campaign might be:

Soon all of New York will be saying "Fanny Who?"

The director was to be Leon Russom, who I knew as a fine actor when he had been a replacement in *Futz*.

We picked the historic Cherry Lane Theater on Commerce Street in the West Village, and I thought I would look into Patricia Zipprodt to design the two gowns Jane would wear. As the multiple-award-winning designer of *Cabaret* and *Fiddler on the Roof* and numerous top Broadway productions, operas, and ballets, Ms. Zipprodt was, for me, without equal. I made a cold call to her, and she invited me to her beautiful fifth-floor loft on University Place.

She was theatrical (though not affected), with beautiful flaming red hair and a wonderful sense of humor. She had actually started her career Off Broadway with the long-running productions of *The Blacks* and *The Crucible*, which had been directed by Word Baker. We hit it off splendidly, and I left the script with her.

A few days later, she called and said, "I will be happy to dress your lady."

The elegance and style of the production were carried over into a series of small dinners for our little group hosted by Jane Marla Robbins, with appropriate wines selected by her coauthor, Terry Belanger, a connoisseur who also provided us with lovely menus beautifully hand lettered on parchment.

On opening night a flamboyant actress friend of mine arrived with a stunningly handsome young man. "I have a very special opening night present for you," she said. "This is Henry."

Having never been offered a living present before, I was very flattered but, with all the hectic activity in the lobby, I did manage to decline. Which was just as well because a short time later she married Henry.

Stewart Mott, the noted philanthropist, presented himself at the box office with two dozen red roses and said that he wanted "the producer to present them to Miss Robbins during the curtain call."

As she took her bows, I nervously walked out on stage. Jane pulled me to her and whispered, "Kiss me, back away, hand me the roses, and then bow to me."

The first image of bowing that came to mind was Judy, so I curtsied, and the audience laughed.

Jerry Schoenfeld called the next day. "Come to my office, Albert," he said. "I'm going to teach you how to bow, Albert." He always said my name twice.

The reviews were decent, though not over the top, and we fashioned one, rather awkward, usable quote from Clive Barnes in the *Times*.

"Not since Roy Dotrice in *Brief Lives* have
I been so taken with a one-person play."

We used it so much that Roy Dotrice came to Broadway in *Brief Lives*.

Miss Zipprodt and I had a dinner with Jerry and Pat Schoenfeld at the Horn of Plenty, and I mentioned to Jerry that negotiations between her representative, the distinguished attorney Arnold Weissberger, and Jack Schlissel, general manager for David Merrick, for her services on *Mack and Mabel* had come to a halt. The very next day she was to meet alone with Merrick to see if it could be sorted out.

"Do you have any helpful hints?" I asked.

Jerry advised her, "At a certain point, Merrick will begin to speak quietly. However quiet he gets, just make sure that you speak more quietly than he does. You will get everything you want."

The next day, she called to report that it had worked. I told her to call Jerry right away and thank him, and he, too, was delighted.

Shortly after *Dear Nobody* got underway, I signed on as the general manager of *Let My People Come* at the Village Gate. It was a schitzy trip to go from tits flying at the Gate to Jane Marla Robbins resplendent in her Patricia Zipprodt gowns at the Cherry Lane.

CHAPTER 9

Naked at the Gate

In the spring of 1973, Earl Wilson Jr. and Phil Oesterman were at a crossroads in their careers. Both were in Houston, Texas. Earl was doing a singing gig at the famed Shamrock Hilton Hotel, and Phil and his companion, Jim Sink, were operating The Flower Children, a successful florist business.

Their meeting was to be a catalyst for what each really wanted.

Earl is the son of the widely known syndicated columnist and his wife, Rosemary (known affectionately in the columns as "the B.W." for "Beautiful Wife"). He had already written hundreds of songs and longed to establish himself as a successful songwriter. He had begun at age twelve tinkering on the white baby grand in the family living room, which theretofore had been a "prop," played only rarely by famous hands at his parents' glamourous parties.

His mother encouraged him to take piano lessons, but, instead of learning to read music, he made up tunes and took them back to the piano teacher. His young words and music were sophisticated because that is what he knew from the songbooks that adorned the piano and from hundreds of Broadway opening nights.

At fourteen, Earl had two songs recorded and became the youngest member of ASCAP. He recorded "This is Earl Wilson

Jr." for Mercury Records, appeared on *The Tonight Show* and *The Ed Sullivan Show*, and played successfully in hotels and nightclubs, including the Maisonette at the St. Regis in New York.

By 1971 he had readied his first full-length musical, *A Day in the Life of Just about Everyone,* which sadly opened and closed in one week at the small Bijou Theater in midtown. After that, Earl returned to the club circuit which was, by now, nearing the end of its era.

Phil Oesterman, born in Dallas, had moved to Houston when he was twelve. He shortly met up with Tommy Tune in a ballet class. Despite a no-charge policy for boys, Phil and Tommy were the only ones. Tommy was a tap dancer who wanted to be Gene Kelly. Phil wanted to be a director.

Phil made several stabs at New York in the years that followed, most notably in 1963, when he insisted his friend Tommy come with him.

After three years of knockabout jobs in touring and stock, Phil landed his first, and Tommy his second, Broadway show, *A Joyful Noise,* a John Raitt starrer. Tommy was a chorus dancer, and Phil assisted the producer, while enjoying a discreet affair with the show's young choreographer, Michael Bennett.

Gradually Phil moved toward his dream of directing and in 1969 had an Off Broadway success at the Provincetown Playhouse with *Geese,* two one-acts by Gus Weill which dealt with hetero- and homosexuality.

Following a successful production of *Geese* in San Francisco, Jim Sink had a serious accident that left him in a coma for two weeks, and the two returned to Houston for Jim to heal. The Flower Children sustained them.

During his engagement at the Shamrock, Earl was the houseguest of Maxine Mesinger, noted columnist of the *Houston Chronicle* and longtime friend of the Wilsons and of Phil Oesterman.

"I've got someone I want you to meet," Maxine told Earl enthusiastically, and he soon found himself at Phil's mother's house performing *A Day in the Life* for Phil. As he went along, Phil made comments and suggestions. He told Earl, "I know how to make this work."

They put together a production in Houston that spring that Phil produced and directed.

With a rave from Ann Holmes in the *Chronicle* and ecstatic word of mouth, the show ran for three months. Phil already had an idea for their next project.

"I'm going to produce a sexual musical for Off Broadway," Phil told Earl. "You're going to write it, and it will be the biggest hit in Off Broadway history."

"I can't do it," Earl responded.

Phil was adamant. "Just write one song."

Pushing aside his own reservations and his serious concerns about what his parents would think, Earl came back the next day with his first song, a bold effort he wrote in forty-five minutes called "Come in My Mouth." Phil was knocked out. By July, Earl had enough material for an entire show.

Back in New York, they got together with a group of non-union actors, working on a shoestring for five months. The actors were provided with subway tokens and the promise of a job should the show be produced.

A few weeks into rehearsal, Phil declared, "It's time to get naked," and one night when Earl's parents were out of town, the company assembled in the Wilson penthouse at the Parc Vendome on West Fifty-Seventh Street. Earl greeted them at the door by candlelight. The rehearsal ran until 3:00 a.m., by which time everyone had reached a comfort level.

"This show has to play the Village Gate," Phil told Earl.

They went to the Gate's owner, Art D'Lugoff, hat in hand, asking for every concession they could get: no rehearsal rental, no rent deposit. D'Lugoff, taken by their youthful enthusiasm, was talking deal when they decided to pull out the *piece de resistance.*

Earl went to the piano and performed "Come in My Mouth" for the stunned D'Lugoff, who became physically ill. "Are you crazy?" he shrieked.

A bit shaken, they did a run-through of the show for Tommy Tune, who told them, "It's perfect—don't touch it." With a full head of steam, Phil went back to Art, who badly needed a tenant. "I have a show," he told D'Lugoff, "It's ready now." Art booked it and agreed to no deposit and no rehearsal rental.

With a famous venue secured, Earl's parents arranged a backer's audition for their friends at the Parc Vendome, where only weeks earlier, the "naked" rehearsal had occurred. The potential investors ate, drank, gathered up their furs and left quietly. His mother Rosemary sat in a corner, smiling. "This is a hit," she said. "How much will it cost?"

"Ten thousand," Earl volunteered. Similar shows at the time were costing one hundred thousand or more. "If you cut 'Come in My Mouth,' I'll put up $3000, and your producer friend over there can raise the rest," she said, throwing the ball to Phil. The song stayed in, and Rosemary wrote a check.

"The rest" was secured in the form of a bank loan for new refrigeration equipment for The Flower Children. Earl Wilson then uttered the same words to his son that had once been said to me. "There is only one press agent for you, and that's Saul Richman."

With Saul on board, the show began a preview period that would never end. There would be no opening night, and the critics were never to be invited.

My first exposure to *Let My People Come* was an ad in the *Village Voice.* I found the ad ugly and the title off-putting. Then I had a call from Saul, who said, "Albert, I'm doing a show you will love. *Let My People Come.*" "Yuck," I responded.

In his office, I could see that Saul's enthusiasm for the project and for "the boys" was genuine. "Look at this coverage," Saul was saying, knowing that next to good box office, press was what I loved most. He showed me a desk full of tear sheets from all over the place, the most striking being the centerfold of *Women's Wear Daily* splashed with photos of the cast in full frontal taken by a camera the size of a cigarette pack.

"The Baron de Rothschild was there the other night with Oscar de la Renta," Saul continued. "And," closing in for the seduction, "there is no general manager. They could really use someone like you." My curiosity was piqued.

I sat in the back of the half-empty club with my agent friend, Howard Rosenstone, anticipating titillation. What we saw was certainly sexual, but it wasn't prurient. And though it wasn't essentially political, it was doing what great political theater is supposed to do. It was changing me. It was joyous and healthy, and by the time the cast sang the finale, "Let My People Come," I felt relief from the years of shaming and manipulation by politicians and religion.

"What do you think?" Howard asked me. "I think it's sweet," I answered. There was an innocence about it. I not only *wanted* to manage it, I *had* to.

Saul arranged for me to meet Phil Oesterman, who had moved into a studio apartment on East Forty-Eighth Street. I stepped from a pouring rain into the small apartment to find three cast members rushing around doing things for Phil with a great sense of urgency. He was a well-built, attractive, masculine man in cowboy boots, with a nicely trimmed beard and a slightly leathery air. As we shook hands, the rain stopped, and the sun came out, which he took as an omen. "The sun came out," he said, and disappeared into the shower for an hour.

I was exasperated by the wait, and, as I sat watching the three actors, it occurred to me that he must be some kind of Svengali. *I hope I never fall into that relationship with him,* I thought.

When he emerged, clad in a large beach towel, we shared our enthusiasm for the show and its future, and I gave him ideas about how I would manage it. He said Actors' Equity was leaning on them to put the show on a union contract and that he and Earl were in favor of it. I concurred. I was hired.

The next step was to meet with Art D'Lugoff and to learn how to navigate the Village Gate, which, with its 430 seats and nightclub format, was the largest and most challenging venue I had yet played, and D'Lugoff was a giant who was as legendary as his club.

In an effort to gather information, I spoke to Lily Turner, the general manager of *Jacques Brel Is Alive and Well and Living In Paris,* which had a six-year run at the Gate. I knew Lily would be outspoken and opinionated. "There is always the air of the padlock," she said ominously, "and Art may sometimes come to the show for an advance to keep his club operating."

I first became aware of the Gate when I read *Variety* as a teenager and saw the weekly listings of the acts under "Cabaret Bills." Then later, when I was in college, Nina Simone's recording of "Porgy" had played constantly on the campus jukeboxes.

When I came to New York, the Village Gate was the center-piece of a two-block strip on Bleecker Street that included Circle in the Square, The Back Fence, The Bitter End, Cafe au Go Go, and Kenny's Castaways. Above it was the notorious Mills Hotel, chock-full of unruly welfare tenants. Just around the corner was the tiny Sullivan Street Playhouse, where *The Fantasticks* continued its record-breaking run. From my vantage point at the San Remo, the traffic on Bleecker and MacDougal never moved.

Bleecker Street, which was the main stem of the Village, was named by and for the Bleecker family because the street ran through their farm. In 1808, Anthony Bleecker and his wife deeded to the city a major portion of the land on which Bleecker Street sits. The street had also been the home of New York's first notorious, openly gay bar, The Slide, open from the 1870s into the turn of the century. It was in what was now Kenny's Castaways, across from the Gate.

Art D'Lugoff had opened his club in 1958, and his bargain-basement lease for the three floors, said to be $19,020 annually, ran until 2020. He was a left-wing political activist and an impresario who presented Paul Robeson in his final Carnegie Hall concerts and Billie Holiday at the Loew's Sheridan Theatre when existing New York cabaret laws kept her from playing clubs because of a drug conviction.

Primarily because of Holiday's arrest, a law was passed in the '50s mandating the fingerprinting of all performers who appeared in New York City cabarets. Despising this law and its racist overtones,

D'Lugoff spearheaded a successful campaign to get it overturned, paving the way for the return of Frank Sinatra and many other great saloon performers who had stayed away from New York clubs for years.

His first concerts were folk singers at midnight in the original Circle in the Square location on Sheridan Square, and he and Ted Mann had an often-contentious relationship. Art added twelve folding chairs for one of his concerts. Mann hit the ceiling but kept the chairs for his own presentation the following night. In 1960, the two wound up directly across the street from each other when Mann moved Circle to 159 Bleecker.

At the Gate and the upstairs Top of the Gate, Art D' Lugoff had presented every top jazz artist and major comic of the era. He put Woody Allen on 150 times and helped him shape his act. "Hold the mic like it's a bottle of seltzer," he advised. The young Bob Dylan came by to perform his songs for D'Lugoff, who told him, "The songs are good, you got no voice." With performers of temperament like Nina Simone, Miles Davis, Bill Cosby, and Lenny Bruce, there had been much aggravation over the years. "When you're dealing with artists," he once advised me, "the thing to be is unavailable."

And the Gate was the town hall of Greenwich Village. Show D'Lugoff a left-wing cause, he would give you a stage and a room. Show him a controversy, and he would provide a forum for its participants.

The night before we were to meet, I hit the Oak Bar at the Plaza with Max and Helen Jacobs and shared with them my angst about meeting the following morning with this man who I found larger than life. As the evening wore on, I excused myself to go to the bathroom and never returned.

So now here I was sitting across the table from Mr. D'Lugoff in his rathskeller. There is nothing quite like the aroma of a nightclub at 10 o'clock in the morning. It smells like cigarette smoke trapped in dried whiskey with a Clorox chaser. But Art was immediately engaging. He was smart, hip, playful, knew talent, and knew his business, half of which he had invented. At one point I said, "I hear things can get a little rough around here."

"Who'd you talk to," he asked, "Dorothy Olim?"

I checked with Dorothy, and she told me the animus between them was so thick that she had once told her producers to sign a Gate lease without revealing she was their manager. When she later appeared there for a meeting, Art said, "She's the manager? I'm giving back the deposit check."

"Before you give back a check," Dorothy responded, "we'll all be dead."

After my meeting with Art, I walked around the Gate, exploring the myriad caverns and passageways. There were payphones everywhere, all of them ringing with people desperate for tickets because they couldn't get through to the box office. Phone reservations were the new convention, and the Gate hadn't caught up with it.

A check of the box office revealed that there was one person and two phone lines to service the entire premises, which, including the upstairs, had a total of eight hundred seats. The two lines were on hold whenever there was a customer at the window. I ran to Art and told him we had to add four more phone lines and two more people to handle the activity. He was all for it.

The box-office gross the week I started was $15,000. The week after the installation of the phone lines and the staff increase, it went to $27,000, the following week $35,000. *Let My People Come* was off and running.

Toward the end of that first week, I had a call from Phil Oesterman. "I have, um, the car," he said. "I'll pick you up at eight." When he arrived, I found that "the car" was a stretch limo. We had a beautiful Maine lobster dinner followed by a visit to The Eagle's Nest, New York's premiere leather bar—in what became our nightly routine. In only one week, Phil and his show had taken over my life, which at that point was much to my liking.

The Gate staff were hip people who shared a great sense of humor and a genuine love for Art. They were a gestalt of his personality, and, like Art, they were not neat; they spilled over the edges. They were a colorful lot of international characters. They looked like the crew of a pirate ship.

And there were the Village fixtures. Meurice, a tall gentleman with a long gray beard who looked like Father Time and came into Village establishments selling newspapers he had found in the trash, usually the *Village Voice*. The Flower Lady, immortalized in song by Phil Ochs. A sweet, winsome woman who offered corsages that no one seemed to buy and then retreated to her waiting Cadillac. And Eddie the Cop, the savvy cop on the beat who'd known everybody for years.

The Gate was famously full of structural poles. People had complained about them since the beginning of time. Because of the nudity in *Let My People Come* and the resulting higher ticket prices, the complaints had become more intense.

There was an usher I used to watch who rarely disappointed. One night early in the run, a man was complaining loudly about a pole blocking his view of the stage. The usher was there to placate. "The moment the show begins," the usher informed him, "the poles go up into the ceiling." "They go up into the ceiling?" the gentleman repeated skeptically. "Yes." *I can't wait to see this,* I thought.

The lights dimmed, the show began. The man looked at the pole and up at the ceiling. Nothing was happening. He looked around at the other poles, and nothing was happening with them, either. He summoned the usher. "You said these were supposed to go up into the ceiling," he insisted. "Sir, I am so sorry," the usher apologized. "They're broken."

At a sellout on a Saturday night, we had to seat people in a small, rarely used section by the theater entrance that we called the Royal Box. A young man and his girlfriend were seated there, and after a few moments she felt something dripping on her face. The usher was called over.

"There's something dripping on my date," the man complained. Just then, she sniffed it. "Honey, it's piss!" "There's piss dripping on my date!" the man exclaimed. "Don't worry," the usher reassured. "The plaster keeps the shit from coming down."

As the show reached the hit category, celebrities found their way. Yoko Ono preferred to watch from the stage manager's booth.

Top Broadway directors Gower Champion and Tom O'Horgan saw the show repeatedly and had special stools placed unobtrusively in a back corner, affording them an open view of the stage and audience.

Sammy Davis Jr. came to a Sunday matinee with a large party that included his wife Altovise and Linda Lovelace, the star of the notorious porno movie *Deep Throat* that was celebrated in one of our songs. The atmosphere was electric and was kicked up a notch when Bob Dylan was discovered sitting quietly at an empty table near the bar.

At intermission, I was nearby when Davis came over to Dylan. "You and I are in different bags," he began but was unable to finish. Dylan looked up at him and made a vomiting sound. Davis, stunned, walked away disconsolate.

After the show, Art, who had known Dylan for years, told me he wanted to speak to me.

As I took him in, I thought he looked druggy and paranoid. " I want to make a film of this," Dylan said. "You want to make a movie of the show?" I asked. "No, that song in the bar. I want to film it. I like it."

The song was "Take Me Home with You," the touching plea of a gay man alone at closing time, sung by Larry Paulette. "I'll talk to the producer and see about it," I said. "Give me a contact."

Phil was aware of Dylan's behavior and didn't have an immediate response. After a few days, he told me to make the call and tell Dylan's assistant that, when Dylan apologized to Sammy Davis, he would give the request his consideration. That was the end of it.

Henry Fonda brought his wife Shirlee in a party dressed to the nines that included the actress Liv Ullman and the distinguished press agent John Springer. I had arranged with Springer for a *Village Voice* photographer to get a shot of Fonda with Earl and Phil after the performance.

However, as we watched, it became apparent that Fonda was hating every minute of it. Seated behind him, Liv Ullman, her hand over her mouth, was enjoying it thoroughly.

Mischievously, I told the photographer to crawl over to the Fonda table during the curtain call and ask Fonda if he would have his picture taken with Earl and Phil. The moment arrived, and as the final applause died down, the Village Gate audience heard the unmistakable voice of Henry Fonda screaming, "NO, I WILL NOT! IS THAT CLEAR?"

Georgie Jessel, the Jewish star whose career spanned vaudeville, pictures, and television, arrived an hour early in a faded military uniform. I sat with him and his friend upstairs on the terrace, fascinated to be with the man who had given Judy Garland her last name. Celebrity sightings were not a shoo-in for an item in Mr. Wilson's column but, with Jessel, I thought I might be able to construct one.

I excused myself, ran downstairs, and asked the musical director if he knew "My Mother's Eyes."

"No."

It had been Jessel's well-known signature song since his vaudeville days in 1929. Had he heard of Georgie Jessel?

"No ."

I sang the song slowly for him. He wrote down the notes while I wrote out the words.

"Go to the office, and Xerox this for the cast," I told him. " When I hit the door with Jessel, I will have the spotlight swing around to us. Give me a drum roll, and the cast should then run onstage and sing 'My Mother's Eyes.'" I went back upstairs and continued my conversation with Jessel, checking downstairs every few minutes to see how it was going.

All went according to plan. I hit the door with Jessel, the spotlight swung around, the audience immediately recognized him as well as the opening strains of the song, and gave him a standing ovation, which moved him to tears. We got a paragraph in Mr. Wilson's column. Art D'Lugoff, hostile to Jessel's right-wing politics, exclaimed, "I'm ruined. Georgie Jessel got a standing ovation in my place."

"Miss Bare America" arrived nude in a stretch limousine. She sat in front of the Gate with a cop next to the car door waiting to bust her the minute she got out. After half an hour of this, I went over to Saul Richman, who just happened to be standing nearby.

"And what is the expense for this non-event?" I asked.

"Give her $50, and she'll leave," Saul replied.

"Darling . . ." It was Tom Eyen. "I want you to come over for a chic lunch." And a chic lunch it was. Avocados stuffed with baby shrimp in a remoulade and a soothing iced tea. A lovely April day, and we ate on the roof outside of his penthouse on lower Fifth Avenue. He wanted to know all about *Let My People Come*.

One of the things that set Tom apart was his enjoyment of other people's success. He was drawn to it. And he was one of the few who had used Off Off Broadway as a place to hone his craft for the marketplace, not as an end unto itself.

But his first Broadway venture had gone badly. He had been the coauthor and replacement director of *Rachael Lily Rosenbloom (And Don't You Ever Forget It)*, an ill-fated musical starring Ellen Greene as a Bette Midler prototype that had closed in previews, despite having Robert Stigwood and Ahmet Ertegun as its producers. With that trauma seemingly behind him, he was now looking with fresh eyes to the future.

What did I think of a commercial production of *Why Hanna's Skirt Won't Stay Down*? Could I find a producer for it? *Hanna* was an Eyen classic that had established Helen Hanft as "the first lady of Off Off Broadway." It had been done successfully at the Caffe Cino and La MaMa, and more recently as a hot one-shot midnight performance at the Astor Place during the *Dirtiest Show* run in 1970. Helen, as the working girl who stood over a breeze hole in a carnival sideshow, had been at the top of her form, with the cult audience cheering her every gesture.

I felt positive about it and thought it could be an inspired choice for the Top of the Gate. Tom looked at the room and agreed, commenting that it was well suited to the carnival atmosphere of his play.

To produce, I went to Bruce Mailman's friend Michael Harvey, a former stockbroker, whose first producing effort had been *Score*, which briefly introduced Sylvester Stallone to Off Broadway audiences. Michael had good access to money, was sensible, and would stay out of Tom's way and let him do his work. He had seen the midnight showing and snapped it up. As rehearsals got underway and Tom launched into his creative process, it was apparent that he was fighting a losing battle with the unprocessed rage he still felt about the stillborn death of *Rachael Lily.* The cast, who had all done the show with him before, were badly shaken by his erratic behavior.

The actress playing Hanna's sister, Sophie, retreated into an alcoholic stupor and had to be replaced by her understudy. The actor playing the Adonis, thinking we were going to close at any moment, was stealing his own shirts to collect the insurance. (I caught him on the third one.) And dear Helen Hanft, a trouper, dug in and returned Tom's anger pound for pound. As we lurched forward, I kept remembering the midnight Astor Place performance and praying we could somehow get back to it.

The first preview couldn't have been worse. Just as we began, the air conditioning broke down, and the July heat was stifling. The audience was peopled with *Hanna* and Helen buffs, but the response was flat, and, incredibly, the show seemed to have become dated in a mere four years. People crawled over chairs and under the black velour drapes to escape. To add to it all, Helen shrieked that Al Carmines, who sat at a front table with his feet propped up against the stage, had been "glaring" at her from beginning to end. Al, unfortunately, was not a person who wished others well when he was not involved.

Tom and I looked at each other. We couldn't deny the disaster that had just descended.

"This show needs $20,000 worth of gimmicks," he said.

"Darling, we don't have that kind of money."

"Darling, this is Broadway."

"Tom, this is not Broadway. This is the Village Gate. You're making everyone fucking crazy."

"Fuck you, Albert."

We had two or three more previews, fully air conditioned, but the show seemed to worsen. Tom and the cast were no longer speaking. We were in a state of paralysis.

One light moment occurred when Dustin Hoffman (who had been a dishwasher at the Gate) arrived on a Saturday afternoon with Murray Schisgal and a young woman with a crew cut. They were there to see *Hanna* and *Let My People Come*, looking for actors for Schisgal's play *All Over Town*, which Hoffman was to direct on Broadway. Hoffman and the young woman ran giggling through the Gate like it was their playground, and, at one point, as I was walking by the grand piano, I tripped over something.

I looked down to see Hoffman and the crew-cut lady under the piano rolled up in a pile of velour. Hoffman looked up and said, "We're chatting."

I sat with Michael Harvey on the terrace of the Gate and told him I didn't think the show could continue with Tom as the director. There was only one person I thought could improve the situation and who would be acceptable to Tom. That was Neil Flanagan. Like John Herbert MacDowell, Neil was a veritable saint of Off Off Broadway and a well-established actor and director on and Off Broadway. Neil had seen *Hanna* dozens of times in its various incarnations and was well acquainted with all the principals involved.

Additionally, he was a healing force, would have a wonderful eye for what needed to be done, and had great diplomatic skills. Michael said he would trust my judgment. I told him I would handle it with Tom.

Tom and I were always honest and direct, and I gave him a hardline assessment of where we were and what I thought was the solution. He didn't like the idea of being ousted as director, but if it needed to happen, he was receptive to Neil as his replacement. I suggested he cut himself off from the cast for the remainder of rehearsals, discreetly attend previews, and give his comments only to Neil.

The whole feeling at the Top of the Gate changed overnight. Neil Flanagan was able to work wonders. But one night on the sidewalk in front of the Gate, Tom approached me. He looked like a pitiable beggar. It was hard not to look away.

Unleashing all of his frustration and turmoil, he cried, "I hate you, Albert!" I shudder at the recollection. It was not a moment you would ever want to have with anyone.

The show never reached the level of its earlier glory, but Neil had brought it to a workable performance level. It opened to good reviews and managed a respectable 127 performances.

Sometime in the late spring of 1974, I got a call from an agent. "I have someone who wants to do *Let My People Come* in Cleveland."

"Nice," I said.

"It's the Mafia."

"I'll take it to Phil and see how he feels," I responded.

In my naivete, I thought we could do business with the Mafia as long as we didn't compromise ourselves by breaking any laws, and Phil said he would be guided by me. I spoke to the man in Cleveland, and he sent an aide to New York for a lunch at Steak and Brew.

"We find ourselves in a certain tax situation," the aide imparted, "and we don't want to pay based on box-office gross. We want to make the same flat payment every week."

"No problem," I said.

"It will be in cash," he explained. "In a paper bag." He noticed that I thought that was funny. "No," he clarified, "an old paper bag."

I tried to be serious, but I realized the falling action had set in and it was now time to blow this off. "I have to tell you that whatever you pay us will appear on statements filed with the attorney general of the State of New York. It's required by New York State law." We never heard from them again.

Years later I learned that "old paper bag" is a mob term for unmarked bills. This would be money from a bank robbery, for instance, originally marked and then sold to the mob for far less than its cash value, deep-sixed for ten years, and then resurfaced unmarked.

There were many such approaches by the mob to do the show, some far less gracious. "Poland, fly your ass to Miami Beach. Put your ass in a hotel," was one.

We elected to stay on the straight-and-narrow. Our first production outside of New York was a co-production with Harold Fielding at the Regent Theatre in London in August of 1974, with Phil directing and our original musical director, Billy Cunningham, repeating his invaluable contribution. Billy was three-hundred-plus pounds of black brilliance and my frequent dinner companion at the Horn of Plenty in the Village. With his sweet face and his Jheri curl wig, I had dubbed him "the world's largest Hershey's Kiss."

During the London rehearsals, Phil called me person-to-person collect every night at the Gate box office for the daily grosses. It was a cost-free call because I would reply that I was out but could be reached later at the following two numbers: the first number was the gross for the performance; the second was the total for the week-to-date.

Phil produced our original cast album himself on our own label, Libra Records. Distribution was a constant tug of war. The record stores, we soon learned, don't pay you for product until they need more of it. However, we set up a concession at the Gate and in our other theaters, which did very well with the album and with a snazzy souvenir book designed by Lorraine Borden of Great Scott Advertising.

Saul Richman and I had our first and probably only fight during this time. He wanted to bring in Ray Lussa, the main purveyor of souvenir books on Broadway and the road, to operate the concession. I felt that, as general manager, it was rightfully my domain. Finally, a meeting was arranged between Lussa and me in his office.

Lussa looked tough, and it was clear he thought he had the upper hand. I made my case, and eventually he asked, "Where do you get off thinking you know anything about concessions?"

"I learned from the best in the business," I answered. "And who the hell is that?"

"L. M. Jacobs," I answered.

Lussa was dumbfounded. "Alright, I'll tell ya' what," he said. "I'll print the books, and you sell them." "Sounds like a good fit to me," I said.

Not only were we a good fit, but he said it was probably the first time he had ever gotten an honest count. We became friends. He went out of his way for me from then on, and he was the kind of colorful Broadway character I liked.

Phil had been longtime friends with Allan Carr, then notable as a friend to the stars, a giver of outlandish Hollywood parties, and the manager of Ann-Margret. Saul and I were called to a meeting with Phil and Earl, and Carr and Bobby Zarem, and informed that Carr and Zarem were to be put on weekly retainers. Bobby was an already legendary international press agent. He was to do "special publicity," and Allan was to seek "special situations" for the show.

Their first undertaking was to provide a glittery assortment of titled royalty and British stars for the London opening. Saul and I rolled our eyes as they rattled off an endless list of names we knew would never materialize. While I enjoyed Bobby, I hated Allan on sight.

One Saturday afternoon, I was on a Village Gate pay phone to London, speaking to Phil, who reported Carr had told him I was never around and no one was minding the store. As luck would have it, Allan was at that very moment upstairs at the Top of the Gate frolicking with the Adonis from the show. I told Phil to hold on and brought Allan to the phone.

I looked him square in the eye as I spoke to Phil. "Allan, I have Phil on the line in London. He tells me that you tell him I'm never around and there's no one minding the store here. Can you get on with him now and elaborate on that?" I thrust the phone in Carr's face.

"Phil, I'm confused. I don't know how this happened. Albert's on top of everything here. If you got a different impression, I'm sorry. He's here right now on a Saturday afternoon." Allan handed the phone back to me.

"Well, what would you call that?" Phil asked.

I glared at Allan Carr and said, "High faggotry."

For the London opening, Zarem and Carr delivered one celebrity: Ann-Margret. It was, however, a rousing evening, loved by the opening night audience and followed by a spectacular yacht cruise on the Thames, circling the city in all of its nighttime splendor. Earl and Rosemary Wilson were there with Maxine Mesinger, who was the unofficial godmother of our show. Being in their company was a real romp.

Throughout my time on the show, I had occasion to be with Earl and Rosemary Wilson for dinner, at parties, and occasional club and show openings. They were well-known as the ultimate New York sophisticates but were in actuality two very uncomplicated people from the Midwest, straightforward and accessible, who thoroughly enjoyed but were unflapped by the glamorous world in which Earl traveled and wrote about, with Rosemary at his side.

At dinner, strangers who recognized Earl from his film and television appearances felt free to sit with us for a drink. The Wilsons seemed totally comfortable with it. Rosemary and I were drinkers, and we often wound up in a corner chatting by ourselves.

With *Let My People Come* a hit in London, Phil began to discuss bringing Charles Pierce to the Top of the Gate for his New York debut. Pierce was a longtime West Coast institution, known for his sublimely funny impressions of Bette Davis, Joan Crawford, Mae West, and, most notably, Jeannette McDonald, soaring over the audience in a flower-bedecked swing, lip-syncing "San Francisco." Oddly, he had never played New York, and Art was eager to have him at the Top of the Gate.

Phil was now securely in the everything-he-touches-turns-to-gold category. *Let My People Come* was an international hit, he practically owned *After Dark* magazine, and Patrick Pacheco coined the moniker of "Old Leather Beard" for him. He was red-hot, and his friend Tommy Tune, whose career was in a lull after his Tony-winning performance in *Seesaw,* came on board along with his companion Michel Stuart to help launch Charles Pierce.

Phil flew Charles to New York in October and asked me to take him to lunch at Maxwell's Plum and map out our plans for him. We would open him at the Top, arrange multiple bookings on *The Tonight Show,* and Phil would then offer him a management contract for television, films, and concerts. Charles was a seasoned pro who had been around for years, and he was stunned to see these possibilities for himself in what he knew to be a limited field.

The first idea that Tommy and Phil hatched for Charles at the Top of the Gate was to combine him with Ethel Smith, a virtuoso organist who was an MGM featured name from Esther Williams pictures who had a hit with "Tico, Tico" in 1944. Phil, Tommy, and I, along with Jim Sink and Michel Stuart, swung down to Florida to pay Ms. Smith a visit. Her apartment in Palm Beach was all white, with what appeared to be white fur carpeting. There were myriad photos of her with most of the A-list MGM stars. She immediately dubbed us *The Cartel*, and, after a chat, she sat down at her organ and played up a storm.

She was very welcoming and eager to work after a few decades of downtime. She and Charles both loved the idea of the double bill, and, naturally, it would be advertised as "Charles Pierce and Ethel Smith: Together Again for the First Time."

Ethel was to have a small, tiered, revolving stage off to one side. With its wrap-around scooped drapes, it resembled a wedding cake, but instead of a bride and groom on top, we had Ethel with her organ. Phil and Tommy determined that she would speak only in French. Charles's stage would extend to Ethel's, in runway fashion, for the entire length of the horizontally shaped room.

The planned opening on New Year's Eve meant lots of rehearsals during the holidays, including an exasperating one on Christmas Eve. Tension was rising on all sides, and I sensed trouble when Phil remarked to me, "Ethel is our mother. Charles is the one we wish was our mother."

Phil had a sadistic side, and by the final week of rehearsal, Ethel had willfully engaged it. This was, after all, a woman who had dropped a flower pot from a third-story window onto the head of her husband, Ralph Bellamy. She now began to see herself as the victim of a gay conspiracy.

"Albert, this microphone makes my voice sound shrill," she said to me in a grating voice. "Ethel, I'll give you Charles's mic." And I replaced hers with Charles's. "This is much better," she said, in the exact same grating voice.

The evening began with Ethel Smith standing in the middle of the opening night audience speaking in French. I realized that some people might think she was Charles. Most were at a total loss for whatever she must be saying. As she moved up the steps to her little, round, wedding cake stage, the gauzy circular drapes rose and took her three mic stands with them. Surrounded by three hanging, swinging mic stands, she reverted to English, glared at the audience and screeched, "Sabotage!"

Charles Pierce was spectacular. Before he went on, he metamorphosed himself into a person named Celene, and it was Celene who did the act. From his entrance to "Beautiful Girls" from the *Follies* overture, to his finish swinging out over the audience as Jeannette, it was a complete triumph. I'm sure, for many in the audience, it was the happiest New Year's Eve of their lives. The evening was so lopsided in Charles's favor that after four weeks, Ethel and her organ were sent packing back to Palm Beach.

During his record-breaking Gate engagement, I must have seen him one hundred times, enough to establish him in my mind as one of the great entertainers. And I declared him " the silliest person I know," which I deemed a high honor. All the critics raved, led by Clive Barnes of the *Times,* who compared Charles to a Hirschfeld cartoon, calling him "a fantastically funny and outrageous man" whose material "has the taste of wit and style to it."

In January of 1975, just as his two clubs were flourishing as they hadn't in years, Art D'Lugoff was the recipient of a notice from the

New York State Liquor Authority informing him that his liquor license was "hereby revoked" pursuant to a state law forbidding the serving of alcoholic beverages in the presence of total nudity, which it considered lewd. The enraged D'Lugoff was a fighter who wouldn't let the state dictate his entertainment policy. He requested and got a stay, and hearings were scheduled.

Betty Friedan, Alvin Toffler, Garson Kanin, *The New Yorker* critic Brendan Gill, and Joseph Papp were among the luminaries who testified at the hearings, most of them taking the position that *Let My People Come* was not lewd or indecent and was, in fact, "a valuable social document." Friedan stated that it was "joyous and affirmative about human sexuality," with Toffler, author of the best-selling *Future Shock,* weighing in that it was "not dirty, just happy and healthy." It would be nearly a year before a decision was rendered. In the meantime, business continued as usual.

I invited Charles Ludlam and his company to see Charles Pierce, and they came back many times. Ludlam attended a glittering party in Pierce's honor given by the scenic designer Douglas Schmidt that attracted the Wilsons, Carol Channing, Andy Warhol, and Craig Russell, among others.

Saul Richman told us that *The Tonight Show* was having a blackout against female impersonators, so those appearances never materialized, nor did the personal management contract. As Charles filled the Top of the Gate, Phil went on to other things, the most immediate of which was to present his dear friend Tommy Tune on yet another stage at the Top of the Gate in an ill-conceived act directed by Tommy's companion, Michel Stuart. Stuart was a prominent member of the original cast of *A Chorus Line* and had danced on *The Judy Garland Show.* He and Tommy had been together for several years.

Stuart believed that Tommy was primarily a singer, not a dancer, and that was the focus of the act. Tommy certainly sang well enough, but the electricity flowed when he tippy-tap-toed. And Tommy Tune wears a white tux like no one else.

The work process was contentious, with Michel dividing and conquering us all in the name of "protecting" Tommy. Michael Bennett came by to put his two cents in. William Elliott, a handsome and talented alumnus from La MaMa, did the orchestrations for the nine-piece orchestra, which, in a money-saving effort, we prerecorded, paying the musicians the one-time-use Local 802 recording rate.

Audiences saw Bill sitting alone at the piano, but they heard a full nine-piece orchestra. I was sweating bullets the night the head of the musicians' union attended. But he either did not notice or, if he did, chose not to pursue it.

With three shows running in an internationally famous venue, Phil Oesterman's hold on the New York entertainment scene seemed assured.

Then came opening night.

Tommy Tune came out on stage in a bathing suit. The audience, which included the Schoenfelds, who were there at my invitation, was stunned. I was enraged. I told Rob Wallner, who was now my apprentice in ATPAM, to tell Tommy that he owed Phil Oesterman $30,000—the cost of putting on the show. He did, and Tommy marched up to me and said, "If I could, I would dance nude before God."

The *Times* review by John S. Wilson was headlined, "Tommy Tune Sings with Little Success 'Atop' Village Gate." That about covers it. Multitudes of great triumphs lay ahead for Mr. Tune, beginning a year later with his direction of the long-running androgynous musical hit, *The Club,* right across the street from the Gate at Circle in the Square.

There were now cracks in the relationship between Phil and Earl. Earl had recently married, and Phil felt that Earl's new wife had become a wedge in their friendship. In addition, Phil had asked me to find someone who could direct other productions of *Let My People Come.*

I came up with Otto Pirchner, who had notably assisted Ron Field on the Broadway production of *Applause.* When Otto directed the New Orleans production of the show, he and Earl became fast friends, adding to Phil's growing resentment and insecurity.

Then there was the matter of moving the show to Broadway. Phil was hell-bent on that. Earl, wisely in my opinion, was not. The ship was presently sailing smoothly, but I was certain that Phil and Earl were on an unavoidable collision course that was about a year away. I didn't want to be around for it, especially with my producer having a position I couldn't support.

On the immediate agenda was the Paris production, to be presented in the basement cabaret of the famed Olympia vaudeville house by Fernand Lumbroso, the top Paris impresario, whose political leanings gave him the European exclusive to the major opera and dance companies from Russia and China, and Bruno Coquatrix, the Olympia's legendary owner.

Mr. Lumbroso was nearing seventy and a close friend of the show's lawyer, James Mosher, who was on board before I joined the production. Not the lawyer I would have chosen, but he brought us this enchanting and brilliant man, who I loved from the first moment we met.

Fernand Lumbroso was a Jew from Spain who came to Paris in his twenties with his sister, Odette. His high-profile career as an impresario and talent manager had spanned decades. He was a short, stout man whose face reflected intelligence and humor, who wore very fine, understated clothing, his hair combed back, his tinted glasses resting comfortably on top of his head. He had a low-pitched nasal voice and a distinctive manner of speech. He was openly gay and took great delight in the many pleasures of *Let My People Come*. It was readily apparent to Phil that Fernand and I would work well together, and he delegated much of the preliminary Paris preparation to me.

I engaged my old friend Jay Kingwill to replace me as New York general manager during my time away, with Rob Wallner staying on as company manager.

Since the word "people" had a communist connotation in France, we needed a new title. The show in Paris would be called *Leve-Toi Et Viens,* which translates as "Stand Up and Come."

Two nights before my trip, I had a 2:00 a.m. call from Phil. He and his companion Jim were having a raging fight, and I was summoned to the apartment to break it up. I had never seen Phil so angry. He was belching smoke like a factory smokestack. I watched this for a moment and realized that he now totally dominated my life. I had placed myself at his beck and call. My desire to break out had become almost physical. The night before I left, I told Jay Kingwill to "get a good sense of how you like this because I may not be coming back."

I arrived in Paris on April 30, 1975, my thirty-fourth birthday, and was picked up at de Gaulle Airport by a crazy Lumbroso assistant who drove his tiny open-air sports car at 80 mph, sometimes on the highways and often on the sidewalks. Being close to the ground made it seem even faster.

We arrived at the Spectacles Lumbroso offices, where I was introduced to Fernand's sister, Odette, who was his general manager, and Fernand then whisked me away to a birthday dinner at the Club Sept on Rue Sainte-Anne. The Sept was a unique spot even for Paris. On one side of the divider was the chicest restaurant in all of Paris, and on the other, a smart, sophisticated European bar tended by a small, distinctly French bartender with close-cropped gray hair. In the large basement below were hundreds of readily available male hustlers under the supervision of a low-level mob boss. The after-dinner birthday treat was the drag show at the Alcazar.

I stayed in an "airline" hotel in the Opera section. It was near the Sept, where Fernand, Odette, and I had dinner nearly every night. During the day, I was in preliminary auditions at the Olympia, working with the designers and the crew, and developing promotional ideas with the press department. I was given an assistant who startled me by arriving with the script of *Futz* under his arm.

"What are you doing with that? " I asked. " It is a wonderful play, and I have translated it. I hope to do it at a small theater in Paris."

"Well, I was one of its producers in New York." "*C'est fantastique.*"

I fell in love with Paris, frozen in time, and filled with beauty, style, and, most of all, care. The shop windows, beautifully designed and spotless, the parks perfectly manicured, and the street cleaners out every afternoon mopping the streets. And I loved the French people. I felt a strong connection with their humor. I found them animated and charming.

The meetings with Fernand and M. Coquatrix in Coquatrix's offices at the Olympia were entirely in French, with Fernand translating what he thought I needed to know. Coquatrix was built like Charles de Gaulle, his chest like a football field. Next to him on an easel was a large chalk drawing of Liza Minnelli. Though I would learn that Lumbroso and Coquatrix had been estranged for twenty years, the meetings were filled with the camaraderie and laughter of two old friends.

Everything had proceeded with amazing smoothness. There were good actor choices for Phil to look at, the sets were ready, and the French press was excited about the show. Fernand told me it was the first time he had ever enjoyed working with Americans.

With Phil's arrival, all of that changed. He didn't like the Olympia Cabaret, he didn't like the rehearsal space, he didn't like the actors. He yelled at all the bewildered French people around the show, and he treated the Lumbrosos like dirt. The goodwill I had built up was decimated by Phil's inexplicable rage. I felt paralyzed.

In this atmosphere, casting was finalized, and rehearsals got underway. At night, I was expected to accompany Phil and Jim to Paris cafes and nightclubs, where I had to endure his endless rantings against these people who had devoted themselves to his show with the same love everyone had always given it. All of the things the show represented so beautifully were mocked by his behavior.

One night, after hours of clubbing and a slew of drinks, I found myself at the breaking point. Still unable to stand up to him, I felt trapped in a phony existence. I determined that the only solution was to take a leap across the Atlantic. When Phil and Jim dropped me off at my hotel, I jumped into a cab to de Gaulle Airport, arriving there at about 3:00 a.m. The airport, to my surprise, was not the twenty-four-hour operation I had imagined. It was open but empty.

My luggage remained at the hotel, and my bill was unpaid, but I had to get out. I was determined to get the next flight to New York. I called Rob Wallner and told him to call Phil at 10:00 a.m. Paris time to tell him that I had left Paris and was leaving the show. I would work out the return of my luggage and payment of the hotel bill with Fernand.

I got on an 8:00 a.m. Air France flight feeling shell-shocked but relieved. When I arrived at my apartment in New York, the phone, as I expected, was ringing. "I am so, so sorry," Phil said.

"I couldn't stand it, Phil. I had to get out."

"I understand. I totally understand. But how will you live?" "I don't know," I said.

"I want you to keep your weekly ten percent of the concession at the Gate." Here was Phil showing his generous side, and I realized I was glad there was still a friendship. I also knew and accepted that there would be an ongoing connection with the show that I still loved but was too burned-out to manage.

"That's very generous and very much needed," I responded. "Jim and I will get your luggage back to you and take care of the hotel," he offered. I called Fernand and Odette to tell them what I had done.

"We understand totally the situation. And we love all that you have done, and we love you," Fernand said.

Three weeks later, as they were driving to Fernand's country house, Phil asked Fernand to stop the car so he could relieve himself. Fernand got out on the driver's side to catch a breath and was hit and hurled into the air by a passing car. He was rushed to the hospital in critical condition, and after several days, it was discovered that he had suffered a broken neck. I got an urgent phone call from Odette, who blamed Phil and said everything about him was trouble.

Miraculously, Fernand made a full recovery.

In the meantime, my friend Gilbert Price had been cast in a leading role in the Broadway production of the Leonard Bernstein and Alan Jay Lerner musical *1600 Pennsylvania Avenue,* and he gave me the honor of asking if I would become his personal manager. We had remained close since our time at the Theatre Wing, and Gilbert was having an interesting career.

Langston Hughes had created *Jericho-Jim Crow* especially for him, directed Off Broadway by Alvin Ailey in 1964. After his breakout performance a year later on Broadway in *The Roar of the Greasepaint—The Smell of the Crowd,* he briefly became a fixture on the Merv Griffin and Ed Sullivan television shows, and went on to two Tony nominations for roles in *Lost in the Stars* and *The Night That Made America Famous.*

I enthusiastically accepted his offer and went to his longtime agent, the highly respected Milton Goldman at ICM, whom I had never met. I told Goldman that we were going to need some serious money, and, with Leonard Bernstein giving marching orders that Gilbert be signed before he returned from Europe, I thought we were in a position to get it. At the composer's request, Gilbert had performed the role of the Celebrant in Leonard Bernstein's *Mass* in 1971.

Milton Goldman's response was, "The quote for the boy has always been $1,000."

"First of all," I advised, "he's not 'the boy,' and we're not going to think of him as a 'boy.' I want you to get $2,500 for him, or we go elsewhere. People know he's your client, but his signed agreement with you has lapsed, and I don't think you want him moving on right now."

Another thing I wanted, unusual for the time, was a rider calling for additional royalties for Gilbert in the event one of his songs on the cast album was released as a single. This I left to our attorney Ina Meibach, who Gilbert appropriately referred to as "the gladiator." Milton buckled down and got him $2,750 for the out-of-town tryout, and $2,250 in town, going to $3,000 after recoupment of the production costs. Ina secured the recording royalty, which, amusingly, they later begged us to give back.

I sensed trouble when Gilbert asked me to join him and his longtime friend Warren Allen Smith for dinner. Warren, whom

I had never met, had been the owner of Variety Arts Studios, the most successful rehearsal studios in Manhattan during the '60s and '70s. Gilbert frequently introduced conflict and even sabotage when things were going too smoothly. As we started dinner, it was clear that Warren was there because Gilbert wanted him to drive a wedge between us, which he was more than willing to do. He was very proprietary of Gilbert, and I was treated as an intruder.

The following night, Gilbert showed up at my apartment to inform me that he now "wanted God to be his personal manager." My services were no longer needed. I was enraged and sent the spice rack crashing to the floor but told him I was willing to terminate provided we signed a rider requiring full payment of my commissions from *1600 Pennsylvania Avenue*. He agreed. I wrote the severance agreement on the spot, and, at the top, he drew a cross and wrote "JMJ" for Jesus, Mary, and Joseph.

I soon discovered that Warren was in charge of his finances and, while I got all payments due me, they were always weeks late, and I sometimes had to call Warren and beg for them. The show was not a success. Later, when Gilbert signed to be the standby for *Pippin,* he moved in with me for two weeks, as he always did, to have me run lines with him. We were still friends.

In November of 1975, *Let My People Come* opened a successful engagement at the Whiskey A Go Go in Los Angeles. I was now well-rested, and Phil brought me out there to act as a consultant for launching the show. Rob Wallner, his ATPAM apprenticeship with me now complete, was the company manager.

During the time we were in Los Angeles, the building housing the Village Gate and the adjoining Mills Hotel was sold. The new owner was a man named Louis Evangelista, of the Bronx. It was Evangelista's intention to evict the welfare tenants from the hotel, convert it to luxury apartments, and get rid of the building's long-term bargain-basement tenant Art D'Lugoff.

On December 4, the State Liquor Authority announced its decision with respect to the disposition of the liquor license. They found three-to-two against the Gate and determined, in a statewide decision, that "the serving of liquor and total nudity are incompatible." Michael Roth, chairman of the SLA, described the show as "lewd and indecent" if decidedly "not obscene."

Neither Roth nor any member of the SLA had ever bothered to see a performance of *Let My People Come.* Legitimate theaters were specifically exempted from the ruling.

Art and Burt D'Lugoff filed an appeal, and the Gate was granted a temporary restraining order against the cancellation of the liquor license. That appeal was to drag on through most of 1976.

On December 18, a fire destroyed the Blue Angel nightclub, taking seven lives. It was not the Blue Angel of Nichols and May and Kaye Ballard, but a tacky, fly-by-night operation exploiting the name of its famed predecessor. As a consequence, Mayor Abe Beame launched a vigorous high-profile campaign to determine what other Manhattan cabarets might be "firetraps."

Evangelista began an all-out assault on the Village Gate after the Blue Angel fire. Art arrived one morning to find that additional pillars had been installed in the audience section without his prior knowledge, larger than the ones that were already there. Evangelista said his engineers had determined they were a "structural necessity." Another cold winter morning, Art arrived to find that the boiler had been shut off and a thick brick wall had been built around it. The aggressive acts of the new landlord and those of the State Liquor Authority in combination with the Blue Angel fire were about to merge into a perfect storm. Although Jay Kingwill was now the general manager of the show, there was a role for me to play in the events at hand.

Lily Turner had taken a long-term lease on the now-empty Astor Place Theatre. I had previously alerted her manager, George Elmer, that we might need to move the show in there "on a dime." Our plan was that I would call George, and he would immediately open up the Astor Place. There was a tuned piano and lighting equipment enough to illuminate the stage.

Early on Friday, January 2, 1976, Art called me and said, "You better get over here—I think something's gonna happen here." During the forty-eight-hour hiatus after New Year's Eve, Evangelista's people had come into the Gate and installed an elevator shaft in front of the walk-in beverage refrigeration and, more important, had dropped another shaft in front of a fire exit, totally blocking it. As if by magic, the city building inspectors appeared that afternoon. They told Art D'Lugoff they would return within hours to close him down.

On Friday nights, *Let My People Come* played two performances, at seven and ten. The first show went off without a hitch. But as the sold-out audience emerged into the small Gate lobby, they found themselves in the middle of a riot of police, firemen in raincoats, and the early arrivals for the 10 o'clock show. At the epicenter of this chaos was a bemused man from the Buildings Department handing Art a court order to close down immediately, as Louis Evangelista shouted at him from the sidelines. I dubbed it *The Keystone Cops Meet the Marx Brothers.*

Art D'Lugoff wadded up the court order and threw it at Evangelista as he yelled, "Goddam Mafia scum. Fucking Mafia scum." Eddie the Cop said, "That this man walks around is the Eighth Wonder of the World."

I fought my way through the melee and into the box office to call George Elmer. I told him we needed to have the Astor Place ready to start the show by 10:30, thinking that, with luck, we'd be on by 11:00.

Suddenly, he balked. "I have to talk to Lily," he said. "What?" I said, "George, this is an emergency. This is happening NOW, for God's sake."

He said he had to "check" with Lily and would get right back to me. My mind flashed on my last conversation with Lily, and I immediately realized this was a revenge fuck. I had offered her a tenant for the Astor Place at a rental she considered insulting, and she had slammed down the phone. Fortunately, I had asked Saul Richman to come, thinking there might be something press worthy, and Saul was an old friend of Lily's.

The phone rang. "It's Lily Turner for Albert." I briefed Saul on what needed to happen and told him to take the call. I didn't have to explain the urgency. It was all around us. Lily told Saul I was a dis-respectful and rude person, she didn't know if she wanted this show in "her theater," what about the insurance, the *this,* the *that.* It was a cliffhanger, but Saul was persuasive, and within minutes he prevailed.

Saul called a fleet of yellow cabs, which he often did on open-ing nights, and I got the box office to make up a slew of envelopes with $1.25 in them that we gave to each group of four to cover the eight-block cab ride to the Astor Place. The 10 o'clock audience was quick to catch on, and, by this time, they were up for it. They had become part of a New York adventure. The show went on at the Astor Place at 11:00. I don't think we made the Guinness World Records, but I doubt that any show has ever moved as quickly.

The front-page headline in Saturday' s *Daily News* was, " Village Gate Shut By City."

There is a doctrine in New York City law called "Self Help" that permits an owner to take emergency measures to correct a situation that has caused him to be closed down or has seriously jeopardized his business. Invoking that clause, Art called up an old sparring partner of Joe Louis who brought in a crew of burly men. They broke through the blocked fire exit and the other Evangelista "renovations" with sledgehammers. The show resumed performances on Tuesday, with drinks being served.

My part in this was to sit with Art in his office for the weekend and put him on the phone with every reporter, every wire service, every TV newscaster and radio commentator I could find. I dialed them one after another, and, when they came to the phone, I asked, "Can you hold for Art D'Lugoff?"

Art was a born media figure, authentic, very New York, and his wit remained intact no matter what. He was backed by his brother, Burt, a stalwart who was a doctor in Baltimore and always at Art's side as wise counsel and ballast in these matters. In its front-page story, the *Daily News* ran a photo of Art on the phone with a wooden carving behind him that said, "This too shall pass."

When we finally finished the last phone call, I looked at Art and said "Mensch."

I looked at Burt and said, "Mensch." Burt looked at me and said, " You say mensch, I say mensch."

The bond of my friendship with the D'Lugoffs was now golden.

After those first intense days of 1976, I was burned out. I have always loved projects and people that grab me by the tail, but I also have a fear of being overtaken and losing myself in the process. I continued to keep track of things, but from a distance.

The State Liquor Authority appeal dragged on and kept the specter of a Village Gate shutdown and/or a show eviction looming for months. Phil, in his mind, was headed for Broadway. Earl was opposed, but, on the other hand, he didn't want his show to be homeless.

The relationship of the two men continued to deteriorate, and the clouds around the Village Gate undoubtedly contributed to a drop in business, leading to financial instability that Phil thought could be solved by a Broadway move he was certain would bring the show a new audience. In the spring, the Internal Revenue Service began an action against Phil for nonpayment of his personal taxes.

On July 7, *Let My People Come* began a disastrous run at the Morosco Theatre on Broadway. It's a subtle but powerful fact that, to succeed on Broadway, a show needs the support and goodwill of the Broadway establishment. *Let My People Come* arrived on Broadway an unwanted orphan in a storm of its own making.

There was no money to pay for things. Earl had declared himself an enemy of the move and took Phil to arbitration over his handling of the show and its finances. Very soon, the production found itself in the same situation with the IRS as its producer, and it staggered to a halt on October 2 after 128 Broadway preview performances, never formally opening.

With the producer and the producing company in bankruptcy, the rights to *Let My People Come* became an asset of the IRS and were put up at an auction attended by only two people, Earl Wilson Jr. and Otto Pirchner, who had changed his name to Otto Maximillion. Otto was the sole bidder on the rights and immediately turned them over to Earl, who has continued to enjoy the benefits of productions of his show all over the world, including ten-year runs in Toronto and Philadelphia. The State Liquor Authority move against the Village Gate had become irrelevant and was dropped.

CHAPTER 10

"Why You Want That Chichi Stuff? Get a Cab"

Catching my breath, I went into therapy, went to the gym, and, after seeing Gilbert and others walk into Phebe's looking like movie stars, I became a regular with a doctor in Brooklyn named James D'Adamo. Going to him was very hush-hush at the time, but the results were spectacular. He was a practitioner of the holistic approach of empowering the body to heal itself through nutrition, vitamins and herbs, foot baths, and high colonics. I skipped the colonics.

All this self-focus and the sudden abundance of leisure time led me to write an autobiographical play called *Normal* that started with my childhood, went through forming the Judy Garland Fan Club, and ended in New York with the Stonewall riots. Writing it overtook me in the way I liked.

The process was absorbing and intense, but the feeling of exposure and vulnerability was palpable. I went through several directors before it even went into rehearsal—good directors like Lawrence Kornfeld, Eugene Lesser, Ron Faber, and Mark Bramble. I ended up choosing an actor who had never directed, Mark Baker, just coming off a spectacular Broadway debut in the title role of the Chelsea Theatre Center revival of *Candide*.

Mark put together a wonderful cast that included Mink Stole, and Edith O'Hara generously gave us her Thirteenth Street Theater. I stayed completely away until the invited dress rehearsal. The small theater was packed, and I was pleased to see that even Tom O'Horgan attended. However, I was horrified by what was on the stage. Mark had taken it in an avant-garde direction that I never intended. The scenes at the Midwestern family dinner table, for instance, were set in a Japanese motif.

I met with Mark afterward in Edith's apartment above the theater and told him I was canceling the production. He left and returned with the cast in what became a very impassioned confrontation. They had devoted themselves to my play, were not being compensated, and now I was cutting it off before their efforts could have a life. I thought they had a point, and, while I thought the choice not to go on was mine to make, I agreed to pay them one week's salary at the current Equity Off Broadway rate out of my own pocket.

Max Jacobs had read but not seen the play and liked it very much. He agreed to put up half the capitalization for a full Off Broadway production at the Cherry Lane. The process enlightened me about what playwrights must go through, and I saw that, in my own instance, I had evolved into an unbearably vulnerable nutcase. Max's investment sat in the bank, untouched.

In the meantime, my old friend, Jay Kingwill, had gone into partnership with Jack Schlissel. Schlissel was the dean of Broadway general managers, not only because he had been David Merrick's manager from the beginning, but because of his knowledge, savvy, and stature in the industry.

Jack and Jay offered me the company manager position on the Broadway revival of Tennessee Williams' *Sweet Bird of Youth* starring Irene Worth and Christopher Walken, and produced by my friend, Michael Harvey, at the Harkness Theatre. I had really wanted to confine my career to Off Broadway, but there was no work for me there at the moment. So I took it.

I had become friends with Bricktop, and on opening night, I gave her regards to Tennessee Williams, who was her longtime friend. "How is that dazzling creature?" he asked.

I had read of Bricktop's legendary clubs in Paris and Rome, so I was eager to go and see her perform when she came to New York in 1975 to play Surabaya, an intimate, upstairs room on the East Side. She was singing elegantly as I walked by. I nodded, and she nodded back.

She was now eighty-one, and her performance was pure intimacy. She sang a song in her inimitable style—a mix of jazz, lowdown, and sophistication—then sat with people, had a drink and an engaging conversation, and moved effortlessly on to the next song and the next table. She was light skinned, freckled, with her famous matted-down red hair, and a countenance of unmatched radiance. Her repertoire included the best of the American composers and songs that were hers alone.

Eventually, she came to my table. As she sat holding my hand, she said, "What do you want to hear, Baby?" I said, "I want to hear whatever you would sing for Judy Garland." She got up and announced that "of alllll the great stars I have met, I never met Judy Garland, but I'm going to sing the song that *I like*." She performed a medley that opened a cappella with "I'll Always Be Somewhere Forever Your Friend," followed by "Thank You for the Flowers," and, joined by Hugh Shannon on piano, "You Better Go Now." It was an exquisite portrait of need, ultimately overwhelmed and defeated by the fear of intimacy.

When she finished her last set, she sat with me, and we talked, drank Remys, and sang to each other until 6:00 a.m. She told me about her life growing up in West Virginia, the daughter of an Irish maid and a black barber, who cut the hair of only the wealthiest white clientele. At night, when she heard her father beating her mother, she said to herself, "No man will ever do that to me."

She ran away to the Theatre Owners Booking Association, or TOBA, the black vaudeville circuit in New Orleans, and eventually opened a club in Chicago that featured Louis Armstrong as its opening attraction. "The mob drove me out of there, Baby, after one week."

When she was singing and dancing at the Cotton Club in Harlem, a Frenchman presented himself and asked if she would come to Paris and be the saloon keep of his club, Le Grand Duc.

She agreed and arrived at the club at 3:00 a.m. just as the janitor was sweeping out. "This is nice," she said, looking around. "Where is the big room?" "This is all there is," the janitor told her, and when she started to cry, he made her a sandwich. The janitor, who later wrote about it, was Langston Hughes.

After her enormous personal success at Le Grand Duc, she moved on to open her own room, Chez Bricktop, which quickly became *the* club in all of Europe, attracting titled people as well as the cream of world culture and literature from the 1920s through the mid-1940s—Cole Porter, the Fitzgeralds, Hemingway, Dietrich, John Steinbeck. Porter wrote "Miss Otis Regrets" for her. King Farouk of Egypt asked her how it felt to have her "little black freckled hand in the hands of the royalty of the world." "It don't feel like nothin', Baby," she said. "It's just there."

Shortly before 6:00 a.m., she laughed and said, "Considering the hour, would you mind taking me home?" "I would be greatly honored," I replied. I discovered that she lived where I had once lived, the Dorchester Towers on Sixty-Eighth and Broadway. As we were saying goodnight, she took my hand and said, "You have something very special, Baby. I don't know what it is, but keep it."

We saw each other often for the rest of her life. She had terrible arthritis and heart problems, and often had to cancel at the last minute, but there was nothing like being with her. She was a fully realized spiritual person, which she combined with real sophistication and a ferocious appetite for all the things that money can buy. She raised a lot of money for the Catholic Church. Her priests called her The Holy Hustler.

She loved giving small dinner parties in her apartment, cooking amazing soul food while wearing her apron and kerchief. After a delicious banana pudding dessert, she would retreat into her bedroom, change into an elegant golden gown, and return to perform a sublime twenty-minute song set accompanied by a tape recorder.

She asked me to escort her to the launch party for Jean-Claude Baker's *TéléFrance* cable-TV show at the Regency Hotel. With a sense of occasion, I asked, "Do you want me to get a stretch?" "Oh, Baby," she demurred, "why you want that chichi stuff? Get a cab."

At the swank party, she was reunited with Stéphane Grappelli, the French jazz violinist, and they memorably performed a duet. As she was singing, she fell backwards, but I caught her, and she went on without a hitch.

I tried to reach her once when she was in a New York hospital. They didn't have her registered under Bricktop or under Ada Smith, her real name. I thought, *there is no way she can be there without the entire hospital being aware of her*, so I described her. "Oh, that's the Countess du Conge," the operator exclaimed. "Just a moment." "Well, hello Countess," I said. "That was my only marriage, Baby. It was brief because I learned quick."

I replaced Rob Wallner as company manager of the revival of *Who's Afraid of Virginia Woolf?* starring Colleen Dewhurst and Bricktop's dear friend Ben Gazzara, and directed by the playwright Edward Albee. It was a stunning production, with Albee wisely emphasizing the humor, as the shock value of the original was now diminished by audience familiarity with the material and the evolving toughness of the culture itself.

It played the Music Box, an intimate gem of a Broadway theater, co-owned by the Shuberts and Irving Berlin. Every night the treasurer called Mr. Berlin to read him the box office figures for the day. I sat there marveling that a great American institution was listening on the other end of the phone.

One night, I asked if I could say hello to Irving Berlin. "Of course," he said.

"Mr. Berlin, I have a young man here who would like to say hello to you. Our company manager, Albert Poland."

"Hi, Mr. Berlin. We would certainly be honored if you would come and see our show."

"Young man, at my age I'm lucky if I can take a good shit!"

"Oh. Well, thank you, Mr. Berlin."

I could only imagine "God Bless America" swelling up from the floor of the small attic room at the Music Box.

After *Virginia Woolf*, there was still no demand for me Off Broadway. Jay and Jack saved the day. They moved me into their office, and I served as house manager for *A Party with Betty Comden and Adolph Green* at the Little Theatre on West Forty-Fourth Street, next to Sardi's. It was my first and only house manager experience, and I wanted to get off on the right foot with Arthur Cantor, the show's producer.

He called me into his office and told me that the façade of the theater was dirty. "Get it cleaned right away," he said.

I turned to Bruce Mailman, who was the maven on all such matters. Bruce would know how to clean it. "Go to the grocery," he said. "Get a loaf of white bread and roll it into a ball. Take the ball and roll it up and down the front of the building." So, of course, I did. And absolutely nothing happened. Except that the matinee crowds on West Forty-Fourth Street were amazed to see a man rolling a loaf of bread up and down the front of the Little Theatre. When I called back, Bruce's foreman answered the phone. "You did it, didn't you?" he said. "We knew you would do it." And he and Bruce fell on the floor laughing.

After the run in New York, Betty and Adolph had a two-week subscription booking at the Mechanic Theatre in Baltimore, and Arthur Cantor asked me to go with them as company manager.

Larry Bussard, the stage manager, and I went down a day early to look at the theater and to catch Katharine Hepburn in her closing performance of *A Matter of Gravity*. I had seen her do it on Broadway and thought her every bit as remarkable as I expected. On the train ride, I told Larry the story of the Judy Garland Fan Club.

As we sat in the theater, three women in front of us were carrying on at great length about stalking Katharine Hepburn. Jumping onto the hotel elevator with her, knocking on her door and hiding; they were cackling like the *Macbeth* witches. One of the voices was vaguely familiar and, in an amazing coincidence, a closer look revealed that it was Pat McMath, who had taken over the fan club from me. She was quite embarrassed by what I had overheard, but we managed to have a bite after the show. She revealed that Judy had disbanded the fan club one morning at 3:00 a.m. in a hotel lobby where Pat was lying in wait for her. I could easily understand why.

The first day of the Comden and Green engagement found Betty with severe laryngitis. The three of us raced across town in a speeding cab, got her treated, and she went on. They took me to supper every night after the show, splitting the bill between them, and taking turns assuming the odd penny. They told great stories from the golden age of MGM musicals, including one about a tribute to the two of them at Mike Romanoff's restaurant in Hollywood after the opening of *Singin' in the Rain*. Evoking Anita Loos, Betty said, "You can't imagine what it was like for a girl to come down the staircase to see all of Hollywood at her feet."

They spent a great deal of time, even in cab rides, writing the lyrics for the songs Madeline Kahn would sing in *On the Twentieth Century*. Their technique was amazing and meticulous. "The 'aw' vowel sounds good in her voice on that note." I had to wonder how many of their latter-day contemporaries knew or even considered such things.

I now had my own desk in the Schlissel/Kingwill office. Next came the Brecht-Weill musical *Happy End*, starring Meryl Streep and Christopher Lloyd, for which I served as company manager. Meryl Streep was widely respected in the theater community and was someone we knew would be, but was not yet, a star. Her film career hadn't really begun. She and John Cazale were a happy couple at that time, and Cazale and his best friend Al Pacino could usually be found hanging out in Streep's dressing room. *Happy End* was her last Broadway show as of this writing.

CHAPTER 11

A Life in the Theatre

A Life in the Theatre (1977)

The first time I laid eyes on David Mamet was at a party in my Dorchester Towers apartment in 1967. The Gateway Playhouse had asked me to direct *The Fantasticks* for their Barn Theater, and I passed it along to my very talented roommate, John Long. At the closing night cast party, I was particularly struck by one of the actors who seemed especially happy to be there, and asked, "Who is that adorable little chublet?"

"Oh, that's David Mamet," John said. "He was the Indian. He wants to be a writer!"

And write he did! Less than ten years later he had begun to shake things up with his unique and sometimes profane voice in the provocative *Sexual Perversity in Chicago*, an Off Broadway success at the Cherry Lane, and in the critically acclaimed Broadway run of *American Buffalo*, unfortunately cut short by the producers when he refused to adjust his royalties for operating losses.

In the late summer of 1977, I was visited at my desk by Jane Harmon and Gerald Gutierrez. They were the producer and director, respectively, of a new David Mamet play, *A Life in the*

Theatre, scheduled for fall production at the Theatre de Lys. The noted actor and director Ellis Rabb would co-star with the young Peter Evans, highly acclaimed for his performance in *Streamers* at Lincoln Center.

Gerry was tall, cute, adorable, and very boyish as he drank his coffee from a large paper cup. Jane was petite, very attractive in a Scarlett O'Hara kind of way, and all business. They met while assisting the producers and director of John Houseman's Acting Company production of *The Robber Bridegroom* by Alfred Uhry.

They sparked each other to the point that Gerry gave Jane the Mamet script and, after discussions with him and with Mamet, she determined to produce it Off Broadway as her first producing effort, with Gerry in his New York directorial debut.

Harmon rightfully felt that the critics, led by Mel Gussow at the *Times*, were poised to give Mamet the crown. Gussow had been his champion, and it was essential that the opportunity to anoint belong to him. Therefore, we set our opening date opposite the Broadway opening of *Dracula* because the *Times* had a strict policy that its critics could have only one byline on review mornings. The "first string" critic would be obliged to cover the Broadway opening, leaving Gussow, the second-stringer, to cover us.

Then *Dracula* changed its opening date. We changed ours. They changed it again. We changed ours. "The *Times* knows what you are doing," said our press agent Betty Lee Hunt. "They are not happy."

I was now paying Jack Schlissel $75 per week for my desk. His opening-night telegram said, "Your rent goes to $100 after pay-off. Love, Schlissel."

I showed it to Ellis, who thought it was funny. "It's not funny," I said. "It's a legal document."

My opening-night gift from Jane was a handsome leather briefcase. She was watching when I opened it, and we both knew what it meant. I had forever carried papers around in a manila envelope because some small part of me still wanted general managing to be temporary until I could once again return to acting. The briefcase represented a commitment.

I was standing next to David Mamet in the lobby when John Simon came through. "John," David said, tugging at his sleeve, "It's a comedy. You can laugh." Simon winced, and I said, "My nightmare just came true."

The party was at the Village Green, and the bitchy queen at the door wouldn't let David in without an invitation. Pushing the door queen aside, David defiantly took ten steps in, turned around, and left. I learned from that experience that the show must have someone on the door to handle these situations but, alas, that night it was not the case.

The next day brought, without exaggeration, an explosion of rave reviews that were led, as Jane anticipated, by Mel Gussow in the *Times*. Gussow called the play "a glorious new comedy" and Mamet "an eloquent master of two-part harmony" and "an abundantly gifted playwright" who "brings new life to the theater."

Jane and I were impassioned people, and our relationship was honest and direct. We spent the advertising meeting that morning screaming at each other over the size of the first Sunday *Times* ad. I demanded that it be a half-page, the weight of which would establish us as a major hit and enhance the value of the subsidiaries. Jane insisted we were a hit without it and it was a waste of money. To prove her point, she asked me to call the box office every five minutes and, of course, each time the phone lines were busy. "See?" she said.

Our account executive, Matthew Serino, asked if I could join him in the next room for a moment. "You would think she would be happy," he said.

"This is as happy as she gets," I answered.

We went back, and I eventually prevailed. And we became a huge "hot ticket" hit that commanded excellent deals for subsidiaries and other productions. After ten months of sold-out performances, Ellis and Peter taped the show for *PBS Great Performances* and left to do it in Los Angeles.

Jose Ferrer, who replaced Ellis, was an Academy-Award- and multiple Tony-Award-winning star who had been away from the stage since 1965. Jane thought a TV commercial would be the ideal way to launch his return. Television commercials were cost prohibitive for Off Broadway, but Jane found Mike DeLuise's Interart, a small agency that could produce a commercial of good quality for only $5,000 and do a package on *The Today Show* for $1,500 a week. Ferrer, who commanded top dollar for TV voiceovers, gave us his services at scale, and our sell-out business continued.

Jose was a real renaissance man. One of the highlights of his career as an actor, director, and producer in the theater was the iconic production of *Othello* in 1943 as Iago opposite Paul Robeson in the title role and Uta Hagen as Desdemona. His marriage to Hagen was broken up by her affair with Robeson during the run, but he still had a very high regard for her. Whenever it was important that he give a particularly good performance, we told him, "There is a rumor that Uta is coming tonight." It worked like magic.

Jane was the perfect producer for me. She was challenging and knew how to get my best work out of me. I loved our process together, even when it could be exasperating. One Sunday morning, I decided to sleep in and took the phone off the hook. A repairman arrived in short order. I didn't even have to guess who sent him.

A Life in the Theatre was the biggest Off Broadway hit in several years and launched auspicious careers for Gerry and Jane. And I was once again, for the moment, in the Off Broadway driver's seat. I was also doing Jack Heifner's *Patio/Porch* and *Vanities*, and Tom Eyen's *The Neon Woman* starring Divine at Hurrah Disco.

Jack Schlissel called me into his office. "Get out of here," he said. "You've got four shows. You're tying up the phones. No one can get through for our shows. Put up a shingle."

I told Max and Helen at Sardi's that I thought it was time for me to open my own office. "Why don't you use the money I gave you for your play?" Max asked. And so he staked me in my big move.

On the day I opened my new office, I got a telegram from Jack Schlissel. "Come back, little shiksa," it said. "Love, Schlissel."

The Neon Woman (1978)

In the early spring, Tom Eyen came to me with a show called *The Neon Woman* starring Divine. It was playing at the Hurrah Disco on West Sixty-Second Street. He wanted to leave it where it was but convert it to an Actors' Equity Off Broadway run. I was overjoyed that the pain of *Hanna* seemed to have been left behind.

At the time, Bruce Mailman was preparing to open his New St. Mark's Baths on St. Mark's Place and Third Avenue and had asked me to do the interviews and hiring of staff. I bought a hockey shirt at Trash Vaudeville next door that had the name "Street Anderson" on it, and that's the name I used. A desk was set up for me in the steam room, which was not, of course, operational.

Thinking the conversion of *Neon* would be a cinch and not impose on his time, I went to Bruce and he and Ina Meibach put up $50,000, and it became an Off Broadway run. When I approached Bruce and Ina, the show was playing to packed houses, peppered with big stars, with everyone sitting on pillows. I had failed to notice that it was the same people coming over and over.

In short order, the trendy crowds moved on, and that, combined with Divine having chronic throat problems that caused him to cancel the two performances each week that would have put us in profits, put the show into hard times.

The owners of Hurrah were crazy about Divine, and, in the middle of all the New St. Mark's activity, Bruce went in and spent ten hours making a deal with them to take over *The Neon Woman* for exactly what it had cost him and Ina. An unfortunate choice for the club, however, because it shortly drove them into bankruptcy.

Are You Now or Have You Ever Been? (1978)

As a generous nod to my great affection for Judy Garland, Jerry Schoenfeld invited me to be his guest for the long-anticipated opening night of Liza Minnelli in *The Act* at the Majestic.

On that brisk October evening, my first encounter in the lobby was with Rosemary Wilson, who was astonished at how well I looked and asked, "Albert, what have you had done?" I laughed and told her I had done it myself, with the help of James D'Adamo and the gym.

My seats were in a box, and what a view it afforded: a living diagram of the Broadway hierarchy, who was seated where, who were they next to, and who kissed whom. Everyone kissed Angela Lansbury, but Angela Lansbury kissed Rosemary Wilson. Elizabeth Taylor arrived early and walked bouncily back and forth across three center rows before finally landing in her seat. Sammy Davis was a one-man party in his fifth-row aisle seat.

Mr. Schoenfeld, in a brash display of confidence, sat himself next to the *Times* critic Richard Eder, who would write that the show "displays the breathtaking presence of Liza Minnelli, and her command of a force that is the emotional equivalent of what a good coloratura achieves in top form." Frank Gero had been Liza's production stage manager for her Broadway debut in *Flora the Red Menace*, and she had approached him to handle the same chores for *The Act*. Unavailable, he had recommended his son, Mark, and a well-publicized romance had ensued. By the time *The Act* closed in July, the couple had begun a long engagement.

In December, I was asked if I would step in as replacement company manager on *Are You Now or Have You Ever Been?*, the Eric Bentley adaptation of transcripts of the McCarthy hearings, which Frank Gero was producing at the Promenade Theatre. I had the time and was happy to do it.

I immediately liked Frank and his wife, Woji, who were both in the show, as was Avery Brooks, who was giving a smashing performance as one of my heroes, Paul Robeson. The famous 1952 letter from Lillian Hellman to the House Un-American Activities Committee (HUAC) was read by a succession of guest stars, among them Colleen Dewhurst, Tammy Grimes, and Dina Merrill, who came in for two- or three-week stints.

Soon after I joined the production, the traditional January lull set in, and Frank said to me, "I have a surprise in store." He then wrote something on a small piece of paper and showed it to me. It said "LIZA."

I was, of course, ecstatic. And a few days later, I was typing up a contract for Liza Minnelli as Lillian Hellman for three weeks at Off Broadway Equity minimum. Frank was well-aware of my history with the fan club, and on Liza's first night, he took me to her dressing room and introduced me. "This is Al Poland, Liza; he was president of your mother's fan club." "I know," Liza said. "I still have my *Garland Gazettes*. Do you have yours?"

"I do," I said.

"Nancy Barr has a club for me," she said, "patterned after yours."

I told her I was thrilled to be working with her and wanted to make her stay as comfortable as possible. We had a wonderful, cordial relationship. But there was a nuance that let me know that she knew my heart was with her mother and that my feelings for her emanated from that.

One night after the show, she invited me to go to Studio 54 with the cast and a group that included Diana Ross, Halston, Kay Thompson, and Steve Rubell. There was a lot of excitement as we were waiting to leave the theater. Kay Thompson kept locking herself in different rooms, and I would hear her pounding on the door and let her out. "You are just everywhere," she said. Caressing my leather jumpsuit, she added, "And I adore your jacket."

I admired the cologne Halston was wearing and inquired as to what it was. He answered imperiously, "It is *Heroin* from my fall collection." Steve Rubell carried a small liquor box filled with candy bars that he ate one after another. Finally, everyone had left, and I stayed behind to lock up the theater. Liza came back by herself and asked, "Are you coming?" "Oh, yes," I said, pleased at her thoughtfulness.

On the Sunday night of Liza's first week, we had a pouring rain, inside of the theater and out. We put seventeen buckets onstage, and the actors had to speak above the noise it created. I was horrified to see Liza having to deal with this, but she did, with great humor. I lay awake that night, seized by the idea that the Promenade roof was probably rotten and could be in danger of collapse. I was terrified at the thought of Liza coming to harm on my watch.

I told the house manager of my concern. He did, in fact, think a roof cave-in was imminent and also suspected that the plywood risers that supported the theater seats were rotted and extremely dangerous.

I called Jeff Wachtel, the manager of the Century Theatre in the Century Paramount Hotel on West Forty-Sixth Street, and got right to the point. "Can we begin performances on Tuesday?" I asked.

"Why not," he said. The Century was originally Billy Rose's Diamond Horseshoe and had recently reopened as a small theater in the Broadway area.

I gave Frank Gero my manifesto for moving and told him I was convinced we could do so without missing a performance. I had priced a bus service to bring Promenade arrivals to the Century. Frank was appreciative and gave the plan an emphatic "yes." The jaded show attorney was another matter. "What do you care?" he said. "You got insurance."

Having been at the opening night of the first incarnation of the Promenade, I had now prevailed over its closing, which happened with our final performance there on Sunday, February 4, 1979.

As promised, we reopened at the Century on Tuesday. At rehearsal that afternoon, Liza gave me a big hug and thanked me. "This is one way to get to Broadway!" she quipped. Louise Lasser, recently of the television show *Mary Hartman, Mary Hartman*, who was to be the next Lillian, came down on the bus. The following day I met her at rehearsal. As I watched from the bottom of the long, winding staircase, she did teeny-tiny baby steps all the way down. She came to within an inch of my face and whispered, "I don't do stairs."

Following Liza's closing-night performance, she invited the company to a small club on East Seventy-Second Street. We had the back room all to ourselves while Joe Derise, a prominent Sinatra arranger in the '40s and now accompanist extraordinaire for star parties, played every song in every key and style, as everyone took a turn at the mic.

Eschewing her usual hard-driving, show business style, Liza sang in a light and jazzy manner, which she seemed to very much enjoy, and she and Avery Brooks did some stunning duets. Late in the evening, one of the actors said, "There is someone here who can really sing, but no one knows it. Albert, will you sing for us?" I thought, *I've either got to pass or get up and knock 'em dead.*

Naturally, I chose to give it a try. I sang "Blues in the Night." Everybody cheered, and Liza ran up and hugged me and asked, "Where did you learn to sing like that?"

"David Sorin Collyer," I said. He was also Liza's voice teacher.

"Isn't he the best? Sing more."

I sang "I'm Always Chasing Rainbows," and when I got to the line "Some fellas look and find the sunshine, I always look and find the rain," it reminded everyone of the leaky night at the Promenade, and they laughed.

Liza then sat on the piano bench and sang "Just Imagine" right into my eyes. It's about imagining that someone loves you who really belongs to another. She duplicated Judy's interpretation of the song phrase for phrase. She then pulled away from me and sang it as herself, never looking at me again.

The next day, we videotaped *Are You Now or Have You Ever Been?* I went to greet Liza, and she looked at me as though she had no idea who I was.

The Price (1979)

I sat with Jack Schlissel at his private party at Sardi's for *The Grand Tour*, a Jerry Herman musical starring Joel Grey that had opened that January night at the Palace. Jack was the producer. The reviews were coming in, and they weren't good. Jack was mellowing after a few drinks and in a reflective mood.

"Ya' know," he said, "Billy Rose used to say this is a 'horse's cock' business."

"What could he have meant by that?" I asked. "Have you ever seen a horse's cock?" Jack replied.

After decades as Broadway's top general manager, he had been taking a stab at producing, and it wasn't going so well. He observed, correctly I think, that the business wants you to stay in the capacity that first proved useful to it. It resists an upward move.

He told me how he had started life as a theatrical accountant and his first job as a manager had been a tour of *Death of a Salesman*. Thinking for a moment, he said, "Jack Garfein has an Arthur Miller play that I can't take on right now. I think the two of you would be very good together."

Arthur Miller. Just months earlier I had been enjoying a frozen hot chocolate at Serendipity 3, the ultimate "delight" place in the East 60s, when I spotted him across the room. On my napkin, I had written, "You are the greatest American playwright. You have written *Death of a Salesman*, the greatest American play." I signed it and gave it to the waiter, instructing him to deliver it after I left.

Jack Garfein. I remembered seeing him in *Photoplay* as part of Hollywood's '50s obsession with The Actors Studio and his marriage to the movie star Carroll Baker. Most of all I remembered running to see *The Strange One*, a picture he directed starring Ben Gazzara. I was a high school student. The picture looked to be homoerotic, a word I didn't know, but a quality I was drawn to. Being the only one in the theater added to my feelings of specialness and isolation.

And now twenty years later, Mr. Garfein walked into my office. He was a short man with the same kind of build as Kazan and Jose Ferrer. I wondered why all these men had the same body. And he had a handsome face that looked carved out of stone, like it belonged on Mount Rushmore.

Jack Garfein, born in Czechoslovakia, had lived through the horrors of eleven concentration camps, ending in Bergen-Belsen when it was liberated by the British in April 1945. All of his family members had perished. He had the burden and the blessing of being the only survivor at age fourteen.

Brought to New York by a group of caring sponsors, he developed an interest in the theater. Sympathetic to his situation, people provided him with opportunities, and he delivered on them. He became a founding member of The Actors Studio and made a smashing directorial debut on Broadway with *End as a Man*, which was his ticket to Hollywood, where it became *The Strange One.* He numbered among his close friends James Dean, William Inge, Henry Miller, Elia Kazan, Harold Clurman, Samuel Beckett, and Arthur Miller.

Garfein was presently teaching acting at the Actors and Directors Lab and operating the Harold Clurman Theatre on Theatre Row, a row of small non-profit theaters on West Forty-Second Street. A revival of the Miller play *The Price*, running there in a production directed by John Stix, had garnered better reviews than the original, and Garfein wanted to take it to Broadway as its producer. I saw it and concurred.

I have never met anyone as steeped in world culture, art, and literature as Jack Garfein. I knew early in our first meeting that I could really devote myself to giving him the best I had to offer as his friend and general manager.

We selected a June opening date at The Playhouse, a five-hundred-seat Broadway theater far west on Forty-Eighth Street. *The Price* had been a sellout hit at the Clurman, and Miller, who had been out of town during rehearsals, jokingly told the *Times* that maybe that was why it was a hit. There was possibly a grain of truth there, because, over the years, Miller had gained a reputation for giving the actors notes that undermined their process with the director. I mean—how do you ignore a note just given to you by Arthur Miller?

John Stix brought the play to full bloom with its stunning cast, Fritz Weaver, Mitchell Ryan, Scotty Bloch, and the great Yiddish theater star Joseph Buloff. The opening-night ovation went on forever. Jack and I were standing on either side of Arthur, and we gently gripped his arms to thrust him forward toward the stage. He at first resisted, and then, just as he took a step forward, the applause stopped.

Clive Barnes wrote that this play was "Arthur Miller's best." Unfortunately, by that time, he was writing for the *Post*. Richard Eder's *Times* notice was a mixed-to-negative, surprising after Mel Gussow's very positive review for the Clurman production, and, shockingly, he called Miller's speeches "high-flown and plodding at the same time." But the *Times* brass were there in full on opening night and contributed to the triumph with their visible enthusiasm.

A Miller play needs the *Times*, and while we had some strong weeks, the overall length of the run was hurt by Eder's review. I called Arthur Miller every Sunday to give him the figures for the week. Once, when I reported a good week, he asked, "Where do you think our audience is coming from?"

"First," I answered, "Jews of all classes. Then students, then tourists."

"Isn't that everybody?"

"Well," I inquired, "do you consider gentiles to be students or tourists?"

When I reported a bad week to him, he asked what happened. I said, "You know, Arthur, there are as many reasons for bad business as there are days in the year."

"True," he agreed, and told me about his experience when his first major play, *All My Sons,* was out of town in Boston in the winter of 1947.

It had opened to rave reviews, and he phoned the box office early the day after opening to check on business. "Well, you know, Mr. Miller, we're having a blizzard, so it's very quiet here."

"Oh, okay."

The next day, he got up and, noticing that the blizzard had stopped, waited a discreet amount of time and called again. "So, how is it today? It's better?"

"Well, Mr. Miller, the roads haven't been plowed, so it's still pretty quiet."

The next day, he heard on the local news that the roads had been plowed. "I hear the roads have been plowed; how is it today?" he asked hopefully.

"Well, Mr. Miller, the way I figure it, people's garage doors must be frozen shut."

I cherished Joe Buloff and spent as much time as I could in his dressing room. He told me he had a repertoire of six hundred roles in the Yiddish Theatre. He said they used to give a free burial if you bought a season ticket. And, at times the show was stopped, and family matters were thrown open to audience opinion. "My daughter wants to marry him. What do you think?"

Buloff was the most shameless scene stealer ever. While other actors were talking, he would cross one leg over another and constantly adjust it or adjust his pant leg. Or he would look around inquisitively. He knew every scene-stealing trick in the book.

One evening he said, "Tonight, Molly Picon will come. She can buy and sell us both, but she wants a special price." Molly Picon was a major Yiddish and Broadway star of the time. "How much are the tickets?" he asked.

"Twenty-one dollars."

"You'll charge her eight dollars."

I waited for her in the lobby with her ticket, handed it to her, and announced, "Eight dollars, Miss Picon." She gave an approving nod and handed me the money.

Arthur Miller reluctantly agreed to do a half-hour interview with Dick Cavett. Jack and I went to the taping with Arthur and his wife, Inge Morath, the great photographer. It went so well that Cavett asked if he would do another half hour. He looked to Inge who gave her approval, and, he proceeded to do two.

Early in the run of *The Price*, my friend Bruce Mailman came to me and said, "Dear, I want you to have money," and told me he wanted me to take over the booking of the Astor Place Theatre. He was moving on to other things, among which was the creation of The Saint, an ambitious gay disco in the old Fillmore East building on Second Avenue in the East Village.

He instructed, "Write a contract, put whatever you want in it, and I will sign it." I wrote a short three-paragraph letter agreement giving myself a generous participation in all income accruing to the theater as a result of the productions that played there. The last paragraph stated, "If you're unhappy, you'll tell me."

Bruce looked at it, signed it, and said, "I would never sign an agreement like this with anyone but you."

Modigliani (1979)

In the spring of 1978, I caught *Modigliani*, a play about the painter, by Dennis McIntyre, at the tiny Courtyard Playhouse on Grove Street. I loved the play. The close camaraderie of Modigliani, Utrillo, and Soutine romping through the Paris of 1916 reminded me of our own downtown theater community. They were artists who were raw, uninhibited, and full of passion, like us. And, like us, they lived by their wits.

Still under the spell of the play, I found my way to a nearby French bistro, where I had a lovely supper, a nice Bordeaux, and indulged myself in the fantasy of moving *Modigliani* to the Astor Place Theatre. The next day, I arranged a meeting with McIntyre and his director, Allen R. "Craig" Belknap. Dennis was a tall, sensitive man with glasses who looked undefended, which made you care for him. Craig helmed Direct Theater, the nonprofit theater company that produced *Modigliani*. I liked them both, and at the conclusion of our meeting, I told them I would commit to producing the play with Craig as director.

The formidable Ted Mann was also after the rights for Circle in the Square, but McIntyre's agent, Howard Rosenstone, advised Dennis to go with me. "Albert is hungrier," Howard said.

Modigliani had an interesting history. Years before it was ever produced, Lane Smith had done a scene from it at The Actors Studio that electrified those present, including Al Pacino, who found a phone number for Dennis and called him the next day. Pacino thought Modigliani could be a great film role for him and asked for and received a script, which further heightened his interest.

A short time later, Dennis presented himself to Pacino at the Cedar Tavern, where both were habitués. The Cedar was a legendary haven on University Place for some of the best contemporary writers, painters, and actors extant—kind of a downtown Elaine's. In that atmosphere a friendship evolved between Pacino and McIntyre that always somehow returned to Pacino's fascination with Dennis's play.

When *Modigliani* was finally produced by Direct, Pacino came to see it with his friends Robert De Niro and Harvey Keitel. Dennis thought that Pacino was obsessed with the role but also frightened of it. He predicted that Pacino would have a prolonged flirtation with it but would never actually do it.

Stephen Sondheim saw the play several times on Grove Street and wrote Dennis a highly complimentary letter in which he expressed his admiration for the play's authenticity. Sondheim took Richard Seff, a real-life theatrical agent who played Modigliani's agent, to dinner after a performance and told Seff he hadn't thought a play could be written about a painter. He was soon to write a musical about one.

Jason Miller, the Pulitzer prize-winning author of *That Championship Season* and Oscar-nominated actor for *The Exorcist*, told Dennis in a late-night Cedar Tavern conversation that he might be interested in playing Modigliani onstage. I arranged for Jason and Craig to meet.

Jason sent word that he would love to do the role, but not with Craig as the director. I decided to at least give it a Sardi's try and arranged a dinner with Jason and his lawyer, the estimable Robert F. Levine.

Knowing that Jason and I were both big drinkers and that the evening could become volatile, I asked Vincent Sardi to give us a table in the back. I winked and confided, "There may be a spectacle."

Actually, Jason and I hit it off very well, enjoying each other's company but not mincing words. I told him my commitment to Craig was absolute. "Of the three of you, only one has a Pulitzer," Levine observed. "What are we talking about here?"

I countered by asking Miller the following. "Let's say you do the play. Will Craig Belknap be the director on opening night?"

His answer was an immediate "No."

Levine excused himself. Jason and I decided to continue our evening at McBell's, a Village watering hole below Eighth Street on Sixth Avenue, where we stayed until well past closing time. When I awoke the next morning, I was curled up on my kitchen floor with my Maltese nestled against my stomach.

When Jason called on Monday, I picked up the phone and said, "I would think not."

"Yes, I would think not," he agreed and added, "Michael Moriarty is playing jazz piano at Reno Sweeney tonight. Do you wanna catch him with me?" We had another terrific night, and I never saw Jason Miller again.

After a long and thorough search, we picked Jeffrey DeMunn and Mary-Joan Negro for our leads. With the funding in place, we went into rehearsal in the fall of 1979. The money raising had taken longer than I had hoped. Max Jacobs and Jerry Schoenfeld came in right away, but months went by before I found my producing partners, Seymour Morgenstern, a well-regarded tax accountant, and Arthur Bartow, a seasoned theater man from the Theatre Communications Group, whom Seymour entrusted to represent his interests.

I thought Dennis and his fiancée, Karen Riedel, would enjoy Nancy Christopherson, and indeed they did. The four of us became frequent dinner companions.

Nancy engaged in a bit of mischief. When we lived together, Nancy showed me a portrait she had painted of Richard Bellamy, a noted gallery owner and art innovator, with whom she had a brief, tempestuous marriage in the late 1940s. Now, several years later, she reintroduced the painting to me as a portrait of Modigliani and offered it for use in the advertising for the show.

Without reminding her of our previous conversation, I said, "Yes." As Bellamy was alive and active at the time, I have often wondered how he felt seeing his portrait all over the city with *Modigliani* written next to it.

The play ended with Modigliani in a drunken rage, slashing seventy of his paintings with a knife and then suddenly, in a moment of self-resurrection, he converts the energy of his rage into inspiration as only a great artist can. He holds a mirror in front of his face and sketches intensely, pauses, looks at it, his confidence restored, and says, "I, I am, Modigliani." I made an arrangement with the Art Students League at Cooper Union to turn out 560 paintings a week for this purpose.

At Jack Garfein's suggestion, Ruth Morley, fresh from the film of *Annie Hall*, did the wonderfully authentic costumes, looking like the characters had been wearing them and sleeping in them for weeks.

Most of the reviews were raves, but the crucial one was Walter Kerr in the *Times*. Kerr didn't like it, feeling that without the famous names we would have no interest in the characters onstage. Our fight was cut out for us, but fight we did. I cut every possible financial corner and promoted the show to the hilt. And the company was right there with me.

Modigliani was on many Top Ten lists and ran 119 performances. Keith Barrish took an option on it for Al Pacino, but, as Dennis predicted, Pacino never made the film.

CHAPTER 12

"Grab Your Honey and Sashay Down to the Village Gate"

Sometime during the summer of 1979, the D'Lugoffs invited me to a Sunday brunch at the Village apartment of their friend the photographer Norma Holt. When the day arrived, I was hung over and decided to sleep in. The phone rang. It was Burt D'Lugoff, whose authority was never in doubt no matter who he was talking to, not least including his brother and me. "Get over here. We're throwing this for you."

"I'm hung over."

"I don't care—get over here. We have a surprise for you." And he hung up.

Resentfully, I dressed and went.

The "surprise" was a crudely made audio tape of a show Art had just seen in New Orleans called *One Mo' Time*. He loved the show and thought it was an ideal prospect for the Gate. It was a backstage-onstage story about a night on the TOBA circuit in 1920s New Orleans.

TOBA, the Theatre Owners Booking Association, was the circuit for black vaudeville performers playing in the South for black audiences in the 1920s and '30s. Usually the theater owners were white, and the living conditions for the artists were less than those accorded their counterparts in white vaudeville. The performers dubbed it "Tough On Black Asses."

In *One Mo' Time*, we are witness to the bickering in the dressing room and the interplay with the white theater owner, interspersed with authentic onstage performances of songs and comedy sketches of the period. Crude as the tape was, the magic came through. I was crazy about it and glad that Burt had coerced me into coming.

Art had a master chef's sense of ingredients, whether for his club or a show, and he invited Jerry Wexler into the mix as a coproducer. When he was a *Billboard* reporter in the late '40s Wexler coined the term "Rhythm and Blues." In partnership with Ahmet Ertegun, he built Atlantic Records into a major force in the recording industry. He successfully produced many of the major acts in the second half of the twentieth century, among them Ray Charles, Aretha Franklin, Wilson Pickett, and Bob Dylan, and he had an eye for out-of-the-mainstream authentic talent. The D'Lugoffs, Jerry Wexler, and I went to New Orleans to see the show.

One Mo' Time was written, directed by, and starred Vernel Bagneris, a handsome young Creole gentleman of talent in abundance in all three capacities. He had surrounded himself with a small cast of uniquely talented comediennes and singers and one crusty white guy as the theater owner. The musicians, put together by Orange Kellin and Lars Edegran, two gifted young transplants from Sweden, were the best New Orleans had to offer.

The performance was a highly entertaining and funny slice of black entertainment history, and the four of us agreed that little was required to bring it up to New York standards. The actors needed a physical style and the scenery and lighting a serious upgrade. The costumes, by JoAnn Clevenger, a New Orleans native, were spectacular.

The next morning, I had an early breakfast with Vernel Bagneris at The Coffee Pot, where we were tended to in his accustomed New Orleans style by Miss Pearl. Vernel was very attractive, insouciant, androgynous to the point of appealing to both men and women, and the keeper of a sublime Creole wit. His bronze skin was complemented by a loose-fitting Hawaiian shirt that hung comfortably on his lean frame.

At one point during our charming repast, he paused and sat back. "I do have to let you know one thing." he said. "If people yell at me, I fall to pieces."

Smart! I thought. *The heavy artillery has just been neutralized. I think I'm going to love this guy.*

Surprisingly, Jerry Wexler's first contribution to the show was not musical. He brought us our choreographer, Pepsi Bethel, a dexterous and witty practitioner of vernacular dance who was on the committee when the Lindy was invented. Pepsi was to become a major ingredient.

At my suggestion, we engaged the talented La MaMa designers Elwin Charles Terrel II, for the set, and Joanna Schielke for the lighting. Charles was currently collaborating with Bruce Mailman on the complex design of Bruce's ambitious disco, The Saint. Joanna was also providing the lighting design for *Modigliani*.

I budgeted *One Mo' Time* at $75,000 with a 20 percent overcall provision, meaning that we could ask the investors for an additional $15,000 if we found it necessary.

My old friend Steve Gardner, who operated the Hit Show Club, called me for a favor. Hit Shows printed and distributed the "twofers," or two-for-the-price-of-one coupons, that shows ultimately came to need at a certain point in their runs. He was a Runyonesque character and one of the most-loved gentlemen in the theater. He never asked anything of anyone, so I was eager to be of help. "I have a little girl, Albert, and I want you to help her. I trust you, and I want you to guide her."

The "little girl" was a young woman, Shari Upbin, who was then married to Hal Upbin, the head of Chase Manhattan Realty Trust. She wanted to buy an Off Broadway theater and produce a season of plays, which I thought to be too ambitious for someone with no experience.

My best advice to Shari Upbin was to join the producing team of a show that was in the early stages of raising money. She could learn while being a part of it. We would look until the right project could be found. There were probably a dozen rejects before *One Mo' Time* came along.

I urged her to take it. She came in with 10 percent of the capitalization and surprised me by tying it to the condition that she be employed as the production stage manager. Again, no experience, but in short order, she was ensconced in the stage manager's booth. At one point, she threw her back out trying on a pair of French jeans and asked to be able to call the show from a mattress. I told her there would be no charge for the pea.

The first production meeting of any show is an important moment. Each person's responsibilities are defined, and everyone is eager to establish their authority and stake out their turf. For this solemn occasion, the D'Lugoffs selected Sammy's Roumanian on Chrystie Street.

Art and Burt, Jerry Wexler, Shari Upbin, and I were there representing the production. Vernel arrived with his representatives, Michael Hertzberg, an activist lawyer with a briefcase and an intensely serious disposition, and Carl Colby, whose father, William Colby, was then head of the Central Intelligence Agency.

As we laid out our production plans, endless mounds of delicious, heartburn-inducing Jewish food arrived, and a thin man with thick glasses played an electric piano and sang in Yiddish. If the customers liked his songs, they threw small white plates that shattered on the floor in front of him. Art introduced us to Stanley, the owner, who had won the place from Sammy in a crap game. Stanley walked around imperiously, his martini perched on his fist. I ran to the pay phone to call Bruce Mailman to tell him I was having the silliest dinner of my entire life.

The New Orleans actors and musicians arrived for rehearsals at the Gate in late September. Co-starring with Vernel as Papa Du were Topsy Chapman as Thelma the ingénue, Thais Clark as Ma Reed the comedienne, John Stell as the white theater owner, and Sylvia "Kuumba" Williams as Big Bertha, the head of the company.

Kuumba arrived with no voice, barely a rasp. She had blown it on a film in Mississippi that required her to scream for several days. I took her aside and told her she must have vocal therapy and that the production would pay for it. I suggested David Sorin Collyer, who taught a number of stars and who had successfully dissolved nodes through vocal exercises. "I don't believe in singing lessons. I'm a natural singer. My voice will come back." And she refused the help.

Having been a professional singer with a "legit" technique, I could listen to someone's voice production and know if there would be difficulty doing eight shows a week. Kuumba, at this point, wasn't up to doing one.

Thinking I knew who I was dealing with, I pulled a little trick. I called Denise Rogers, a La MaMa actress and favorite of Ellen Stewart, and asked if she would be interested in understudying. I got her to Vernel, and the next day I asked her to sit quietly in the back of the Gate during rehearsal.

It took Kuumba about five minutes to notice a woman of her same physical type sitting in a corner. "Albert Poland."

"Yes?"

"Who is that?"

"That is your understudy, Miss Kuumba."

"Call that voice teacher. I want to go to him now."

It had worked, and David had her voice in shape in no time. She never missed a performance.

The ingredients in the New York production were coming together brilliantly. Pepsi Bethel brought just the right touch to the choreography, establishing the period and giving each actor a physical style that emanated from them. Elwin Charles Terrel brought a humorous, period look to the set, and Joanna Schielke lit it in Technicolor. JoAnn Clevenger's upgrade of the clothes rounded out an altogether inviting and authentic Village Gate production.

Milly Schoenbaum, a friend of the D'Lugoffs and a veteran of Morton Gottlieb's successful Broadway comedies, was the press agent. She came up with a brilliant idea that was to reap rewards for the entire run. Only two years before, *Roots* had made television history. She asked Vernel to prepare a well-researched piece to accompany the initial press release, which he titled "The Roots of *One Mo' Time*." It not only placed the show and the music in a historic perspective but opened the door for the music press to cover us.

Lars Edegran and Orange Kellin, who also did the orchestrations, were internationally respected in the jazz universe, Lars as a pianist and Orange as a clarinetist. Rounding out the orchestra were New Orleans veterans John Robichaux on drums, Walter Payton on tuba, and music legend Cladys "Jabbo" Smith on trumpet and vocals.

In the 1930s, Jabbo had been a rival to Louis Armstrong, but Armstrong was backed by the mighty Joe Glaser and his minions. Having no such backing, Jabbo's record sales and bookings flagged, and he spent his career on the fringes, highly respected but little known, with a more-than-casual relationship to alcohol. Yet, in 1979, his playing and singing were still virtuosic, and he was to be a consistent show stopper in *One Mo' Time*.

The word "nigger" occurred twice in Vernel's script as part of the backstage banter among the on-stage characters. We tried to persuade Vernel to cut it. As white people, we did not yet understand that, among black people, it could be an endearing and even affectionate term. All we heard was the pain.

Vernel argued vigorously, and eventually it was settled by deleting one of the usages. The remaining usage occurs when the company is alone in the dressing room, and Ma Reed, reminiscing fondly about a past romance, says, "Honey I ain't seen that nigger in years."

We all agreed that *One Mo' Time* should be sold on television. Tommy Schlamme shot wonderful footage of the show, and Vernel did the narration in his inimitable, flavorful accent and voice. Our buyer was Michael Kubin of Corinthian Media, one of the largest media buyers in the country. As an Off Broadway show, his bulk-rate buys made it possible for us to mount an effective campaign without breaking the bank.

The opening, on October 22, 1979, was a Village Gate blowout of a night. Only the *Times* review by John Corry brought us back to earth. He found the show stereotypically racist and referenced Amos and Andy by example. Art was enraged and used every bit of his considerable clout with the *Times* to let them know it.

The wrong was righted when Frank Rich, the new first-string critic on the *Times*, came to a Saturday night performance. He wrote, "*One Mo' Time*, which correctly bills itself as 'The Great New Orleans Musical,' arouses the audience at the Village Gate into a state bordering on delirium."

The rest of the reviews were sparkling and offered a goldmine of quotes, our favorite being Marilyn Stasio's in the *Post*: "Grab your honey and sashay down to the Village Gate!" The commercial wrapped up with Emory Lewis's quote, "I hope it runs forever!" The hard-to-please John Simon described the three ladies as "laser beams" and declared, "I could easily see it two mo' times."

Business was good but not what I thought it should be, which I attributed to the lukewarm sound system designed by Carl Seltzer. We had a hot show on stage, and the sound, by the standards of the day, did not match it. I had done other shows in the Gate and knew that a higher volume was possible, but Seltzer argued that, with this combination of singers and musicians, it was not. "A higher level will give us constant feedback," he insisted.

I felt it had a serious impact on us. For the first three months of the run, the checkbook was consistently $15,000 overdrawn. Only by careful coordination of the deposits and the payroll were we able to keep going. The company manager was a nervous wreck. I told her not to worry. No one was going to come and arrest her.

It was only when Shari Upbin departed the show as production stage manager that it was discovered there was no problem in raising the sound level. Duane Mazey, an experienced sound designer and stage manager, came in and adjusted the levels within minutes. I found Carl Seltzer and read him the riot act. He said he was trying to "protect the integrity of the sound." He wanted the show to sound like it would have in 1920.

With the sound raised to hot 1979 levels, the audience response was heightened. The show began selling out and stayed there for most of its three-and-a-half-year run at the Village Gate. Later on, Seltzer did further damage by engineering the in-person cast recording at the Gate.

Jerry Wexler knew well his place in music history but, by this time, had begun to think of himself in the past tense. He knew when he signed on with us that a cast album would be expected, but he did not want to intrude on Warner Records, his present home label. So, instead of a Wexler-produced studio album, we had a Seltzer-produced live album. The actors sound like they are singing through a tin can and the audience seems miles away. The D'Lugoffs liked Seltzer. I thought he was pompous and devoid of talent. Primarily as a tribute to Jerry, we received a Grammy nomination for Best Original Cast Album.

In the meantime, the show was exploding all over the place. We had two touring companies, a first-class national tour starring Vernel, and a bus and truck in which Papa Du and the white theater owner were understudied by the same actor, a savings I have always admired.

Early in the run, I told Art I would be happy to understudy the theater owner and that, every time we had a losing week, I would waive my salary. I passed the audition with Vernel. Whenever I went on (about twenty times), there was a list of managers and lawyers who were to be notified. Over the run, I saved the production about $20,000.

Vernel left the *One Mo' Time* touring company in the late fall of 1980 to film the role of The Accordion Man in Herbert Ross's *Pennies from Heaven*. The glorious cast included Steve Martin, Bernadette Peters, and a singing and dancing Christopher Walken.

At about this time I did a little show called *A Matter of Opinion*, memorable for the following reasons. It was written, directed, and produced by the same woman. We had narrowly escaped a cast mutiny when I convinced her it needed another director and replaced her with Shari Upbin. We did it at Donald Goldman's Players Theater on MacDougal Street. I got my good friend Charles Randolph-Wright into it so he could get his Equity card. A year later he was in *Dreamgirls* on Broadway and has evolved into a spectacularly talented playwright and director who works all over the world all the time. At the opening night party, Shari told me, "Whatever I did to you, you have more than paid me back." I love Shari like family, but she did have a point. Donald Goldman said, "Did you book this into my theater because you hate me?" And Marilyn Stasio wrote in the *Post*, "You can tell how bad a show is by the number of suicides in the audience."

Vernel returned to us in May of '81 filled with the discipline of his Herbert Ross experience and put the original cast back into rehearsal for Germany's Theater der Welt festival performances, to be followed by the London West End production in August. He cracked the whip in a way that took everyone by surprise, and by the time we reached Germany, no one was speaking to him.

As the result of a sensational cast appearance on *Bio's Bahnhof*, a television talk show produced in an abandoned train station in West Berlin, all of the Theater der Welt engagements were completely sold out. At Deutsches Schauspielhaus in Hamburg, calls were coming in every three seconds. The television appearance had made us the toast of Germany. Art D'Lugoff, swept up in all of the prestige, began speaking in a mid-Atlantic accent.

The tension among the cast, however, was so thick that during a performance in Frankfurt when Vernel accidentally brushed against Thais Clark, she shrieked, "Don't touch me!" But it broke after the final performance, when the entire company convened in my tiny hotel room to celebrate our triumph. We emptied the mini bar at least a dozen times.

From there, the company went into intense rehearsals for the London production at Club Med in Athens, where Orange Kellin had arranged a complimentary ten-day stay. Peter Schneider, who had stepped into the Village Gate production to replace our company manager, who was on maternity leave, was now company manager of the West End production, and was in London preparing for our August 12 opening night.

Helen Montagu and I planned a splashy opening night party at the Savoy, where, thanks to Milton Goldman, I always stayed when in London—fifth floor with the incomparable Martin as concierge.

The opening night party was to be my treat. In the middle of the afternoon, I realized that I had no idea how much it was going to cost. In a sudden state of panic, I mentioned it to Helen, who said "Oh, don't worry about money, daahling," going into her highest soprano register.

Helen produced shows in London and in her native Australia and lived the kind of outsized life that had earned her the title of "The Playgirl of Shaftsbury Avenue" from the British press. She was fun itself. A close friend of Elton John and a regular fixture on Robert Stigwood's yacht, she lived life to the hilt. She was my date for the performance, and we sat amongst a number of the critics, all of whom were her friends. Cameron Mackintosh was there with his mother and his father, who was a jazz trumpeter.

As I watched the show, I quickly saw the method in Vernel's madness in Germany. He had taken the cast to a new level, and Germany had been the warm-up. The performance was the best it had ever been. It was no longer the Village Gate. It was the West End, and the show was more than up to it.

At intermission I was called to a phone. It was Vernel from backstage. At the London producer's request, the cast had been doing a "second line" through the audience and out into the street after the curtain call. It's a New Orleans tradition, a line that follows after a parade, dancing and twirling parasols. For some reason, Vernel had a real aversion to it. "If we have to do the second line, I won't go on for the second act." "Then don't do the second line," I said.

The show was beyond triumphant, and the party at the Savoy went on all night. At 5:00 a.m. the reviews came in. The London critics had gotten the show in a way that the New York critics had not, calling it "an explosion of joy," "a milestone," and "two hours of the most concentrated pleasure within memory." I sat there, drunk as a skunk, and read all of the reviews out loud, stumbling over the words, but no one cared. Vernel told me it was the happiest moment of his life.

The show became a huge West End success, and the cast received many honors, including a Royal Command Performance. *One Mo' Time* continued at the Gate until February of 1983, playing 1,372 performances and, with acclaimed productions all over the world, was an international hit.

The closing night party in my apartment on Bleecker Street topped even the London opening. Two hundred people spilling out into the halls, Raphael D'Lugoff playing up a storm on my upright piano while Ruth Brisbane (the current Big Bertha) stood on top of it, tore off her wig, and sang "Love for Sale" for all it was worth. The cops arrived at 4:00 a.m.

I asked, "Who complained?" They replied "Everybody," looked around, and said, "Enjoy yourselves." It was the perfect capper to the closest, most loving relationship I have ever had with a company. *One Mo' Time* was the happiest experience of my life.

CHAPTER 13

Manager Overboard

Das Lusitania Songspiel, Table Settings (1980)

At the end of 1979, Christopher Durang and Sigourney Weaver were on a roll. Chris had an Off Broadway hit with *Sister Mary Ignatius Explains It All for You* and Sigourney, his classmate at the Yale School of Drama, was on the brink of major stardom with the release of *Alien*. The two adored each other and thought it the perfect time to bring back their Brechtian cabaret, *Das Lusitania Songspiel.*

Almost as a favor, Garland Wright asked producer Milton Justice if the pair could audition fifteen minutes of it for him. Milton had taken over the *Vanities* run at the Westside Theatre and made it a hit all over again, and Garland was its director. Milton asked me to come along and, thinking we were going to end up doing it, I suggested we bring our press agents, Betty Lee Hunt and Maria Pucci.

The four of us were knocked out. It was irresistible. Durang and Weaver together were pure magic.

Sigourney could give it only six weeks, so it had to be done on the cheap. To save on rent, we went to the Westside management and sold them on doing *Das Lusitania* as a "late night" after the

Vanities performance. Milton and *Vanities* author Jack Heifner bankrolled it themselves. I put the budget at $7,500.

We would do six performances a week at 11:00 p.m. and, with the fifty-minute running time, the audience would be out by midnight. There was no scenery to speak of, but Sigourney was resplendent in a beautiful red gown, with Chris a bit rumpled in a slightly oversized tux. We began previews in late December, and, by the time we opened on January 10, 1980, the show was at capacity and stayed there. Tickets were $7.

The critics were beside themselves. Frank Rich selected it as one of the season's highlights. After-theater nightlife had returned to Manhattan—it was the town's smart ticket.

Stephen Sondheim, whose current *Sweeney Todd* was spoofed, came to see it and returned the next night with Leonard Bernstein. Thanks to my friend Helen Montagu, half of London came through our doors, starting with Sir Laurence Olivier. Richard Gere, who was appearing on Broadway in *Bent*, called to ask if we could possibly hold a seat for him as he couldn't get there until 11:15. Meryl Streep, another Yale classmate of Chris and Sigourney, came several times. People loved discovering it and returning with friends.

Milton and I had become pals, and one night he told me that Sigourney had invited him to a supper with her parents and asked if I would come along. Her father was a distinguished-looking gray-haired gentleman. We took one look at him, determined that he was an insurance salesman from Connecticut, and ignored him all evening.

I later told a friend about it. He gasped. "Do you know who her father is? Sylvester 'Pat' Weaver." As president of NBC in the '50s, Weaver had created both *The Today Show* and *The Tonight Show*.

Milton and I had a late drink one evening with the great actress and teacher Stella Adler. She was a mentor of Milton's, and he would later become head of her Los Angeles acting school. Adler had an imperial bearing that was mellowed by her honeyed blonde hair and her welcoming manner. She had just come from a Liza Minnelli concert at Carnegie Hall.

"How was Liza?" I asked.

She shook her head and, after a moment, added, "Her mother."
"Did you and her mother ever meet?" I asked.

"Yes, I was brought to MGM in the early '40s to be an acting coach, and they were taking me around the lot, when suddenly, there was Judy. She was sipping a milkshake. We were introduced, and I gave her a long spiel about what I was doing there and said I hoped we would work together. She took me in as she looked up at me over her milkshake. Then she held it out to me and said, 'Want some?'"

Milton and Jack made another $7,500 on their *Das Lusitania* investment, and Sigourney frequently cited it as one of the happiest times of her life. In 1992, she approached Milton about doing it again. We were all very excited, and I did a budget. Only twelve years later, it would cost $135,000. We chose to stay with our memories of it coming together so magically when Chris and Sigourney were the king and queen of late night in Manhattan.

Four days after the opening of *Das Lusitania*, I opened *Table Settings*, a delightful comedy set around the dinner table of a Jewish family, written and directed by James Lapine in an auspicious Off Broadway debut. Stephen Graham, the son of Katherine Graham, publisher of the *Washington Post* and *Newsweek*, produced it with Joan Stein and Luis Sanjurjo.

Joan had an old-fashioned Jewishness that I adored. She was vibrant, haymishe, and had a sense of humor worthy of Fanny Brice. During our interview, she revealed that she worked during the day as a waitress on the Bowery. I said, "We'll get a *Times* story on that, for sure," which David Powers, our superb press agent, managed with ease. Stephen had a professorial air for one so young and was classy and brilliant. Luis, born in San Juan, had been an executive assistant to Mike Nichols. He was the group cheerleader.

With sparkling reviews, led by Walter Kerr in the *Times*, the show was a successful launch for James Lapine and for his three young producers, all making their debuts. Stephen and Joan and I went on to have a long history together, while Luis became a successful agent at ICM.

Shortly after opening, *Table Settings* moved from Playwrights Horizons to the Westside Theatre Upstairs. I now had five Off Broadway shows running, three of them at the Westside.

Sometime during the summer, Stephen Graham brought Peter Sellars, a young director friend, to my office. Sellars was currently attending Harvard, and Stephen wished to help him get a start in New York. The meeting with Peter was most peculiar, and after about forty-five minutes, I looked at him and said, "I keep thinking that one of us is kidding."

Wanting to be of help to Stephen, I called Ellen Stewart to see if a slot at La MaMa might be possible. "I have open slots, Baby, but Mother has no money." I called Stephen to see if he might be willing to underwrite, and he came up with $15,000. I called Ellen back. "Can Mother make do with $15,000?" "Mother can," she answered.

And so, on October 23, 1980, Peter Sellars made his New York debut at La MaMa with an opus entitled *A Day in the Life of the Czar, or I Too Have Lived in Arcadia*. When I saw the bubble wrap on the floor, I couldn't wait to see what was in store.

On the triumphant opening night of *Das Lusitania*, I reached a Waterloo, although water had nothing to do with it. Before the show, Milton Justice and I went to Curtain Up, the restaurant across from the Westside, where I downed three glasses of white wine.

A few minutes after we arrived at the theater, Milton told me that Cheryl Crawford said the ladies room was filthy. Sensitized by the alcohol, I thought, *Who the hell does he think I am, the ladies room attendant?* The fact that the estimable Ms. Crawford was making the complaint made it even more insulting. Incensed, I walked out on my own opening night. And into a seamy Times Square dive where I proceeded to get roaring drunk.

Months, perhaps years, earlier I had suspected that I was an alcoholic. I drank almost daily, but always after six, with my dinner, which allowed me to remain functional. I went to restaurants where I was known, and the framed posters of my shows surrounded me. My career was the part of my life that people saw, and, as long as my career flourished, I thought I could get away with drinking more than my fill.

With this walkout, "career-as-enabler" was over.

The opening night of *Modigliani* had been a warning. The photo with Jerry Schoenfeld that I didn't remember. And there had been the Sardi's party that Milton Goldman gave for Jose Ferrer's return to the stage in *A Life in the Theatre*. On that occasion, I cornered Arlene Francis and dragged her to a pay phone to call my mother, who adored her. And the dinner at Peter Luger with Vernel, Peter Schneider, and Milly Schoenbaum where I had become belligerent with my dear friends and with the waiters.

Now, after my opening night walkout, I awakened with the hangover of death and all these memories ricocheting in my head. I called a friend I knew who was in a program of recovery. The call didn't surprise him. "Will you help me?" I asked. I met him in a large church basement on Park Avenue.

There were about two hundred people listening to a woman with a Bronx accent whispering into a microphone. She was talking about God. I connected. I had a catharsis of tears that lasted through that gathering and into a second smaller one that immediately followed.

I went every day. Having no hangovers was a wonderful feeling. And I loved the people. I watched and listened, but I did not participate. I didn't join in because I hadn't accepted myself as an alcoholic. After nine months of increasing isolation from everyone in the fellowship, I walked out and picked up where I had left off.

It would be eight years before I came back.

CHAPTER 14

On the Brink

Arriving for the historic 1980 opening night of David Merrick's *42nd Street* at the Winter Garden, the first person to catch my eye was Fred Nathan, the show's press agent. He was no longer the pudgy, pimply-faced boy of yore, but gaunt and handsome, and totally in charge of the hectic press and celebrity arrivals that are part of major openings.

The next person I saw was Jerry Schoenfeld, angrily shaking his finger at me because my dear friend, coauthor Mark Bramble, had arranged aisle seats at the opposite end of the same row he was in. How dare I! My date for the evening was Helen Montagu, in from London, who was also a close friend of Mark.

With seasoned stars like Tammy Grimes and Jerry Orbach, a first-class design team, and Gower Champion at the helm, the show was a wow from start to finish, a Merrick blockbuster of a caliber that hadn't been seen since his heyday.

After eleven curtain calls, the applause reached a crescendo when Mr. Merrick joined the cast onstage. He put up his hands to stop it and said, "No, no. This is a tragedy." Thinking it was some of Merrick's wicked humor, we all laughed.

"Gower Champion died today," he said and put his head in his hands. He turned abruptly and rushed over to embrace Wanda Richert, who played Peggy Sawyer, and with whom Champion had been having an affair.

A shockwave passed over the audience. The cast, who had spent months working with Champion, was hearing this for the first time, with all of us watching. Jerry Orbach yelled, "Bring it in!" and the curtain came down.

Helen Montagu and I walked up and down Broadway for forty-five minutes trying to deal with what we had heard. On the one hand, it was shamelessly exploitive. On the other, totally appropriate. Champion was a showman, and so was Merrick.

Fred Nathan had alerted the press that Merrick was going to make an important announcement at the end of the show, and the print and television coverage was massive. Within minutes, the news was all over Broadway, and the box office take the next day would be the largest to date in Broadway history.

As Helen and I arrived for the opening-night party at the Waldorf, the cast of Michael Bennett's *A Chorus Line* was performing a tribute to Gower Champion. They were followed by the cast of Bob Fosse's *Dancin'*. Merrick sat off to the side at a table by himself, drinking white wine. At one point I went over to him and said, "Mr. Merrick, I'm a downtown kid, but for whatever it's worth, I think you are the greatest producer of the century."

He stood up and threw his arms around me and responded, "It's worth a great deal. I have had a love affair with the theater, until lately largely unrequited. Tonight was very difficult for me."

I went back to Helen, who said, "I'm going to have a word with David." Helen and David had been friends and good gossipy pals ever since she was head of the Royal Court and David had imported plays from there. I sensed she might be a woman with a mission.

They sat together, undisturbed for the better part of an hour. As we were leaving, Helen turned to me and said, "Well, darling, it's done. I've the London rights. And probably Australia."

"Darling," I said, "That's fabulous. Let's go to Cowboys and Cowgirls."

Cowboys and Cowgirls, on Fifty-Third Street near Second Avenue, was the best hustler bar that ever existed. The hustlers and johns had the kind of camaraderie I had seen at the Sunday country brunches in France with Fernand Lumbroso's circle of friends and their young companions. Commerce to be sure but good conversation, and in many instances genuine and lasting friendships.

We arrived, and I was immediately collared by Lester Persky. Lester was one of the funniest men I knew, and with his handlebar mustache, he looked like a comic villain in a melodrama. When he talked, he inevitably ran out of breath before he finished his sentences, which caused him to either choke or crescendo. He had evolved an approach to film investment as a tax shelter, and his film producing credits included *Hair*, *Equus*, and *Yanks*.

"Albert," he said, yelling above the din, "Truman is number one on all three lists. His book *Music for Chameleons* is number one. I want to produce him on Broadway in an evening of readings from his work."

"Lester," I yelled back, "no one wants to hear that voice for two hours. Having a best seller has nothing to do with filling a Broadway house."

"I'm telling you, I'm going to do this, and I want you to help me."

"Not a good idea, Lester," I reiterated.

We were joined by a young man. "Oh, Albert, this is Tim. Thanks to Tim, Tenness-eee-eee is writing again." Suddenly the place was quiet except for Lester, who shrieked, "SHE'S WRITING!"

A couple of weeks later, I again ran into Lester, and he was still after me about Truman Capote. "I've told Truman you're brilliant," he said. "You're the perfect person to do this with me."

"Lester, it's just not realistic."

But with his persistence, Lester had planted the idea in my head. While I was in Paris producing *Ain't Misbehavin'* for Fernand Lumbroso, I tried to figure out how it could work. When I returned in October, I tried out an idea on him.

I suggested that instead of a Broadway house, we put Truman in the three-hundred-seat Mitzi Newhouse at Lincoln Center and do it over the Christmas holidays. I thought the imprimatur of Lincoln Center, the smaller capacity, and the holidays would all work in our favor. I envisioned the ad being the beautiful René Bouché pen-and-ink drawing of Truman.

Lester liked it and arranged a meeting with Capote at his United Nations Plaza apartment.

Not surprisingly, Capote was utterly enchanting. He was very white, translucent almost, as if there were light pouring out of him. He loved my idea.

"Well," I concluded, "the next step is for Lester and me to meet with Richmond Crinkley." Crinkley had had a prestigious producing career and was a protégé of Roger Stevens. His tenure at Lincoln Center was controversial because there was absolutely nothing going on. Supposedly, there were renovations to the Vivian Beaumont but otherwise no activity of any kind in either theater. A Woody Allen play had been announced, but no dates were set.

Crinkley, a Southerner, loved the idea of bringing in Truman for Christmas at the Newhouse and was sure his board and Woody Allen would approve it, which they did.

Truman invited me for a celebratory lunch at the "discreet French restaurant" across from United Nations Plaza. Discreet it was. The only other guests were Jackie Onassis and two lady friends. They were all wearing blue jeans and white flannel shirts. Truman did a running monologue about everyone in American literature—you could jump in and out or just listen, it didn't matter—while Michael McKenzie took a photograph every thirty seconds.

"Albert, you should have a very dry Manhattan made with Southern Comfort," Truman said. "It's the drink that sent me into AA."

I was on my second one when Truman excused himself to go to the men's room. I guessed that he and Jackie were on bad terms and that, as she had to cross directly in front of our table, she would now leave without having to face him. Sure enough, seconds after Truman excused himself, Jackie and her friends departed.

A few days later, I got a call from the noted producer and manager Nelle Nugent, who was in Washington for the tryout of *Amadeus*. "You know me," she said. "I get right to the point. What in the hell are you doing walking around Lincoln Center?" She and Elizabeth McCann were the resident general managers.

"Lester Persky is producing Truman Capote there, and I'm his representative," I answered.

"You mean you're his *agent?*" she said sarcastically.

"I'm his general manager."

"The only general managers at Lincoln Center are Liz and me. If there is a show, we are the general managers. If you want to work with us, fine. But we're the general managers. I'll draw up budgets, and let's meet in two days."

I called Lester to apprise him of the Liz and Nelle situation and, additionally, to discuss how I was to be paid. His assistant told me he was "island hopping in Hawaii and could not be reached." When he finally called back, I started to discuss my fees, and he told me Richmond Crinkley should pay me.

The following morning, Richmond told me Lester should pay me. That afternoon I met at Lincoln Center with Nelle Nugent, who brought her company manager, none other than my former union apprentice and longtime friend, Rob Wallner.

We sat down, and Nelle said, "Production budget." Rob slid it over to her.

"May I have a copy, too?" I asked. Rob looked at Nelle, and, after she nodded, he slid one over to me. Needless to say, I was seething.

"Operating budget," Nelle said, and Rob slid a copy to her.

"May I have one, too?" I again asked. Rob looked at her, she nodded, and he slid one over to me. I was totally fed up and decided it was time for a little prank.

The next morning, I arranged to have breakfast at Elephant and Castle with Brent Peek, who was a manager in Liz and Nelle's office. I pretty much told him the situation and said I was now going to take him to meet Truman. If he and Truman hit it off, I was prepared to get the hell out of Dodge.

We sat with Truman for an hour, during which he regaled us with tall tales, including one about his male cousin having a long affair with Anita Bryant's husband. "Why don't you tell Liz Smith?" I asked. "Why don't I tell Liz Smith?" he repeated vacantly, almost as though the thought had already left him.

When I was sufficiently satisfied that he and Brent would get along, I sent Brent on his way and told Truman that I was leaving the project because neither Lester nor Richmond were willing to pay me, and I was insulted and fed up. Truman, as I expected, was furious. I left it to him to break the news to Lester and Richmond.

Lester located an island telephone and called an hour later. "Truman is enraged. What have you done? You must reconsider."

I told him I was finished.

A few weeks later, Truman called and asked if I would be his guest at the opening and at the after party at Halston's loft on Fifth Avenue. I was very touched and, of course, I accepted. I took my assistant, Erik Murkoff.

It was deer hunting season in the audience. I have never seen so many empty seats at an opening. Truman was a frail, sympathetic figure on the stage, and his performance was earnest but didn't quite hold for the hour and a half.

Erik and I arrived early at the party, and there were few people there other than Truman.

He was wearing strange, beady-looking sunglasses that covered only his eyelids.

He approached me and asked, "What did you think, Mr. Poland?" "I was very moved by the evening, Truman," I said. "Well," he said, sounding slightly sarcastic, "coming from you, that's very high praise, indeed." He then put his drink on the radiator and left the party. It was a very dry Manhattan made with Southern Comfort.

The party began to pick up, and Rob Wallner came over to me several times in an effort to be friendly, but I wasn't having it. Lester saw what was going on and said, "Albert, go easy on young Rob."

Finally, Wallner came over and sat down on my lap. I hurled him to the floor and walked out. He followed me, and I had a screaming match with him on the sidewalk about his abhorrent behavior with the ice maiden, Nelle Nugent. I was enraged by what I considered to be his betrayal of a loyal friendship.

The next morning in his *Times* review, John Corry described Truman onstage as being an "elderly child," an image I found to be very touching.

Barely one month after the opening of *42nd Street*, Bruce Mailman opened The Saint, his spectacular gay disco in the building that had formerly housed the Fillmore East on Second Avenue and Sixth Street. The opening was one of the highlights of the season.

Above the enormous dance floor of The Saint was an actual functioning planetarium dome which, as the evening and the drugs took hold, made it feel like you were dancing in the cosmos. And to one side was the old balcony of the Fillmore where, in keeping with the convention of the times, there was a hotbed of sexual activity. The club had been brilliantly designed and constructed by Bruce and Elwin Charles Terrel II.

Fernand Lumbroso called it "a cathedral for our times," which was exactly what Bruce had intended. He considered the dances to be Dionysian rites embracing some of the darker aspects of sexuality and human nature. It was a part of Bruce that I was very much aware of but did not participate in. For its participants, it was a celebration of the highest order.

Who, amongst the revelers, was to know that the limits of gay liberation had now been tested and we had lost?

In 1981, the New York theater was minutes away from becoming part of world pop culture. The audience was still the "theater audience" for the most part, and "the theater" was "the theater." And the *New York Times* still held sway over all the goings-on.

So, when Craig Lucas put together an evening of Sondheim trunk songs called *Marry Me a Little* at The Production Company and John S. Wilson, the *Times* music critic, gave it a glowing review, not only was the tiny Off Off Broadway theater stretched to capacity, but producers were looking at it in terms of a possible commercial transfer.

To Wilson, these were not your ordinary trunk songs. They were Sondheim trunk songs, and they had been discarded from his early work as well as his important Broadway successes, not because they were bad songs but because they just didn't fit. Additionally, Wilson felt the chronology of these choice rarities presented an interesting insight into Sondheim's development as a composer.

The show used the songs, with no supporting dialogue, to explore the separate lives and problems of two New Yorkers sharing a one-apartment set. Not major dramatic stuff, but Wilson felt that "the skill with which Craig Lucas and particularly Suzanne Henry fill out the vocal and emotional demands of this musical sketch make it an unusually moving evening."

It was an ideal Off Off Broadway review. It had the aura of discovery.

Young Diane de Mailly had contacted Flora Roberts, Sondheim's representative, about moving it. Seeing that Diane was a first-time producer but liking her, Flora steered her to me. Diane was very serious, attractive, and had class. I called Flora to get a read, and she said, "If you're on the show, we'll go with Diane."

Deservedly a legend in the business, Flora's walls were filled with Tony and Drama Critics Circle Awards for her authors, composers, and directing clients, almost without missing a year, and her comments during rehearsals and previews were eagerly sought by both clients and producers. In addition to Sondheim, she represented Susan Stroman, Alfred Uhry, Arthur Penn, Tina Howe, and Maya Angelou. Flora began her career as an assistant to Kermit Bloomgarden, an historic Broadway producer, who she had urged to produce *Death of a Salesman*.

We occasionally went out for dinner and often wound up singing into the night at a small piano bar. After a few drinks, there was no stopping us, and like everyone else who went to piano bars, we favored Garland and Sinatra. Late in the evening at a Sardi's party, we even serenaded Jerry Schoenfeld. She sang "Get Happy," and I sang "My Funny Valentine."

At one point during the Sondheim negotiation, she began pounding on her desk and bellowed, "Will someone get me a cookie?" She leaned in and whispered, "I've quit smoking. Can you tell?" Someone brought her a cookie, but the *Marry Me* negotiation remained unfinished. Not unusual. It was part of the way Flora did business.

Finally, she declared, "Albert, just prepare the agreement. You know what the terms should be. Prepare it, and send it over here." I imagined how a negotiation between Flora and me would go and wrote down the result. It was signed and returned within a week, without one word changed.

I suggested to Diane the Actors' Playhouse on Sheridan Square because of the heavy traffic, and I thought the intimate theater would be charming for the production. I also had a long-term lease on the big billboard above the cigar store on the Square and was making it available to my shows at cost. *One Mo' Time* was on the billboard, and I convinced Art D'Lugoff to share it with *Marry Me*.

I also suggested to Tommy Schlamme that Jonathan Schwartz do the voice-over for our commercial. Schwartz, son of the noted American composer, Arthur Schwartz, was a major New York radio personality and had a very recognizable voice and a close identification with the best of American popular and theater music.

Mitchell Maxwell loved Sondheim and literally gave us his stylish WPA restaurant in Soho for the glittering opening-night party. Sondheim, Carl Reiner, Tammy Grimes, Phyllis Newman, Jerry Orbach, and Morton Gottlieb were among the attendees.

In a column item about the opening, the *Times* noted that it was an evening of firsts: the producer's first production, Sondheim's first Off Broadway musical, and "surely the first time that that many people had tried to squeeze into the WPA restaurant."

The only letdown was the re-review in the *Times* by Mel Gussow. Gussow found no fault with the underlying material but felt that the two performers and even the piano player were not up to Sondheim's musical level. Faced with that disappointment, combined with the discovery of new Sondheim gems, Gussow felt "sorry-grateful."

The *Times* essentially had gone from telling people to come, to telling them not to come. It is a risk you take in moving a show. A new critic can be assigned who won't like the show, or the same critic can change his mind. Without *Times* support, we struggled to a respectable ninety-six performances.

Stephen Sondheim was involved from start to finish. When RCA recorded the exquisite original cast album, he was there every moment with Thomas Z. Shepard, his traditional cast album producer, to lend his expertise. For Craig Lucas, it was the beginning of a notable career as a dramatist of conscience and daring.

Just as *Marry Me* was going into production, I had a surprising call from Michel Stuart.

He was going to produce a play by Caryl Churchill called *Cloud 9* at the Theatre de Lys. Tommy Tune would direct, and he and Tommy wanted me to be the general manager.

I was shocked to say the least. "We had such a bad time of it at the Gate. I can't understand why you would want me."

"Because you're the best," Michel insisted. "Let me read it, and I will come back to you."

The script arrived with a bottle of Cristal, and I read it that night. I thought it was beyond pretentious, and I called Helen Montagu, who had produced it at the Royal Court in London.

"Daahling, the critics were wild about it, and it ran two weeks," she said. "As for myself, I felt as you do."

I called Michel Stuart, thanked him profusely, and passed. But I took note of his confidence and easy assurance about the project, so different from the divisive person I had known at the Gate. I kept thinking I might be making a mistake.

When the first preview rolled around in May, I ran to the de Lys. It was exquisite. It was all that I loved about Off Broadway. Of the dozens of shows I have turned down, mostly flops and some hits, *Cloud 9* is the only one I regret.

It ran for 971 performances and launched Tommy and Michel as a team. They were to go on to even greater success with *Nine*, a Maury Yeston and Arthur Kopit musical adaptation of Fellini's *8½*, which won a raft of Tony and Drama Desk Awards and ran on Broadway for two years.

During the run of *Cloud 9*, Lucille Lortel, "acceding to innumerable letters, phone calls, and demands from her friends," renamed the Theatre de Lys after herself. The occasion was commemorated by an evening at which she was also declared, once and for all, the Queen of Off Broadway.

And there was another major development for the Theatre de Lys and Off Broadway. Sometime in the spring I got a phone call. "This is Ben Sprecher," the caller declared. "I'm the new manager of the Theatre de Lys for Lucille Lortel." The voice was not warm. It had a hard edge I had never heard in our community. In just those few seconds, I recognized in him an adversary and a harbinger of change for Off Broadway.

"We got a new water fountain," he said, "and I wanted to know if you could use the old one at the Astor Place."

Wow, I thought, *this is a political act.* The guy is new in the community, and his opening salvo is to offer me his hand-me-downs. And yet, we didn't have a water fountain at the Astor Place. "Is it broken?" I inquired.

"No," he said. "It's working just fine."

Erring on the side of practicality, I said, "Yes, we can use it over here. Thank you."

The fountain arrived. He had neglected to mention that the facing was missing, revealing all of its internal plumbing. *An insult*, I thought.

Ben and I were off and running, swapping insults and sidelong glances whenever our paths crossed. He made no bones about the fact that he was solely about dollars, and he used the Lortel as a vehicle to establish himself and push Off Broadway in that direction. I thought it was dangerous and destructive. While the rest of us were running around with our scotch tape, paper clips, and glue, Ben Sprecher was reading *The Art of the Deal*.

CHAPTER 15

Enter Cameron

"This is Cameron Mackintosh. Can you possibly join Tom Lehrer and me for lunch today?"

"It's the best offer I've had all morning."

Cats on Broadway was more than a year away, but the excitement about it and about its young British producer was rapidly reaching a fever pitch. The Shuberts had grabbed it for a co-production at the Winter Garden, and it was continuing to be a huge hit in London.

Tom Lehrer I remembered from 1953, when the older brother of a friend of mine called us into his room and played a ten-inch LP called *Songs by Tom Lehrer*. "The Old Dope Peddler," "Be Prepared," "My Home Town," and "Rickety Tickety Tin" were real eye openers for two innocent seventh-graders in Indianapolis. I never heard them again, but I never forgot them.

At lunch we sorted out that I was there because Cameron wanted to present *Tomfoolery*, his successful London revue of Tom's songs, Off Broadway, and Jerry Schoenfeld had generously pointed him in my direction.

I told Tom my 1953 story and said that, by now, the ten-inch LP must surely be a collector's item, not knowing that he had printed them himself and sold them out of his house. Cameron and I discovered we had a very close friend in common, Helen Montagu. They had co-produced the London production of *Side by Side by Sondheim* when she was heading up H.M. Tennent, Ltd. It was a wonderful, enjoyable lunch.

The following week, Cameron, Tom, and I flew to Vancouver to see a local production of *Tomfoolery*. The audience of Canadian Lehrer fans went wild for the show, but I felt concerned that, with the passing years, the material might now be provincial for New York. My doubts were momentary, pushed aside by Cameron's enormous enthusiasm and his eagerness to know what ideas I had for the Off Broadway production.

I thought immediately of the Top of the Gate. The whole environment, including the Village location, seemed right, and Tom concurred. Not surprisingly, he and Art D'Lugoff had a history. Decades earlier, when he was still performing, Art was his manager and had presented him in concerts at Town Hall and other venues. Lehrer stopped writing and performing in the '60s, noting that, after Henry Kissinger won the Nobel Peace Prize, there was no longer any need to write political satire.

By the end of our trip, I had two wonderful new friends. And on the flight back, Cameron and I decided to share offices in the Theatre Guild building.

I took Cameron to the Gate and arranged for him to meet Art. Sharing a zest for life, mischief, and *mishegas*, the two men hit it off immediately. Cameron thought the Top of the Gate perfect for the show and arranged for Art to have special billing in the advertising.

CAMERON MACKINTOSH
in spite of ART D'LUGOFF
presents TOMFOOLERY

I suggested the married team of Gary Pearle and Mary Kyte to direct and choreograph. They had recently gotten a lot of attention with *Tintypes*, a revue pastiche that sold out at the small York Theatre at St. Peter's Church for several months and then was wrongly transferred to the Golden on Broadway, where it sank. I had seen it several times and thought they were a real find. Gary was the son of Dr. Stanley Pearle of Pearle Vision, and he and Mary were a very attractive, self-assured couple, he directing and she choreographing. After several meetings with Cameron and Tom, it was decided to go with them.

In October, Cameron and I went traveling again, this time with his companion Michael Trench, to visit Tom in Cambridge, Massachusetts, and to attend what turned out to be the very first performance of *Dreamgirls* at the Shubert in Boston. The earlier three scheduled performances had been canceled because Jennifer Holliday was having vocal problems.

The four of us were knocked out. It was a total triumph, and I was delighted when my friends, Tom Eyen and Henry Krieger, the show's author and composer, joined us across the street for a post-show supper.

After the celebration, our little group went to Tom Lehrer's apartment, where we stayed up into the wee hours; Tom played the piano, and I sang. I can't believe I had the nerve to sing "Soliloquy" from *Carousel* for Cameron Mackintosh with Tom Lehrer playing the piano. I certainly didn't think of it as an audition. Later on, when Cameron produced *Carousel*, I realized that he didn't, either.

Just prior to *Tomfoolery* rehearsals, we hit our first bump. It was due to my alcohol consumption. A morning meeting had been scheduled with Cameron, Tom, and Hinks Shimberg, the gentlemanly co-producer from Orlando, Florida. I was shaking and hung over, and clearly not up to it. I told my assistant to tell Cameron I was "ill."

Minutes later the phone rang. It was Cameron. "She's ill," he said. "They're in from London, Cambridge, and Florida, but she's ill. She's ill." And he hung up. *Yikes*, I thought. *He's onto me.* The meeting happened the next day, and I sailed through it. Cameron said, "You more than made up for yesterday."

As rehearsals got underway, it became clear that "the Puhles," as Cameron called the Pearles, were independent and accustomed to being left alone. Cameron, however, was a producer of the old school, a real producer who was going to play a collaborative role in the creation of his show. This kind of "meddling," in their eyes, became increasingly irritating.

One afternoon during the third week of rehearsal, Cameron bounded into the office very upset. "'The Puhles' have banned me from rehearsal," he fumed.

I couldn't believe it. What could have possessed them? He respected their wishes for the duration of the rehearsal period but returned to a fully active role during previews. And "the Puhles" were forever after "the Swine."

Sales were brisk, and in the early weeks of the run, there was an intense rush of fervent, lifelong Tom Lehrer fans. They were wild about the show, but how deep was this audience?

Helen Montagu called and said she was flying in for the opening. In the early weeks of our friendship, Cameron and I took great delight in imitating the lilting soprano Helen affected, and we had begun doing our impressions on the phone to her friends. Frequently, they were actually fooled for a moment. Helen first got wind of it when she made an international call and was asked, "Is that really you or one of those imitations that seem to be going around?"

A couple of nights before the opening, as Cameron, Helen, and I headed for the Algonquin, I launched into my imitation. Having had quite enough, Helen belted me in the mouth with her purse. "Cameron," I yelped, "my lip is bleeding."

"She knows you're onto her," he whispered.

My opening-night gift from Tom was an original issue of his ten-inch LP, which he inscribed, "To Albert, who is himself a collector's item. Love, Tom."

It was a high-spirited opening that was greeted by mixed reviews across the board. The reception was best summed up by Frank Rich in the *Times*. "The charm and intelligence of the songs are still in evidence: the lyrics are almost always dexterous, the pastiche melodies almost always clever. But, with a few exceptions, the bite is gone. Through no fault of his own, Mr.

Lehrer has been outrun by the nasty march of history. What was rude in the days of Eisenhower and Kennedy could almost pass for nostalgia now."[2]

The devout Tom Lehrer audience lasted about six weeks, after which the attendance and level of audience response lagged considerably. It ran 120 performances. Cameron was disappointed, but I think his disappointment was more with the Pearles. I thought much of their work was good and leaned more toward Frank Rich's analysis.

In January, Cameron invited me to the London opening night of Andrew Lloyd Webber's *Song and Dance*, which was to be at the Palace on March 26. And he added, "If you like it, baby, it's yours for Broadway."

I could not have been more honored, or more convinced that I was wrong for the job, for any number of reasons. At that point I had never managed anything on Broadway, let alone a musical for Cameron Mackintosh. Nothing in my experience had prepared me for such an undertaking.

I loved my little niche Off Broadway. It gave me a career of the size I wanted. I believed that the size of a career is limited by the amount of emotional baggage you are willing to take on in order to have it, which, in my case, was finite. I wanted to make a living, but having fun doing it was a top priority. I was afraid of being overwhelmed or having a career that got beyond my control.

In addition, Cameron's passion for work did not stop at six o'clock. I feared that a Broadway musical with him would be a serious intrusion into my drink time.

As March 26 approached, I remained at a loss as to how to deal with Cameron's generous invitation, knowing that turning it down on opening night, with Andrew present and all of the attendant hoopla, would be unthinkable. I prayed for an intervention.

One occurred. When I got up for my early flight on March 26th, I looked out to see the city being blanketed by a heavy spring blizzard. A call to JFK confirmed it. There were no flights. I called Cameron to wish him well without me. He sounded annoyed.

Two weeks later, I flew over and quietly attended a regular performance. As I had suspected, *Song and Dance* was not for me. When I told Cameron, he said, "That's why I love The Peach. You always know what you want."

There was much more to come.

CHAPTER 16

The Musical That Ate Off Broadway

In 1976, Howard Ashman asked his friend Kyle Renick if he wanted to start a nonprofit theater company. Kyle was the business manager of The American Place Theatre, and Howard was an editor at Grosset and Dunlap. Soon after, they took over the floundering WPA Theatre and immediately put it on the map. The opening productions were an Albee adaptation of *Ballad of the Sad Café* and *Gorey Stories*, a revue mentored by Ashman that moved to Broadway. Howard spent the next six years honing his craft as a writer and director, and he began a collaboration with Alan Menken, who he met in Lehman Engel's BMI Musical Theatre Workshop, as his composer.

In 1982, with Howard as author, lyricist, and director, Ashman and Menken created a show that had twenty-five commercial producers in hot pursuit. It was called *Little Shop of Horrors*, and I'll never forget Kyle's breathless phone call telling me he was considering me as a possible general manager. I rushed to see it that night.

What I saw was a certified hit. Hits have a swagger that nothing else has, and it was right there from the very first note of music to the finale.

I ran home to call Cameron in London. He was, of course, asleep. I told him I had found a huge hit. "You have to do it. Everyone in town is after it. I'll get you a tape."

"Call Bernie," he urged.

Bernie was, of course, Bernie Jacobs. I called him that morning to tell him Cameron and I wanted him to see the show. Could he go tonight? He could, and he promised to call on Saturday morning with his report. Jerry Schoenfeld's "If you ever find a *Godspell*" request of twelve years before echoed in my mind, and I thought maybe this was the one.

Excited, I told Kyle I had spoken to Cameron, and that I needed four tickets for Bernie.

He told me that Esther Sherman, Howard Ashman's agent, had arranged tickets for David Geffen the following night. Esther and I were very close, and she was thrilled when I told her about Cameron and about Bernie seeing the show.

Bernie called me early Saturday as promised. "It wasn't my cup of tea," he said, as I sank. "Betty didn't much care for it. The young couple we were with enjoyed it. It has a lot of whimsy. The British like that kind of thing." He added, "But if you want us to come along, we might consider it."

On Saturday night, David Geffen was a no-show.

On Monday, just to be professional, I put in a follow-up phone call to Bernie. I'll never forget his return call. "Albert, I have David Geffen on the line. We will take the show. How much will it cost?"

Not having even thought about a budget, I blurted out the first figure that came to my mind. "Three hundred fifty thousand."

"Do you want to come along, David?" Bernie asked. "Whatever you say, Bernie."

"You've got to leave room for Cameron," I said. "He is the one who suggested I call you."

"Very well. Come to my office on Wednesday," Bernie commanded, "and bring the budgets."

In true Bernie style, he spent the next two days telling the industry he was doing *Little Shop of Horrors*. He would later claim that he decided to do the show when Alexander Cohen, who attended the same performance, told him it would never work. "If Alex didn't like it," he said, "I knew it would be a hit."

I started work on the budgets, and Kyle, Howard Ashman, and I began checking out theaters. It was my first time meeting Howard, and I found him to be rakishly handsome, to the point, and brilliant. He was exhausted from directing the show but focused and intense. We were going into summer, and the only venue available was the Orpheum on Second Avenue and St. Mark's Place.

The Orpheum had a long track record of hits and was fine except that its 299-seat capacity fell short of the economic requirements of the show. Fortunately, the resident WPA set designer, Edward Gianfrancesco, was also an architect and contractor. He told us that the Orpheum could accommodate the addition of a balcony, giving us the capacity we needed.

On Wednesday, I went in for my meeting with Bernie Jacobs. I arrived at his office, which was something out of MGM, to see him sitting at his desk with toilet paper stuck to his cheek. In the middle of it was a small red stain. He was yelling into the phone.

"Mr. de Rothschild, I can't hear you! Mr. de Rothschild, I am in the business of selling tickets. No, I cannot give you free tickets. Mr. de Rothschild, I can't hear you." And he hung up.

"Did he want a pair of comps to *Cats*?" I queried.

"A pair? He wants an entire house. He's doing a fundraiser, and he thinks I should contribute the tickets. What is he, anyway? Just a Jew with a 'de' in front of his name."

Watching this unabashed man with toilet paper stuck to his face, I had my first realization that Bernard B. Jacobs was a man who was himself at all times.

"Do you have the budgets?"

"Yes, but Bernie, I have to tell you something. You don't have the rights."

"Well, what does he want?" Bernie barked.

"What are you willing to offer? There are twenty-five people chasing after it, but you are you."

Within seconds. Bernie structured an offer. It acknowledged who everyone was, the value of what they brought to the table, the value of the property, and the need to be competitive with the other bidders.

"The offer is brilliant," I told him. "If I can't deliver it, I won't be on the show."

He looked at the budgets and said he didn't know anything about Off Broadway, so he would have to trust that I knew what I was doing.

"By the way," he said, looking at my flat top, "how do you get your hair to stand up like that?"

"Actually," I said, "when I get on the elevator to come and see you, it's lying down."

Esther Sherman and I were well matched, and we went into rehearsal with an unresolved royalty point on Howard Ashman's director contract. I wouldn't budge, nor would she. The third morning, Kyle called in a panic. Esther had pulled Howard out of rehearsal over the open point. "Just sit tight," I told him. "Don't do anything or say anything to anybody."

At 5:00 p.m. Esther called, irate. "Do you not realize that I have pulled the director out of rehearsal??"

"I do," I responded. "If I were the author, I would be furious." "Send the agreement," she snapped. "And fuck you."

During rehearsals, the William Morris Agency, which represented Howard and *Little Shop*'s star, Ellen Greene, threw an industry-wide stag party, and Bernie and Jerry invited me to be part of the Shubert table. The entertainment was to be Alan King and Buddy Hackett.

Before the performance, I sought out Alan King to tell him of my fond memories of Detroit in 1957, when he opened for Judy Garland and was so gracious to all of us.

He remembered the fan club, and we had a wonderful reminiscence. I had come full circle. It was twenty-five years later, I was talking to Alan King, and I was in show business.

When I returned to the table, Phil Smith, who was the Shubert Executive Vice President, said, "You had quite a conversation with Alan."

"I was president of the Judy Garland Fan Club, and he was very kind to us many years ago when she played Detroit."

Phil then astonished me. "I was her house manager at the Palace in 1951," he told me. We talked the entire night, and it was the beginning of a decades-long close friendship.

David Geffen and I met for the first time on opening night in front of the Orpheum. He was understandably nervous. He was the producer of a show he had never seen. I assured him he would be very happy. The opening "Skid Row" number was greeted with rousing applause, and we were off and running.

At intermission David Geffen made a bee-line for me, gave me a big hug, and said, "Albert, it's a great big smash." After the performance, we had our opening night party—wine and cheese in the lobby of the Orpheum.

The reviews were spectacular. Not just raves, spectacular. Business was solid, but I told the producers we would not have a sellout week until October. We were in the middle of July, and I had enough Off Broadway experience under my belt to talk about buying patterns with certainty.

Tommy Schlamme outdid himself on our TV commercials, and they became famous in their own right. Like *One Mo' Time*, *Little Shop* was sold primarily on television.

The stars came in droves, and I gave the house manager a Brownie Hawkeye camera. He was to take the photo and get the film to our press agent, Milly Schoenbaum, who would have it rush-developed and get it to the press. For each photo he took, I gave him $25. If it ran in the paper, an additional $25. The following months and years brought Steve Martin, Eddie Murphy, Mary Tyler Moore, Harry Belafonte, Steven Spielberg, Robert Redford, Barbra Streisand, Sidney Poitier, Lucille Ball, Dustin Hoffman, Bette Midler, and many others.

Almost as if by magic, October brought us our first sellout week. And we stayed in that position for years. The show would now make a profit of six to eight thousand dollars a week. I was happy. I had always considered three to five thousand dollars to be a good weekly profit for Off Broadway.

As we enjoyed our first sellout week, *Cats* opened on Broadway.

I had flown my mother and father in from Michigan, and we attended opening night with Art D'Lugoff and his wife, Avital. Twenty minutes into the performance, my mother leaned in to me and said, "Isn't this monotonous?" Otherwise, it was an evening of high glamour.

I introduced my parents to David Merrick, Earl and Rosemary Wilson and, most important, to Arlene Francis, my mother's favorite actress.

My mother said dancing with her son at the Waldorf that night was a highlight of her life. My father had a long conversation with Art D'Lugoff. Politically and culturally, they were poles apart. When Art and Avi went out on the dance floor, I looked at my father. "Do you like Art?"

"Why, I love him," he said. "The man is *life*."

The following day, Bernie showed me the accountant's statement for the first week of *Cats*. In one week it had made an operating profit of $186,000. I was stunned. The critics' reviews were mixed-to-negative. The next day Bernie had a tag line placed under the title in all the *Cats* advertising: "Now and Forever." Howard Ashman said there was only one man who would put that in an ad after those reviews.

After the great success of *Cats*, the phone call from Phil Smith was inevitable. "Bernie wants you to come over here to discuss the implementation of the new ticket prices."

I urged Cameron to come with me. "We have to fight this," I told him. Bernie had brought up increasing our ticket prices several times, but I had so far stemmed the tide.

Bernie started. "Phil keeps saying to me, 'Why do you let Albert push you around?'"

"You will destroy my turf," I said.

With Cameron sitting in total silence, I realized we were dealing with a fait accompli.

We raised the ticket prices. I bore enormous guilt. I felt like I was now complicit in the things I accused Ben Sprecher of doing.

And I wasn't the only one who felt Off Broadway was being damaged. In the middle of dinner, my good and revered friend Dorothy Olim attacked me. Dorothy was the conscience of Off Broadway. I went home and cried all night long.

In addition to the new ticket prices, Bernie wanted the royalty participants to defer 20 percent of their royalties to hasten recoupment of the production costs. I battled to no avail with Esther Sherman and Scott Shukat, who represented Alan Menken and the choreographer Edie Cowan. I called Bernie to tell him, and he got Esther Sherman on the line and read her the riot act. Before it was over, she had agreed.

He called me back. "You've got to be a killer, Albert. You've got to be a killer. You're not tough enough, Albert. But I love you." Vintage Bernie.

I grew to love him very much. He was a great motivator. I found myself lying awake at night thinking of things to do for the show that would please him. He constantly told me he loved me and, equally important, I had his trust. He gave me free rein to run the show. As a matter of procedure, I called for his approval before I made any major decisions, especially financial ones. The usual answer was, "Whatever you say, Albert."

At Christmas, Howard Ashman gave me a large handmade doll of Judy Garland as Dorothy. It meant a lot because we both loved her so. With it was a note. "Albert. Christmas is always a good excuse to get sentimental (for me, anyway). And this, of all Christmases, is a special one for me. You've done so much toward making that happen and I just hope you know that none of your care and work and time and smarts, none of the above, goes without notice, deep deep appreciation, and an inner smile from me. Thank you. May we be part of each other's lives many Christmases more. May you have all the wonderful things you deserve. Love, Howard."

Just after the first of the year, Jerry Schoenfeld told me that the Shubert Organization was going to take over the management of the National Theater in Washington and asked if l would join others in the industry in writing a reference letter for them. It was an effortless undertaking. His and Bernie's direction of Shubert had been exemplary.

A short time later, Stephen Graham and Joan Stein approached me with their new partner, Alison Clarkson, about a commercial transfer of *The Middle Ages*, a wonderful A. R. Gurney play about a WASP family, trying out at the Church of the Heavenly Rest.

Given Graham's *Washington Post* connection, I thought it was the perfect moment to combine the producers with Shubert and took them in for a meeting with Bernie. Shubert came in with one-third of the capitalization and took billing. The young producers were as thrilled as was I. Bernie chatted with them amiably and asked each one what they did. When Alison told him she was Richmond Crinkley's assistant, he quipped, "Richmond Crinkley needs an assistant?"

Neil Mazzella had been the technical director for the old WPA Theatre on the Bowery and a regular at Phebe's in its heyday. In 1980, he went Upstate to open a union scene shop and took his downtown spirit, his long hair, and his motorcycle with him. He now called and told me he could get *The Middle Ages* set built on a nonunion basis, necessary for Off Broadway, at a rate competitive with the nonunion shops, and when the show moved to Broadway, he would touch it up and give it a union stamp. I liked him and his offer and, flattered by the possibilities of the relationship, I grabbed it. It was the beginning of a lifelong, golden friendship.

Stephen Graham threw a lavish opening night party at his penthouse, and when I saw Jerry Schoenfeld having a long conversation with Katherine Graham, I knew the Shubert investment had been recouped in goodwill. The play, with a star turn by Andre Gregory, ran 110 performances.

By spring, it was time to consider the first *Little Shop* production outside of New York. Bernie and I thought it should be in an eastern city like Boston. David Geffen wanted it in Los Angeles, and he prevailed. We scouted for theaters, and I was heavily in favor of the Roxy, a Village Gate-like cabaret where *Rocky Horror* had run for years. Howard ruled it out immediately. "I don't want glasses tinkling during my show," he said.

Largely because of its proximity to UCLA, the producers chose the Westwood Playhouse. No location in Los Angeles was ideal because the town was completely spread out and was full of so-called "Equity Waiver" theaters that offered shows at $10 a pop within blocks of people's homes.

Milly Schoenbaum, our superb press agent, was employed by a large public relations firm owned by Lee Solters and Sheldon Roskin. Solters was now based in Los Angeles and had heavyweight clients like Frank Sinatra, Barbra Streisand, and Michael Jackson. He personally wanted to handle *Little Shop* in LA, but, for reasons he did not explain, Bernie wanted nothing to do with him. Solters applied substantial pressure to Milly to at least deliver a dinner with me, and I convinced Bernie that it was the politic thing to do.

At the dinner, Solters went out of his way to charm me and was brimming with ideas for selling the show in Los Angeles. I liked him and would have gone with him. There was clearly a reason he was at the top of his profession. I reported back to Bernie, and he was still adamant. He favored Judi Davidson, who was indisputably the top theater press agent on the West Coast.

When Milly told Lee Solters of the decision, he said, "I'm going to get them if it's the last thing I do."

I joined Howard in Los Angeles at the beginning of rehearsal. As the opening neared, Jerry, Bernie, and Phil Smith arrived. They were relaxed and happy. Jerry, dressed casually in a cardigan sweater, took me for a long drive through Beverly Hills. "Behind those windows, Albert, are some of the wealthiest people in the country," he said.

"And what are they doing behind those windows?" I asked.

"Clipping coupons."

Little Shop opened in Los Angeles on April 28, 1983. Before the show, Jerry Schoenfeld spotted Dan Sullivan, the *Los Angeles Times* theater critic, and called him over to introduce me. I winced as he said, "Dan, I want you to meet the king of Off Broadway. "Well,"

Sullivan exclaimed sarcastically, "I'm always happy to meet the *king* of anything."

After the blowout performance, Howard asked all of us to come into the auditorium. He and Alan had a new song they wanted to do for us. It was called "Sheridan Square," and we were hushed as they sang it so plaintively. It was about the blight of AIDS on what had been for decades one of the happiest gay areas in Greenwich Village.

The epidemic was now claiming its first victims. Even with available medication, it was a matter of time. Having it was a death sentence. Stuart White, an early companion of Howard and a founder of the WPA, was to die in July after a long illness. The theater community was devastated by the epidemic. The gay community was devastated and terrified.

The next day Dan Sullivan savaged us in the *LA Times*. He said, among other things, "This show thinks it's so funny, it doesn't need an audience." The other reviews were all superlatives, but Sullivan's review hurt us, and *Little Shop* did not perform to our expectation. I continued to wonder who or what caused Dan Sullivan to write that damaging review.

Did Lee Solters have a word with him?

We returned to New York just in time for awards season, and we won everything—the Drama Critics Circle, Drama Desk, and Outer Critics Circle Awards for Best Musical of the Season.

My old friend Michael Feingold, drama critic of the *Village Voice* and head of its Obie Awards committee, was at the Drama Critics Circle Award. I went over to him with my third martini in my hand and opened with, "This will never win an Obie because it's not in a basement, more than three people have seen it, and no one from the *Voice* has ever slept with any of us."

"Oh, sour grapes," Michael responded. "Albert's right," Esther Sherman chimed in.

"The only award you've given to a commercial show in the last ten years was *Bloolips* for Best Costumes." Glancing over at Lucille Lortel, who was standing nearby, I added, "We'll get our own awards for *commercial* Off Broadway."

I brought it up the next morning at a meeting of The League of Off Broadway Theatres and Producers. The Lucille Lortel Awards. Everyone liked the idea. George Elmer asked, "Do you think Lucille will go for it?"

"Go for it?" Paul Libin replied. "She'll pay for it."

As it happened, that night was the opening of a double bill of Beckett one acts, at the Clurman, co-produced by Lucille and Jack Garfein. At intermission, I approached Lucille on the sidewalk and told her of my idea.

"How much will it cost, dear?"

Lucille asked Ben Sprecher to call me, and we began a series of meetings about the awards. I found myself beginning to like him. He was arrogant, but so was I. And smart with a quick sense of humor. He arrived at the third or fourth meeting looking forlorn. "You're not going to believe this," he began. "Lucille thinks the first award should go to her."

"Oh, God," I replied, "I forgot who we were dealing with." The Lortel Awards came to a screeching halt.

In August, I got a call from Jeremy Ritzer, a veteran casting director who had become a skilled producer. I had very much enjoyed working with him on his successful Cherry Lane revival of *Entertaining Mr. Sloane*. He had acquired the Broadway rights to the film *Smile*, which he intended to make into a musical. Marvin Hamlisch was on board as the composer, and he needed a book writer and lyricist.

I told him, "I might have just the person for you. What would you think of Howard Ashman?"

He responded, "I was hoping you would say that."

I approached Howard and Esther. They liked the idea, and Howard joined the project.

At the same moment, Ben Sprecher opened the newly refurbished Promenade Theatre, from which I had rescued Liza Minnelli five years earlier. He brought his brand of professionalism to it and made it the most sought-after and most expensive theater Off Broadway. But this time, he was working for himself as co-owner. Producers, without exception, wanted to put their shows there.

The synchronicity of Ben Sprecher's approach to theater operation and the lucrative *Little Shop* profits were driving Off Broadway from scotch tape and paper clips toward the realm of big business. Bernie was ready for yet another increase in ticket prices.

"It's the Jacobian Theory," I said, resigned. "What's that?" he asked.

"What goes up must go up."

When Michael Jackson first saw *Little Shop* at the Westwood, we approached him about some photos with the cast. "If you'll hide me at intermission, I'll do it," he said. And he was good for his word. Now he appeared at the Orpheum in the middle of a performance wearing a surgical mask and accompanied by seven bodyguards. "No one must know I'm here." he said. "Who would ever guess?" I answered.

Howard Ashman called me in the fall to say that Jeremy Ritzer wasn't coming up with the money for *Smile*. Did I think the Shuberts would be interested? With the success of *Little Shop* and *A Chorus Line*, I was absolutely certain they would. They funded a workshop, with Howard directing, to the tune of $200,000. It was the talk of the town, but they were not happy with the result and dropped it. The Shuberts do not like to be the deliverers of bad news, and Howard heard it through the grapevine. There was no meeting, no phone call, not even a letter.

A few weeks later, I gave a small party at my apartment. Howard and Esther were there, and Jerry Schoenfeld arrived. He walked immediately over to Howard. "Don't come near me!" Howard screamed. "I don't want to talk to you. I'm not interested in anything you have to say."

Jerry pulled me aside. "Does he want a career in the theater?"

"Jerry," I retorted, "you dropped *Smile*, and no one said one word to him. He's angry. He's hurt."

In a complete turnabout he asked, "Should I apologize to him?"

"I would stay completely away from him for the rest of the evening," I advised. For the next hour, Jerry sat chatting quietly with Esther, then he left.

Howard Ashman's companion, David Evans, passed away in the summer of 1986. Howard had stayed by his side as the illness progressed. He was grateful to the St. Vincent's Hospital Supportive Care Program for providing hospice care to his friend and for the support group he participated in for those grieving the loss of loved ones to AIDS.

Howard asked me if I would join him to co-produce a benefit to raise funds for the program. The result was *Showstoppers*, "a show of concern and support," and Edward Albee, Vernel Bagneris, Kaye Ballard, Christopher Durang, Dolores Gray, Ellen Greene, Marvin Hamlisch, and Alan Menken were among the performers. We raised fifteen thousand dollars.

The David Geffen-produced film of *Little Shop* premiered in New York at the end of December. Howard wasn't that happy with it, but it should be said that Howard's happiness was never a slam-dunk. The movie did well at the box office and drove our business way up for several months.

In the fall of '87, business dropped sharply. After a month of operating losses, I called Bernie and told him I didn't see it coming back. It was as if the public had suddenly had enough of us and moved on.

No playwright has ever agreed with the decision to close a show, this one included. "You're closing it too soon," Howard protested.

"Howard, we have run five and a half years!"

"I'm telling you . . ."

When *Little Shop of Horrors* closed on November 1, it had run 2,209 performances and was the highest grossing show in Off Broadway history.

In the summer of 1983, our company manager Nancy Nagel Gibbs had taken the first of two maternity leaves and was replaced for three months by Peter Schneider. During that time, Peter struck up a friendship with Howard Ashman and Alan Menken that was to have an impact on the entertainment industry none of us could have possibly imagined. After Peter left us, he moved to Los Angeles where, in 1985, he became the first president of Disney Animation.

He brought Howard Ashman and Alan Menken along with him, beginning a ten-year renaissance at Disney that changed the history and importance of animation forever. The films they made together, *The Little Mermaid*, *Beauty and the Beast*, and *Aladdin*, set world box-office records and won multiple Academy, Golden Globe, and Grammy Awards. *Beauty and the Beast* was the first animated featured to be nominated for the Academy Award for Best Picture.

After the 1990 Academy Awards, where they collected two Oscars for *The Little Mermaid*, Howard told Alan that he was HIV positive. Peter instructed the animators on *Beauty and the Beast* that they were now to work with Howard in New York. With time, the reason became apparent. His health was deteriorating rapidly.

Near the end, I spent an hour alone with Howard at St. Vincent's Hospital. His sight was going, and he said everything was as if by candlelight. We spoke fondly of our time together and agreed that, with *Little Shop*, we both became what we had been becoming.

It was our goodbye.

Howard died on March 14, 1991. He was forty years old.

CHAPTER 17

Shouting in the Town Square

Bernie Jacobs could talk of many things, but by the mid '80s, he had three favorite topics.

Cameron, whose international productions of *Cats* had moved the theater into the mainstream of world popular culture, and who Bernie sometimes referred to as "The Wooden Spoon" because of his penchant for stirring things.

David Merrick, about whom Bernie had an endless supply of larger-than-life firsthand stories. By then, Merrick had suffered a debilitating stroke that made him virtually impossible to understand for much of the time, and he was living with Mark Bramble. The stroke was the result of a serious addiction to cocaine that began when Merrick was producing *The Great Gatsby* film in Hollywood in 1973. The emergency medics had arrived to find him unconscious in a bedroom allegedly strewn with white powder.

I wrote a gossip column in *The Saint* newspaper under the name of Hedda Poppers, and, in a blind item, I expressed my sadness about "a drug-induced stroke" suffered by "the greatest producer of the century."

Merrick found it on Mark's coffee table and read it. "This is the blond one," he murmured, according to Mark.

During the three months Merrick stayed with Mark, Bernie Jacobs arrived in his limousine every weekday at 11:30 and stayed with him for an hour—an example of Bernie's loyalty to people he cared for.

Bernie loved gossip and asked me several times if Merrick and Mark were lovers. I was incredulous at the thought and gave him an emphatic "No." "And I will tell you why," I said, laughing. "NO interest whatsoever."

Michael Bennett, the young genius whose talent Bernie Jacobs worshiped, and who had put millions in the Shubert coffers with his productions of *A Chorus Line* and *Dreamgirls*. Despite protestations by both parties, the relationship had distinct father-and-son characteristics. In this instance, the father was both fascinated and disheartened by the antics of his naughty son.

Bennett would call Bernie at 3:00 a.m. slurring his words and saying whatever was on his mind. Bernie took the calls and always listened.

At the time their relationship began, Bernie, by his own admission, had a fundamental misunderstanding of the nature of homosexuality. He thought it was just a matter of finding the right girl and had urged Bennett in that direction with Donna McKechnie. When it didn't work out, Bernie felt responsible and came to realize that "finding the right girl" was not the answer.

Bernie had more recently been put out with Michael for not committing to direct *Chess*, a musical by members of ABBA, which Shubert intended to produce. Michael would appear to be heading toward a "Yes," and then it would be a decisive "No." It had gone back and forth like that for months and through myriad meetings in London and New York. One day, Bernie had had enough and lost his temper. Bennett grabbed him and dragged him to the bathroom. He tore open his shirt, revealing Kaposi's sarcoma. Michael Bennett had AIDS.

Bernie was beyond devastated. He immediately began to seek out ways to bring the public's attention to the growing pandemic and to pursue support and care for its victims. It was all a way of showing his love and support for Michael.

John Glines and Lawrence Lane came to me with *As Is*, William M. Hoffman's beautifully written play about the impact of AIDS on a heretofore happy group of friends in New York City. It was a drama of enormous social consequence and, coming as it did from Off Broadway, it seemed the perfect vehicle for my Broadway debut. I thought of Bernie and took it to him, and we went to see it together at Circle Rep on Sheridan Square, where it was directed by Marshall W. Mason, Circle's artistic director. Bernie turned to me at the end and said, "I'll give you a hundred thousand and the Lyceum."

Hoffman and his agent were there. I asked Bernie if we could tell them, and he said, "Fine."

They were obviously very happy, and the agent said, "Thank you, Mr. Shubert." Bernie responded, "I'm not Mr. Shubert—I'm Bernie Jacobs."

John Glines was a great man of the theater. In 1976, he had started The Glines, a theater company "devoted to creating and presenting gay art to develop positive self-images and dispel negative stereotyping." The Glines was unique of its kind and was a prolific producer of quality gay plays of every stripe. In 1983, The Glines production of Harvey Fierstein's *Torch Song Trilogy* won the Tony Award, making Broadway history. It also made Tony history when John introduced his producing partner, Lawrence Lane, as "my lover."

I took John Glines and Larry Lane to meet Bernie, and while we were waiting to go in, John hit me with, "Lucille Lortel is coming in with $125,000. See if Bernie will match that, and I would also like him to take producer billing." That was a lot to hear seconds before we went into the meeting, but okay.

Bernie spoke of the importance of doing *As Is* on Broadway. The mainstreaming of AIDS awareness was central to his desire to do the show. The disease was still stigmatized. There was very little in the public media. "If you want people to hear your message," Bernie emphasized, "you shout it in the town square, not on a side street."

He agreed to upping the Shubert investment to match Lucille's. When I raised the question of billing, he looked intensely into my eyes thinking, I believe, of what it would mean to him, especially in terms of Michael, and what it would mean to us. After a long moment, and without breaking the interlock of our eyes, he said slowly, "I'll take billing."

So, it was done. We had half of the $500,000 that was needed and the prestige of The Shubert Organization as a co-producer.

My author negotiations for *As Is* were the first on the new Dramatist Guild Approved Production Contract (APC) agreement. The basic minimum as well as the maximum terms were specified in the agreement and were non-negotiable. It was a very complex almost obsessive document. Its primary architect later murdered his wife and jumped out the window.

Still, I found it a brilliant agreement, and, most important, it gave shows a break when they were struggling and gave authors a reward when the show was flourishing. It was ideal for this production, which I thought would be in the struggling category.

One month after *As Is* opened at Circle Rep, Larry Kramer's play about AIDS, *The Normal Heart,* opened at Joseph Papp's Public Theater downtown. The Public Theater was far and away the major contributor to world theater at that time. Significantly, Papp believed Broadway could support only one AIDS play and wisely kept *The Normal Heart* downtown, where it ran for 294 performances.

When you are doing a cause-oriented play, I believe it is essential to ensure that it will have a respectable run. This is done by having a healthy financial reserve or access to loan capital in the event of operating losses, and by all involved pitching in to keep the weekly costs as low as possible. There is more at stake than just running a play. The cause itself must be respected.

I took that approach in my deal making for *As Is*. I conformed Marshall Mason's director agreement to the structure of the Dramatist Guild APC. If the show struggled, he took the minimum terms allowable by the Society of Stage Directors and

Choreographers. If the show flourished, he got the advantageous terms of the agreements to which he was accustomed. Mason and his agent, the highly respected Robbie Lantz, agreed with the approach and went along with it.

Sam Cohn, the justifiably legendary "super-agent," was another story. He represented two of the actors and was adamant they be paid as if they were Sam Cohn clients in a commercial hit. I was equally firm in my position.

There were some fiery conversations, my particular favorite being when he screamed, "Germany is in America!"

"Cheap shot," I fired back. At the first rehearsal, when I introduced myself to an actor who was one of Sam's clients, he looked at my blond hair and said, "I thought so."

One evening just before seven, I got a call from the stage manager. Marshall Mason had told him we needed to add a sound operator and was very upset that one was not on board. I knew that the aggregate amount of time of our sound cues fell within the range that could be handled by the electrician without having to hire an additional man, which would have added about fifteen hundred dollars to our weekly costs.

I called Phil Smith, informed him of the situation, and asked if Bernie could meet me at the theater right away to handle it. "Yes," Phil said. "Bernie is busy right now, but you go ahead, and he will meet you there." I went to the Lyceum. Bernie never appeared, and I realized he thought I should handle it myself, which I did, and the matter was settled.

I called Phil back and thanked them both. "Did you solve it?" he said.

"Yes."

"Good, because if you had brought Bernie in, the crew would have forever thought of you as a weak sister." It was a confidence-building moment for me.

As Is opened May 1, 1985, the day after my forty-fourth birthday. It was my first Broadway show. Before the show, I took a bottle of Remy Martin to the Shubert offices, and we drank a toast. Later, at the Sardi's party, our press agents Betty Lee Hunt and Maria Pucci poured a bottle of champagne over my head.

The reviews ranged from spectacular to supportive. The press was all over us. Being on Broadway was an enormous help, and the presence of *The Normal Heart* Off Broadway added to the momentum of getting AIDS awareness into the mainstream. *As Is* won the Drama Desk Award and was Tony-nominated as Best Play.

The Drama Desk Awards were very prestigious and were held in the glamorous Rainbow Room atop Rockefeller Center. Lucille Lortel asked me to escort her, and I did so, gladly. When Bill Hoffman, our playwright, got up to receive the Best Play Award, it was clear that the audience was with him with all their hearts, and it was a moment for us all.

However, as we got on the large elevator to leave, Lucille began to rant. "Why wasn't I there, dear? I should have been up there. After all I have done. All my *years* of supporting Circle Rep." The large elevator went quiet. I felt hurt for her but also irritated with her shallow egotism.

"Lucille," I said as we got into the car, "you really let yourself down when you act like this. You're bigger than this. It just doesn't have the importance that you put on it." She quieted down but was in a sulk all the way back to the Sherry Netherland.

John Glines arranged for us to tithe three dollars from the sale of every ticket to AIDS organizations, divided equally among the only three that existed at the time: AIDS Medical Foundation founded and headed by Mathilde Krim, Gay Men's Health Crisis (GMHC), and the AIDS Resource Center.

In July, the world spotlight was thrust on AIDS when Rock Hudson appeared with Doris Day on her cable TV show, incoherent and showing the ravages of the disease. Within a week, he released a statement confirming that he had it. Elizabeth Taylor, motivated by her friend's illness, started an organization devoted to AIDS research in Los Angeles, which merged in September with Mathilde Krim's Foundation and became the American Medical Foundation for AIDS Research (AMFAR) of which Taylor was acknowledged as Founder.

Rock Hudson died on October 2. Press and television cameras flooded the back of our theater as the cast and audience stood for a moment of silence at the end of the performance. Watching it all, John Glines observed that "Bernie had it right. The cameras are here because we're in the town square."

Fan club members backstage in Detroit, 1957 (l to r) Tom Cooper, me, Judy, Gordon Stevens, Martha Shepherd, Pat McMath, and Robert Rosterman.

Sing Along with Santa, Eaton's Dept Store, Montreal, 1963. Puppetry came in handy during my salad days.

Max Jacobs   Louis M. Jacobs

With Larry Ross in a stock production of *West Side Story*, 1962. Two weeks of my dancing, and they made me the press agent.

With Helen Millikan, my fourth-grade teacher—guest of honor, Indianapolis opening night.

David Cryer and Walter McGinn in *The Fantasticks* tour, 1966.

At Theatre de Lys with Word Baker and David, 1967.

Gretchen Cryer and Nancy Ford.

Now Is the Time for All Good Men Columbia Cast Album recording session. Ed Kleban (left) and cast, 1967. Eight years later, Kleban took Broadway by storm as the lyricist of *A Chorus Line*.

A May 3 *Fantasticks* anniversary party at the Sullivan Street Playhouse. There were forty of these. With (l to r) Tom Jones, Lore Noto, Tim Scott, and Harvey Schmidt.
Lou Manna

The Peaches Intimate Revue in the Judson Church Garden, 1973. (l to r) Madeleine leRoux, Al Carmines, John Vaccaro, Rosalyn Drexler, and The Peaches.

Tom O'Horgan   *Daniel Nicoletta*

Charles Ludlam

Let My People Come. Earl Wilson, Jr., Robert Blume, Art D'Lugoff, Shezwae Powell, and cast celebrate the 800th performance at the Village Gate, July 2, 1976.

Hale Haberman

The Cartel at the Fontainebleau With (l to r) Jim Sink, Michel Stuart, Tommy Tune, and Phil Oesterman, 1974.

Rudolf Nureyev and *Times* critic Clive Barnes visit Charles Pierce backstage at the Top of the Gate, 1975

With Ellen Stewart and Bruce Mailman on East 4th Street.

With Liza at the Promenade Theatre, on our way to Studio 54, 1978.

With Truman Capote, 1982.
Michael McKenzie

With Arthur Miller during previews of *The Price* at the Playhouse Theater, 1979.

Vernel Bagneris in *One Mo' Time!*   *Barbara Y. E. Pyle*

One Mo' Time! Original Cast (l to r) Thais Clark, Orange Kellin, Sylvia "Kuumba" Williams, Vernel Bagneris, and Topsy Chapman, 1979.   *Barbara Y. E. Pyle*

Royal Command Performance. Elizabeth II greeting (l to r) Topsy Chapman, Thais Clark, and Sylvia "Kuumba" Williams, 1981. *Doug McKenzie*

With Art D'Lugoff, the legendary entrepreneur and proprietor of the Village Gate. Art believed that in the second half of the 20th century, Greenwich Village was the cradle of world culture. If that is so, he was a major contributor. *Avital D'Lugoff*

A Life in the Theater team. (l to r) David Mamet, Gerald Gutierrez, Jane Harmon and production assistant Eileen Wilson, 1977.

Tomfoolery, 1981. Tom Lehrer (center) and the production staff. (l to r) Connie Coit and Alice Galloway, Stage Managers, Nancy Nagel Gibbs, Company Manager, me, Milly Schoenbaum, Press Agent, (seated) Mary Kyte and Gary Pearle, Directors.

Carol Rosegg

Little Shop of Horrors creators Howard Ashman and Alan Menken are visited by Roger Corman, who was responsible for the low budget film that spawned the big musical hit, 1982.   *Sam Siegel*

Forever Audrey. Ellen Greene and Howard Ashman.   *Peter Cunningham*

Los Angeles opening, 1983. With David Geffen, Bernard B. Jacobs, and Kyle Renick.
Lee Salem

Los Angeles opening. With (l to r) Milly Schoenbaum, Martin P. Robinson, Alan Menken, Ellen Greene, Howard Ashman, and Paul Mills Holmes.   *Lee Salem*

We had multitudes of celebrities at *Little Shop*, but Michael Jackson was among the most delightful. We asked him for a photo, and he said, "Yes, if you will hide me during intermission."

Howard Ashman   *Kyle Renick*

With Alan Menken at Howard Ashman Memorial, May 6, 1991.

William Lauch

The producers of *The Middle Ages* in the Shubert offices (l to r) Alison H. Clarkson, Joan Stein, Stephen Graham, and (seated) Gerald Schoenfeld, 1983.

Gerry Goodstein

Gary Sinise, brilliant director of the Steppenwolf production of *Orphans* at the Westside Theater, 1985.

With Lucille Lortel, *Orphans* opening night. *Sam Siegel*

As Is was my first Broadway show. So proud to do it with Bernie Jacobs. Here on opening night with Bernie and his beloved wife, Betty. 1985.

Anita and Steve Shevett

Producer John Glines presents first *As Is* tithing checks to Mathilde Krim, Robert Morgan for GMHC, and Rodger MacFarlane for AIDS Resource Center.

Gerry Goodstein

CHAPTER 18

Steppenwolf

David Mamet and Steppenwolf had both emerged from the thriving Chicago theater scene to make an enormous impact on New York—and both had the lively, upstart audacity of the city of Carl Sandburg's great poem. Steppenwolf was an acting ensemble founded in 1974 at precisely the same moment Mamet was founding one of his own—the St. Nicholas Theater Company—whose emphasis was more in the direction of playwrighting.

I had done *A Life in the Theater* with Mamet in 1977. Steppenwolf came to my attention when a man nearly out of his mind with excitement called me from Chicago in the fall of 1980.

He had just seen Lanford Wilson's epic *Balm in Gilead* by a theatre company called Steppenwolf. He was a lawyer who admitted to knowing nothing about producing shows, but he wanted to bring this to Off Broadway, and someone told him to call me. It had a cast of twenty-nine.

For me, this kind of passion is what it's all about, and I told him I would look into it.

I first called my friend Peter Schneider, then the managing director of St. Nicholas, and asked if he had heard of Steppenwolf. "Oh, yes," he said. "They're very serious. Very dedicated."

Steppenwolf had been created by three young local actors—Gary Sinise, Terry Kinney, and Jeff Perry—in a church basement in Highland Park, Illinois. It was named for the Herman Hesse novel because somebody happened to be reading it at the time. They were building an ensemble in which everyone could do everything, and they seemed like my kind of shitkickers.

I worked diligently to come up with a dream budget that had no roots in reality. If the show were doing really well, the actors came perilously close to making a living. Maybe I thought it would somehow open the door for the production to really happen. I sent it off to Steppenwolf for consideration.

And now, a few weeks later, Gary Sinise was standing in front of me in my office in a bandanna. A charismatic figure to be sure, cool and intense, with piercing eyes and a penetrating voice. He looked like a pen and ink by Cocteau. He distinctly remembers wearing a suit, but if it was a suit, it sure looked like a bandanna—and jeans and a shirt—to me.

"I'm sorry, man," he said earnestly. "We talked about this, but the company just can't live on this." Clearly, the project at hand was lost, but we talked for an hour or so and wished each other well. I was knocked out that he had taken the time to respond in person.

Since that first meeting in 1981, Steppenwolf, like Mamet, had become a force to reckon with in the New York theater. First, in 1982 with Sam Shepard's *True West*, which Gary had directed and occasionally acted in and which ran 762 performances at the Cherry Lane, followed by *And a Nightingale Sang*, 1983, directed by Terry Kinney at Lincoln Center, and *Balm in Gilead*, which made it to Circle Rep in 1984, directed by John Malkovich, introducing Laurie Metcalf in an unforgettable twenty-minute monologue. My phone caller had been right. *Balm in Gilead,* more than anything before it, left a permanent imprint of Steppenwolf's galvanizing ensemble style on New York audiences.

Now they approached me about a Lyle Kessler play called *Orphans*, which David Singer, a lawyer, Gary, and Russ Smith, the former Steppenwolf executive director, wanted to produce Off

Broadway under the banner of Wolfgang Productions. They would be joined by Dasha Epstein and Joan Cullman.

Gary was to be the director with ensemble members Terry Kinney, Kevin Anderson, and John Mahoney comprising the cast. Mahoney, a vibrant man approaching middle age, had only recently come to acting from a decade of being the editor of a medical journal. He was to have a spectacular career.

The story, such as it is, concerns two young orphan brothers living in a North Philadelphia slum. The younger (Kevin) lives at home on a steady diet of fast food and TV, more or less imprisoned by the older (Terry), who provides by holding up victims at knifepoint during the day. When they are joined by a mysterious Chicago mobster (Mahoney) who is also an orphan, the three of them experience for a moment what it might have been like to have the families they never had.

Sam Cohn represented Gary, and he and I had a somewhat better time of it than we had on *As Is* because *Orphans* was being done on the assumption that it would be a commercial success. And Sam knew that I shared his belief that his client was a genius.

One of the conditions of my being the general manager was that I take on Russ Smith as the company manager. Russ, who had more than a passing resemblance to Dick Tracy, was, if anything, overqualified for the job and he had the kind of rough-riding spirit that I liked. His presence helped make it a golden time for everyone in the office.

As Is opened May 1, and *Orphans* was to open May 7. On the Saturday between, I was booked to be the sole speaker for Fred Vogel's FEDAPT program at, of all places, the Lyceum. The program was a series of lecture Q&A's for (mostly) young people looking for a future in producing for the theatre. I would be alone on the stage in front of five hundred people from 1:30 to 5:00. When I agreed to the booking, I had no idea I would be carrying with me the stress of opening two shows on either side of it.

I called my nutritionist, Allen Pressman, to ask how I could deal with my nerves. He said that when he was lecturing, taking a couple of L-tryptophan worked for him. I was familiar with it as an enzyme that was also a muscle relaxer, so I took two of them at about 1 o'clock, and everything was fine.

At 3:15, we took a ten-minute break. At 3:45, the L-tryptophan wore off. I was taking the group through the complexities of an Author's Agreement when I looked up and saw five hundred faces leaning forward, hanging on my every word. I started hyperventilating and speeding. After two minutes of that I told Fred I would have to take a break.

"We can't take a break," he said.

"I *have* to take a break," I said and got up and walked backstage. I looked in the bathroom mirror and said, "Pull yourself together. You have no choice. Go out there and finish, and then you never have to do one of these again." That worked. I was able to go until 5:00. And I never did one again.

My *Orphans* opening-night present to Sam Cohn was a fifth of tequila with a worm in it accompanied by a note that said, "Please note the tiny agent in the bottom of the bottle." While Lucille Lortel and I chatted in the lobby, a photographer came by and said, "I want a picture of the king and queen."

"Who's the king, dear?" asked Lucille.

In the *Times*, Frank Rich was rhapsodic about the evening, calling the Steppenwolf style "a sizzling, idiosyncratic performance style as brawny, all-American, and blunt as the windy city that spawned it" and the three actors "riveting as they rip themselves apart with a raw ferocity that is Steppenwolf's theatrical answer to the esthetics of rock and roll." He regarded Kessler's play as "a taut trampoline for its levitating performers."[3]

Orphans was a pure Off Broadway experience, and audiences flocked to see it. Albert Finney fell in love with it and said, "I have to do it in London." On June 2, Steppenwolf was presented with a special Tony Award for Regional Theater Excellence.

Albert Finney wanted Terry and Kevin to do the show with him in London, so we rehearsed it in New York at Circle in the Square on Bleecker Street. Finney and I became pals, and, after the final rehearsal, I decided to throw a party in my apartment, which was only two blocks away.

It was a blowout, and John Mahoney, John Guare, Bernie Gersten, Gregory Mosher, and Jerry Zaks joined us on the eve of what was to be their triumphant Lincoln Center revival of *The House of Blue Leaves*, with Mahoney as its star.

By 2:00 a.m., the only people left were Albert Finney and me. And a half bottle of red wine. But no clean glasses. That didn't stop us. "Pour it in me bloody hands, Albert," Finney said. We finished the bottle pouring it into each other's hands and slapping it into our mouths. "I want to help pay for the party," Finney said, and endorsed his rehearsal paycheck for $287 over to me.

Alan Pakula made a film of *Orphans* starring Finney, Kevin Anderson, and Matthew Modine. It was one of those rare instances when the movie grossed less than the play, which had made it into the hit category and was the beginning of Steppenwolf's meaningful stretching of all of my theater muscles.

CHAPTER 19

Sam Shepard Returns

After the consecutive failures of *Zabriskie Point, Operation Sidewinder*, and my *Unseen Hand* and *Forensic* double bill in 1970, Sam Shepard and his bride O-lan Johnson took their newborn son, Jesse Mojo, and went into hibernation in Nova Scotia, Canada.

The years that followed, which they divided between London, New York, and the farm in Nova Scotia, were chaotic and fraught with marital difficulties. There was his long and public affair with Patti Smith, who was at that time a Theatre Genesis poet. She had wanted Sam to become a rock star, but when it didn't happen, she seized upon the dream and became one herself. When the romance was over, he and Smith remained the closest of friends, and Sam returned to his family.

Looking for a fresh start, Sam and O-lan relocated with their son to the Bay Area in San Francisco, where Sam became playwright in residence at the Magic Theatre. Safely outside the purview of the New York critics, he produced some of his best work, including *Curse of the Starving Class, Buried Child*, and *True West*.

In 1978, he landed an important acting role in Terrence Malick's poetic masterpiece *Days of Heaven* that immediately established him as a significant actor in films. Other film roles followed, and in

1983, he reached full star status with an Academy Award nomination as Chuck Yeager in *The Right Stuff*.

Sam began a romance with the film star Jessica Lange in 1982, and in 1984, he and O-lan were divorced.

Lewis Allen and Stephen Graham called me in the early fall of '85 to say that they were going to produce *A Lie of the Mind*, a full-length Shepard masterwork, which dealt with the lives of two families in the "gritty West." The producers had raised with Sam the possibility of directing it himself, and he had responded that, to do so, he would require certain things. "I would need Albert to be the general manager," he said. Obviously, I was blown away to be remembered and immediately said yes.

With all the heat around Sam, we were able to assemble a dazzling cast: James Gammon, Harvey Keitel, Geraldine Page, Will Patton, Amanda Plummer, Aiden Quinn, Ann Wedgeworth, and Rebecca De Mornay. With all this prestige, the Promenade Theatre was essential. I didn't even have to pick up the phone. Ben Sprecher called me.

As Sam's New York arrival date drew ever closer, I had to deal with the fact that, although I loved Sam, I was in awe of him, and he intimidated me. He was hip. He seemed to be in on something that I wasn't and never would be. It was unsettling.

I had a series of dreams that helped work out my fears. As the dreams progressed, each became less threatening. One of the most fearful involved the first day of rehearsal. A burned-out light bulb hung from a fixture on the high ceiling of the rehearsal studio, and Sam pointed to it and stopped everything until I had replaced it. The cast looked on in horror as I climbed toward it on a rickety stepladder. The last dream was the least fearful and even a little funny. I was driving though Las Vegas and saw a big hotel marquee that read "SAM."

I arranged for Sam and Jessica to stay in Jack Garfein's luxury apartment in the building adjoining the Harkness Theater, which was within walking distance of the Promenade. They drove to New York from their home in Albuquerque and, as instructed, the garage attendant called me when they had arrived safely, at 3:00 a.m.

Two days later, we had our first production meeting with Sam, Lewis Allen, Stephen Graham, and me. Sam directed everything to me, ignoring the two producers. *This is not good*, I thought. My producers were both fine gentlemen, but protocol was protocol.

After our meeting, I took Sam to look at the rehearsal studio. He liked the space, but as we were leaving, he looked up. "There's a bulb out, Al." "There's a bulb out," I told the man at the front desk. "We'll take care of it right away," he said.

Lewis and Stephen joined us for lunch at the Gaiety Delicatessen near my office in the Theatre Guild building. Sam had the roast beef and complained to the waitress. "This roast beef is tired." "You're tired," she shot back. "Yes, actually, I am," he agreed. When I saw her the next day I asked, "Do you know who that was?" "Yeah," she sneered, "Sam Shepard. What do I care?"

After the production meeting, the dynamic changed. The producers claimed their rightful place with Sam, and my relationship with him was compartmentalized. The first indication was the handling of the cast read-through of the play on the first day of rehearsal. I began to get the feeling that I wasn't to be included and finally asked Lewis Allen. He responded that I was not and followed with, "Sam is afraid it will get to be a crowd."

I came to the beginning of rehearsal for the meet-and-greet and found we were missing Amanda Plummer. Geraldine Page beckoned to me. She peered up from under her upside-down sailor cap. "Amanda is frightened," she suggested. "You must go to her apartment and fetch her."

I hopped in a cab and went to Amanda Plummer's apartment in Soho. She was up, fully awake, and in good spirits. She had a dental appointment that morning and had simply fallen asleep. We made friends in the cab ride uptown, and, as the reading began, I slipped out.

Marion Finkler, who had been Jack Schlissel's assistant, was my company manager. She was my equal in every way. I told her the only thing we had to do was make sure Sam got everything he wanted. While we were doing the show together, Marion computerized my office. Through the quirk of fate of her being there, we became one of the first offices to go on computer. It revolutionized the way we did everything. Agreements and budgets that used to take weeks could be done in hours.

At the beginning of the second week of rehearsal, Sam called to tell me he wanted a group called the Red Clay Ramblers to compose and play live music for the play. They were somewhere in North Carolina. He wanted them at rehearsal the next day.

At my first budget meeting with the producers, I had a line item labeled "Music" and the figure next to it reflected live musicians. Lewis Allen pointed out that there was no music in the show. "Wait," I had insisted. And we left it in. I told Sam. He laughed and said, "You know me, Al."

The Red Clay Ramblers were at the Promenade the next day at 2 o'clock. They were a group of five who started in 1972 as a traditional string band and evolved a very eclectic musical style with a touch of theater in the mix. They watched rehearsals every day and composed the score on the spot.

Sam, who continued to view the press as hostile and intrusive, agreed to do only three major interviews: *Newsweek*, the *Times*, and the *Village Voice*. The *Newsweek* interview, granted on Sam's condition that it would not be a cover story, was extensive and conducted by its theater critic, Jack Kroll. On the Friday before it hit the stands, Sam got wind that he was to be on the cover and went ballistic. He called Jack Kroll and told him he was coming over to bust him up and break all the furniture in his office.

Kroll called his friend Lewis Allen in tears. "I'm so upset I'm going to pull the story," he said. Allen laughed it off, knowing that pulling a story on Friday for a Monday issue of *Newsweek* wasn't really rooted in reality.

Sam called me at home that Monday night. "Guess what I'm doing?" I said. "I'm looking at you in shades on the cover of *Newsweek* and talking to you at the same time."

"Yeah, I'm doing the same thing," he said, sounding much more relaxed about it.

Rebecca De Mornay, originally cast as Sally, had begun to make a name for herself in movies, notably in *Risky Business*, but had no stage chops. Sam needed me to fire her. The role became a break for Karen Young, a downtown actress who went on to have an extensive career in film and television.

When Sam had told me he wanted Harvey Keitel, I started to tell him that Harvey was difficult. They had a history together, and he interrupted me to say, "I will take care of Harvey." "Oh, really," I marveled. "From your front porch in Albuquerque?"

A few days into rehearsal, Sam told Harvey he wanted him to do a Western accent. "A Western accent?" Harvey asked.

"Yeah."

Keitel laughed and avowed, "If you wanted a Western accent, why'd you hire a New York Jew?"

Harvey became a father during the run and was overjoyed, as were all of us for him. As a consequence, he missed a fair number of performances during the six-month run. Two little old ladies who bought tickets to see him saw the understudy sign on the way into the performance. "Every time I buy tickets to see Harvey Keitel in a show, he isn't in it," one of them exclaimed.

I negotiated Sam's author and director agreements with Steve Mark, a skillful lawyer engaged by his new agent, Lois Berman. Sam's former agent, Toby Cole, had seemed like a perfect fit for Sam. Toby had long since retired, and I couldn't connect Lois Berman with him at all. She was smart enough but seemed like someone you would encounter at bridge club.

When, after a long negotiation, signature copies of the agreements were finally ready, I called Berman to tell her they would be delivered to her.

"Would you mind taking them to Sam yourself?" she asked. "To be honest, I'm scared of him," Berman confessed. "We never see each other, and our conversations are very quick. Usually he calls me from pay phones at gas stations."

So I gave the agreements to Sam on a break during rehearsal and told him to take his time and look them over. He asked for a pen and signed them.

"Don't you want to look at them?" I asked. "I trust you, Al."

The dean of all paparazzi, "Doc" Simon, was at every preview and placed about seven celebrity shots in the *Post*. The columns and magazines ran items. Jessica Lange had a baby with Mikhail Baryshnikov, and my favorite item was in *Time* magazine: "At intermission of *A Lie of the Mind*, the Baryshnikov baby played unattended on the Promenade stairway while Geraldine Page was refused an orange drink by the concession because she was twenty-five cents short." I told Ben Sprecher that his business acumen had now attained national prominence.

Ben and I were, at that point, practically best friends. Hits bring people together, and Ben and I were completely caught up in the energy of the production and having frequent dinners and phone conversations. The day the box office opened, it had taken in $27,000, the record for Off Broadway at that time.

Robert Woodruff is, in my estimation, the best director of Shepard, and Sam asked to bring him in to work with the cast for two weeks during previews. Sam's direction was solid, but it lacked the peaks and valleys that Woodruff, who had directed the Pulitzer Prize-winning *Buried Child*, was able to bring.

The audience response during previews was disconcerting. The show was in three acts and was four hours long. The audiences arrived wanting the show but became restless as it progressed. There were a number of walkouts and we began to wonder if we had *The Emperor's New Clothes* on our hands. Our spirits were buoyed on the day of the opening, however, when someone from the *Times* told our press agent David Powers, "I hope your box office is ready for what's going to happen tomorrow when the review comes out."

I made a prediction to my staff. "Tonight there will be fisticuffs thrown at the opening-night party. If the reviews are bad, it will happen inside the party. If the reviews are good, it will happen outside. And the thrower of the fisticuffs will be Sam Shepard."

The party was upstairs at Sardi's, and Sam was off in a corner with his own small group that included Danny de Vito and others. When the *Times* review came in, I went over to Sam, who was by this point well-oiled. Remembering our last opening night together, I asked, "Well, how do you feel?"

"I'm ecstatic, Al," he said mockingly, and I knew we were on our way to the dark side.

Later, as he left the party, "Doc" Simon snapped a picture of Sam, who responded by punching him in the face, breaking his glasses, and punching him in the stomach, rupturing a blood vessel. The following day, as lines were forming around the block at the Promenade, Simon, who had been invaluable to us, issued a warrant for Sam's arrest.

In the meantime, if the audience wasn't yet ready for Shepard, the critics were. Wall-to-wall superlatives, with Frank Rich of the *Times* leading the pack. "'A Lie of the Mind' is the unmistakable expression of a major writer nearing the height of his powers," Rich wrote in a review of stature that placed Sam and his play in the context of great American literature. The box office take that day was $37,000, another Off Broadway record.

A Lie of the Mind went on to capture the same triple-crown as *Little Shop of Horrors*: The New York Drama Critics Circle, Drama Desk, and Outer Critics Circle Awards for Best Play. I called Flora Roberts, whose clients had collected these awards for decades, and told her I now had a sample of her wallpaper.

The audience response was a different matter. There were many walkouts, and advance sales had begun to drop. People in the apartments across the street from the Promenade had a new hobby. During the intermissions they looked out their windows to count the number of walkouts.

We had an emergency advertising meeting to develop a counter strategy and decided there was none and that it would be a waste of money. Nancy Coyne had an interesting idea for a TV spot: a voiceover as a camera followed a lanky, young man in a cowboy hat and boots walking toward the long line in front of the Promenade Theater. We chose instead to do a regular "maintenance" campaign, keeping up the appearance of a hit. It was the right choice, and by the end of the run, the show had paid back its investment.

In March, Geraldine Page took a two-day leave to attend the Academy Awards. She was nominated as Best Actress for her role in *A Trip to Bountiful* and was actually in competition with Jessica Lange, who was nominated for *Sweet Dreams*, the story of Patsy Cline, co-starring our own Ann Wedgeworth. When Page won and returned to us one day later, it just seemed like part of the magic synchronicity that surrounded the production.

In April, Sam called to tell me he was coming in to be inducted into the Theater Hall of Fame. "You better dress up like Sam Beckett," I advised. "There's a warrant out for your arrest."

"What?"

"For beating up 'Doc' Simon after the opening night party."

"To tell you the truth, I don't even remember it."

On June 2, the day after our closing, The Red Clay Ramblers went into a studio and recorded *The Music of Sam Shepard's A Lie of the Mind* for Sugar Hill Records. It was all original music written and performed by the Ramblers: Tommy Thompson, Jim Watson, Mike Craver, Jack Herrick, and Clay Buckner, except for the closing piece. That was a plaintive Stephen Foster parlor song called "Hard Times Come Again No More," performed hauntingly by "The Hard Times Chorus"—which was actually our star-spangled cast performing under the radar.

CHAPTER 20

Mike Nichols Has a Flop

*A*t Christmastime in 1984, Jeremy Irons and his wife Sinead Cusack threw a party in their Riverside Drive apartment for the Royal Shakespeare Company, then in New York performing *Much Ado About Nothing* in rep with *Cyrano de Bergerac* at the Gershwin Theatre.

The evening's centerpiece was a small *divertissement* called *Standup Shakespeare*, created and performed by Ray Leslee and Kenneth Welsh, which, in an atmosphere of good food and drink energized by the holiday season and the presence of the celebrated guests, was a delight to one and all.

It caught the imagination of one of the most illustrious guests of the evening, Mike Nichols, who saw potential for something more. With a slew of directing credits that included *Who's Afraid of Virginia Woolf?*, *Carnal Knowledge*, an Academy Award for *The Graduate* and Tonys for the Broadway productions of *Barefoot in the Park* and *The Real Thing*, among many others, Nichols was at the very top of the pantheon of all-time greats. After the holiday soiree, Nichols began two years of developmental workshop sessions with Leslee, who composed the music, and Welsh, who wrote the book. Nichols felt that *Standup* might make Shakespeare accessible to a new audience.

Early in 1987, his agent Sam Cohn brought the project to Jerry Schoenfeld with an eye to a Shubert-backed Off Broadway production. Jerry called me to see if I would be the general manager. Naturally, when he said "Mike Nichols," I readily agreed.

The first thing I did was chase down video of the project that I looked at after hours in my office. Not only did I not like it, I felt it was a project for which there was no audience. It was Shakespeare in a cabaret style, and I felt that Shakespeare and cabaret were disparate audiences. Leslee's songs were tuneful, but Kenneth Welsh's book was pun heavy and required some advance knowledge of Shakespeare, which I did not have. I called Jerry and Bernie, who were still in, and rushed over to their offices.

"Why are we doing this?" I asked.

"Because it's Mike Nichols," Jerry responded.

"Is it good to have a flop with Mike Nichols?"

"I agree with Albert," Bernie said. Nonetheless, we went ahead with it, and I stayed on because I, too, was eager to work with Mr. Nichols.

I was nervous as Jerry and I cabbed through Central Park for our first meeting with Nichols. I needn't have been. We sat down, and the conversation began with the two men discussing, at some length, their respective nervous breakdowns. I thought, *This must be a way of expressing mutual trust.*

The Nichols wit was on display and seemed to be fundamental to his attitude toward everything. Wit is, for me, an invitation, and I relaxed and was drawn to him.

He expressed a preference for Michael Bennett's Theatre 890 as a home for the production. He had just seen the opening night of Lanford Wilson's *Burn This* there, and it and John Malkovich's performance were fresh in his mind. Theatre 890, on Broadway at Nineteenth Street, was a beautifully designed 299-seat Off Broadway house with a Broadway-sized stage. Michael Bennett intended it as a tryout space for promising works that would allow them to move to a Broadway house, as *Burn This* was about to do, without major changes in direction, scenery, and lighting designs.

Now that Shubert interest was established, we sat in Bernie's office with Jerry and Sam Cohn. As usual, Sam wanted everything. After an hour, Bernie, who didn't care for Sam, departed and left the balance of the negotiation to Jerry and me. Later, when Bernie reviewed the deal, he thought Nichols's royalty for touring productions was half a point too high.

Touring productions? I thought.

The agreement was put in practice but never signed by either party. I was to learn that having one unresolved point was a tradition in Jacobs-Cohn agreements, even signed ones.

Whenever Nichols called me, he began the conversation with "Al . . . Baby . . ." which I thought must be a reference to a character, possibly an agent, in an old Nichols and May routine.

We hit our first bump when *Standup Shakespeare* was announced in the second paragraph of the Friday *Times* Onstage, and Off column. Nichols called me. He was furious. "I have *never*, I repeat *never*, had the second paragraph. If Bill Evans had been our press agent, we wouldn't be having this conversation because it never would have happened. I want him on the show. He's done every one of my shows. I want him hired today."

I defended Milly Schoenbaum, who had been my suggestion with the Shubert blessing.

But Nichols was immovable. I called Bernie and told him Nichols wanted to fire Milly. "Can we call him and try to save her job?" I asked.

"Absolutely," Bernie said.

So, we made the call, and it was to no avail. But I did get a call back from Nichols. "You and Bernie Jacobs have just wasted eleven minutes of my life," he said. "Eleven minutes I will never have again. Now, get me Bill Evans."

We did, and Bill Evans, a well-established first-class Broadway press agent, was also a fine gentleman who became a lifelong friend.

At some point during the second week, Nichols called. He was concerned. "The better I make this, the worse it gets," he said, confirming my thought that *Standup Shakespeare* had peaked as a party piece. If you took it beyond that, you risked losing what charm it had.

Preview business was slow and the audience response lackluster. There was a meeting with Nichols, Jerry, Bernie, and me to discuss whether to pull the plug or allow the show to open for critics.

Nichols landed on the side of letting it open because he felt the creators were owed reviews for their efforts. We posted closing notice five days prior to opening, which gave the authors their reviews and allowed us to close the following day.

We opened on a Saturday night. My phone rang at 10:00 a.m. that morning. It was Mr. Schoenfeld. "Albert," he said, "you've hated this show from the beginning, Albert."

"Will I see you tonight?"

"No, I can't be there."

"Uh huh."

On Monday the reviews came out, and Gussow of the *Times* was enthused over Ray Leslee's musical contribution: "In Mr. Leslee's talented hands, Shakespeare has soul," but not in the book by Kenneth Welsh, about which he wrote, "the dialogue is troublesome" and "often too whimsical for words." The overall reviews, while affording occasional quotes, were not supportive enough to turn the tide, and we remained closed.

Standup Shakespeare was the final theatrical production to play Theatre 890. Michael Bennett died weeks later, on July 2, 1987.

CHAPTER 21

Steel Magnolia

At the end of March, *Steel Magnolias* opened at the WPA Theater to a scattering of mixed notices. Mel Gussow limited his praise in the *Times* to the stage setting by Edward Gianfrancesco. The audience, however, was loving the play. My friend Kyle Renick, head of the WPA and the originating producer of *Little Shop of Horrors*, asked if I would come and have a look.

I found every reason in the world to do the show. First of all, I loved it. It had everything. Humor, heart, and a story that was genuinely touching. The playwright Robert Harling, a young Southern gentleman from Natchitoches, Louisiana, was moved to write it by the passing of his sister from complications of type 1 diabetes and childbirth. The serious theme was juxtaposed with the setting of a chatty, Southern beauty parlor.

I was sure that if we could stick around long enough for word of mouth to kick in, the show would be a popular hit well beyond the "theater audience." And, with an all-female cast, it was a woman's show. Women are the decision-makers when it comes to buying theater tickets, and many stock and amateur companies are run by women looking for roles for themselves. There was also the likely possibility of a film sale.

I invited three or four people to performances at the WPA, each of whom was capable of raising the money and providing a proper production. None was interested, names upon request. I thought I was bad luck as a producer, but good luck as a manager, and so I turned to Kyle.

"You are currently the producer of one of the biggest hits in Off Broadway history," I told him. "You produce it. I know you can raise the money."

Kyle was slightly daunted, but I had enough confidence in him and the project for both of us. He began raising the money, and each time he met with success, he called me. The calls became more frequent until all of the funding was finally in place. My budget anticipated that we would initially have substantial weekly operating losses.

Steel Magnolias was clearly an ensemble piece, but the key role was Shelby, based on Robert's sister Susan, played at the WPA by Jack Garfein's daughter, the very talented Blanche Baker. Sadly, her agent demanded above-the-title solo billing that was inconsistent with our ensemble vision and, we thought, insulting to the other actors. We had to pass and moved on to Betsy Aidem, who was wonderful in the role.

We booked the prestigious Lucille Lortel and, once again, I was in a Sprecher-operated theater. We uninstalled the turntable that I had installed twenty years earlier for *Now Is the Time for All Good Men*, thus lowering the stage thirteen inches and improving the audience's proximity to the performance. It was important that they feel like they were in the beauty parlor rather than looking up at it.

Pamela Berlin, who had directed the play splendidly at the WPA, tightened things up and made it even better for the Lortel—the most productive use of throwing a show back into rehearsal for a commercial transfer that I had seen.

As performances got underway, Kyle and I carefully monitored the audience response.

Every audience in the sometimes half-full theater told us we were a hit. Seeing the small houses, Robert Harling fearfully approached me several times on the sidewalk in front of the theater. "You're not going to close it, are you?"

I assured him we were not.

Two things happened that majorly improved our fortunes. Still being of a fan club mentality, I decided that the fan club for *Steel Magnolias* would be the mom-and-pop beauty parlors in the metropolitan area. What do people do in beauty parlors while nature is being aided and abetted? They talk. As a result of mailings and phone calls, we filled three performances with shop owners and their employees, and Jeffrey Richards, our well-known press agent, promoted free beauty products to give as premiums. After each performance, there was a discussion with the author and the cast. The audiences felt well cared for, and they were mad for the show. Our advance sale shot up dramatically.

About a week later, Bret Adams, Harling's agent, received a call after hours from someone claiming to be Bette Davis. Adams listened incredulously for a few moments and decided, well, we are in show business—maybe this is Bette Davis.

It was. She had called to tell him that someone had sent her a script of *Steel Magnolias*, and she thought it was the best thing she had read in years. Not only did she want to come and see it, she was going to convince Elizabeth Taylor and Katharine Hepburn to join her in making it into a film.

In the next three days, she gave press interviews to the *Wall Street Journal* and the *Associated Press* and went on *The Today Show* touting *Steel Magnolias* in the way she had to Bret. Again, the box office shot up dramatically, and a few performances sold out. After eleven weeks of operating losses, we had our first profitable week. And two weeks later, our first sellout week. It would stay that way for more than two years.

Miss Davis arrived in a limousine and was, as we had expected, in a bad mood. The first thing I saw was a bone-thin ankle jutting out from the car door, and then Miss Davis herself, post-stroke Bette Davis, who did her best to seem put upon by the one photographer who had shown up. "Oh, I should have known," she carped.

Our elderly treasurer, an admirer for many years, came out to the sidewalk to greet her.

She glared at him and made a face. It was as funny as it was unpleasant. By the end of the performance, word was out all over the Village, and there were police blockades with several hundred people behind them.

The house manager went to her. "Miss Davis, I'm going to take you out the side entrance. There are hundreds of people waiting to see you on Christopher Street."

"Oh, good," she said. "I'll sing 'I've Written a Letter to Daddy.'"

With success, we noted a change in Robert Harling. He dumped Bret Adams as his agent and went to John Breglio, one of the best, and certainly the most high-powered lawyer in the theater. Robert was spending a lot time with Breglio and also sought out Fred Nathan, who was at the peak of his powers as press agent of all the Mackintosh and Shubert shows.

Other producers approached Harling for the touring rights. We had determined that we weren't going to do the tour ourselves but would let Robert license the rights and retain our contractual financial participation as the original producers. John Breglio negotiated with me on behalf of the touring producers.

The *Little Shop* touring producers had voluntarily given me production and weekly fees. Because I felt I had been a major contributor to *Steel Magnolias*, not to mention the fact that it was even done, I asked for more than I was given on *Little Shop*. Breglio didn't seem to think I was entitled to anything. I became hurt and angry, and called Robert Harling to tell him so. I also canceled a party I had planned to give for the company. At the time, Harling seemed sad to hear these things, but his feelings were soon to harden.

These events were a body blow to my ego, and my drinking accelerated and became depressive. Increasingly alarmed that I was about to go out of control, I had to take decisive action. I reserved a bed at a rehab facility in Pennsylvania and made a commitment for twenty-eight days. The only person who knew was the show's company manager, Peter Bogyo, who told people, at my request, that I was on vacation.

Rehab came just in time, and I was ripe to receive it. Thanks in large measure to my group therapist Steve Fecho, I emerged entirely ready to devote myself to the program of recovery, which continues to enrich my life as I write this, thirty years later.

I got a recovery sponsor and, because parties are such an integral part of show business, I always took him with me. At a *Steel Magnolias* party a few weeks after I got back, Kyle's assistant at the WPA ran over to us to say Robert Harling had been bad-mouthing Kyle and me and even questioning our honesty and integrity. Attacks on my honesty take me right to the red zone, and ordinarily this would have been a perfect excuse to go right to the bar and fuel up for a tirade. But in this new life, I simply grabbed my sponsor and said, "Let's get out of here."

Days later, we received a letter from John Breglio, on behalf of his client, requesting an audit of our books. Our attorney, Elliot Brown, immediately fired back a letter welcoming such an audit and recommending "the sooner the better." We advised that if they wished to use the show's accounting firm, Rosenberg, Neuwirth, and Kuchner, the cost to Harling would be $7,500. That was the last we heard of the matter.

Making conversation one day when they happened to be at the theater at the same time, Kyle casually asked Harling if he was working on any new plays. "Yes," he answered. "*Pigs from Hell*. It's about Off Broadway producers."

In sobriety, I recognized that my financial demands on the *Magnolias* tour had been excessive. I wrote Harling a letter apologizing for my overreaching, which was my only wrongdoing. There was no response, and the estrangement remained permanent.

In the meantime, Elizabeth Taylor came to the show with five young men in attendance. There is a line in the play about her, spoken by Margo Martindale as Truvy. "When it comes to pain and suffering, she's right up there with Elizabeth Taylor."

Curious to see how Taylor would react, I stood in the back of the small theater. When Margo delivered the line, the heads of all five young men swiveled in her direction awaiting her response. She threw her head back and roared, and the young men then joined in with her.

Ray Stark put together a deal to acquire the film rights. His representative called me in June of 1989. "The money and Dolly Parton have just come together, and we have to do the film now."

I told him making the film now was fine, but our agreement with Harling called for a restriction on any showing of the film worldwide for three years following the date of our official opening (which would be June 20, 1990) or the date of the closing, whichever would first occur.

Shooting began that summer with Sally Field, Shirley MacLaine, Olympia Dukakis, Daryl Hannah, and Julia Roberts joining Dolly Parton. Robert Harling wrote the screenplay. At that same moment, *Steel Magnolias* became the most-produced play in stock and amateur theaters, a position it held for several years.

In the fall, I had another call from Ray Stark's representative. "We are going to need to exhibit the film in December to qualify for next year's Academy Awards."

"That's just not possible," I responded. "We have to protect the New York production. And a film release will kill it."

There was a series of phone calls that happened to coincide with indications the show in New York was slowing down. By late October it looked like we would be fortunate to get past the first of the year, and I began bargaining with the representative.

"We'll give you what you want," I proposed, "in return for a one-time payment of $500,000."

"I'll take that to Ray Stark," he replied. He called me back within an hour, which, no matter what he had to say, was an indication of interest. "Ray is unhappy. He's going to call you." Clearly a scare tactic.

"That's fine, but he will be wasting his time. We're sticking to our position. So, again, tell him to call, but let him know it's a complete waste of his time."

Two hours went by, and the man called again. "Will you accept $400,000?"

"Yes," I said without hesitation, knowing that the closing of the show was imminent. So, we got $400,000, which, pursuant to the Author's Agreement, was distributed as 60 percent to Harling and 40 percent to the production.

We had been sending out monthly profit distributions of $50,000 to the investors for about two-and-a-half years. They had become accustomed to them, and when our business dropped, the investors called to say, "I didn't get this month's distribution." "That's because there *weren't none*," I said.

Steel Magnolias closed on February 25, 1990 after 1,126 performances.

Although the estrangement from Harling and his treatment of us were unhappy making, Kyle and I still experienced a great deal of joy from *Steel Magnolias*. I loved the play, and I thought the decision to do it, and our decision process during the run, were superb. That was enough.

Years later Robert Harling was on a panel with my dear friend Vernel Bagneris. During the discussion, Harling spoke badly of me. Vernel approached him afterward. "You know," Vernel said, "Albert Poland is a very good friend of mine."

"How unfortunate," Harling answered.

Steel Magnolias was given a revival on Broadway in 2005 which ran for 159 performances.

CHAPTER 22

What's the Worst That Could Happen?

Please listen to me when I tell you to never, ever be the first show to play a brand-new theater. The Criterion Center, formerly the famed Criterion movie palace on Broadway at Forty-Fourth Street, was converted into two handsome small-scale legit theatres in 1989 by B.S. Moss Enterprises, which had owned the property for decades and were experienced entrepreneurs in Broadway real estate.

My friend Steve Warnick, who had produced *Tomfoolery* and *Little Shop* successfully at the Charles Playhouse in Boston, had relocated to New York and brought to my attention a small musical called *Starmites* that was playing at the American Stage Festival in Milford, New Hampshire. It was a space-age comic strip that was the brainchild of Barry Keating, who wrote the music and lyrics, with an assist from Stuart Ross who co-authored the book.

I thought it could really cook in the 399-seat Minetta Lane down in the Village and took it to Bernie Jacobs. We went to New Hampshire together, and he agreed to come in for a third of the $750,000 capitalization. However, as I began nailing down the weekly operating costs, it was clear that 399 seats were not going to be enough to make the show economically viable.

When the *Times* broke the story about the conversion of the Criterion, I thought its new 499-seat theatre might be the solution. I hadn't been to the Criterion since my friends and I gawked at the 1960 gala premiere of *Pepe*, the international film starring Cantinflas and a host of Hollywood stars in cameos. Judy Garland sang in it but didn't appear, and every time we saw an empty limo pull up, I said, "Oh, look. It's the Voice of Judy Garland."

The theatre, called Stage Right, which had a three-quarter stage surrounded by a raked configuration of 499 seats, was spectacular. And the numbers would now work. People were vying for the space, and I told Bernie that we needed his clout to get it. I asked if we could meet with Charley Moss in his office. He agreed, and it worked. When Moss left, we had the theatre.

The budget was now $1,250,000 to address the costs of the new theatre and the Broadway location. I was able to negotiate a fair contract with Actors' Equity and for the musicians with John Glasel, the head of local 802, American Federation of Musicians. Bernie called and asked that Steve Warnick and I come to see him.

Bernie and Robert Wankel, then Shubert Vice-President, Finance, were present. Bernie began by saying that he thought *Starmites* was worth $750,000 but not $1,250,000. He then added, "But I don't want to say 'no' to you, Albert."

It took me a few minutes to realize he wanted me to let him out of the show. I took Steve into the next room and told him that was now what we must do. Bernie remained an ally, but it was a body blow to the production.

Our contract with Moss required that we rehearse in the theatre, which was still under construction. All around us were the noises of hammers and saws and machines. There were at least five days when the fire alarm went off for the entire day. We were told that the fire department was conducting tests and nothing could be done.

The theatre manager stayed in his office with his cat. His answer to every question was the same. A withered and withering "I don't know." It was like being in an orphanage with a passive-aggressive headmaster.

The theatre had a "deluge curtain" as the Minetta Lane had when it had first opened. Deluge curtains are disasters waiting to happen. The curtain covers the entire stage and orchestra pit area and theoretically releases tons of water when there is a fire. Twice, our curtain was released, and no fire had been required. Thousands of dollars of musical instruments and set pieces were destroyed. Only through the superb efforts of Jolyon Stern, our insurance broker, were we able to collect both times.

I sat down to watch the dress rehearsal with Scott Shukat, who represented Stuart Ross. We had become friends as a result of his representation of Alan Menken on *Little Shop*. I had been raving to him about *Starmites*. The lights came up on the first scene, and a window rig came crashing to the floor. Worse than that, the show was not playing. I think it was a combination of the vastness of the seating area and watching what was clearly an Off Broadway show in the middle of the Broadway theater district. Scott left quietly after the first act.

The reviews were good, not great, with Gussow in the *Times* finding that it had not fulfilled the promise of its past productions. Whatever the reviews, the fact was that, in this new setting, it did not have the impact that won me over in New Hampshire. Nonetheless, it received six Tony nominations, including Best Musical.

The day the nominations were announced, John Glasel of American Federation of Musicians Local 802 called me, raging that he would never have given me the deal we had agreed upon had he known the show was Tony eligible. And a Broadway League representative called to say that there had been a request to count the seats to make sure there were 499. On the Tony telecast, the conductor took the tempo twice as fast as it had been in rehearsal. The cast looked like windup toys.

CHAPTER 23

Trouper

J ane Allison was from Indianapolis but was a singularly New York creature. Vivacious, part phony, part hanger-on, she was plugged into all of the shallow cultural events of the city, realized the ridiculousness of it all, and wrote about it in a column called "Hoosier in Manhattan" in the *Indianapolis News*. She was part of a group of fringe journalists and near-celebrities for whom life was a continuous junket.

We first met when she wrote about *Now Is the Time for All Good Men* and, as I was an active New Yorker transported from Indy, she continued to write about me from time to time. Hers was the kind of life that you dropped in and out of.

At one of Jane's soirees in the summer of 1988, there was someone I had wanted to meet for a long time. Kenneth Elliott, who, with his college friend Charles Busch, had hit shows running on MacDougal Street for the better part of the past three years. With *Vampire Lesbians of Sodom* and *Psycho Beach Party*, written by and starring Charles, and directed, produced, and general managed by Ken, their Theatre in Limbo company had become part of the Off Broadway landscape and was one of the few remaining vestiges of the Off Broadway that I loved.

I made a bee-line for Ken, who, like me, was there because of the Indianapolis connection. He was an effortlessly elegant and gentle man, not at all the frenetic hipster I might have expected. I immediately asked him about the weekly costs for their shows. "Breakeven is about eleven thousand dollars," he answered, unheard of in 1988. Comparable shows would break at twenty to twenty-five thousand dollars.

The low operating costs and the resulting low ticket prices were key to making their shows affordable to the gay subculture that was in large part their audience.

The Busch troupe had a kinship to two other downtown companies that I loved. Charles Ludlam's Ridiculous Theatrical Company and Tom Eyen's Theatre of the Eye. All three had an ongoing troupe of actors, with Eyen and Busch reaching out to the marketplace more than the esoteric Ludlam. The troupe members became audience favorites who gave their followings what they came to expect, time after time. All three companies incorporated movie, cultural, and historical references into their work that were immediately familiar to their savvy gay audiences.

Sparked by my encounter with Ken, and being a longtime Busch aficionado, Kyle Renick suggested that the four of us have dinner together.

Kyle told Charles and Ken he had been thinking of a "Silly Series" for the WPA and asked if they had anything suitable. By chance, they had discovered a forgotten '30s gown in Charles's closet and had been toying with the idea of a Norma Shearer figure trapped by the Nazis. But they worried that it might be too outrageous to take further. For Kyle, it was outrageous enough to be the perfect opener for his new series.

With minor tweaks by Theatre In Limbo's resident designer, B. T. Whitehill, the existing set for the show that had just closed would work perfectly for the new show and satisfy the ever-present need for thrift. As Charles later said, "Kyle had the set, and I had the gown." Ticket prices were low, and as a further enticement to Charles's audience, a late show was added on Saturday nights.

Accustomed to rehearsals in the hectic Limbo Lounge in the East Village, Charles, Ken, and company were elated by the formality of rehearsing *The Lady in Question*, as it was now called, on a real stage in a real theater. The result was the best work the company had done to-date, and we all agreed to put our efforts behind a commercial transfer to be co-produced by Kyle and Ken.

We secured a mid-July booking at the Orpheum. In June, we took a page from John Glines and created a float for the Gay Pride Parade. The crowds cheered as Charles rode by surrounded by young men in lederhosen, with the rest of us running alongside, passing out discount coupons as if our lives depended on it. The day cost us three thousand dollars and generated fifteen thousand in ticket sales.

We were delighted when Lambda, the organization for gay civil rights, called and wanted to buy an entire house for a fundraiser, but "the committee" first had to read the script. The phrase "goose-stepping lezzies" was not to their taste, and they demanded it be cut. Charles refused, with the rest of us backing him up, and we lost the sale.

As we got into previews at the Orpheum, it was clear that, with the addition of a brilliant new set by B. T. Whitehill, the company and its designers had reached a new level of production away from its Off Off Broadway roots and closer to the Off Broadway mainstream of that time. Everyone rose to the occasion, and the critics responded in kind with spectacular raves across the board. In a surprising turnabout from his largely negative take on *Psycho Beach Party*, Frank Rich, in the *Times* ended his superlative review by calling Busch "a star."

As expected, there was a rush at the box office. As always, I monitored the first few performances to see if our audience was in step with the reviews. The first Saturday night we had Sam Cohn, who brought Meryl Streep, and Lester Persky, Madeleine le Roux, and Holly Woodlawn. *This is our audience*, I thought. But there was cause for concern. The response, especially in the first act, was not saying "hit."

It was as if a large part of his core audience had not made the upward transition with Charles and his company. With all of the universal acclaim and higher ticket prices, perhaps he no longer belonged to them in quite the same way. After about six weeks, business began to soften.

No longer scotch tape, paper clips, and glue, commercial Off Broadway had become spreadsheets and marketing. Advertising and theater costs had increased drastically. Our breakeven was in the $30,000 range. Even for Theatre In Limbo, a break-even of $11,000 was no longer possible. Higher ticket prices were a given. It was the theater's part of the Reagan Revolution, and it seemed to happen overnight. Even more daunting was the thought that a significant number of Charles's audience may have been lost to AIDS.

I wanted to try a TV commercial. Tommy Schlamme had moved on to a producing and directing career in film and television that led him to three Emmy Awards and included the enormously successful series *The West Wing*. For *Steel Magnolias*, I had found another man of enormous talent who was just starting out as Tommy had been. His name was Paris Barclay, and he produced some brilliant 1930s film noir spots for *The Lady in Question*. He, too, went on to Emmy Awards and a distinguished career. If sometime someone asked, "What kind of a general manager was Albert?" and the response was, "Well, Tommy Schlamme and Paris Barclay did his television commercials," I would be perfectly happy.

The Lady in Question closed at the Orpheum on December 3, 1989, after 165 performances. Charles remarked to me, "It looks like I can only count on a six-to-eight-week run from now on."

And for a brief time, that was the case. But Charles Busch is a talented and resourceful man. He would seek out and find a larger audience.

CHAPTER 24

The Grapes of Wrath

"The production at the Cort (is) an epic achievement for the director, Frank Galati, and the Chicago theater ensemble at his disposal . . . pure theater as executed by a company and director that could not be more temperamentally suited to their task. As Steppenwolf demonstrated in *True West*, *Orphans*, and *Balm in Gilead*—all titles that could serve for *The Grapes of Wrath*—it is an ensemble that believes in what Steinbeck does: the power of brawny, visceral art, the importance of community, the existence of an indigenous American spirit that resides in inarticulate ordinary people, the spiritual resonance of American music, and the heroism of the righteous outlaw."[4]

With his eloquent *Times* review, Frank Rich confirmed what Stephen Eich had known—that a Broadway production of *The Grapes of Wrath* would establish the Steppenwolf Ensemble as a major force in the American theater.

Eich was the dynamic thirty-four-year-old managing director of Steppenwolf, and, for the prior two years, he had been putting his considerable efforts and abilities behind two massive projects: getting *The Grapes of Wrath* to Broadway, and undertaking a fund drive to raise the capital to break ground for a brand new 515-seat theater for Steppenwolf in Chicago.

Eich and his wife, Rondi Reed, had joined the company in 1979, she as an actress and he sitting at a desk next to Russ Smith, then the executive director. Eich became the managing director in 1983, a year after Smith's departure. Randall Arney succeeded Gary Sinise as artistic director in 1987, when Sinise left the post to pursue a career in New York. Their styles complemented each other perfectly: Eich filled with outsized ideas, high energy, and drive; Arney smooth, ingratiating, and laid back. As Frank Galati put it, "Steve does the heavy lifting, and Randy does the goo."

When Eich first spoke to me about *The Grapes of Wrath* as a Broadway prospect, I thought it was undoable. A cast of forty-one? "You'll get rave reviews, and it won't make a dime," I declared. And who would be willing to risk the fortune it would take to do it?

At that point, it was still early in the game. Frank Galati, the associate artistic director of the Goodman Theatre, another Chicago company of national consequence, had just come to Gary Sinise proposing to write and direct an adaptation of *The Grapes of Wrath* as a co-production by Steppenwolf and Goodman. Eich and Sinise immediately recognized how indigenous it was to the Steppenwolf style and wanted it to be Steppenwolf's alone. Galati, a Steppenwolf ensemble member, agreed.

Frank Galati, who had begun adapting novels for the stage as a professor at Northwestern, sent a long and eloquent handwritten letter to John Steinbeck's widow, Elaine Steinbeck, seeking her permission to adapt *The Grapes of Wrath*. It went into considerable detail. His adaptation would be built around the elements of earth, wind, fire, and water, and would include an interweave of elemental music on saws, Jew's harps, banjos, and the like. Mrs. Steinbeck must surely have had a stack of such requests, but Galati's letter and the reputation of the Steppenwolf production of Steinbeck's *Of Mice and Men*, directed by Sinise, won the day. She said yes.

The Grapes of Wrath opened at the five-hundred-seat Royal George Theatre in Chicago in the fall of 1988. AT&T provided a sponsorship of $100,000 and, at a total cost of $500,000, it was the most ambitious Steppenwolf production to date. They were out on the high dive.

Hedy Weiss penned an unqualified rave in the *Chicago Sun-Times*, finding the evening "breathtaking" and "wrenching" and insisting that it should have an extended life in this country and abroad. Richard Christiansen, on the other hand, wrote in his largely negative review in the *Tribune* that the production was "sluggish" and that "admiration for its effort must give way to disappointment with the results."

Buoyed by the Weiss review but badly dispirited by the Christiansen notice, Frank Galati, Steve Eich, and Randy Arney had an all-or-nothing meeting the next day to determine whether or not their monumental undertaking had a future. Eich, calling a halt to the gloom, brought the group's focus back to his original goal of getting *The Grapes of Wrath* to Broadway.

In that event, Galati wanted more work time, and, with the mixed Chicago response, Eich thought the key to getting to New York was to launch a successful and prestigious London engagement. And then there was the money to pay for these things. That would have to come from the venues themselves.

Eich skillfully put a plan in place that satisfied all of these requirements. It would play the La Jolla Playhouse in San Diego in May/June of 1989 and, only days later, become the first American attraction ever to play the National Theater in London as part of INTERNATIONAL 89, a festival of world theater companies, produced by Thelma Holt. Eich had initiated a relationship with Holt and flown her to Chicago, all in a matter of days. She embraced the production and would see to it that every aspect of its London engagement was given the best of care.

I finally caught up with *The Grapes of Wrath* at La Jolla. I was there because Rocco Landesman, on behalf of Jujamcyn Theaters, made a contribution of $50,000 with the sole stipulation that he could see a budget for a Broadway production, which Eich asked me to do.

Even in his unbridled enthusiasm, Steve Eich could not have prepared me for the magnificence unfolding on the stage in San

Diego. As I sat with the children and grandchildren of the people who had victimized and exploited the characters being so authentically portrayed in front of us, I felt it to be the finest dramatic offering I had ever seen. The stature of the performances by Gary Sinise as Tom Joad, Terry Kinney as the lapsed preacher Jim Casey, and Lois Smith as Ma Joad were met by every aspect of the production around them.

I would do the budgets. I hoped I could possibly be the general manager. And I had to get *The Grapes of Wrath* to the Shuberts. Steve sought a relationship with them for Steppenwolf as well.

Days later as he stood next to my desk and we finished reviewing my budget, I said, "Now watch this." I called Phil Smith and said, "Phil, I'm with Steve Eich from Steppenwolf. He has asked me to prepare a budget for *The Grapes of Wrath* for Jujamcyn. Would you mind taking a look at it before I send it over there?"

"*Not at all*, Albert."

My budget called for $1 million, at that time on the high side for a drama. But the cast, now thirty-eight, had to be transported to the city, and the physical production, which included fire and rain, a truck, and a small creek, was costly. Within days of reviewing the budget, Bernie and Phil flew to San Diego, and Phil called me from the Los Angeles airport to say they wanted the show.

"Do you think I could possibly be the general manager?" I asked.

Phil Smith responded, "Why shouldn't you, Albert? Why shouldn't you?"

It would be my second Broadway show and my second Broadway show with the Shubert Organization. We would play the Cort Theatre on West Forty-Eighth Street. It was on the "other side" of Broadway but was a beautiful house with an illustrious history that began with Laurette Taylor in *Peg O' My Heart* in 1912.

The Grapes of Wrath went on to the National in London, where it exceeded expectations. "As shatteringly perfect a piece of American theater as you are likely to experience in a lifetime of trans-Atlantic travel," wrote critic Jack Tinker in the *Daily Mail*. "You would have to have a heart carved out of granite not to be moved by this magnificent production," wrote the *Sunday Express*'s Clive Hirschhorn. The company was the toast of London and reached a level of prestige that paved the way for the journey to New York.

In the meantime, as I delved further into the financial realities of bringing *The Grapes of Wrath* to Broadway, I found that my original budget was off by a shocking $500,000. The total costs were going to be $1.5 million. I was a nervous wreck. I worried that I might be a goner as I presented it to Bernie and Phil over lunch at the Polish Tea Room in the Edison Hotel. Bernie looked at it and was unflapped. "I knew you were off, Albert, but I'm glad you found it yourself."

Putting the deals together for the show was challenging and exciting. I had to keep the costs to the bone, and, given that necessity, it is essential to have a producer who is willing to "walk away." Bernie always had that in his back pocket, and we did it twice on *The Grapes of Wrath*, once with Sam Cohn on Gary Sinise's deal, and once with Gilbert Parker acting on behalf of Frank Galati. In both instances we felt that we had gone the distance and threatened cancellation of the production.

When I told Sam we were walking, he said, "Why are you telling me this? Why didn't Bernie call me himself?"

"I'm speaking for Bernie," I asserted.

Sam called back twenty-four hours later and fumed. "We accept. And ask them when they're moving their offices to Delancey Street." Delancey Street is a famous discount Jewish business section on New York's Lower East Side.

Within minutes, Sam called Bernie to arrange their traditional open point. They would revisit Gary's deal when the show became a "hit." Gary and Terry Kinney were on a "favored nations" basis, meaning whatever one got would also be given to the other. Their long history with Steppenwolf had been a major consideration in the negotiations.

Gilbert Parker called back, too, but was more gentlemanly. He made no reference to Delancey Street.

On the first day of rehearsal, Frank Galati welcomed the cast and began by gently suggesting that they gather their props and savor them for a few moments. He is a renaissance theater man of tremendous skill with only one known fault. Doesn't return phone calls. I told him to change his answering machine message to "Please leave your name, phone number, and the year you called."

In the technical end of the theater, there are five departments: carpentry (the set), costumes, electrics (lighting), props, and sound. Interestingly, the "creek," which Jim True dove into at one point in the action, fell under the jurisdiction of electrics because, prior to the invention of electricity, the "footlights" were candles floating in a trough of water. The intensity of the illumination onstage was regulated by raising and lowering the water level, placing water forever in the domain of the electrics department.

At three hours and ten minutes, we had a long show, but the audience response during previews was rousing, and we were already running at a weekly profit. On the Sunday before opening, the *Times* honored us with a half-page Hirschfeld caricature of the company that was a striking departure from his usual, inimitable style.

On opening night, Steve Eich, Randy Arney, and I stood in a doorway on West Forty-eighth Street across from the Cort. As we watched the glittering first-nighters arrive, we were bonded together by the realization that it was finally happening.

Inside, as the lights went down, the audience sat in rapt silence from the opening solo on the saw to the final moment in the barn, after which they erupted into a standing ovation that went on for eleven curtain calls.

We took over all four floors of Sardi's, and, when the eagerly awaited Frank Rich review came in, floor by floor, the place went wild. It was the first time a review had been on page one of the *Times* Weekend section. When it's your show, such details become important.

It was an especially happy night for Elaine Steinbeck. She was our champion, and Steve Eich gave her an acknowledgment on all of our posters and major advertising: "Presented with the kind permission of Elaine Steinbeck." Elaine was of the theater, having been the first woman to be a stage manager on Broadway, notably for the original production of *Oklahoma*. Born in Austin, Texas, she was sophisticated and totally real. She recalled the opening night Sardi's party for *Pipe Dream*, a Rodgers and Hammerstein musical based on Steinbeck's *Sweet Thursday*, for which the reviews had been dismal. This night was a much happier time. It was happy for me, too. The show was open and on budget.

We had a spirited advertising meeting the next morning but found ourselves up against a major obstacle. Jerry Schoenfeld didn't believe in advertising. Especially in the *New York Times*. I am of the Merrick school that you advertise heavily when the critical acclaim has just landed and public awareness is at its peak. You make it a tight ticket. Later you can pull back and allow word of mouth and a maintenance advertising schedule to carry the show.

Mr. Schoenfeld either thought that, because this was a Shubert-produced show, it would sell tickets, or he was engaged in a testosterone contest with the *Times*. He seemed to have a special resentment over spending money with them. We had *Times* support, *Times* readers were our audience, and that was where we needed to spend our advertising dollars. Knowing we had a great show and having superlative reviews made it all the more agonizing to have to fight to get ads in the paper.

It came as a great shock to me because I had more than five years of Bernie Jacobs approving every advertising expenditure I proposed on *Little Shop of Horrors*. Bernie was now taking a less active role, and Jerry and I were locked in a continuous, tug of war.

We got eight Tony nominations, including our three stars Gary, Terry, and Lois Smith, as well as Frank Galati for Best Director, and Best Play.

Elaine Steinbeck and I had become friends and frequent dinner companions, and we went to the Tony Awards together. I had begun the week obsessed with winning Best Play and found that I was making myself crazy. By the time I had convinced myself it didn't matter, we won.

What a thrill it was to sit there with Elaine and to hear both of us thanked in the acceptance speeches of Steve Eich and Bernie Jacobs. When he picked up his Best Direction Award, Frank Galati spoke movingly and eloquently of the recent Tiananmen Square protests in China.

Steve Eich prearranged for everyone involved with the production to meet afterward at the Cort for an onstage photo. This is an example of what he is willing to do that others are not. The result is a stunning shot of a huge group of people taken moments after we had made theater history together.

The Tony Ball was a special occasion for all of us, besieged with congratulators and well-wishers. I introduced Frank Galati to Tommy Tune, who had also won that night for his direction of the musical *Grand Hotel*. They were great admirers of each other's work, and Tommy had been a very vocal champion of our production from opening night on.

Hearing my name on national television at last confirmed to my parents that I was in show business. There was lots of local fuss about it in my hometown of Big Rapids, Michigan. Articles and an editorial in the local paper, and Schuberg's on Main Street, which still has the best burgers in the world, requested an autographed poster for the dining room.

Five days after the Tonys, I was stricken with appendicitis and spent a grueling week in the hospital. My very first visitors were Phil Smith and Bob Wankel. I had been told I should start walking as soon as possible. "Do you mind if we take a walk around the halls?" I asked. They helped me out of bed, and, as we walked through the door, there was a group of nurses clustered around it. "No pictures, please," Phil Smith said. "Judy has had a long night."

Fred Nathan, our press agent, called me in the hospital. The dearth of advertising for *The Grapes of Wrath* had become so widely discussed that Alex Witchel was doing a story on it for the *Times*. She wanted to talk to me. Alex was a skillful journalist, and we knew each other very well. It would be impossible to hide my feelings from her. "Tell her I'm in intensive care," I told Fred. "There's no way I can speak to her about this."

In Alex's lengthy article in the *Times* on July 2, she noted that "some Broadway executives and disgruntled show personnel say that to succeed at the box office 'Grapes' needs a barrage of upbeat advertising, which would cost more money than the producers are already spending." She continued, "They say that instead of actively selling the show, the producers are sitting back and waiting for a miracle at the box office. As one employee of the production said, 'When even the stagehands go around saying, The show is a hit; why don't they advertise?' you know you're in trouble."

The article then included a refutation of those comments by Jerry Schoenfeld and Rocco Landesman with their own sets of "facts," "figures," and expertise. Jerry confirmed my worst fears about his views on advertising. "To my mind, all television advertising does is establish a show's image for the mass market,' Mr. Schoenfeld says. 'It's a reference that doesn't show an imminent box-office response. As for radio and print ads, we've been involved with nine shows this season, and I've tracked them to see the effect both have on sales. In my judgment, it's been minimal. Don't assume that taking out big ads guarantees success. When the street is up, business is up, ads or no ads.'"[5]

Since there was so little advertising, I wanted us to be well protected in what there was. I got an advance copy of an ad for six Shubert productions that was to run in the Sunday *Times*. Our show was in the bottom row on the spine. I ran over to Phil Smith's office to complain. I smacked the ad so hard it fell to the floor.

"Albert, leave," Phil commanded.

"I don't want to leave," I protested. "I want my show to have the treatment it deserves." "Well, you come in here all pumped up with adrenalin."

"I'm sorry, all I want is better placement for my show."

I went from nearly being kicked out of Phil's office to having lunch with him and Bernie at the Polish. "Albert fights for his shows," Bernie said, and we were given an upgrade in our ad position.

Fred Nathan was now the top press agent on Broadway, doing all of Cameron Mackintosh's productions and many Shubert ones. He was a close friend and confidant of many of the top people in the theater, including Bernie and Phil. I was finding his performance on *The Grapes of Wrath* to be seriously lacking. He was going through the motions, with no visible results. I didn't know until later that he had begun a serious personal and professional descent that would end tragically.

In August, Sam Cohn called Bernie, declaring that the show was now a "hit" and that it was time to readdress his client, Gary Sinise. To most people's thinking, a "hit" is a show that has repaid its investment and is headed toward profits. *The Grapes of Wrath* had recouped $500,000, or one-third of its investment. Bernie so informed Sam and told him there would be no salary increase for his client. Sam responded that, in that event, Gary would be leaving the show when his contract was up on September 2.

I don't know what Sam had promised Gary, but over a dinner we had at Frankie and Johnnie, our regular haunt, Gary was bitter about it and felt he had not been treated properly. "I feel like a chump," he said. Soon after that, Gary left Sam, which knowing how Sam had fought for him, made me sad. Despite our frequent fights, one of the reasons I most loved Sam was his love and reverence for talent. And Gary's performance as Tom Joad had established him as an actor to be reckoned with.

In early August, Phil Smith called a meeting with Fred Nathan and me to tell us that *The Grapes of Wrath* would be closing on September 2. On the surface, the decision seemed harsh and cynical. At that moment, we were still making solid weekly profits, and the audiences were responding with rousing standing ovations at every performance. As a business decision, it was defensible. Gary was leaving, and September is traditionally a terrible month at the box office.

It was unlikely that we could continue the run without substantially dipping into our accumulated profit, and more than likely that the amount expended would never be recouped. Throwing the show back into rehearsal to replace Gary would be costly. Still, it was devastating.

I asked Bernie if he would break the news to the company in person. "I'll do whatever you want, Albert," he responded. But the day before that was to happen, the closing date was leaked to *Newsday*. He did speak to the cast but was not the deliverer of the news, as I had hoped. It was a sober and punishing moment.

In its last week, *The Grapes of Wrath* made an operating profit of $98,000. On closing night, many of the cast remained onstage, crying, unable to fathom what had happened to them and to their show.

Taking it all in, Frank Galati said to no one in particular, "This is an example of how cruel the theater can be."

Under the guiding hand of two great men of the theater, Steve Eich and Frank Galati, *The Grapes of Wrath* was the high-water mark of my artistic experience in the theater. It was what I was here for. It was what I came to do. It was what Tennessee Williams meant when he described the theater as "the purest form of religion."

CHAPTER 25

Reckoning

After *As Is* and *The Grapes of Wrath*, I was no longer a top Off Broadway general manager, but an Off Broadway general manager who had done two Broadway shows. I knew that, in a certain way, this was a diminution of my brand. Further, as a byproduct of rising production costs, there was a new breed of competition emerging Off Broadway in managers like Richard Frankel who were willing to raise money and assume a producer role. I was not, though I understood that projects I would have gotten in the past might now pass me by.

In addition, I realized that I had been twenty-six until I was forty-eight. My reference points had stayed the same, people looked the same, people were doing the same things they had always done. Suddenly, at forty-eight, all of that had changed. People looked and acted older, they were divorced, they had moved away, they had left the business. Many had died. AIDS was robbing us of people who had brought inspiration and magic. Greed, made so fashionable by the Reagan years, was rampant. In the new technological order, transactions had become more important than relationships. It was as if people thought there was no tomorrow.

I decided to take a hike, if not permanently, at least for a while. I would close my office on April 30, 1991, when I turned fifty. I would direct my attention inward, to my own health, which mercifully, I still had.

I had dinner with Bruce Mailman to tell him of my decision, and he greeted me with some news of his own. He had been diagnosed. The words had an undeniable inevitability, but that didn't make them any less shocking and hard to grasp. AIDS was not a foreign war. It was right in front of us and all around us. Howard Ashman and Tom Eyen were seriously ill, and Charles Ludlam and Michael Bennett were among the hundreds who had been lost.

Gilbert Price came to me in the early spring with no place to live and suffering from dementia. He was an outpatient at St. Vincent's, and had left home because he thought his brother was sending rays through his body. I took him in. He was also struggling with crack addiction, and I took him for help. I dealt with his paranoia by calling him on it every time it came up, and he was responsive to that. But when I found crack vials in the apartment, I had to protect my own sobriety and arranged for him to stay in the vacant apartment of a friend. He left there after three days and moved to the YMCA on West Twenty-third Street, where he was kicked out.

He came to see me and told me he was going to Vienna to stay with friends. He said it was the last time we would see each other. He told me he planned to die there. Rife with Catholic guilt, he said his passing would be attributed to something else.

In December I received a postcard from him with the Sacred Heart of Jesus on the front. "Dear Albert, I love you. I have a lot to tell you about my experiences in Germany and Austria. I think of you a lot. I have been off of you know what since I left New York. I asked Jesus what to send you and he told me to send this photo of Him. I'll write again soon. I love you Albert. Thank you and God be with you. Love, Gilbert"

A few days later, when he surprised me with a transatlantic phone call, I teased, "You know, Gilbert, Jesus and I had actually discussed another photo." We both had a good laugh. On January

8, I read in the *Times* that he had been "found dead" on January 2. Found dead.

He was the purest "God performer" I ever knew. An open channel, unobstructed and unfiltered. I suspect that is why Langston Hughes fell in love with him. And why, one night when we were having dinner together at the Five Oaks in the Village, James Baldwin, who was sitting across the room alone, looked over at Gilbert and bowed to him three times, each bow lower than the last. It took my breath away. I said to Gilbert, "Did you see that?" "Yeah," he said. "That's because he knows about Langston."

Only days after Gilbert's passing, the relentless and unmerciful nature of the AIDS epidemic was driven home once again when my assistant told me that "Anthony Tunick's sister" was on the phone. It was Anthony who, thirty years earlier, stayed up all night with me in my college dorm and convinced me that my future was in New York and not in a classroom. Gilbert had been our first New York friend.

In 1991, someone's sister calling could mean only one thing.

"Anthony is in hospice," she said "and we don't know how much longer. I wanted you to know." "I'll be on the next plane," I said.

I gave him a long embrace. "With all the meaning," he said. He spoke with difficulty. We shared conversation and periods of silence. I told him how much it meant to me that we had come to New York together. I told him I was sorry for any hurt or grief I might have caused him along the way. "You made life exciting," he said.

The only time I cried was when I was telling his sister about our fights.

We spent several days together. Then we said our goodbyes. "Think of me," he said. I walked through the door but backed up and smiled so that he could have "another look at me." It was a reference to *A Star Is Born* that I knew he would recognize.

He died early the next morning.

I was gasping for air. The fact that I was healthy was meaning less and less. It would never be possible to have our full measure of happiness again. Where in the fuck was God?

Into this malaise came an almost life-saving phone call from Ellen Stewart, who said, "Baby, I have a show for you." I ran down to La MaMa, and Ellen and I sat together and watched *Blue Man Group Tubes*. I thought it had everything going for it to be a big, long-running Off Broadway hit. My "retirement" precluded my taking it on as general manager, but I grabbed it for the Astor Place, which I would continue to operate after my office had closed.

Dates were set, and contracts were signed for *Blue Man Group* at the Astor Place. I did one last show. I opened Harvey Fierstein in Robert Patrick's *The Haunted Host* at the Actors' Playhouse as a freebie for my friend Lawrence Lane, who had split from his partner John Glines. I worked on it until my office closing in April, then Larry took over. I came back to join the float in the Gay Pride Parade, primarily to show off the results of my months of dieting and hard work at the gym.

In June, I left for Paris with Helen Jacobs and her daughters, Lael and Zoe, and we had a glamorous French holiday headquartered in our hotel on the Ile St. Louis. Two weeks later, I returned to Paris on a first-class flight, courtesy of Bernie Jacobs, to a beautiful Neuilly apartment, courtesy of my friend Jean Dalric, and complimentary acting classes at his small studio in Montmartre, courtesy of Jack Garfein.

I came home to a lovely note from Ellen Stewart. "Dear Albert, love child of mine, I know that you know your Mama is out there, and the winds are blowing in all directions. Thank you for putting your arm in mine so I can try to stay in the road that we have been traveling all this time. Love, Ellen."

A significant marker for a sabbatical, a retirement, or whatever it was going to be. But the theater and I weren't finished with each other. Not yet.

CHAPTER 26

An Enemy of Playwrights

"**I** have the play that is going to pull you out of retirement."
It was Steve Eich calling from Steppenwolf, and the play was *The Song of Jacob Zulu*, by Tug Yourgrau, a white South African Jew who came to the US when he was ten. His play was the heartbreaking story of Jacob Zulu, the young son of a preacher whose spirit is first broken then driven to madness by the unrelenting brutalities of apartheid. In desperation, he plants a bomb in a shopping center, killing six and injuring scores of others.

As I sat through the electrifying opening night at Steppenwolf, I felt the calling that Steve Eich had predicted. The utter savagery of the events portrayed onstage juxtaposed with the delicate voices of Ladysmith Black Mambazo in the role of a kind of Greek chorus made for a stunning evening of theater. The final scene of young Jacob hanging from the gallows was heart-wrenching, the events onstage heightened by the fact that, as we watched, apartheid was actually coming to an end in South Africa.

It was the playwright's first dramatic effort and relied heavily upon the transcripts of the actual trial, but the presence of Ladysmith Black Mambazo, who had first come to prominence in Paul Simon's *Graceland* album, stamped the evening as an authentic

South-African experience, and the elements had been blended perfectly by the director Eric Simonson.

I rushed to take Bernie Jacobs and Phil Smith to Chicago to see it the following week. Bernie committed to it on the spot. Shubert would come in as a co-producer, put up half the capitalization, and furnish the Plymouth, one of its flagship playhouses, for an opening in the spring of 1993. I told Steve Eich I would do the show.

Soon after I began work on *Jacob Zulu*, my producer friend Michael Harvey engaged me to manage an Off Broadway production he hoped to present of his friend Edward Albee's play, *Three Tall Women*. I sent it to Jerry Schoenfeld, who I thought might be interested in coming along.

In the meantime, raising money for *Jacob Zulu* was not an easy chore. Jujamcyn came in for $50,000. We showed a piece of video to James Nederlander, who said, "I don't know what it is. Is it a play? Is it a musical? Is it a dance piece? I don't know what it is." Jimmy would not be coming in.

Within days of our meeting with Jimmy, there was a funny but distressing *Jacob Zulu* meeting with Bernie, Jerry, and Phil. Bernie was sitting at Jerry's desk, and Phil was in a chair off to the side. There was no focus, and no one was looking at each other. The agenda I had passed around was ignored, and into this disarray walked Jerry Schoenfeld, reading aloud, in a tone of mockery and scorn, from the script of *Three Tall Women* I had sent him. I was taken aback by the entire scene.

In an uncharacteristic moment of understatement, I said, "I'm thinking we should do this another time." As I left, I said to myself, "This show ain't happening."

The next day I got the call. Mr. Schoenfeld said he now felt that *The Song of Jacob Zulu* was a bad investment. The cast of twenty-eight, combined with the royalties required by the unions, did not allow for a sensible path to recoupment. The change was sudden. The budget totals were the same as they had been for months.

Whatever the reason and however sudden it was, Shubert was out, and we were canceled. Bernie announced it officially in Bruce

Weber's *Times* column the following Friday. Had Jimmy Nederlander had a word with Jerry Schoenfeld?

Steve Eich went into fighting mode.

"Go back to the budgets," he urged, "and be really creative with the royalty structure. Forget about the union requirements; come up with something that will prioritize the investors."

I sent Steve half-a-dozen royalty alternatives. He picked one that he thought had an impact but was within the realm of fairness and asked me to fly out to sell it to the Steppenwolf board. Prior to recoupment of the production costs, the plan called for minimal, flat weekly payments to the author, director, and producer, thus diverting a large portion of pre-recoupment royalties to the investors until they had recouped their money. After investor recoupment, the author and director were given a richer deal than they would otherwise have received.

Under this scenario, Eich proposed to his board that Steppenwolf itself would act as producer, but he emphasized that there was a potential downside with the Dramatists Guild. The Guild was known to expel author members who violated its minimum contractual requirements, and Steppenwolf's own relationship with the Guild could be jeopardized. As Steppenwolf was a theater of playwrights, it was crucial that the board go into these arrangements with their eyes open. Board approval was unanimous.

In a private meeting in November, Eich presented the bold proposal to Tug Yourgrau, Eric Simonson, and Randy Arney. He stressed to Yourgrau that his participation would likely mean his suspension from the Dramatists Guild. If he elected not to go along, his position would be respected, but Steppenwolf could not move forward. The men were seated in a circle. When Eich finished, they placed their fists in the middle, one on top of the other, to indicate agreement. All of the parties were in.

On Broadway, all signed author agreements are required to be sent to the Dramatists Guild, where they are given careful scrutiny and returned to the producer with a list of changes the Guild demands in order to "certify" the agreement. The Guild does not recognize an agreement as legally binding until it has Guild certification.

We would clearly be operating under an uncertified agreement. I stressed to Peregrine Whittlesey, Yourgrau's agent, the risks to her client as a Guild member. Whittlesey assured me that she and Tug would stand with us and that the agreement would be signed, irrespective of the Guild's position.

Within hours after Yourgrau's signed agreement was filed with the Guild, Steve Eich and I were summoned to the Guild offices. Present were executive director Dana Singer and the Guild lawyer. Peregrine Whittlesey was in Bermuda but was present on a round speakerphone that looked like it had just landed on the conference table.

Singer first expressed an appreciation for Steppenwolf's history with playwrights and our efforts to mount a large production with the intrinsic social value of *The Song of Jacob Zulu*—a production she felt would be best served on a standard Guild APC agreement under its minimum terms.

We stated that Peregrine and her client had agreed to the terms of the agreement as filed. Peregrine, in a change of position and aligning herself with the Guild, prevailed on us to reconsider. After a few minutes of that, I lifted up the phone receiver, dropped it into its cradle, and we walked out. Dana Singer chased after us to the elevator screaming, "Does Steppenwolf want to be the enemy of playwrights?"

Our battle had become the talk of Broadway. That afternoon, we were called to a meeting in the Shubert conference room. Jerry Schoenfeld marched in, with Bernie Jacobs and Phil Smith behind him. "Bloodied but unbowed," Mr. Schoenfeld declared. Admiring and congratulatory of our efforts, they would now come back to the show as investors to the tune of $600,000, and the Plymouth would be ours. It was a brief moment of triumph.

The Guild was on fire. When I returned to my office, Bruce Weber of the *Times* was on the phone. His entire Friday column of February 19 was devoted to *The Song of Jacob Zulu* vs. the Dramatists Guild. Bernie Jacobs supported us to the hilt.

The Guild and its members were railing, with Tug Yourgrau in the *Times* piece smugly playing the role of a neutral innocent: "Told that it sounds as if Steppenwolf gave him an ultimatum, he replied: 'I think there were times in the negotiations where it was this is it. I might experience that as an ultimatum. They might experience it as negotiation.'"

Tug's words caused us to look further, and we discovered that there had been a deception. In an effort to make Tug's position more sympathetic to the Guild, Tug and his agent told the Guild that we had come to them in January, *after* the full investment was in the bank, and said, "Now, take it or leave it." It was as if the fair play and goodwill of the November meeting had never existed.

When I confronted Whittlesey about this deceit, her response was, "I told you we would go along with you. I didn't say how we would do it." Things got much worse.

On February 26, a group of Islamic terrorists detonated a truck bomb below the North Tower of the World Trade Center. It was intended to knock the North Tower into the South Tower, bringing both down and killing thousands of people. It failed to do so but did kill six, and the shocking sight of hundreds of bloodied and injured people fleeing the buildings established New York and the country as now being vulnerable to terrorism. *This has just killed us*, I thought. Who will care about why our young man became a terrorist when we have just seen at close range what they can do?

David Rothenberg, who was a widely respected, socially conscious man of the left and had been a Broadway press agent for many years, handled our press. After the public brawling with the Guild, he restored some dignity to the proceedings.

The preview audiences were rapturous in their response, always a standing ovation, and many times singing the South African National Anthem with the company at the end. I watched and was moved by every performance, proud of what we had done.

Frank Rich's *Times* review of *The Song of Jacob Zulu* was a disappointment. He very much liked Ladysmith Black Mambazo, but throughout he kept returning to the script, which he described as "most easily embraced by those who don't mind some boredom in pursuit of a good cause." There was not an iota of the ticket-selling energy of a positive Rich review.

We now knew the outcome of our struggle and strife.

The next day, Steve, Randy, and I went to the ad meeting at Serino/Coyne. I observed, "Well, let's see, we have a play about a terrorist, and we've just had a terrorist attack, we've been dragged through the mud by the Dramatists Guild, and we have a negative *Times* review." Howard Kissel, my friend on the *Daily News*, astonished me by writing, "These people are in favor of terrorists." We picked what quotes we could find and went to my office to lick our wounds. Tug Yourgrau came by with his wife and said, "If there is anything I can do, please let me know." Steve Eich said, "You've done enough, Tug. You really have."

I sought Phil Smith's advice as to how to drum up an audience. "Put out one million discount coupons in Harlem," he suggested. Almost immediately, we got full houses. And they were 60 to 80 percent black. I was thrilled. But at $20 per ticket, we couldn't make any money. The response from the audiences was worth a great deal, but we were rapidly depleting our reserve funds. Whenever someone points to a standing ovation as a hopeful sign for their show, I tell them *The Song of Jacob Zulu* got one at all sixty-two performances.

With Steve and Randy next to me, I announced the closing to the company. I will never forget the heartbreak on our assistant stage manager Femi Sarah Heggie's face as she shook her head "no."

There was an aftermath.

In the early summer, David Richenthal, a young lawyer whom I felt to be a promising producer, called me to say that he and Jerry Schoenfeld, on behalf of Shubert, were going to co-produce *The Kentucky Cycle*, the double bill of Pulitzer Prize-winning plays that had been done at the Mark Taper. They wanted me to be the general manager. I laughed to myself because at one point I was sharing a cab uptown with Gordon Davidson, who was the Taper's artistic director, and he said, "Why don't you produce *The Kentucky Cycle*?" I had replied, "Gordon, no one in this town gives a flying shit about Kentucky."

Jerry, who hadn't read the plays yet, gave copies to me and suggested we both read the first one that night. We talked the next day and agreed that we both loved it. We read the second one the next night. He didn't like it and dropped out, but I stayed on. A week later, David Richenthal got a phone call from the attorney for the Dramatists Guild.

"I want to advise you," he postured, "that the Guild will never certify any agreement if Albert Poland is the production's general manager." David reported this to me, and I replied, "What do you want to do?" "I don't know," he said, "but it's a concern."

Two weeks later he called again to say he had just gotten another call from the Guild counsel reiterating the Guild position. "Well, what do you want to do, David?" I asked again.

"You're annoyed with me," he said.

"David, it's your show, and you have to be free to produce it the way you want. So, why don't I just remove myself? And wish you well."

Several months later, I was representing Nat Weiss on an Off Broadway musical called *Zombie Prom*, and I got a call from the agent who represented its authors, who told me that the Guild lawyer had called him with the same information he had given Richenthal. There seemed to be an ongoing attempt by a representative of the Dramatists Guild to jeopardize my livelihood, and I thought it should be brought to the attention of the Board of Directors of the League of Off Broadway Theaters and Producers. I called a special meeting.

There was one board member who was missing, another general manager whose office was in the same building as mine. I went to him directly after the meeting to share the information about the actions of the Guild lawyer. "I have to disclose something to you, Albert," he said. "He is my best friend."

That was it. I had had enough and called a powerful friend to ask what could be done. He told me that it was a violation of the RICO

Act for one person to attempt to influence another in such a way that a third person is deprived of a livelihood. He called me back a short time later. "I have spoken to my friend, William O. Bittman. Bill is a high-ranking lawyer in Washington, and he is prepared to walk this into the Justice Department should you want him to."

I am a union man, and I had no desire to do anything to jeopardize the Dramatists Guild, but I was damned if I would be treated like this. I called a close lawyer friend who did occasional work for the Guild and told him of the situation. I shared with him, "in strictest confidence," that I was minutes away from letting William O. Bittman walk the matter into the Justice Department.

Lo and behold, it stopped.

My friend Nancy Christopherson once said that the production process of a play often replicates its plot. If that be true, *The Song of Jacob Zulu* had illustrated it brilliantly.

CHAPTER 27

Past and Present

During the American Revolution, 1776-1783, the philosopher-author Thomas Paine published nineteen pamphlets known collectively as *The American Crisis* or simply *The Crisis*. They were written in the language of the common man and effectively bolstered the morale of the American colonists. The house where Paine wrote *The Crisis* pamphlets was located at 59 Grove Street in Greenwich Village.

In 1935, Marie Du Mont, a French-Austrian woman who had worked in, sung in, and owned a number of New York speakeasies, opened a nightclub at 59 Grove Street. Mme. Du Mont called her place Marie's Crisis, and it became a popular Village watering hole and the longest-running piano bar in the city. Its denizens, talented or not, sober or not, sang way into the night. Cynics called it "the place where show tunes come to die," but it was a Village classic.

In this place, some two hundred years after Thomas Paine wrote his inspirational papers, a group of talented young men began to gather every day in the late afternoon at a table by the stairs. Their mission was to write something that would lift the spirits of the gay troops, "to provide," in director Phillip George's words, "a USO show for the AIDS crisis."

The magnet that brought them together was Howard Crabtree, a singularly talented, silly, and fabulous man himself—and his overstuffed closetful of elaborate and eccentric costumes that cried out to become a musical revue.

Phillip George saw the costumes as metaphors for aspects of gay life. A collection of parasols and top hats inspired "A Lovely Day for an Outing." A huge nose sang a wandering love song to a tissue ("the first time you blew me"). A banana attempted to join an army of meat and potatoes ("the new recruit is a fruit"). An invisible dance troupe sang "if you have a skeleton in your family closet, teach it how to dance." Tinkerbell sat in a gay bar and lamented, "It's tough to be a fairy."

They named the opus *Howard Crabtree's Whoop-Dee-Doo!* and the goal was to do four 11 o'clock performances at the Actors' Playhouse on the set of Julie Halston's one-person show in the spring of 1993.

The late-night crowds were high spirited and hungry for what the show had to offer. In the audiences were Fred Barton, who had achieved success as a performer in his own one-person show *Miss Gulch Returns*, and producer John Glines, who thought *Whoop-Dee-Doo!* had a future beyond its 11 o'clock performances.

Glines told the company that if it could be mounted for a regular run at the Actors' Playhouse for $25,000, he was in for half. Fred Barton joined the show as musical director and vocal arranger when Glines signed on.

Stephen Holden wrote in the *Times*, "What kind of shows might Florenz Ziegfeld have produced had he been gay and grown up in the age of the Ridiculous Theatrical Company, Charles Busch, and Ru Paul? That is the clever premise behind the musical revue *Whoop-Dee- Doo!* in which an ensemble of nine men parade around dressed up as everything from a giant scotch tape dispenser to a dinner setting complete with tablecloth. In this all-male sendup of the Ziegfeld Follies, what is lacking in expensive glitz is made up for in campy ingenuity."[6]

When Fred Barton approached the Actors' Playhouse the next night, he noted a large crowd on the sidewalk. *Oh, no,* he thought, *someone has been hurt*. It was the box office line—the show was a hit. The reviews were not quite raves, but they were "money" reviews that let its audience know what it was, that it was fun, and that it was there.

Shortly after the opening, John Glines asked me to come and see it and, if I liked it, to join in as the general manager. I loved it. After the rough going of *Jacob Zulu* and the movement of Off Broadway into the commercial realm, *Whoop-Dee-Doo!* was a return to the Off Broadway that first won my heart.

I thought the show represented the best the gay spirit had to offer: humor as a survival mechanism with a sweet gay soul. There was something old fashioned and homemade about it, and yet young audiences were flocking to it, too.

I called Cameron Mackintosh and told him I had the perfect place for him to spend his birthday: the Sunday matinee of *Whoop-Dee-Doo!* He believed me, came to see the show, and loved it, as I knew he would. He backed it for a production at Kings Head in London, where it opened to enormous critical and audience acclaim.

Michael Wright wrote a valentine in the *Daily Telegraph*. "Go see this ultra-camp super-splurge shoestring extravaganza as soon as possible. It does for musical revue what Einstein did for physics. I've never seen anything like it." One of *Whoop-Dee-Doo!'s* achievements that I most cherished was the return of camp ownership to us. It had been very much flattened by its entry into the public domain.

When it closed on February 20, 1994, the little show that started with a closetful of eccentric costumes and some meetings by the stairs at Marie's Crisis had won Drama Desk Awards for Best Musical Revue and Best Costumes, had run for 271 performances at the Actors' Playhouse, and made a lot of people happy, including those of us who participated in it.

As Greg Evans said in his *Variety* review, 'Howard Crabtree's Whoop-Dee-Doo!' proves that vaudeville ain't dead, it's just been to the powder room."

Days after *Whoop-Dee-Doo!'s* closing, Ben Sprecher addressed a meeting of the League of Off Broadway Theaters and Producers.

He wanted to bring the Tony Awards to Off Broadway. The group's opposition was raucous, with Richard Frankel coming close to throwing a punch. My own position was, of course, adamantly opposed—favoring the specialness of Off Broadway over its inevitable commercialization—and, given the reaction from the community, I thought the issue was dead. It was anything but.

"I'm going to canvas the Off Broadway nonprofit companies," Ben told me the following day. "There may be support there." And for the next year, that is what he did.

At this point Ben owned two Off Broadway theaters, the still-in-demand Promenade and the less-successful Variety Arts on Third Avenue just below Fourteenth Street. He was now ready to sell and stated outright that making his theaters Tony-eligible would drive up their value in the marketplace and be essential to attracting his target buyer, The Shubert Organization. I couldn't believe that one man would sacrifice an entire industry for these selfish ends.

I knew that Jerry Schoenfeld would be opposed to Off Broadway Tonys, but at this point, given his own detractors, that alone would not keep it from happening. Frank Rich and the *Times* never wrote a treatise about it, but there were occasional sprinklings of support. Broadway producer Roger Berlind, in favor of it, took me to lunch. I told him I hated the idea and paid for the lunch.

As a byproduct of these discussions, Bernie looked me in the eye and told me it was time for Off Broadway to have union stagehands. "A level playing field," he called it. He was studying me carefully as he spoke. I glared. I never heard about it again, and it didn't happen.

In December, after nearly a year of relentless campaigning, the matter was put to a vote by the Off Broadway League Board. League president Barry Grove joined Ben in support. The Roundabout Theatre Company was Tony-eligible because it was in the 499-seat Criterion Center in Midtown, and Barry wanted parity for Manhattan Theater Club, a long-running Off Broadway institution for which he was the executive producer. The Board vote was two in favor, eight opposed, and one abstention.

The wisdom of the Board was not sufficient for Ben, and he now wanted to bring the matter to the entire membership. A meeting was scheduled at the Westside Theatre on January 5, 1995. Ben would speak in favor of the motion, and I would speak in opposition. When I saw the large turnout, I knew this was an important issue, and I was optimistic about the outcome.

Then Ben arrived, wired up to a portable electrocardiograph machine. "I'm being tested for possible serious heart trouble," he said. "I won't be able to speak today, but Barry will take my place." I marveled at the invention.

Barry Grove began with, "I am not passionate about this" and made his case. The League should actively seek to participate in the Tony Awards, specifically being represented in three categories: Best Off Broadway Play, Best Musical, and Best Individual Performance. He felt it would mean invaluable national promotion for our industry.

"I *am* passionate about this," I began, and fervently made my case. I told of the negotiation I had with John Glasel, the head of musicians Local 802, regarding *Starmites*, the first attraction to play the 499-seat Criterion Center in the Broadway area. All things considered, negotiations with John were generally reasonable, and we came to a deal we both thought to be eminently fair.

The day Tony nominations were announced and *Starmites* received six, Glasel called up and read me the riot act. "You didn't tell me your show was Tony-eligible," he said. "I would have never agreed to that deal" (a strong illustration of my point about unions seizing the moment). The Dramatists Guild has a "standard minimum" Off Broadway agreement, ready and waiting, that is well beyond our reach. This would provide the perfect opportunity for them to pounce. Others would follow. I wrapped up with, "We are not 'Little Broadway'—we're Off Broadway and happy to be."

The vote was sixty-three opposed to Off Broadway Tonys and ten in favor. This battle, at last, was over. Ben Sprecher, in the meantime, was wooing Jerry Schoenfeld and had convinced him, against the opposition of Bernie Jacobs and Phil Smith, that Shubert should build an Off Broadway theater on Forty-Second Street that Ben would operate.

It would be called the Little Shubert.

CHAPTER 28

Yoko

*W*hen David Geffen called in the spring of 1993 to ask if I would help Yoko Ono put together an Off Broadway production of her autobiographical musical, *New York Rock*, I leapt at it, wanting to help her and excited at the prospect of getting to know her.

From her childhood in World War II Japan on, Yoko Ono had endured a life of wealth and trauma, nurtured through it all by a creative spirit that could not be extinguished. After the assassination of John Lennon, she finally got away. She took their son Sean and moved to Switzerland for two years. She was now back living in the apartment at the Dakota and ready to embark on a new project.

"So," I said, "I just come to the Dakota and ask for you?"

She giggled. "Yes, you just come to the Dakota and ask for me." An assistant invited me to park my shoes outside the door and seated me in the living room with the famous white piano. Yoko came in smoking a thin mentholated cigarette and was never without one for the hour and a half of our first meeting. She smoked them halfway down then used them to light the next one. She was open, direct, and honest. I was drawn to her.

The apartment was like an enormous mansion in the country. The carpeting throughout was white and pristine. All of the rooms were huge, with high ceilings, typical of the Dakota. There was one room with just a mummy in it for which I was told that she had paid one million dollars. The seller told her it was her in another life.

I left with a draft of the *New York Rock* script and a demo tape of the songs, which she and Sean had recorded. It was a gentle, somewhat idyllic portrait of her life with John Lennon. New drafts of the script and revised demos of the songs began arriving frequently. She asked that I not copy the demos and that they be picked up after I was finished listening to them. I respected her requests. Sean's singing on the demos was remarkable.

My first and only choice to direct *New York Rock* was Robert Woodruff. He had started the Eureka Theater in San Francisco and was the definitive Shepard director, having directed Sam's Pulitzer Prize-winning *Buried Child*, among many others. We were longtime friends, but the only time we worked together was when Sam brought him in to fine-tune his own direction of *A Lie of the Mind*. I thought Robert could bring Yoko to the core of anger that must surely be at the heart of her play, which could have made it truly exciting. Sadly, he declined.

She hired a car and driver, and we spent a wonderful day looking at theaters, both nonprofits (all of whom wanted the show) and commercial spaces. She was wearing her Yoko sunglasses, and every time we emerged from the car, the universe stopped. I had been with a number of stars by that time but none as intensely iconic as Yoko. Workmen jumped from scaffolds to get her autograph, cabs crashed into the cars in front of them.

Kyle Renick and the WPA struck the best chord with her. In the great Kyle tradition, he had researched her entire career and listened to the complete Ono Box while making extensive notes. He really wanted the show. That and our track record of success together attracted Yoko to Kyle and his theatre. He gave us a date in the spring of '94, so we had plenty of time to find our director.

Sam Havadtoy, a British-born Hungarian-American interior designer, painter, and gallery owner, was Yoko's live-in companion. He was well known for being part of an artists' circle that included, among others, Yoko, Keith Haring, Andy Warhol, and Jasper Johns. He had done the décor of the Dakota apartment but had a falling out with the Lennons about a year prior to John's murder.

Seeing the shocking news on television, he rushed to her side and, in a break with his male companion, remained there for twenty years. He was enormously devoted but not subservient, a ballast and clearly a stabilizing influence.

Our search for directors proved difficult. Yoko wanted someone from the avant-garde, but no one we met with seemed to fit. I am sure some were frightened or intimidated. I told my old friend Phil Oesterman about our difficulties. "What about me?" he said. I told him I would consider it.

Following the calamitous end to his successes with *Let My People Come* and Charles Pierce, Phil had worked as an associate director with his friend Tommy Tune on one Broadway hit after another. I was close enough to Phil to know that his contribution to these shows had been substantial, and he seemed to have emerged whole in the years since the *LMPC* chaos. He was eager for a project of his own, and I felt that he might offer the kind of focus I had been looking for from Woodruff.

I was giving Yoko an objective overview of him in her kitchen when the phone rang. Sam said, "It's someone who says he's Paul McCartney." Yoko was surprised. "I haven't heard from him in a year." She went to the phone and proceeded to cross-examine the caller for about five minutes, after which she put her hand over the receiver, said, "It's him," and left us for about an hour.

When she returned, she said McCartney had called about a seven-hour anthology series he, George Harrison, and Ringo Starr were putting together for ABC, which he laughingly described as "three old whores looking back." He sought her blessing and participation, which she gave.

We finished our discussion of Phil, and I took copies of the material to give to him in preparation for their meeting. Phil knew how to woo, and he was at his wooing best in his early collaboration with Yoko. They were able to put together a first-rate cast and, at Kyle Renick's suggestion, we engaged as our musical director and orchestrator the young, supremely talented, and attractively arrogant Jason Robert Brown, who would later collect Tony Awards for his scores of *Parade* and *The Bridges of Madison County*. Jason put together such a kick-ass band that "rockers" (as Yoko called them) from all over town flocked to the show just to hear them.

Yoko was totally accessible, working collaboratively with everyone, and really getting to know the company. She brought in her own sound people, who gave the show a studio-quality rock sound in the small WPA Theatre.

Since the goal was a production that would move to an Off Broadway theater, we had agreed that Yoko would do no press for the WPA production, saving it for the move. A fool's errand. The phones rang off the hook with press requests, and Yoko, an innate press hound, was eager to respond to every one of them. Once the floodgates had opened, there was no stopping her. I'm sure *New York Rock* was the first Off Off Broadway show to be on the cover of the weekend Arts sections of newspapers in the provinces.

When it came to advertising, however, she was conservative. I suggested that, in the *Times* ABC Directory, we bill it as "Yoko Ono's *New York Rock*." "No," she said, "they'll think it's me screeching or something." I showed her a beautiful logo with artwork of her in the Yoko sunglasses. She vetoed that. "That's Mrs. Lennon," Sam added. Indeed, whenever we were out without her sunglasses, she went unrecognized.

The ride with Phil Oesterman was a bumpy one. I had commented to him over the years that when he and Tommy were in production, there always seemed to be some company member who was "the enemy." I now saw that at close range. There was a new one every week. Phil would describe each of them as "evil, the devil incarnate" and turn on them abusively. I did my best to be a mediator but ultimately found his behavior indefensible.

I arrived one afternoon to find the set in place. It was unmistakably the platform and poles from *The Fantasticks*. I was startled and confronted Phil about it. "As Tommy and I always say," he postured, "we borrow, but we pay back with interest." A mildly clever response, but the fact was it was the iconic set from another, very famous show.

At the invited dress rehearsal, the audience was knocked out by the songs, but the dialogue seemed naïve and stilted. Before the Sunday preview matinee, I took Yoko and Sam to lunch at the nearby Empire diner. I complimented Yoko on her many talents but told her I didn't believe they extended to dialogue. She blanched. "We all want this to be a success," I said, "and I have a suggestion."

"What . . . ?" she said with a slight edge.

I proposed that we take out all of the dialogue for a few performances and see what portions of it we could not live without. The songs could carry the story. Her short answer was "no." Sam backed me and urged that we try it. He said that some of the lines made him cringe. Yoko huffed a bit, but ultimately agreed. She finished her tea, excused herself, and said she wanted to "say hello" to the cast before the matinee.

"Albert is cutting all of your parts," she told them. Experiment over. And not surprising. Yoko was a woman for whom control was, quite literally, a matter of life and death. She was the child of a father who died of alcoholism, and during World War II in Japan, her quick-witted hiding of her siblings had literally saved all of their lives time after time.

Sam was devoted to *New York Rock*. Often, when we rehearsed at night, he would man the phones at the WPA and take the phone reservations himself after the box office had closed. Despite everyone's efforts and the huge amount of attendant publicity, the show never sold out at the tiny 137-seat theater.

The press on opening night outdid anything I had ever seen. There were several hundred paparazzi, and, when Yoko emerged from her car in front of the theater, they closed in on her like a flashing, moving chrysalis. I thought, *This is what fame is about: somewhere in the middle of that is little Yoko.* By the end of the performance, we had the *Times* review. It was written by Stephen Holden in a tone of mockery and condescension. He found that the show "belongs to the jerry-built music-theater genre in which a story is pieced together around existing songs" and without "fully drawn characters or dialogue that could be confused with everyday speech."

Yoko and Sam read it and told the driver to put it in the trunk.

Yoko gave a classy opening night party and made sure everyone had a photo moment with her. The reviews were largely uncomplimentary, and attendance was not up to what we would have hoped, both of which I attributed to a continuing, unjustified bias against her. She asked me to meet her for lunch with a budget for an Off Broadway move and had in mind a big opening night with A-list rock glitterati in attendance. I arrived with the budget but counseled her not to take it beyond the WPA. She listened.

At the closing performance, she rushed up to me. "Go in there—they are performing it with a sort of vengeance." I did. The cast, angry that their hopes of moving ahead in a show by Yoko Ono had been dashed, were performing in a torrent of rage that made it the most effective performance of the run and gave it an edge it had not previously had. Their vocal performances are preserved on a Capitol original cast recording.

I love Yoko. I found her to be open and vulnerable. She does not have the tough skin you might expect. What she has is infinite inner strength, and she understands the nature of power—when and how to use it, who has it, how to sit next to it, how to cozy up to it. I saw her a couple of times after our work was done but realized she had a life filled with priorities and knew that she would move on.

I loved her comfortable relationship with her son. Sean Lennon was very involved with *New York Rock*, recording all the demos and present for rehearsals, many of which were in his studio on Broome Street. He and his mother are clearly each other's champions.

With the passing of time, the public bias against Yoko has diminished, and her talent as a composer has gained significantly in stature and respect, with many important contemporary composers listing her as an influence.

Shortly before this writing, Sean performed at a large fundraising dinner for the Caron Foundation at Cipriani on Forty-Second Street. Caron has major centers for the treatment of alcohol and drugs and is a cause dear to the hearts of both Yoko and me. When he finished performing I ran backstage to say hello and send my love to his mother. I reminded him of our journey together on *New York Rock*.

"Oh, yes," he said. "That was a happy time."

CHAPTER 29

Bruce

Bruce Mailman died on June 9, 1994, after what seemed like a long illness. Early on we had seen each other as often as possible, but gradually he began to tire more easily. Then came his first hospital stay. He gave instructions that there were to be no visitors, but his companion, John Sugg, his close artist friend Boris Fedushin, and I went anyway. He was sitting in the middle of his bed like a Buddha. He smiled and said, "It was very sweet of you to come, and it will be very sweet when you leave." That was Bruce. John and Boris gave him round-the-clock care at home, but for several months before he passed on, he was no longer there. The Bruce we knew had left us.

In the fall, I produced a memorial service at the Astor Place that was attended by the illuminati of the downtown scene. Al Carmines and some regulars of the Judson Poets Theater were set to perform, and Al told me beforehand that some people weren't going to like what he had to say. His words were hurtful, but I chalked it up to his resentment about the royalty cuts on *The Faggot*, as well as Al's childish need for attention when the focus was on someone else.

He categorized Bruce with Cole Porter and Noël Coward, both of whom he considered brilliant, but bitter, and the inimitable David

Vaughn sang Coward's "Parisian Pierrot" by way of illustration. The song depicts a gloomy figure celebrated by a society he views with scorn and contempt. Larry Kramer, seated in the balcony, greeted the song with a loud "BOO" and yelled, "When are you going to say something nice about Bruce?" Al and I had been longtime close friends. We saw little of each other after that, but when he hit me up for a loan a few years later, I gave it to him without hesitation.

Ina Meibach and Mark Bramble spoke, and Henry Krieger sang "We Are a Family" from *Dreamgirls*. In 1976, Bruce brought Henry and Tom Eyen together for the first time to musicalize Tom's *Dirtiest Show* into *The Dirtiest Musical in Town*. It had starred Nelle Carter, and Peter Schneider was his general manager.

Helen Montagu and I spoke, and Ellen Stewart again berated us for what Bruce had written about her in our book. When it was over, Bruce's dear friend, the charismatic restauranteur Keith McNally, provided a sumptuous buffet in the lobby, and the inner circle was invited for supper at his exclusive "44" in the Royalton.

The day after the memorial service. I had a letter hand delivered to Ellen. I told her how sorry I was that, after twenty years, she was still finding *The Off Off Broadway Book* a source of pain. I wrote, "If I have never apologized to you for this hurt, please allow me to do so now."

A short time later, the phone rang, and it was Ellen. "What is this letter?" she said. *"What is this letter?"*

"Ellen," I said, "I would really like—"

"Do you want to be on the board of La MaMa?" she interrupted. "We already have too many white people."

"Do you want me on the board?" I asked.

"Yes."

"Well, how can I resist such a charming invitation?"

I found the board meetings impossible and resigned after a year.

CHAPTER 30

A Producer Is Born

Jeffrey Richards was one of the most successful press agents in town. By early 1995, when he decided to try his hand at producing, he had flacked for more than 150 shows on and Off Broadway, many hits among them.

People either liked him or hated him, but he got results. His mother, Helen Richards, was a distinguished general manager who had previously been a press agent. The Broadway Jeffrey was born into was a street of gumption and grit, crowded with stars and fourteen newspapers, etched definitively and for all time by Clifford Odets and Ernest Lehman in *Sweet Smell of Success*, his favorite movie.

We had a big hit together with *Steel Magnolias*, so I was delighted when he took me to dinner and asked if I would general manage *The Compleat Works of Willm Shkspr (Abridged)*, his first effort as a producer. The play was a condensed madcap compendium of all of Shakespeare's works. Not particularly to my liking, but Jeffrey's encyclopedic knowledge and inherent smarts made me think he could be an effective producer. He was savvy and had the knowledge to operate in any area of the industry. He also knew what he didn't know, and for that he was willing to trust my knowledge and experience.

Jeffrey was playful and fun. He was, however, hard to get to know. I constantly felt I was dealing with a created persona in search of a result. He frequently told outrageous lies as though they were facts and, after he had scrutinized your response, he would reveal that he had just made the whole thing up.

Ben Brantley, in his generally positive *Times* review of *Shkspr (Abridged)* echoed some of my feelings when he said the show "speaks, quite loudly, to the sophomore in all of us. This is such stuff as frat-house revues are made on, but if the level of sophistication here is only groin high, there is also a gung-ho vitality that is often impossible to resist."

Like *Tomfoolery*, the show had an initial burst in attendance then tapered off, never to return. It closed July 1 after 164 performances. A seemingly inauspicious beginning for a man who would become an archetypal producer for the beginning of the new century.

CHAPTER 31

Great Ones

It was a masterstroke of synchronicity when Sam Cohn called Steve Eich to propose that Steve Martin's first full-length play, *Picasso at the Lapin Agile*, have its world premiere at Steppenwolf. "We want to start this with you," Cohn said, "but Steve wants to start it small."

Eich had just the spot for it. The paint was drying on Steppenwolf's new three-hundred-seat studio theater, and the premiere play had yet to be selected.

Set in the old Lapin Agile Tavern in 1905 Paris, the play is Martin's comic vision of a meeting between Picasso and Einstein, nearly hijacked by the arrival of Elvis Presley as a cosmic visitor from the future. Martin renders a rich and compelling portrait of the twentieth century, painted in the exquisitely funny dialogue he provides for three of the men who shaped it.

The Steppenwolf production of *Picasso*, directed by Randall Arney, with a cast of ensemble members including Rondi Reed and Tracy Letts, opened to critical and audience acclaim and was held over for six months. It was followed in October of 1994 by a sold-out extended run at the Westwood Playhouse in Los Angeles.

At my suggestion, Joan Stein came on board as Eich's producing partner in LA, and Jerry Schoenfeld signed on for Shubert to partner in an Off Broadway production at the Promenade in the fall of 1995. It was time to talk to Mr. Cohn.

As a gesture of respect, I always started major negotiations with Sam sitting with him in his office, laying the groundwork. His associate at that time was Victoria Traube, who I adored. I thought the two of them were the best in the business, and our sparring sessions together were delicious and fun. Vicky, the daughter of Mildred and Shepard Traube, founding members of the Society of Stage Directors and Choreographers, had grown up in the theater. I could never forget her mother's kidnapping of Word Baker during rehearsals for *Now Is the Time for All Good Men*.

At Jerry Schoenfeld's request, the second meeting with Sam was held in the Shubert conference room. Unlike Bernie, Jerry liked to get involved with my doings as general manager, and the meeting was a bumpy affair. Jerry took over, and it turned into a battle of wits because I thought I could do better and kept interrupting him. Finally, he said, "Will you excuse us?" and took me outside.

"Obviously, Albert, you think you can do better than I am doing. I don't want to cramp your style, Albert. You take this over, and we will keep our investment in the show but withdraw as producers." He was neither angry nor emotional. We went back in, he informed Sam of the change, and I finished the deal. We continued to treat Jerry as a partner, but all of the decisions would be ours.

Everything about Steve Martin was class, beginning with his enormous talent and extending to his collaboration with every member of the team. If you were one on one with him, it was a serious discussion; with two or more, he was "on," and you became an audience. His public thought it knew him intimately, and he had an easy relationship with them. Whenever we had dinner with him, mothers stopped by the table and placed their babies in his arms. As we continued talking and eating, he held them, patted them, and gave them back with no words exchanged, not even so much as a thank you.

During a lunch I had with him, a man came over and said, "We have been here for over an hour, and you haven't done one funny thing."

"Well," Steve said, "What can I tell you? It's the old me."

Steve's West Coast press agent was a nightmare. We were offered the cover of the Fall Preview Issue of *New York Magazine*. The press agent told them, "Steve Martin has no interest in being on the cover of *New York Magazine*." She told the *Times*, "Steve Martin has no interest in being interviewed by the *New York Times*." Our skillful show press agent, Alma Viator, rescued us from those and other Hollywood gaffes.

During that season, I would have the distinct pleasure of being the general manager of productions in all three theaters under Ben Sprecher's control. At one point during the run of *Picasso*, Steve Eich and I wanted to do a reading of a new play on a Monday night at the Promenade. Ben quoted me a rental of $3,000. I was appalled and called Steve to tell him. Steve gave me special instructions, and I called Ben back. "Will you take $2,500?" I asked.

"Yes," he said.

"We pass."

Two days after the *Picasso* opening, I opened my second hit of that season, Uta Hagen's much-heralded return in *Mrs. Klein*.

In the fall of 1995 when David Richenthal and Anita Waxman took Uta Hagen to the Lucille Lortel Theater to star in *Mrs. Klein*, she was seventy-five and about to celebrate her sixtieth year in the theater. Her career began in 1937 when she played Ophelia opposite Eva Le Gallienne's Hamlet.

In the early '40s, Hagen appeared with Paul Robeson and her then husband, Jose Ferrer, in the legendary Broadway run of *Othello*. In 1947, she met her future husband, Herbert Berghof, and shortly thereafter she joined him on the staff of his HB Studio, beginning one of the longest and most distinguished teaching careers in the American theater. The marriage and professional partnership with Berghof lasted until his death in 1990.

Hagen had collected Best Actress Tony Awards in 1951 for *The Country Girl* and, more notably, in 1963 for her celebrated portrayal of Martha in *Who's Afraid of Virginia Woolf?* Other than a monologue she performed from *Charlotte* in A Herbert Berghof Retrospective at the HB Studio theatre in 1992, Hagen had not appeared on a stage in New York City for nearly ten years.

When William "Billy" Carden, a young actor and director, took over as head of the HB studio theater in 1994, he began raising the idea of Hagen acting again. If he could find a project for her, would she act? She told Carden she was actually dying to.

Carden suggested *Mrs. Klein*, a play he knew by Nicholas Wright. Melanie Klein was a prominent Austrian-born psychoanalyst noted for her impact on child psychology. The play builds to a fiery confrontation between Klein, her own daughter, and her assistant over responsibility she may bear in the death, possibly a suicide, of her son. Carden got the rights to perform it in the HB studio theater for sixteen performances in April and May of 1995.

The small space was packed with Village cognoscenti and dedicated theater lovers. The agent Bill Craver, who had been invaluable in helping to secure the rights, brought producer David Richenthal, who immediately wanted to move it Off Broadway. He took Hagen to dinner the following night.

"She smoked a lot of cigarettes, coughed in my face, and said, 'Yes,'" Richenthal recalled. He returned with Lucille Lortel, who joined him as a co-producer and generously held her theater empty for the entire summer so that *Mrs. Klein* could play there in the fall.

There was a standard clause in her theater booking contract that provided Lucille with producer billing to the effect of "Produced by Special Arrangement with Lucille Lortel." Though no producer responsibilities were required of her to back it up, it afforded her the option to later claim a producer credit in her epic-length bio. For *Mrs. Klein*, in addition to holding the theater, she actually came in with a small investment.

Lortel's agreement with us called for co-producer billing next to David on a line with no other names. But for our opening *Times* ad, we had elected to use movie-style "run-on" billing, which put several people's names on every line.

When Lucille received the advance ad proof, she called Ben Sprecher to complain. Ben asked David to call her, and David explained to her that we were using movie billing.

"If I wanted movie billing, dear," she said, "I would do movies."

Amy Wright continued in her role as Paula the assistant, and Laila Robins joined us as Melitta, the daughter—both remarkable actors who could hold stage with Uta. As the first read-through was about to start, the house manager of the Lortel ran anxiously down the aisle and stopped the rehearsal. "Excuse me," he said to Uta Hagen, "there is no smoking in the theater."

"No smoking," she demurred, "no actress." He scurried away without even mentioning her dog.

I adored Uta. She had a wonderful sense of humor, we both smoked, and it was the natural thing for me to devote myself to her. Ben Brantley, the *Times* critic, had written an advance squib to the effect that a Hagen appearance on a New York stage was the equivalent of Halley's Comet, and I was constantly giving her the glowing reports from the box office. "I'm used to having managers tell me how well Billie Burke did last week," she said. "This is wonderful."

A half hour before the first preview of *Mrs. Klein*, Uta asked the stage manager to get Billy Carden. "My peephole," she said. "There's no peephole. I need my peephole." The set designer made a hole in the upstage velour and put a flap over it. Every night, five minutes before curtain, Uta peeked through it to have a look at her audience. "I need to sense who they are," she said, and, indeed, her acting technique was projected through a stage presence that was inclusive of the audience and made them feel that she belonged to them.

Ben Brantley in the *Times* placed Hagen's performance among legends. "Each generation of theatergoers tends to feel it has just missed out on the really great performances: by Duse, say, or Laurette Taylor, or John Barrymore. For those of us now hitting middle age, that wistfulness embraces Julie Harris's Sally Bowles, Kim Stanley's Cherie in *Bus Stop*, and Ms. Hagen's Martha. Well, it seems we haven't arrived too late at the party after all. Ms. Hagen is now in a role she says she believes she was meant to play, and there's no evidence of diminished fierceness or technique in her performance. Admirers of serious acting who choose to miss it are merely foolish."[7]

The day after opening, the box office took in $44,000, which put us well into *A Lie of the Mind* territory. With a sheaf of solid reviews now in hand, it was time to approach Lucille Lortel about an ongoing problem with her theater. Christopher Street had changed. It was now a noisy honky-tonk. During previews, we had stationed someone in front of the theater to try to control the noise level. People screaming, transistor radios, and firecrackers could all be heard from inside the theater.

"Lucille," I began, "Christopher Street has changed. It's become very noisy, and the noise carries right into the house. I was wondering how you would feel about building up the rear half-wall to the ceiling. Or, hanging some thick velour above it."

There was a long silence, after which Lucille rejoined, "Tell Uta to speak up, dear."

At a production photo shoot, someone suggested a picture of Uta and me. "Oh, yes," Uta said. "The Smokers." As the photo was being taken, she told me a story Bea Lillie had told her about a smoking chorine that is unprintable. I will tell it privately upon request.

The Off Broadway production of Dana Rowe and John Dempsey's new musical, *Zombie Prom,* went into rehearsal at the Variety Arts Theatre in late January of 1996, produced by the legendary rock attorney, Nat Weiss, and directed by Philip Wm. McKinley, a director with worldwide credits in his New York debut. But at that very moment, a phenomenon was beginning that would have a seismic impact on Off Broadway in the months to come.

Rent opened at New York Theatre Workshop on January 26, 1996, two days after its author, lyricist, and composer, Jonathan

Larson, died of an aneurysm. The Workshop had been founded in 1979 by Stephen Graham, who remained one of its prime benefactors. *Rent* was an edgy musical fashioned after *La Bohème*, which the author targeted at the MTV generation. It was greeted with an explosion of critical and audience support and quickly became the standard against which every new musical would be measured for the rest of the season.

Months earlier, I had walked out of a reading of *Rent* after twenty minutes. The Workshop's Artistic Director, Jim Nicola, who is a friend, was in the lobby. "Leaving?" he said. "Yeah," I said. "These people," referring to the characters in the play who were squatters, "think they're entitled to something for nothing."

I didn't like them.

The Sunday in February that *Zombie Prom* ran its first *Times* ad, we were engulfed by one full page after another of *Times* editorial devoted to *Rent* and its impending move to Broadway. Never before had the *Times* accorded such an abundance of space to a single production. It was the bold beginning of a Broadway avalanche that would bury Off Broadway by the end of the season.

Zombie Prom preview audiences were ecstatic, but there were no ticket sales. We were, in the vernacular, "sold out of comps." And I observed out of the corner of my eye that sales for my two hits, *Picasso* and *Mrs. Klein*, were softening.

Ben Brantley's *Times* review was a negative, dismissing the show as bland and not sufficiently edgy.

Other reviews for *Zombie Prom* were good to mixed but not enough to ensure survival in the evolving Off Broadway desert.

It was scary to me that the show I had walked out of was the biggest hit in decades and that the one I thought was a big winner was a flop. My taste was my taste, but it was suddenly far out of what had become the mainstream. Were the outer edges of the parade passing me by?

During March and April, an astonishing eighteen Broadway productions opened, all vying for Tony attention and buying ad space with which Off Broadway couldn't possibly compete. *Rent* and

Bring in 'da Noise, Bring in 'da Funk were among them. The press focused entirely on the new Broadway product, and Off Broadway found itself all but forgotten. Advance ticket sales for *Mrs. Klein* and *Picasso* came to a screeching halt.

On June 12, there was a *Times* piece by Peter Marks with the headline "Why Commercial Off Broadway Is All but Wiped Out, for Now" that told our story. Eight Off Broadway productions had closed within weeks, and four of them were mine. In the *Times* story, Ben Sprecher irked me by publicly second-guessing our decisions to close *Picasso* and *Klein*. "I really don't understand," he said. "Their grosses were terrific. I think they were closed prematurely."

We could have stayed in Ben's theaters, begging him for rent concessions, and struggling through the summer. Instead, we chose to take both shows to San Francisco, where they made big profits. *Mrs. Klein* launched a small tour that began at the Geary Theater, and *Picasso* played at Jonathan Reinis's Theatre on the Square, where it racked up a record 408 performances.

Picasso owed a measure of its San Francisco success to Reinis, who knew his city like the back of his hand and was a master promoter. He began with a massive press conference attended by more than seventy local journalists.

Steve Martin was there, but Paul Provenza stole the show. When a reporter asked how he prepared for his role as Picasso, Provenza answered, "I start by moving both of my eyes to the same side of my head."

Uta Hagen in the 1,024-seat Geary was a revelation. Without any new direction, her performance seemed to expand automatically to fill the larger theater and, if anything, was even better than it had been in the 299-seat Lortel.

On June 13, Bernie Jacobs' eightieth birthday was celebrated at an industry-wide luncheon at Sardi's. The afternoon was memorable for Nancy Coyne's heartfelt tribute to his wife, Betty, beloved by one and all, and the late arrival of David Merrick and his girlfriend

Natalie Lloyd, who tiptoed eerily through the restaurant looking for a table.

Days later, his birthday was again celebrated at a more intimate gathering at Peter Luger that included his wife Betty, Alvin and Marilyn Cooperman, Ron and Isobel Robins Konecky, Dasha Epstein, Cary Calvert, and me. It was a relaxed evening of warm, wonderful fun with people who loved Bernie very dearly. A few weeks later, he and Betty took the whole family on a three-week Alaskan cruise.

Shortly after the family returned to New York, he went into the hospital for additional major heart surgery. Late in the morning on August 27, I received a call from Jerry. He was crying as he said, "Bernie died today." I rushed to the offices. Lee Silver and Jerry's longtime assistant, Betty Spitz, were there with him. Jerry and I embraced, and he gestured toward the papers on his desk. "None of this really matters," he said. "None of this matters at all."

I have rarely loved anyone as much as I loved Bernie Jacobs. He was as endearing as he was wise. "Dead is dead," he always said, and that quote is even in a book of daily meditations published by Hazelden Press. What he meant was death is absolute, it's over, and after a moment you are forgotten. I am among the people who think of him every day. I never had a more loyal friend and, when you think of his position, loyalty was not a realistic expectation. He came into my life with the same force as Judy Garland.

I had a dream about him a few years later. I was on a bus: I looked back and saw him seated across the aisle. I began to cry and said, "You're here." He looked at me and, in his Bernie way, he said, "I'm here, Albert." I woke up crying when I realized it meant he would always be with me. I told my therapist about it, expecting some profound explanation. "Isn't it wonderful how they come to us?" she said.

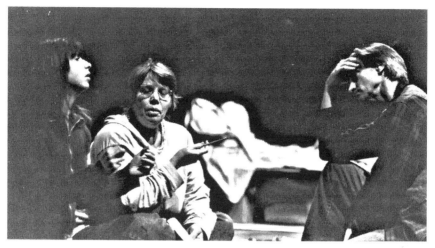

Tech rehearsal. Anne E. Militello, Lighting Designer (left), Ruth Kreshka, Production Stage Manager (center)—part of Sam Shepard's (right) hand-picked production team for his multi-award winning *A Lie of the Mind*, 1985.

Photo by Martha Swope (c) New York Public Library

A Lie of the Mind Cast and Band. (seated on floor l to r) Jim Watson, Clay Buckner, Mike Craver, (second row) Amanda Plummer, Karen Young, Aiden Quinn, Anne Wedgeworth, James Gammon, (standing) Jack Herrick, Geraldine Page, Harvey Keitel, Will Patton, and Tommy Thompson, 1986. *Anne E. Militello*

Brunch on the Titanic. Mike Nichols with the company of *Standup Shakespeare*, 1987.

Meaghan Robinson, Charles Busch, and Julie Halston celebrating the jubilant opening night of Charles' *The Lady in Question*, 1989.

The Grapes of Wrath. Producer Stephen Eich assembled the entire company on the stage of the Cort Theater after our triumphant Tony wins for Best Play and Best Director, Frank Galati, 1990. *Kenneth Katz*

Tony nominated co-stars and Steppenwolf co-founders Terry Kinney and Gary Sinise enjoying *The Grapes of Wrath* opening night party at Sardi's.
Cathy Blaivas Photography

Two of the best. Lois Smith, Tony nominated for her unforgettable portrayal of Ma Joad, and Malcolm Ewen, our fine Production Stage Manager—responsible for 38 actors, hundreds of lighting cues, and a creek. *Robyn Taylor Barbon*

Frank Galati and Stephen Eich. *Cathy Blaivas Photography*

With *Blue Man Group* (l to r) Phil Stanton, Matt Goldman, (kneeling) Chris Wink.
David "Squid" Quinn

Paris, 1991 with Helen and Zoe Jacobs.   *Lael Jacobs*

Montmartre with Jack Garfein.   *Clare Euclare*

The Song of Jacob Zulu. Ladysmith Black Mambazo in front of the Plymouth Theater, 1993. *Anita and Steve Shevett*

Joseph Shebalala and Erick Simonson. *Anita and Steve Shevett*

American Theatre Wing "Working in the Theatre" telecast, 1993. (front l to r) Wendy Wasserstein, Dasha Epstein, George White, Isabelle Stevenson, Lucille Lortel, Lynne Meadow. (back) Ben Sprecher, Zakes Mokae, Dorothy Olim, me, and Howard Kissel. *American Theatre Wing*

Picasso at the Lapin Agile, 1995. With (l to r) Randall Arney, Steve Martin, Joan Stein, and Stephen Eich.   *Joan Marcus*

"I had asked for a seabreeze!" (My caption) With the great Uta Hagen and Santa Claus during Ms. Hagen's smashing success in *Mrs. Klein* at the Lucille Lortel, 1995.

The Lion King opening night, 1997, with my cherished friend Peter Schneider, who produced it for Disney Theatricals. The following day the box office took in $2.5 million—a record. As the years went by, *The Lion King* became the highest grossing event in world entertainment history.   *Anita and Steve Shevett*

Bernie Jacobs' 80th Birthday at Peter Luger. June 1996.

With Cameron Mackintosh and Mark Bramble at the smashing Actors Fund Salute to Cameron, 1997. Both of these dear friends were people of fun and mischief.

Jay Brady Photography/Actors Fund

Seeing *The Boy from Oz* in Sydney with Adrian Bryan-Brown, the Dean of Theatrical Press Agents, 1998.

Joan Marcus

A Broadway opening night with Peter Schneider, Bernard Gersten, and Paul Libin.

Anita and Steve Shevett

Happy Birthday—Tarantino Style. *Wait Until Dark*, 1998.

Anita and Steve Shevett

The brilliant Edwardo Machado and Angelina Fiordellisi. *Havana Is Waiting—* a fine play but the first rehearsal was 9/11/2001. *Carol Rosegg*

Gore Vidal's The Best Man. Gore Vidal and Jeffrey Richards at the opening night party at Tavern On the Green, 2000. *Anita and Steve Shevett*

Meet Me in Las Vegas!—With Ellen Stewart for the opening of *Blue Man Group* at the Luxor Hotel, 2000.   *Rebecca Schneider*

Stevie Philips organized a birthday bash for me at Frankie and Johnnie with most of my favorite ladies. (l to r) Stevie, Dorothy Olim, Joan Stein, Betty Jacobs, Jane Harmon. (back row) Irene Burns, Ina Meibach, Helen Jacobs, (kneeling) Dasha Epstein.

Long Day's Journey into Night after closing at the Plymouth Theatre, August 26, 2003. (Front) Vanessa Redgrave, Brian Dennehy. (first row l to r) Philip Seymour Hoffman, Fiana Toibin, Robert Sean Leonard, Philip Cusack, Jane Grey, Christopher Wynkoop, (second row l to r) Bruce Klinger, Sandy Binion, Barbara Rosenthal, Mac Smith, Kathe Mull, me, and Michael Dempsey. *Jay Brady Photography/Actors Fund*

The Boy from Oz, 2003. Across from the Plymouth was the Imperial, where I saw Ethel Merman in *Gypsy*, my first Broadway show. Now, forty years later, I was about to play the Imperial with a big Broadway hit.

The Boy from Oz. Hugh Jackman and his Tony, 2004.   *Anita and Steve Shevett*

Hugh's Sardi's caricature unveiling. (l to r) Stephanie J. Block, Beth Fowler, me, Deborra-lee Furness holding Oscar, Hugh, Maureen Lipman, and David Krane.   *Eileen F. Hagerty*

With *Oz* producers Ben Gannon and Robert Fox at our Tony after party. Two classy, savvy men—working with them was the best of times.   *Brian Abel*

The Company onstage after the closing performance of *The Boy From Oz*, September 12, 2004. If we had enforced the Actors' Equity rule against the taking of photographs, the entire audience would have been thrown out. *Joan Marcus*

Noted director Michael Wilson with Robert E. Wankel, President of The Shubert Organization, at a sparkling Sardi's birthday party for D.S. (Dessie) Moynihan, Shubert Vice President, Creative Projects (at left), 2014.

Gay Men's Health Crisis presentation of Howard Ashman Award to Tom Viola
November 30, 2015. With (l to r) Tom, Cyril Brosnan, and Bill Evans.

Broadway Cares/Equity Fights AIDS

With the great producer and manager Elizabeth I. McCann

Jean Dalric

With Philip J. Smith. Phil was a major force behind The Shubert Pavilion for interim care at the Actors Fund Home in Englewood, New Jersey.

With Philip J. Smith, Chairman of The Shubert Organization.

Anita and Steve Shevett

With Barbara Hogenson, Michael Riedel, and Imogen Lloyd Webber at a Players Club evening of readings from STAGES, 2017.   *Anthony Reyes*

CHAPTER 32

"'Present Laughter' Is Really About Control"

Buoyed by his success with *Mrs. Klein*, David Richenthal decided to go full tilt and produce a Broadway show that actually started on Broadway. No out-of-town tryouts, which by 1996 were rare, no preliminary nonprofit production enhanced with the producer's money, which by 1996 were de rigueur. The show was Noël Coward's elegant autobiographical comedy *Present Laughter*, and David was ready to gamble big.

For the role Coward had created for himself, Richenthal chose Frank Langella, who was in everyone's opinion, including Langella's, the perfect choice. On the risk side, Langella's insatiable need to control was as legendary as some of his performances, and his star power over the years had been largely dependent on the public's interest in the role itself. *Dracula*, his greatest success, had occurred nearly two decades earlier. More recently, he proved a draw with a provocative performance in The Roundabout's revival of Strindberg's *The Father*. The moment when the Langella character slapped his daughter then grabbed and kissed her passionately was not in the script. The audiences gasped. The run was extended. But citing differences with his star, the gifted director Robert Falls fled the production during rehearsals.

To direct *Present Laughter*, Richenthal chose—and Langella embraced—Scott Elliott, the exciting young director from The New Group, a choice that offered bold possibilities, but a director with no previous Broadway experience who would be taking on one of its *monstres sacrés*.

I amused myself by loading up my deal memo to Scott's agent, Sam Cohn, with minimum terms, as I noted what a pleasure it would be to work with Scott on this, his *first* Broadway show. Frank Langella handled his own negotiation, which was intimidating and fun.

David again partnered with Anita Waxman, and the two producers surrounded their star with a superb cast that included Allison Janney, Lisa Emery, Kellie Overbey, and Tim Hopper. Steve Ross, the elegant cafe society star who was a long-time fixture at the Oak Room of the Algonquin, was a splendid addition, playing and singing Coward songs during the scene changes.

In most productions, the honeymoon period lasts until the Thursday of the third week of rehearsal. By that point, trouble of some kind is inevitable. If you are fortunate, it's just a reset to put everything on a more real footing. With Mr. Langella, we barely made it to the end of the first week. The first soured relationship was with Jeffrey Richards, the press agent, who was himself not without fault. They disliked each other on sight and Langella found him duplicitous.

Next was Scott Elliott. As he had with Dennis Rosa, the director of *Dracula*, and with Robert Falls on *The Father*, Langella turned on him and stopped speaking to him. Elliott and Richenthal demanded cuts in the script. Langella was unapproachable. The producers wanted to replace the actress in the role of Joanna, and on this they got resistance from Scott Elliott. She was a standing member of his New Group company, and he wouldn't hear of it.

At this same moment, our other production, *Mrs. Klein*, opened badly in Chicago. The *Tribune* critic saw it while jet lagged after a delayed London flight and described it as "grim." This confluence of elements created one of those moments in the theater when you think everything in the universe is conspiring against you.

David Richenthal, stressed to the max, had a heart attack and was rushed to the hospital. His doctor released him hours before the opening night, reluctantly allowing him to attend the performance but not the party. Instead, David and I had a marketing meeting in a private hotel suite. David's father, the attorney Arthur Richenthal, dropped by to say hello and was horrified to see David smoking a cigar.

The reviews were full of superlatives for Frank Langella's performance, with Ben Brantley of the *Times* slightly less enthusiastic, writing, "The ever-magnetic Frank Langella, who, in a role he was born for, is having an infectiously fine time as Coward's alter ego." Somewhat slyly, Brantley saved his ultimate praise for Allison Janney, who he said delivers the "most fully accomplished performance on the stage."

Scott Elliot had taken the lid off the play's underlying sexuality, which seemed jarring to Brantley but excited Coward's surviving companion, Graham Payn, who thought the play had been liberated. Brantley also faulted an overeagerness he sensed in the direction. In an interesting side note, Brantley mentioned that "Philip Hoare, Coward's most recent biographer, has observed that for all its comic frenzy, 'Present Laughter' is really about control."[8]

Before the first performance after opening, I went to visit Frank in his dressing room. "Are you watching today?" he asked. "I hadn't planned to," I said. "You should watch," he said, "because now I'm going to give *my* performance." I did watch, and his performance was broad and occasionally vulgar. It was a crowd-pleaser for sure, but the elegance of Coward's play and of the character had been sacrificed. The Tony nominators agreed. Langella, fully capable of capturing the award itself, failed even to be nominated.

I was not on the receiving end of Langella's willfulness. I enjoyed him immensely on and off stage, and I like him very much. In my estimation, his obsession to control exceeded even the size of his enormous talent and, while not catastrophic, it did him a disservice.

A few weeks after our closing in April of 1997, Langella called me. "I am going to produce, direct, and star in a major Broadway revival of *Dracula*," he said. "And I want you to be my general manager." I gulped and said, "I would be honored." As I hung up, I thought, *How the hell do I get out of this?* Two months later, Frank called again.

"I haven't heard from you since our last conversation," he said. "I just want to make sure you're really on board."

I took a deep breath. "Look, Frank," I said. "I have to be honest. I adore you, but on *Present Laughter*, you didn't listen to anyone. If you're going to produce, direct, and star in this, I would have three people who weren't listening to me."

"Fair enough," he said.

A few months later, he directed, adapted, and starred in a poorly received revival of *Cyrano de Bergerac* for The Roundabout. He phoned me the day after opening. "I have been thinking of you all morning," he said. "I will never do this again."

CHAPTER 33

Opryland

I was familiar with Dasha Epstein as a producer of such well-known hits as *Same Time, Next Year*, *Ain't Misbehavin'*, and *Children of a Lesser God*, but we had never met until she became involved as a producer of *Orphans*. I was expecting a short woman with hair severely pulled back and feet planted permanently in first position. She was expecting a middle-aged man in a three-piece suit with a cigar. Dasha was instead a very attractive lady of generous heart and adventurous spirit, and I was a very young 44.

Dasha knows everyone, and everyone knows Dasha. She is a spontaneous person, and her requests are sometimes as audacious as her generosity. My office got a phone call one night at six. "I need six tickets for *The Lion King* for *tonight*—for my dear friend the King of Spain." I called the producer, my friend Peter Schneider, and implored him to grant the request. "What name shall I put these under?" he asked. "Spain comma, King of," I answered, and within minutes the King's security descended on the New Amsterdam Theatre.

When I was visiting her beautiful home in Marbella with friends, she said, "Oh, take twenty minutes and go to Ronda." We went up a mountain on a one-lane dirt road, and, when we drove *through* a cloud, it was clear that twenty minutes was an underestimation. At the top, we saw a beautiful bullring and watched part of a bull fight (it was too brutal).

She has the best taste of anyone I know. When Phil Smith moved into a duplex apartment on Fifth Avenue, Dasha and Betty Jacobs did the décor, and it was superb. Her parties in her sumptuous Park Avenue apartment are spectacular. Especially one for Bernie Jacobs' seventieth birthday. David Merrick was there. It was after his stroke, and I stood by as he and Jerry Schoenfeld had a twenty-minute conversation in which Jerry appeared to understand every word he said.

Dasha, Betty Jacobs, and I were nearly thrown out of a performance of *Forbidden Broadway* at Palssons for eating jelly beans. We stopped along the way and bought a bag, which we were nicely sharing, when our waitress (they weren't yet called *servers*) informed us that we could not eat them in the club. After a few minutes, Betty slid them across the table under her playbill and the waitress again stopped us. Betty then pretended to put them in her purse but shared them with us under the table. The waitress had had it with us. She said she was going to call the manager and have us removed. Like naughty schoolchildren, we promised we would stop, and we did.

Dasha called in the spring of 1997 to say that her friends at Gaylord Entertainment in Nashville wanted to bring a show to New York, and she told them I had to be the general manager. *Always . . . Patsy Cline* was a two-hander by Ted Swindley about the legendary country-and-western singer and her ongoing correspondence with a loyal fan. It had been done all over the country. Gaylord, of course, were the producers of *Grand Ole Opry*, the iconic weekly country-and-western concert that had been broadcast live from Nashville since 1925. Every major star in the history of the genre had performed on the *Opry*.

Always . . . Patsy Cline was to be my first and only corporate experience. My contact was John Haywood, entertainment director of Opryland USA and the husband of singer Louise Mandrell. John was a handsome man and a true gentlemen. Not "corporate," nor were any of the other Gaylord people I encountered. Very genuine, totally accessible people. I stayed in the amazing Opryland Hotel, which was ostentatious but in the best of taste. The restaurant in the atrium was breathtaking. I went to Ryman auditorium, where the *Opry* broadcasts took place, but I spent the bulk of the two days talking to the executives about how I thought *Patsy Cline* should be handled in New York. They had already engaged Ken Sunshine, a major press agent for politicos and stars, to handle public relations, but I convinced them that a theatrical press agent (who could handle previews, opening night, and the New York theatre press) should be added and suggested Chris Bono. He and Sunshine got on splendidly.

Unfortunately, in our production, there was a hole where the star should have been. Ben Brantley wrote in the *Times* of our Patsy that "(her) mimetically exact interpretation never registers as fully human. She's a figure of windup graciousness and patented rustic charm, an animated page from a fan magazine . . . her perfectly pleasant voice simply can't expand into Cline's rich, soul-clutching timbres . . . The show is less an instance of resurrection than taxidermy."[9]

The band, under the superb direction of Gene Hicks, was top-notch, and Margo Martindale, an audience favorite from *Steel Magnolias*, played the friend. Cline devotees swarmed the theatre for the first few months, but word of mouth was not sufficient to sustain a run, and the show closed after 191 performances, its potential never fully realized.

CHAPTER 34

Jane

I loved my collaboration with Jane Harmon as producer of *A Life in the Theatre*, so I was thrilled when she asked me to fly to Atlanta during the summer of 1996 to see a new Alfred Uhry play, *The Last Night of Ballyhoo*, at the Alliance Theatre. Her relationship with Uhry had begun in The Acting Company with *The Robber Bridegroom* and had reached a high point when she was the lead producer of Uhry's long-running *Driving Miss Daisy*, which captured the Pulitzer Prize and is the first and only winner of the Academy Award for Best Picture based on an Off Broadway play.

The Last Night of Ballyhoo is a family comedy set in Atlanta in 1939 on the eve of the historic premiere of *Gone with the Wind*. A Jewish family is preparing for "Ballyhoo," an annual event at a country club that accepts only the "right" kind of Jews, meaning German, not Eastern European.

I was awed by the Atlanta performance and thought the play's underlying warmth and humor beautifully paved the way for the presentation of its issues. Afterward, as Jane and I raced through the sprawling Atlanta airport to catch our return flight, she said, "Who knows, maybe we'll even get a nomination."

"I would expect to win," I replied.

For the Broadway move, Jane wisely picked the 597-seat Helen Hayes Theatre on West Forty-Fourth Street, next to Sardi's. The location was perfect, and, as we had no major stars, the small seating capacity afforded us lower weekly operating costs than most other Broadway plays. Ron Lagomarsino was the director, as he had been for *Daisy*. The outstanding cast featured Dana Ivey, Jessica Hecht, Terry Beaver, Celia Weston, Paul Rudd, Stephen Largay, and Arija Bareikis.

Early in rehearsal, Jane, who lived in Weston, Connecticut, was diagnosed with Lyme disease. Her first priority was the production and her investors, and she forged ahead despite our concerns. As a result, she developed bilateral Bell's palsy, a paralysis of some of her facial muscles, which became permanent.

Like many other things in the theater, opening night parties had become elaborate and complicated. Suzanne Tobak established an opening night party business that handled everything to perfection and worked with whatever budget a show could provide. It was no longer just a matter of the general manager picking up the phone and negotiating a price with a restaurant's press agent. The era of one tray of cold hors d'oeuvres had passed.

Jane and I snuck off from the party to read Ben Brantley's *Times* review. Although he felt the play to be "honorably intentioned," he thought it formulaic, old-fashioned, and in over its head on the social issues. He dismissed it as "the theatrical equivalent of comfort food." The play, one of feelings and fond remembrances, was perhaps an overload for Mr. Brantley, an intellectual who sometimes lived in his head and liked his sentiment wrapped in the protective cover of style.

Here, once again, was a *Times* show with a negative *Times* review, but the other reviews were sparkling, and there was enough ammo to mount a campaign. And mount one we did, using Howard Kissel's "You'll have a ball at Ballyhoo!" from the *Daily News* as our energized lead quote.

By 1997, ticket discounting had become an essential element of Broadway marketing. Shows offered discounts by mail, on the

Internet, and at the half price booth in Duffy Square. The top ticket price was now determined by factoring in a theoretical number of discount sales. Going against the trend, Jane held fast that every *Ballyhoo* ticket would be sold at full price. All of our unsold tickets were traded for advertising and marketing. No discount offers, no booth. To the public, we were behaving like a show that was selling out, and, after eleven weeks, we were. An audience survey revealed that 91 percent bought tickets on the basis of word of mouth and 76 percent on the basis of advertising.

Jane and I were intense people. We treated every week as if it were the first, and our spirited "discussions" were part of why I loved working with her. Liz Oliver, one of her producing partners, recalled one discussion in which, after a pause, Jane said, "I'm just anticipating the other shoe." To which I apparently replied, "Jane, you *are* the other shoe."

Ballyhoo was nominated for four Tony Awards: Dana Ivey, Celia Weston, and Terry Beaver for acting, and the production for Best Play. It was a thrill to sit in Radio City and hear Jimmy Smits announce that we had won Best Play, and I was deeply touched when Jane, who proclaimed that Alfred Uhry now had the "triple crown" of the Pulitzer, Academy Award, and Tony, thanked me for my work on the production. When she got home, her son Doug had posted a sign on the door. "TAKE THAT, NEW YORK TIMES!"

Raquel Welch had been the presenter in Terry Beaver's category, and when I asked him if he was disappointed at not winning, he smiled. "No. It was worth it just to hear Raquel Welch say 'Beaver.'"

After we had been running about a year, business began to lag, but we continued to make a small profit. Jane pursued me to ask the author and director for royalty cuts. "How can I do that?" I said. "We are still making a small profit."

"I'm not in this for a small profit," she advised. "See what you can do. Otherwise I'm prepared to close."

I kicked and screamed but went after it.

We reached agreement for a partial but significant waiver. During that period until the show closed in June, it made an additional profit of $250,000, and the author and director had three more months of income. Once again, I had to bow to her. By the time the show closed, it had repaid its investment and made a 134-percent profit. Everyone, including its author, lays this squarely at the feet of Jane Harmon.

CHAPTER 35

"If You Think You Know What Terror Is . . ."

Quentin Tarantino's journey from video store clerk to cinema auteur of *Reservoir Dogs* and *Pulp Fiction* was the stuff of contemporary mythology. In the age of video games, he was a hero, and when producers Alan Lichtenstein and Robert Young approached me in 1998 to general manage a Broadway revival of *Wait Until Dark* starring Tarantino, I couldn't resist.

It was an idea that looked great on paper, and Nancy Coyne came up with a smart ad campaign. Spooky photos of Quentin and his co-star, Marisa Tomei, on either side of an eye chart for print, and a radio spot that began, "If you think you know what terror is (Scream) Wait Until Dark . . ."

Truth told, the Frederick Knott play first produced on Broadway in 1966 was badly dated. A group of hapless hoodlums go through an entire week of elaborate schemes and disguises to extract a doll stuffed with heroin from a blind woman's basement. By 1998, we lived in a more ruthless world. Quentin nailed it when he told an interviewer, "If I had written the play, it would be over in three minutes. I would just put the gun in the blind woman's mouth and say, 'Give me the doll, bitch, or I'll blow your fucking head off!'"

Prior to Broadway, we were to do a three-week out-of-town tryout at the Wilbur Theatre in Boston. Jon B. Platt, who controlled the Wilbur, the Colonial, and the Charles Playhouse, was a Boston powerhouse. He came into *Wait Until Dark* as a partner on the basis that we would play his theater. Out-of-town tryouts, long the stuff of theater lore, were now extinct. Why add a million dollars to the budget to go to Boston when you could endow a production at the Manhattan Theatre Club with $200,000 and get away scot-free if it didn't work?

Wait Until Dark was the only out-of-town tryout I ever did. I loved Boston, and I looked forward to the adventure, despite warnings to be wary of Mr. Platt and the Boston theatrical unions. His theater agreement charged and overcharged for everything imaginable. We tried to fight it, but Platt refused to budge, and my producers wouldn't blow the deal. "We've got Quentin," they said. "Boston will pay for itself."

Yes, I thought, *and the handsome profits that should be accruing to the production will flow neatly into the Platt pocket.*

The balls were constantly in the air, and balls there were. We set the venue for our Boston opening night party, and Platt, without consulting his partners, called the place and canceled it, scheduling it instead in a disco he operated in the basement of the Wilbur. And so it was.

At midnight, our party came to an abrupt end. Strobe lights flashed, music pounded, and the waiters crashed our tables against the wall. Jon B. Platt's disco was now open for business, and there was a long line outside pushing its way in, hoping, no doubt, for a glimpse of Quentin Tarantino. I noticed Platt as we were leaving. "You know, Jon," I said, "I keep hoping to like you."

The reviews, especially for Quentin, were terrible, but he was doing the best box office since Al Pacino had played the Wilbur in *Glengarry Glen Ross* ten years earlier. Good box office covers a multitude of sins, but it's not a cure-all. After the Boston opening, Mira Sorvino broke up with Tarantino, ending their two-year relationship, and his long, prestigious New York opening-night celebrity list began to shrink drastically.

In the meantime, I had no signed agreement with Tarantino. The Broadway advance had now reached $3,000,000, unheard of for a play at that time, and his William Morris agents, who I had known for years, weren't even returning my calls. I complained to Alan Kanoff, head of the agency, with whom I'd had a relationship since *Little Shop of Horrors*. As a result, the responsible agents, my friends George Lane and David Kalodner, sent a huge bouquet of flowers and arrived in person to apologize.

But there was still no contract. I was told it was because there were three William Morris agents on the West Coast who desperately wanted Tarantino to walk. The theater commissions were a drop in the bucket compared to what they could be making on him in a film. I was sweating bullets. If he walked, the show would collapse.

The New York press were all over Quentin. He was totally accessible and always interesting. When David Letterman asked, "You're a director. How can you take direction from someone else?" Quentin responded, "Easy. As a director, I'm an adult. I'm in charge. As an actor, I'm a child. So there's no conflict."

His approach to acting *was* childlike. And inconsistent. Some nights he did it with an Italian accent, other nights with an Irish accent, sometimes even an American accent. To prepare, he came in two hours before curtain and sat in his dressing room in total darkness. He played devil rock and burned incense as he wrote "kill the bitch" on his mirror in lipstick.

The first preview in New York was March 27, Quentin's thirty-fifth birthday. We gave an informal party in the basement of the theater. Instead of cutting his cake, he stabbed it. As he exited the stage door, there was a surging crowd of five hundred people waiting for him. It was to be that way every night.

Our only opening-night celebrity was Faye Dunaway. When I noticed Bridget Aschenberg, the author's agent, eating a bag of peanuts and shelling them on the front walk under the marquee, I said, "I see the bus from the shtetl has arrived."

The reviews held no surprises. Ben Brantley's take in the *Times* was representative. Tarantino, he wrote, "seems to be not so much acting as just hanging out, as though a big Broadway house were a moderately cool place to mark time until the clubs open. He was roasted by critics during the Boston tryout of 'Wait Until Dark', and reports of his inadequacy have not been exaggerated."[10]

Wait Until Dark used up its $3,000,000 advance and closed on June 28, 1998, after 208 performances.

CHAPTER 36

Rehearsals for Retirement

In the spring of 1997, I was in the middle of the best financial period of my career and thought it was time I owned something. The logical acquisition was an apartment, but, as I told Peter Schneider, everything I wanted was beyond my means. Peter was on top of the world. As the head of Disney Animation, he had presided over a glorious renaissance that included such blockbusters as *Who Framed Roger Rabbit*, *The Little Mermaid*, *Beauty and the Beast*, *Aladdin*, and *The Lion King*, which he was now about to bring to Broadway as the new head of Disney Theatrical.

"You've worked hard," he said. "You should have what you want. Find it, and I'll help you." I was touched by this response.

As my search continued into the fall of 1997, *The Lion King* began previews. Peter gave me a large discounted block of tickets to benefit the Caron Foundation, the drug and alcohol treatment program that was the bedrock of my own sobriety. Having been through my drinking years, Peter was a champion of my recovery, and he honored me by joining me for the pre-show dinner, where we heard Robert F. Kennedy Jr. announce that it was the most successful fundraiser in Caron's history. We sat together as I watched *The Lion King* for the first time. I cried from beginning to end, moved by the staggering achievement of this young man I first met a week after he had come to New York and with whom I had so much rich history.

The star-studded opening night was monumental, with Peter surrounded by so many of our loved mutual friends. The only thing that topped the out-of-this-world reviews was the take at the box office the next day: two and a half million dollars, which was the record for a single day on Broadway.

In the early spring, producer Anita Waxman and her husband Albert took over the entire New York Public Library at Forty-Second Street and Fifth to throw a blowout in celebration of the sale of their HMO. Astrologers and tarot readers were lined up along the walls of the main hall. I spoke to an astrologer who told me that in June or July I was going to find a home. I told her of my futile year-long apartment search that had ended in exasperation with a $550,000 windowless loft in Soho. She said, "No, no, this will be a home, not an apartment."

Weeks later in the *Observer*, I saw an ad for a country house in the Hudson Valley. "French Provincial, Romantic, Mini-Estate for Sale by Owner." No button unpushed. I clipped it and put it on the coffee table. Over the next several days, I kept picking it up and looking at it. Despite my friends' protestations that I was a city person, I called the owners.

The following Saturday afternoon, I hired a car and driver to go look at it. Before we even reached the end of the long, wooded driveway, I knew I had to have it. After a tour of the house and grounds and a three-hour chat with the owners, I put together my offer in the car and called the minute I got back. A charming French Provincial house on seven acres with a pool was now within my reach, at half the price of most of the apartments I had seen in Manhattan.

The dream weekend continued on Sunday when *The Lion King* won the Tony for Best Musical, and Peter acknowledged Bruce Mailman and me in his speech. I could hardly wait for our breakfast at the Pierre the following morning to share Peter's well-deserved triumph and to surprise him and his wife Hope with my own wonderful news. I told them all about the house and showed them some photos. True to Peter's promise, they were right there with their help.

That afternoon, the owners accepted my offer.

My friend Bill Hemingway, who owned Alice's Antiques in Soho, had recently acquired a country place in Pennsylvania. "Be careful," he warned me, "it can be seductive." Indeed. I knew it when I felt my heart leap as the Metro North train crossed the Harlem bridge on Friday and eventually Thursday afternoons. It was romantic, comforting, and a respite from the hustle and bustle of New York and the changing theater industry.

CHAPTER 37

Ellen

*E*llen Stewart called to tell me she was going to Las Vegas for the opening of *Blue Man Group* at the Luxor Hotel and asked if I would like to fly out together. "I would love it," I said. "Let's go first class!"

I began making the arrangements, and, a few days later, she called again. She wanted my advice.

"My older sister lives in Las Vegas," she said, "and we have been estranged for seventeen years. I want to know if you think I should get in touch with her."

I said, "Ellen, do whatever you can live with." She gave it some thought and decided that she did want to see her sister. On our flight, I was treated to Ellen's life story as I had never heard it before.

Ironic, after she had been so touchy for so many years over what was written about her in *The Off Off Broadway Book*.

She had grown up mostly in Chicago. Her mother was a skilled seamstress who designed and made the fancy clothes for the debutante balls black working families gave in the palatial homes of their wealthy white employers while they were away during the cold Chicago winters.

Ellen sat on the floor next to her mother, taking the scraps of the beautiful leftover fabrics and designing and sewing clothes for her dolls.

"My two vivid memories of childhood," she told me, "were the strap hanging in the kitchen and the soap operas playing on the radios in every room in the house. Early in my life, my sister poisoned my mother's mind against me, and there was nothing I could do to change it."

She ran away to Detroit when she was seventeen and found her way to a Mafia-operated nightclub that presented all of the top black entertainers to its white audiences. She was charismatic and bright with a good business head, and the owner adored her. He called her "Sunny." When he eventually became ill and died, he willed his position with the club to her. His daughter, in a jealous rage, threatened to kill her, and Ellen ran away to New York City and Saks Fifth Avenue, where she was employed as an elevator operator.

At Saks, wealthy customers inquired about the exotic Egyptian model with the colorful clothes.

She became Edith Lances' assistant, trimming the threads off of Lances' custom-made bras and corsets. Lances quickly saw her great talent and brought her to the attention of management, who sent her on scholarship to the Sorbonne. Upon her return, she designed a clothing line of her own. Everyone at Saks disliked her. She was disdainfully called "Miss Ellen." Both the black and white employees resented her rapid upward progression and her recognition by the young, wealthy clientele who constantly requested her.

She lived on Orchard Street and frequently told her tales of woe to Papa Diamond, who had a pushcart at her subway stop. Diamond told her she would never be happy until she got a pushcart of her own.

Her first Broadway show was *A Streetcar Named Desire*, and she didn't like it. "It reminded me of my mother's soap operas," she said. "It gave me a migraine headache." "So, did you feel that way about everything linear?" I asked. "Yes," she said. "It all took me back to those soaps on my mother's radios."

She left Saks and, with Paul Foster and Jim Moore, found a tenement basement on East Ninth Street, put down a deposit, and opened the Cafe La MaMa on July 27, 1962. Combine Ellen Stewart's non-linear sensibility with doll clothes made out of exotic scraps, and you may find the core of the La MaMa esthetic. An esthetic articulated and amplified by the major writers and artists at La MaMa and one that had a universal impact. She had found her pushcart. And she pushed it around the world.

As we checked into the Luxor, Ellen asked me to be with her when she met her sister. In the meantime, she wanted to see Matt Goldman, Chris Wink, and Phil Stanton, the original Blue Man creators who were busy rehearsing.

She had a gift for them. Busy as they were, they greeted us warmly. She gave them her gift and then chastised them for not inviting her to their Boston opening. That was the real point. She had an almost constant need to portray herself as a victim and to exact a punishment on her alleged victimizers.

I said, "Ellen, they're opening tonight, for God's sake."

"They need to know mother was unhappy," she replied.

We met in the lobby at six to greet her sister, who was to be waiting in front of the hotel. She linked her arm tightly in mine as we went to the front walk, where there was an older woman who looked somewhat like Ellen. They barely spoke, and they couldn't look at each other. They looked down at the sidewalk.

It was painful. I realized that I was along for comic relief but said to myself, *No, whatever this moment is, it belongs to them*. We went to the bar and had a drink, and, soon enough, it was time for the show. With Ellen on one side of me, with her sister and Peter Schneider, who had joined us, on the other, I was seated between two triple Scorpios.

"I don't know about you guys," I said, "but I'm in a rocket to the moon."

Blue Man Group had carefully expanded their show, and it played beautifully in the two-thousand-seat theater. In an era when big New York hits have come and gone in Vegas, *Blue Man Group* is still there nineteen years later. Ellen and I couldn't stand the place. We changed our plane reservations from one o'clock the next afternoon to 6:00 a.m.

CHAPTER 38

Eileen

*E*ileen Heckart began her career in 1943, and, by 2000, she had accomplished more than fifty years of distinguished, idiosyncratic performances onstage and in television and films. A summer earlier, she had appeared in Kenneth Lonergan's *The Waverly Gallery* at the Williamstown Theater Festival.

The play, based on Lonergan's own grandmother's descent into Alzheimer's, was a well-observed, beautifully written second play by the young author of *This Is Our Youth*, which had made a critical splash and run for 240 performances Off Broadway two years earlier. The play was made more meaningful for me because I remembered the lady and her gallery from my Village rounds in my early years in the city. She was one of those people who made the Village the Village.

The festival run had been a bumpy ride. Heckart, now eighty-one, had been in frail health, and Joanne Woodward, a friend of the festival and a board member, had gone on for several performances carrying the script. But Heckart was now eager to bring the play to the Promenade for an Off Broadway run, and producers Anita Waxman, Elizabeth Williams, and Randall Wreghitt were eager to have her. At my suggestion, Jason Robert Brown, fresh from his

Tony Award for Best Original Score for *Parade*, came on board to compose the incidental music.

Though not a hit, it was in many respects a blessed run. We were all set up to have a prompting device in Heckart's ear should she forget a line, but before the first preview, she said, "I'm going to do without it," which she did for the entire run. There were occasional missed lines, but it fit the character, and the actors around her adored her and were able to cover. I adored her, too, and we became pals. Chatting, gossiping, laughing, smoking. We both loved to smoke.

The reviews were decidedly mixed for the production and the play but unanimous in their high praise for Eileen Heckart, and she came away with a slew of awards, including the Drama Desk Award, the Lucille Lortel Award, the Drama League Award, the Obie Award, and the Outer Critics Circle Award. She was also inducted into the American Theater Hall of Fame and received an Honorary Tony for Lifetime Achievement. Like Uta Hagen, Arthur Miller, and others before her, she was highly annoyed that the reward for a lifetime of work consisted of being asked to stand in the audience and take a bow. "If I'da known that's what it was, I woulda told them to *mail* it," she said as we took a smoking break.

Eileen Heckart passed away on December 31, 2001. *The Waverly Gallery* was her last hurrah. And a clarion call it was.

CHAPTER 39

"May I Suggest?"
"No, You May Not"

I n the years following Bernie Jacobs' passing, Jerry Schoenfeld had become the Face of Broadway. It was not by design and was such a natural occurrence and so indigenous to the landscape that no one really noticed. There he was, greeting one and all on opening nights, speaking freely and articulately to the press, appearing suddenly in the wings, unannounced and enthusiastic. On Saturdays, he regularly put on a gray sweater and made the rounds of all the matinees in the Shubert houses.

I ran into him one Saturday when I was doing *Wait Until Dark*. "Have you had lunch, Albert? Join me for something at the Polish."

We had a terrific lunch, and he invited me to go with him to meet his wife Pat at Fendi to buy her a birthday fur. I wound up buying one for myself, which he convinced the salesman to give me at half price.

Early in 2000, Jerry asked me to general manage Claudia Shear's play *Dirty Blonde*, which Shubert was about to transfer from New York Theatre Workshop, a home to consistently outstanding and innovative work under the artistic direction of James Nicola.

James Lapine had taken a *New Yorker* piece about the young Mae West to Dessie Moynihan, Vice President, Creative Projects for Shubert, suggesting it as the genesis of a project for Claudia Shear. James and Claudia conceived it, and Claudia wrote it. At Dessie's urging, Shubert had been involved from the beginning.

The result was a wonderfully creative, collaborative endeavor. Claudia, after her long-run Off Broadway success as writer and star of *Blown Sideways through Life*, had written a multi-layered, insightful work about stars and their fans. Lapine's direction brought it to life with unpretentious clarity. In featured roles, Kevin Chamberlain and Bob Stillman were wonderful, with Stillman contributing the musical direction and a catchy title song. The venue selected for the transfer was the intimate Helen Hayes, which I thought the perfect choice, as it had been for *The Last Night of Ballyhoo.*

In the twenty years since I had served as the general manager of James Lapine's Off Broadway debut as the author and director of *Table Settings*, he had amassed a brilliant career that included three collaborations with Stephen Sondheim (*Sunday in the Park with George, Into the Woods,* and *Passion*), six Tony Awards, four Drama Desk Awards, a Pulitzer Prize, and an artist-in-residence arrangement with The Shubert Organization.

Dirty Blonde was the first in a series of productions requiring that I deal with both Sam Cohn, who represented Claudia in her dual capacities, and George Lane, who represented James Lapine. I believed that this was God exacting a punishment upon me for some wrongdoing I was not aware of. They were two of the toughest agents operating in the theater.

Sam was a skilled negotiator. The first thing he did was ask for the budget, virtually the only agent to do so. He understood it and knew how to read it. Armed with that knowledge, he conducted a negotiation that stretched the realities of the budget to their limits—to his clients' benefit, of course. He assaulted you with facts, figures, and possibilities.

George's technique was abject bullying. He was brutal. He also had the clout of representing nearly every top theater director and was well aware that the advent of inexperienced producers and "producing by committee" made the involvement of a strong director more crucial than ever. The alchemy that great producers once brought to the process now fell to the director, while the myriad list of names that were now billed as producers sat in ad agencies discussing "marketing."

I liked both agents. It began with their passion and their devotion to talent. When George started life as an assistant to Biff Liff at William Morris, he reached out to me with the early plays of Marsha Norman. With his good taste, and fueled by determination and guts, he had now become the head of the William Morris Theater Department, replacing his mentor.

The most problematic negotiation on *Dirty Blonde* was with Ron Gwiazda, a new agent who seemed to think his client, John Carrafa, was God's gift to choreography. Sitting behind him during the dress rehearsal, I watched the actors doing a "grapevine," the most rudimentary of steps, and pounded on Gwiazda's shoulder. "Genius," I said. "This is genius."

From the very first preview of *Dirty Blonde* at the Hayes, it was evident that we had a hit. Something magical had happened to it in the move uptown, wrought, no doubt, by James Lapine.

When I arrived for opening night, Mr. Schoenfeld glared at me. As I got closer, he said, "Is this the way you dress for the opening?"

"The jacket?" I responded, "Ermenegildo Zegna. The shirt? Armani. The ascot? Hermes. The pants? Dockers."

"You're wearing sneakers," he said.

Laying it on thick, I said, "Mr. Schoenfeld, I am a polio victim, and these are prescription." I added, "Are you going to say something nice to me, or am I going to spend the evening in a sulk?"

"I love you," he said, and pinched me on the cheek.

The reviews were spectacular, with Ben Brantley of the *Times* leading the pack. "Mae West has returned in a compact Rolls-Royce of a vehicle called *Dirty Blonde*, the play written by and starring Claudia Shear that opened last night at the Helen Hayes Theater . . . hands down the best new American play of the season."

Once open, Mr. Schoenfeld and I went back to our battle stations over advertising. Getting him to commit to *any* space in the paper was like pulling teeth, and it reached a point where I felt totally ignored. I asked to speak to him after one of the meetings. "I feel like I'm not being given a voice in the advertising," I complained. "Albert," he retorted, "it's one thing to have a voice, but you jump in and say, 'NO, NO, I don't agree.'" And we both laughed because it was true. My style tended to be confrontational, more out of passion than anything else.

"If you were to say, 'May I suggest?' that might be a better approach," he offered.

The following week, Mr. Schoenfeld laid out our plans, with which I didn't agree. I said, "May I suggest—"

"No, you may not," he interrupted. At the end of the meeting, I again asked to speak with him. "Remember last week when you told me if I had ideas I should say, 'May I suggest?'"

"Yes."

"I said, 'May I suggest?' and you said, 'No, you may not.' It's not working."

"It's working for me," he said.

Dirty Blonde was nominated for five Tony Awards, including Best Play and Best Direction, and for five Drama Desk Awards.

Near the end of the run, Bette Midler was invited with an eye toward starring her in a London production. The next day Claudia Shear called to say she wanted a meeting with Sam Cohn and me in Mr. Schoenfeld's office. She was in a bit of a state. "I write things for myself because until I did, no one ever cast me," she told us. "If this show goes to London or anywhere for that matter, it goes with me."

Sam didn't have to say a word. She made her case and made it well. When the show did eventually go to London, Claudia was the star and opened to spectacular reviews.

CHAPTER 40

Voting With Their Checkbooks

I kept telling Jeffrey Richards to give up. "*The Best Man* is a show that does not want to happen," I repeated. He had been trying to cast a Broadway revival of the 1960 Gore Vidal chestnut for months. I was afraid he would segue into one of those delusional producer traps of casting so-called "names" who added up to nothing at the box office. The play needed a cast that would sell it.

In true Richards fashion and just in time for the 2000 election, he landed a cast that collectively meant something at the box office. "A necklace," I called it. The beauty part was they came from all areas of the entertainment world. Chris Noth, currently of *Sex and the City* and *Law and Order*; Charles Durning, beloved veteran of stage and film; Christine Ebersole, Elizabeth Ashley, and Jonathan Hadary from Broadway; Michael Learned from television's *The Waltons*; and, in an inspired bit of casting, Spalding Gray, the noted avant-garde monologist.

The critical responsibility of directing these people was given to young Ethan McSweeny, recently acclaimed for his direction of *Never the Sinner*, a Leopold and Loeb play that Jeffrey had moved briefly to Off Broadway after its run at Stanley Brechner's American Jewish Theater. McSweeny brought with him a stunning rear-view photo of JFK addressing the 1960 Democratic Convention in the vast, smoke-filled Boston Garden at 1:30 in the morning. The photo, never before published, had been in storage in his father's garage for decades. It became our poster.

Jeffrey generously arranged a dinner for six of us at the Union Square Cafe with Gore Vidal and his companion, Howard Austen, who wasn't at all what you would expect. Howard was plain spoken and seemed like someone from the Bronx, which he was. Vidal was an awesome figure who spilled over the edges of the rambunctious cauldron of American politics and letters. Jeffrey said, "I want each of you to take turns sitting with Gore and get to know him a bit."

As I watched, Vidal drank martinis and had rollicking conversations with one and all, but I noted that, witty and informed as he was, his opinions were consistently negative.

Hoping to get a rise out of him when my turn came, I asked, "Are there any institutions you believe in?"

"Aha," he said.

"Because there is one I believe in," I continued. "Alcoholics Anonymous."

"Yes," he said, "and you are a man after my own heart. I come from a long line of alcoholics, and I've been watching and admiring you with your Diet Cokes."

Jeffrey was developing a template for his productions that included the engagement of his office in the triple capacity of producing, press, and marketing. And in what had now become common practice on Broadway, for an investment in the $200,000 range, investors could "buy" their way into producer billing above the title and participation in production meetings where their ideas were listened to and dealt with. Like members of boards of directors, these were people who had been successful in other lines of business. I called them "checkbook producers." There were eight such producers on *The Best Man*.

The first rehearsal was notable because Vidal was reading the role of Ex-President Hockstader in place of Charles Durning, who was due to arrive the following week. Ethan McSweeny stood before the group and made his lengthy introductory remarks, which were striking for their lack of insight into both the political dynamics of the play and the period in which it was set. I watched with angst as the cast of stage veterans visibly withdrew from him. *This play is going to have to direct itself,* I thought.

Journalists and politicos turned out en masse for the opening night. Our stellar cast did what it could, but the reviews were decidedly mixed, with most saying the production seemed tentative and unsteady.

Jeffrey and his office promoted the hell out of the production, and its relevance to the current presidential election kept it in the news. Several weeks before the date of the election, and against my protestations, Jeffrey arranged for a functioning voting booth to be installed in the lobby of the Virginia Theatre. Stunts had always been a part of his repertoire and very often worked. I thought the booth installation impugned the dignity of a Broadway theater, but what did I know? When I dropped by and saw television cameras galore and seventeen members of the press having a wonderful time, I had to salute him.

Thanks to Jeffrey Richards, Gore Vidal had once again become relevant. Like *Dirty Blonde,* the newly titled *Gore Vidal's The Best Man* had landed squarely in the hit category of the 2000-01 season.

CHAPTER 41

"The City Had Become a War Zone"

"**N**ine and eleven. Nine and eleven," I kept saying to everyone. "Power and magic." This was the promising numerology of the date of our first rehearsal for *Havana Is Waiting* at the Cherry Lane Theatre in Greenwich Village.

The Cherry Lane began its fabled history in 1924, when it was converted from a tobacco warehouse to a theater by members of the Provincetown Players, led by Edna St. Vincent Millay. Over the decades, it was a home for the works of every major playwright on the international stage, many of them world premieres. More recently, the theatre had been a birthing place for the young work of Edward Albee, Sam Shepard, Joe Orton, and David Mamet. Tucked away on Commerce Street, it is the oldest Off Broadway theater in New York and, for me, the heart and soul of the Off Broadway movement.

When the actress Angelina Fiordellisi acquired the Cherry Lane in 1996, its place in theater literature was very much in her mind, and she set about to make it a sanctuary for young writers. Its centerpiece is the Mentor Project, a season-long program that matches established dramatists with aspiring playwrights to perfect a single work and bring it to production. The list of esteemed mentors has included Albee, Tony Kushner, Marsha Norman, Alfred Uhry, Jules Feiffer, Wendy Wasserstein, A.R. Gurney, and Ed Bullins.

Eduardo Machado is a Cuban-born playwright who was forcibly airlifted to the US at the age of eight with his brother Jesus and 14,000 other Cuban children as part of Operation Pedro Pan, a CIA construct that separated children from parents who believed that growing up under non-communist rule was more important than family. The traumatized children had no say in the matter.

Machado and Fiordellisi met in 1998, the first year of the Mentor Project, when he directed Heather Hill's *Notes from the Confederacy* under the mentorship of A.R. Gurney. He was then head of the graduate playwriting program at Columbia University. The following year, Machado returned to Cuba for the first time in thirty-eight years, taking with him his closest friend Ed Vassallo. *Havana Is Waiting*, which Fiordellisi helped to develop, is an intensely felt realization of that seminal experience.

The play seeks to pierce the bubble of America's righteous meddling and manipulation all over the globe under the guise of freedom and democracy. The impact of the embargo on the Cuban people, powerless over the will of governments in both countries, is seen through the eyes of Federico, the Eduardo character, his best friend Fred, who videotapes the journey, and Ernesto, a local communist cab driver who becomes their guide—a deeply emotional catharsis for all three. I was engrossed by the play and eager to get to work.

As has been said so many times, September 11, 2001, in New York was a beautiful, sunshiny day.

Our first rehearsal at the Cherry Lane would begin at 11:00, so I went to a 9 o'clock meeting of my recovery fellowship on Perry Street. As I was going in, a young man ran by shouting that a plane had crashed into the North Tower of the World Trade Center. I thought, *Well, my sobriety is more important than that,* and disregarded it. At about 9:15, the same man ran into the meeting room and said another plane had hit the South Tower. *This is history*, I thought, and ran to Sheridan Square, where hundreds of people had gathered to watch the unwatchable.

People of every nationality, listening to broadcasts in every language, watched in shock as an endless cacophony of fire engines and ambulances surged through the crowd. At first, the two unyielding structures seemed remarkably secure, the huge fires for the moment contained.

Hundreds of flat objects floated from the windows, flickering in the sunlight as they drifted. I shortly realized they were people's papers. The fruits of the labors of the people who had worked in the buildings. It made me cry.

I got to a working pay phone and called my house guest, Joing Camero, a sax player from Venezuela. I yelled into the answering machine, "Quick, turn on the TV!" He picked up the phone and said, "Oh, my God"; then he took a shower, and by the time he finished, neither of the buildings was still standing. I saw them fall with my naked eyes. Racked with rage and despair, I could hardly breathe.

Desperate for continuity, I went to the Cherry Lane to see if anyone was there. Directly across the street, a bicycle thief was blow torching a lock and chain and phoning the location to a van that would then come to pick it up. The underbelly of the city continued unabated. I walked home to One Hundredth Street, and Joing and I had dinner at El Malecon nearby. As we ate, televisions on both ends of the restaurant showed the fallen Towers continuing to smoke and burn.

The first rehearsal was held the next day at Ed Vassallo's apartment on the Upper West Side. Angelina Fiordellisi recalled, "We were all in shock and trying to determine if we were at war. The city had become a war zone. There were army tanks on the West Side Highway and Seventh Avenue. Chelsea Piers became the morgue. And the Village smelled like a crematorium for several months. We were literally breathing them in.

"We had to distribute identification cards to prove that the cast and crew were working at the Cherry Lane," she continued, "otherwise they were not allowed past the army checkpoints on Fourteenth Street. Only people who lived or worked there were allowed passage." But, for most of us, continuity seemed a necessity.

In what she called "the worst decision of my life," Angelina decided to stay on schedule. *Havana Is Waiting* opened on October 24, 2001. The Fourteenth Street blockade had by then been lifted, but, despite good reviews, we played to a despairing 10 percent of capacity for our short run. And our lives and the world were forever changed.

Three days before our opening, the *Times* published an interview with Eduardo. "*Havana Is Waiting* is Mr. Machado's most political work, and he said he finds it ironic that it is opening against the backdrop of the United States' new offensive after the terrorist attacks on the World Trade Center and the Pentagon. The play makes a plea for getting past the thirst for revenge, of transcending politics, and its themes now have a special resonance. 'I've been at the mercy of politics my entire life,' Mr. Machado said, 'and there has to be a way to step beyond it, to have *human* interaction.'"[11]

CHAPTER 42

Twin Peaks

Long Day's Journey into Night (2003)

Jerry Schoenfeld was boiling mad. He had given David Richenthal's production of *The Price* its walking papers, but the Arthur Miller revival defiantly continued its run at the Royale. Schoenfeld claimed that *The Price* was an "interim" booking having the theater only until *Copenhagen* was ready to move in, which it now was. Richenthal pointed out that there was no such thing in the theater agreement, and Schoenfeld countered that it was a verbal understanding, which Richenthal steadfastly denied.

While this was going on, I happened to be with Jerry in his office when he opened a letter from Arthur Miller that essentially asked, "Why are you kicking us out?" He read it to me. "Do you want to answer this?" he asked, brushing it off.

His airy dismissal was a pose. His standing with people like Miller meant everything to him, and Shubert was only weeks away from opening its own production of a new Miller play, *The Ride Down Mt. Morgan*, starring Patrick Stewart, which made the timing all the more damaging. But business for *The Price* was declining. Ultimately it was allowed to play out its short run at the Royale, and *Copenhagen* opened there virtually on schedule.

Unhealed wounds were reopened a few weeks later when Patrick Stewart stopped the applause at the curtain call of a Saturday matinee of *The Ride Down Mt. Morgan* to deliver a blistering tirade to the audience attacking Jerry Schoenfeld's "lack of commitment" and "unwillingness to advertise" what had been "a well-reviewed and well-attended production."

Stewart insisted that he had Arthur Miller's full support, later reiterated in press interviews by the author.

Newly angered and humiliated, Schoenfeld was convinced that Stewart would never have done it without Miller's support and that the event would have never occurred were it not for Richenthal "poisoning Miller's mind" against him during the Royale dispute. Richenthal now occupied a place of intense hatred with Schoenfeld that few, if any, had ever entered.

In November of 2000, a glowingly received revival of Eugene O'Neill's *Long Day's Journey into Night*, starring Jessica Lange, opened on the West End of London under the auspices of producer Bill Kenwright. Biff Liff, the revered and respected theater veteran who represented the O'Neill estate, attended the opening. Backstage, Kenwright said something to the effect that he couldn't wait to bring it to New York. Liff graciously nodded, forgetting for the moment that the option for New York belonged to David Richenthal. When Kenwright found out, he was enraged. But there was a signed contract with Richenthal, and nothing could be done. Almost nothing.

When David engaged me as general manager of his Broadway production of *Long Day's Journey* in September of 2002, he was in the process of putting together an extraordinary group of artists. Robert Falls to direct, Brian Dennehy as James Tyrone, Phillip Seymour Hoffman and Robert Sean Leonard as the sons, and for the role of Mary Tyrone, he sought Vanessa Redgrave. My first thought, as always, was to take it to the Shuberts. I was well aware of the ill will with Jerry but naively thought that the prestige of the project and my long friendship with him would override the difficulties.

No such luck. Jerry was immediately opposed to David and his production, and he championed his good friend Bill Kenwright and his production. He telephoned Kenwright in my presence and said, "Albert Poland is sitting with me and asking for a theater for David Richenthal to do *Long Day's Journey*. I have told Albert that if you do not wish me to release a theater to them, I will not do so." Kenwright told Schoenfeld not to give us a theater. I was aghast. I thought it was despicable. After he hung up, Jerry told me of the long and productive relationship he had with Bill Kenwright. "He has brought me many shows," he said. *What about our relationship?* I thought.

There were no Nederlander or Jujamcyn houses available. At every opportunity, I asked Jerry if he had a theater for us. In December, I was chatting with him after a press conference for the opening of the Little Shubert, and *he* introduced the topic. "Have you found a theater?"

"No," I answered. "Do you have one for us?"

He responded with a disapproving frown and slow, smug shake of his head "no." I found it cruel.

In the meantime, the actor deals had to be done, and they were a handful, with Vanessa Redgrave, represented by Sam Cohn of course, topping the list.

Our target date was late spring of 2003. I knew Redgrave would want a dialect coach and suggested Tim Monich, who was then available for that slot but would shortly be booked. She wouldn't commit to anyone. She insisted on five weeks of rehearsal and two weeks of previews. All of this was appropriate and reasonable, except that she had agreed to appear in a film being directed by her son, Carlo Gabriel Nero, right in the middle of it, which would cause us to open after the Tony deadline. For weeks we twisted our brains like washrags to fit seven weeks into four and a half. Finally, she agreed to change the film dates.

The negotiation had been the most exasperating I had ever experienced. Combined with the stress of having no theater in which to put this masterpiece, I was right at the edge. There was a conference call with David and Sam in which I was seconds away from putting the phone down, leaving the office, and never returning. It was in that conversation that the deal was made. We now had the most stellar cast of the season but no theater.

The January 19, 2003, Sunday *Times* "Arts and Leisure" section was delivered to producers and managers' offices late on the Wednesday before, as usual, and the opening salvo of a "Spring Preview" by Ben Brantley gave me exactly the artillery I needed to storm Mr. Schoenfeld's office and stake my claim. Brantley wrote that "Eugene O'Neill's masterwork is the 'King Lear' of the American theater" and "a play of such intensity, gravity, unwieldiness and, yes, greatness that if a production hits even half of its depth-charging dramatic notes, it's a big deal. The odds are automatically improved in this spring's Broadway production, however, by the participation of Vanessa Redgrave, who is portraying the morphine-sneaking mother and who is famous for fearlessly burrowing into darkness to bring a character to light. The promising cast is rounded out by Philip Seymour Hoffman and Robert Sean Leonard as the unhappy brothers and, as their swashbuckling, penny-pinching dad, Brian Dennehy, who collaborated to stunning effect with this production's director, Robert Falls, on 'Death of a Salesman.'"[12]

It was 6:30 p.m., and I called Jerry. "Can I come over there?" I said. "Yes, come right over." I marched in and placed the clipping firmly in front of him. He read it. I didn't wait for a response. "You have a responsibility," I said. "You have a mandate to bring the best of the American theater to the American public. And that's what this play is. I don't care what you think of David Richenthal—this is way beyond that. And what about your relationship with me? We have thirty-five years together. You have done for me, and I have done for you. That should count for something."

He was listening to me and not arguing with me. He respected people for their convictions, and mine were ablaze. "We might be able to put you in the Cort," he said.

I shot back. "You're going to have Vanessa Redgrave arriving every night at a theater on Forty-Eighth Street on the other side of Broadway? Do you want to be there to greet her? I want the Plymouth."

"The Plymouth has *The Frog and the Toad*."

"You're going to put a frog and a toad in the Plymouth and send Vanessa to the Cort? Don't make me gag."

As all of this was going on, he was also taking occasional phone calls. Each time, I would run into Phil Smith's office and report my progress. Phil was rooting for me.

Bob Wankel came in after about half an hour and, sizing up the situation and to break the tension, he said, "Albert, why don't you say to Mr. Schoenfeld, nicely, and in the manner of a request, 'Mr. Schoenfeld, I have a distinguished production worthy of consideration for one of your fine playhouses.'" So, I repeated it exactly as Bob had indicated. Jerry smiled and said, "Awww, say it again."

When I got home, I called Robert Fox, with whom I was working on *The Boy from Oz* and who was highly regarded by Mr. Schoenfeld. I asked Robert to call him in the morning, take his temperature, and give him one last push to give us the Plymouth. Robert called back shortly before noon and said, "I think you're on track." We got the Plymouth.

I was on the Internet on the Saturday before our first rehearsal when an instant message came through from a name I didn't recognize, inquiring about a dialect coach. It was Vanessa Redgrave wanting to know if Tim Monich would start working with her on Monday. "No," I wrote back. "I'm sure he's not available, but I will find someone in short order. Do you want them for about five sessions?" She went to all capital letters and said Sam would be in touch with me. She wanted the dialect coach for the purpose of running her lines, and the coach we secured, the very fine Deborah Hecht, was there for the entire rehearsal period.

On Monday at the "meet and greet" when I introduced myself, Redgrave laughed and said, "Well, that was quite something we had on Saturday."

"It certainly made my weekend," I said. "Shall we smoke?" And we went down to Forty-Second Street and smoked.

We had a top stage manager, Jane Grey, whom I knew from *A Lie of the Mind*, and, by and large, rehearsals went smoothly. I went by the theater to watch the tech rehearsals, and Vanessa was a study in disapproval. I left after an hour.

At the invited dress rehearsal, I thought the three men were ahead of her. Her speeches were nicely structured but didn't seem to connect responsively with the other characters. The audience, of course, was totally awed. Coincidentally, a steel band playing their first spring night on the corner of Forty-Fifth and Broadway could be heard onstage and in the theater. "Will we be having the musical accompaniment each night?" Vanessa shot at me. Given the circumstances, I thought she was more than reasonable.

This battle with the band had been fought before, and, astonishingly, the band had won on a "freedom of speech" issue. Why their freedom of speech was given preference over that of the city's multi-billion-dollar theater industry was a puzzlement. We fought it at the mayoral level, but it was through the cops on the beat that we were victorious. Our bodyguards were ex-cops headed by the mayor's personal bodyguard, and they coordinated with the Midtown beat cops, who persuaded the band to cease and desist for four hours seven times a week.

The other internal issue was a growing conflict about a piece of business Vanessa had created for Mary Tyrone. She entered carrying a silver tray with three fresh fish on it and, after a few moments, she angrily flung the fish to the floor. Robert Falls was opposed, as was David, and it nearly became an international incident. Noted O'Neill authorities were consulted. They didn't think it was something Mary would do.

On Thursday afternoon, the day of the third preview, Vanessa and Brian Dennehy were onstage running lines when Robert Falls said from the back of the house, "Excuse me, excuse me. Vanessa, the tray with the fish will not be on the prop table tonight."

Redgrave went ballistic. "Don't you ever, ever say another word to me!" she screamed. "Stay away from me. I will get an injunction if I have to. Don't you ever come near me." The exchange had an impact.

That night, Vanessa Redgrave found her performance. She was electrifying. As I watched in awe, I thought the blowup must have been part of her process. From there, it only got better and better. Yes, the play was long, but all of us watched every night. Within days, her Mary Tyrone had evolved into the finest stage performance I have ever seen. The men's performances were elevated by hers, and it was clear that a masterpiece was in the making.

Many actors with fine reputations set the way they are going to say their lines and, night after night, it never varies. Vanessa watches, listens, and responds, playing the reality of the situation as it unfolds, allowing that to impact the dialogue night after night. This for me, is the practice of acting as an art, the most demanding and, I would think for its practitioners, the most rewarding.

By the first weekend, the entire two weeks of previews were sold out, as were several performances in the early weeks of the run. On the day of the opening, Sam Cohn sent me an exquisite bottle of red wine, and I had to call his office to remind him that I had a group of friends who would be very unhappy if I drank it. A half hour later, a new gift arrived. I don't remember what it was, but I still have the note which said simply, "OOPS! Love, Sam." During the first intermission on opening night, Sam and I found ourselves standing next to each other at the urinals in the men's room. "Do you still have that bottle of wine?" he asked. "Yes," I said. "Good, I'll send a messenger."

My opening-night gift to Santo Loquasto, who designed our set and costumes, was a framed copy of our original contract for my production of *The Unseen Hand* and *Forensic and the Navigators* in 1970, his New York debut as a designer fresh out of Yale. I had kept it all these years because I knew then that he was destined for greatness. It called for a fee of $300, a royalty of $25 per week, and no assistants.

The opening night audience had the stillness that you only experience at great theatre. I went, as I did to most opening nights, with my dear friends Max and Helen Jacobs. I was accompanied by Irene Burns, also a dear friend who is Helen's cousin. The occasion was especially meaningful because my first encounter with the play had been a production with Max's stunning performance as James Tyrone at the North Carolina Shakespeare Festival.

The next morning's reviews catapulted us into history. They were led by Ben Brantley in the *Times*, who called Robert Falls's production "soul-piercing" and Vanessa Redgrave's performance one "that will never leave the memory of anyone who sees it."

Our production became that rarity you dream of—a theater work of art that sets the marketplace on fire. We had to add extra staff to handle house seat requests, and our superb company manager, Bruce Klinger, had four boxes filled with faxed orders that could not be filled. "House seats" are desirable, preferred seat locations held aside for celebrities and known people in the entertainment industry. People were calling from all over the world saying, "I'm only flying in if I can get tickets."

When Mike Wallace presented us with the Tony for Best Revival, David called Robert Falls to the stage to join him, as the Best Director award had already been given to someone else. Brian won Best Actor and, in the evening's most memorable standing ovation, Vanessa won Best Actress. Laurence Fishburne, who had seen her performance the night before, knelt down on one knee as he presented it to her.

On the heels of all this triumph, I went to Jerry Schoenfeld's office to meet him for lunch.

As we were leaving, the anger I had held back for months poured out. "Are you now sorry that you made me crawl through mud and slime to get you to take a show that will have no empty seats for its entire run?" He wasn't having it. He turned on me and raged right back, "Weren't you HOMELESS!" We were silent in the small Shubert elevator.

Outside on Shubert Alley, he changed the subject, complaining that Rudolf Giuliani wanted to change the name of Duffy Square, home of the half-price ticket booth, to "Sinatra Square." "I think that would be great," I remarked. "He was the greatest singer of the twentieth century." Jerry replied, "What about Bing Crosby?" We had a nice lunch at Barney Greengrass.

Early in August, young Sid King gave his notice. Sid was our production assistant, a catchall title, a glorified gofer I hired because I loved having him around. One of his duties was to be waiting offstage to take Vanessa's hand as she came off in a blackout at the end of Act II. When she got word of his leaving, she was upset and stopped speaking to him. I was called to a meeting in her dressing room. The continuity of having the same person there was obviously important to her, and before the meeting, I arranged with Sid's new employers to let him off for the short time it took to run over to the theater, perform his task, and run back.

On August 14, Vanessa was in Connecticut visiting her sister Lynn, who was seriously ill. Her assistant called her shortly after 4:00 p.m. to say, "Vanessa, the city is in a power blackout." In a classic actress response, she said, "What's that got to do with me?"

"Well," he said, "your show won't be going on, so you don't need to come back."

Toward the end of the month, I stood in the middle of Forty-Fifth Street. On the marquee of the Plymouth was *Long Day's Journey into Night*. Across the street at the Imperial, where I had seen my first Broadway show forty years earlier, was the marquee for my next show, Hugh Jackman in *The Boy from Oz*. For a moment, I was in Broadway heaven.

The Boy from Oz (2003)

On a cold winter's night in 1965, after a sublime evening of Felicia Sanders at the Bon Soir, the little emcee took the stage to tell us we were in for a special treat. "Tonight," he announced, "as an extra added attraction, the Bon Soir is proud to present, in their American debut, Chris and Peter Allen."

As I watched what was a fairly routine, cruise-ship-caliber act with club-date choreography, I took note that the tall one had good eye contact and a smile that seemed to say, "You know, of course, that we are kidding." Months later, I learned that Judy Garland, who had brought them there, had been sitting directly behind me at the bar.

Garland discovered them performing at a nightclub in Hong Kong, where she had retreated in 1964 after a disastrous performance in Melbourne. Taking a special liking to Peter, she brought them to the United States to be her opening act. Peter was soon married to her daughter Liza Minnelli.

Rumors of Peter's gay affairs abounded, and, after the inevitable breakup of the marriage, he began a solo career as a singer-songwriter. The artwork in the ads for those first appearances in the thriving small-club circuit of the 1970s made it apparent he had undergone a personality change and was depressed, if not disturbed. Gradually, that was countered by a more upbeat, hip persona.

By the time I saw him at the Bottom Line in 1976, both sides of his duality were in full flower. He had produced a remarkable body of work that caused John Rockwell of the *Times* to observe that he was "the finest composer and performer to emerge from the cabaret scene in New York in the early-mid 1970s." For an audience, watching an artist on a journey of self- discovery and being invited in was exciting and generous.

I saw him a year later with eight thousand others, performing in Central Park, where he projected the same persona, with an added swagger that smacked against the outer reaches of his vast audience. Under the skillful guidance of his manager, Dee Anthony, Peter Allen became a full-fledged star, went on to sellout engagements at Radio City, and to major international fame and show-business mythology.

As he was beginning his upward climb in New York, Robert Fox and Ben Gannon, both in their early twenties, were starting out in London. Robert was an associate of the prestigious West End producer Michael White. Ben, a transplant from Australia, was an agent representing, among others, Robert's brother, the well-known actor Edward Fox. Ben and Robert began a longtime, close friendship that included their families and would last for the rest of their lives.

Both became distinguished producers, Ben of film, stage, and television, and Robert of stage and film. Ben Gannon returned to Australia in 1980. Peter Allen died of AIDS in 1992.

Moved by the trajectory of Allen's life and career as an Australian and a gay man, Gannon commissioned his friend, Stephen Maclean, to write a biography. In 1996 the two collaborated on a television documentary for ABC called *Peter Allen: The Boy from Oz.*

Renewing acquaintance with Allen's song catalog, Ben called on his friend Robert Fox, who was by then theater royalty on both sides of the Atlantic. "So many of these songs are actually autobiographical," he told Robert excitedly. "I think there is the potential here for a great musical. Will you do it with me?" Fox gave an immediate "Yes."

Their first choice for the role of Peter was Hugh Jackman, not yet a star but well-established with the Australian theater-going public. Fresh off long runs of *Beauty and the Beast* and *Sunset Boulevard*, Jackman was now turning his attention to films, and he declined. After an extensive casting search and two workshops, *The Boy from Oz* opened at Her Majesty's Theatre in Sydney on March 5, 1998, starring Todd McKenney as Peter and featuring Chrissy Amphlett of the Divinyls as Judy Garland.

The Boy from Oz toured successfully for two years and became the top-grossing show in Australian theater history. Jackman, after seeing an early performance, told his wife Deborra-lee Furness he thought he had made a mistake.

I rarely went after shows. Usually they came to me, and, for the most part, I was able to pick and choose. Sometime in early 1998, I read about *The Boy from Oz*. A musical about the life of Peter Allen in which Judy Garland was a major character? I set my cap for it.

General managing Broadway musicals had, over the years, become an enormous undertaking. The financial investment alone was a tremendous responsibility, and, in an attempt to tame the unwieldy greed that now assaulted us from all sides, contractual arrangements had become increasingly complex.

My fears notwithstanding, I felt I would be sufficiently energized by the project to be up to it. And I was savvy enough to know when to pick up the phone and call people for help and guidance. People of my generation were generous that way. We constantly shared our knowledge and experience with each other as members of a close-knit community.

I found out the producers of *The Boy from Oz* were Ben Gannon and Robert Fox and called Jerry Schoenfeld to ask if he would put in a good word for me. He would. When they were soon in New York, I arrived for a Joe Allen's lunch wearing my Fendi fur and my diamond cocktail ring. I thought I should at least look the part, and we had a spirited lunch. We were joined by Ben's companion, Brian Abel. It was clear that, as much as anything, my sensibility and kinship with the period were going to be important.

I was completely captivated by the gentlemen and hoped they felt the same. They were brilliant, elegant, and witty, the kind of people I most enjoyed knowing and the kind of producers I most enjoyed working for. I was hired, and in late spring of 1998, I was flown to Sydney on a madcap flight with Adrian Bryan-Brown, who was to be the New York press agent, and his wife Joan Marcus, the photographer.

Adrian and I both felt the show needed a star for Broadway, and the producers thought an American writer was needed to switch the emphasis from Peter's time in Australia to his time in New York. There was also the question of a director. We soon found that the toxins were still fresh in the waters from Allen's disastrous Broadway production of *Legs Diamond* (1988), and that our top choices weren't going to be available to us. Allen's insistence on writing and starring in *Legs* had caused a split with his manager Dee Anthony, and Frank Rich's vitriolic review in the *Times* was hard for the industry to forget.

I suggested Philip Wm. McKinley, who had directed *Zombie Prom* Off Broadway, and whose talent I liked enormously. Following *Zombie*, I had seen an impressive Broadway-caliber production of *Jekyll and Hyde* that he directed at Kansas City Starlight, and he was now several seasons into directing the Ringling Bros. Circus.

McKinley had a long, free-wheeling interview with Ben and Robert and was hired.

After several false starts with American writers, Robert Fox suggested his London friend, Martin Sherman, who had enjoyed a Broadway success with *Bent*, starring Richard Gere. McKinley flew to London, and they began work on script revisions.

A star, a star, a star. Again, the idea of Hugh Jackman, now a rising star in films, came up. The consensus was that, with his film career gaining momentum, he wouldn't be interested, but Ben Gannon phoned him, and, to everyone's surprise, his response was positive. A meeting was arranged for Jackman and Phil McKinley.

After an exchange of niceties, Phil disarmed him by asking, "What did Andrew, Cameron, and Trevor say to you to convince you not to do the show?" Jackman laughed and said, "How did you know?" They had a lengthy and thoroughgoing conversation during which Jackman revealed his insecurities about playing Broadway. McKinley promised, "I will cover you," and added, "You should do this because it's the first New York show from Australia, it's about an Australian icon, and you will have seventeen songs. There are no other musicals like it."

It was planned that, prior to Broadway, the production would be workshopped. "What if you do the workshop and I come and see it?" Jackman asked. McKinley insisted that they had to go through the process together and that they would then go to Broadway knowing exactly what they had.

Workshop rehearsals began on April 8, 2002, and, at the end of the second day, Jackman told McKinley, "This was absolutely the right decision." By the end of the workshop, Jackman was "a genuine Broadway thoroughbred," in the words of McKinley. "Disciplined and the hardest-working member of the entire cast."

The waiting list for tickets to the four invited performances was in the hundreds. Each one seemed more like a Broadway opening than a workshop performance. Standing ovations all, and Broadway was abuzz that a huge hit was coming in. The Shuberts came in with a substantial investment and promised the Imperial, one of their prime musical houses on West Forty-Fifth Street.

In making Hugh's deal, every conversation I had was with his agent Patrick Whitesell, Whitesell's assistant, and an attorney. I was so amused that there were three West Coast people dealing with me, or at me, that I was unintimidated. The sticking point became the length of Hugh's stay in the show. His people wanted nine months. We demanded a year. We were doubtful that anyone would replace him, and there was no possibility that a big musical could recoup in nine months. When we eventually said take it or leave it, he took it.

My first recollection of dealing with Hugh Jackman's assistant, John Palermo, was a phone call I received before Hugh was due to come in for the elaborate *Oz* photo shoot. "Hi, there are some things Hugh is going to need." "Okay . . ."

"An international cell phone," he began.

"Let me stop you right there," I said. "I know you've just come off a film shoot, and I need to tell you the important difference between film and the theater."

"What's that?" he asked.

"Distribution. We have none. We have a finite number of seats in one theater in one city. That's it. If you have read Hugh's contract, you can see that he is well taken care of. But the kind of extras you're getting at just aren't possible, as much as we might like to give them. It's very important that you understand that and accept it as an absolute."

The air was cleared, and the relationship with Palermo continued on a largely even keel. Hugh was dazzling in the photo shoot, and in the resulting ads created by Greg Corradetti of Serino Coyne, his energy leapt off the printed page.

A lawyer representing Liza Minnelli called indicating that she would like to watch a rehearsal and see a copy of the script. I happily told him Liza would be welcomed to any rehearsal or performance she wished in whatever manner she would prefer but that we were "not letting the script out at this time." I then explained that we had worked together on *Are You Now?* and that I had been the president of her mother's fan club—and thus would not be party to anything unbecoming to her or her mother in any way.

The lawyer called back a few days later to say that PMK, Liza's public relations, would be calling to arrange a rehearsal visit. It never happened.

In rehearsals, Jackman was rapidly finding his performance, but there was concern that he was playing the gay aspect of the character too broadly. Phil McKinley told him, "The way you play gay is to play trying not to be gay." It worked. Just before the dress rehearsal, McKinley told me to go over to the area under one of the box seats and wait. In a few seconds, Isabel Keating materialized, wearing her full Judy Garland makeup for the first time. We both cried.

Three days before our first preview on September 16, our beloved Ben Gannon was diagnosed with cancer. He immediately began chemo, which resulted in complications requiring him to spend time in the hospital. But he was largely available to us and discharged his producer responsibilities at full throttle.

Our advance sale was in excess of $10 million, but we were startled to discover that we were coming into a hostile environment. It was as though new shows had no friends. Before previews even started, *New York Post* columnist Michael Riedel began running a flurry of items about the show that always included the phrase, "Hugh Jackman, swishing around Broadway as Peter Allen, the gay singer-songwriter who died of AIDS." The Internet was now loaded with faceless cyber critics, empowered by their anonymity, who lived only to claw new shows to death before they could even take their first breath. With four weeks of previews still ahead, there were full reviews of *The Boy from Oz* on the *All That Chat* website within hours of our invited dress rehearsal.

Meanwhile, at the *Times*, the toxic legacy of *Legs Diamond* remained. The advance *Times* Sunday piece—which was generally at worst neutral, and at best high puffery—was called "The Boy from Oz You Won't Meet on Broadway." Written by Michael

Joseph Gross, who had attended previews, it compared the Peter of our show, which Gross found idyllic, to his perception of the real Peter Allen, whom he trashed. I read it in advance on Wednesday, October 1, and was despondent. Try as I might, I could not find a *Times* piece about "The Fanny Brice You Won't Meet in *Funny Girl*" or, better still, "The Rose Hovick You Won't Find in *Gypsy*."

The next night, I attended the opening of a *Little Shop of Horrors* revival on Broadway, and, hours later, I was stricken with pancreatitis. It was the most agonizing pain I have ever experienced. My friend Max Jacobs came to my house and took me to our mutual doctor and to a testing lab and then to Mt. Sinai Hospital. It was the beginning of two weeks of not knowing how I would live through the next minute.

The doctor released me from the hospital too early. While staying at the home of Max and Helen, I was unable to ingest anything more than a Popsicle and small sips of soup. Friends rallied round me. Jane Harmon arrived with delicious chicken soup from Eli Zabar's EATS, Peter Schneider literally reached through the phone and held onto me, Stevie Phillips kept saying I should be back in the hospital, and Jerry Schoenfeld asked Paul Marks, the head of Sloane-Kettering, to examine me immediately and offer a second opinion.

Max Jacobs did a smart thing. He faxed this last piece of information to our doctor, and two minutes later the doctor called and put me back in the hospital. I was dehydrated almost to the point of no return and had suffered heart damage. This interaction of my two caring friends saved my life.

I missed the opening night of *The Boy from Oz*, but Phil Smith called during intermission, and I could hear him on the answering machine. He was rapturous and said he hadn't seen an opening night like it since Judy at the Palace in 1951.

The next day, back in the hospital, a videotape arrived, made by Bobby Wilson, of opening night greetings from the company and the opening-night curtain call. Weak as I was, my spirits soared.

The reviews were not at all comforting, except for the expected superlatives for Hugh, who said to Robert Fox, "I couldn't give what they are all saying is a 'great performance' in a lousy show." Although we had no weeks of financial losses, we weren't initially doing the kind of business we had hoped for. When I returned to the show, Hugh sent me a note. "You are a godsend, Albert," he wrote, "and I am honored to be working with you."

Hugh Jackman's performance was astonishing. Working with someone of his caliber is the greatest privilege a career can offer. I must have seen the show thirty-five times, and each time it was impossible not to go back and thank him. He is a generous performer, for me a significant part of talent. His spontaneous ad lib sections with audience members, who he sometimes brought onstage, were consistently unerring.

Barbara Cook was a huge fan, and one matinee Hugh said, "Ladies and gentlemen, we have with us the greatest star of Broadway musical comedy, Barbara Cook." He indicated for her to join him onstage. She stood up and was so transfixed by him, she failed to notice that the audience was giving her a standing ovation. I called her the next day and said, "I don't think you know this, but yesterday you got a standing ovation for a show you aren't even in."

In the month-long Broadway Cares/Equity Fights AIDS audience fundraising campaign, Hugh's solicitations from the stage beat anything I had ever seen. He worked out a routine with Michael Mulheren, who played his father and manager, that was magic. He auctioned off towels, t-shirts, you name it. I saw him raise as much as $37,000 at a single performance.

The first night he got carried away and auctioned off a dinner with himself. "Get me out of it," he said afterward. "I went too far."

In the end he raised $1,236,910, far beyond anything that had ever happened before, and a record broken only by him and Daniel Craig during their Broadway engagement in *A Steady Rain* in 2009.

In the meantime, Michael Riedel did not let up on Jackman and went after Robert Fox personally and Bernadette Peters for her performance in Robert's current Broadway production of *Gypsy*. I took Riedel to lunch. "You are going after the wrong people," I said. "Hugh and Robert and Bernadette are decent. There are plenty of nasty people out there. Go after them. It's going to come back to you, I promise you." He was a friend, and we had a very civil lunch, but my advice fell on deaf ears. He was unstoppable.

Months later, Ronnie Lee, the dean of Broadway group sales agents, produced his annual presentation for three thousand tour operators from all over the country looking to book big Broadway musicals for their groups. Shows paid a $16,000 fee to participate, payable half in advance and half the day after the performance. I thought Hugh's presence would be of great benefit, and I convinced him to appear in it. When we arrived, I saw Michael Riedel backstage. "This is a private showing. If he writes one word," I told Ronnie, "I am not paying you the second half of your fee. And you can sue me until the cows come home. I do not care."

The next day, Riedel wrote that Hugh's appearance was a sign of *Oz*'s sagging box office.

It was near capacity at the time. Ronnie Lee did not get the second half of his fee, and my feud with Michael went on for another year. But, of course, I continued to read his column. One day it amused me so much that I shot him an email. He wrote back within seconds. "Let's have lunch," he said. And it was over.

I once told Hugh's mother in his dressing room that many of us thought she had created an exemplary person. He seemed to have it all in abundance and handled it with modesty and humility. One of the few things that set him off was pretense.

Lincoln Center Library arranged for a three-camera shoot of our show for the Theatre on Film and Tape Archive. As is customary, no one involved in the show would be compensated. I sensed that Hugh was slightly edgy about it. The day came for the taping, and the stage manager was required to read an announcement to the audience. "Ladies and gentlemen, today you are part of theater history. The Lincoln Center Archive is taping this performance for posterity." It set Hugh off.

Patrick Hoffman, head of the Archive, was doing on-spot editing in a trailer parked in back of the theater, and, about an hour into the show, he called me in a panic. "Albert, you've got to get over here. Hugh Jackman is absolutely full of himself, and we're going to have to shoot this again tonight."

I couldn't imagine what he was talking about, but I ran over immediately. He showed me the excerpts. In the ad-lib section Hugh did with latecomers, he said, "You are late. Don't you know that this is an historic occasion? Don't you know that Lincoln Center is taping this for their Archive so it can be seen by the children of the very rich? Actually, it will be on the Internet in two hours."

"Patrick," I said, "this performance is totally unique. Not like any other. There will never be a performance like this again. And you have it." That was the end of that.

When I saw Hugh afterward, he asked, "Did you watch?" "Yes," I said. "It was definitely the supper show."

Clifford Stevens and David Kalodner, two top agents and good friends of mine, approached me at the end of the performances they had seen. "This is the show business we came into," they exalted. "This is the romance, the glamour, and the passion of the industry we came into." And both agreed that there had been no greater Broadway performance since Barbra Streisand in *Funny Girl*. And Hugh was that rarity: a star the audience comes to love.

At the 58th Annual Tony Awards on CBS, Hugh took home the Best Actor in a Musical Tony Award for *The Boy from Oz*. After that, the show did solid turn-away business. He also won The Drama Desk, Outer Critics, Theatre World, Broadway Audience, Drama League, Theater Fan's Choice, and TDF-Astaire Awards for his performance in *Oz*. Later he earned a Primetime Emmy Award for Best Variety Performance for his chores as the emcee of the Tony telecast.

Hugh and I regularly spent an hour together between shows on Wednesdays. Admittedly, he was having the time of his life, but by August, he winked at me, smiled, and said, "I'm never doing a year again, mate." "Well," I said, "I'm glad you learned that on me."

At the final performance on September 12, 2004, the tickets were $200, and we could have sold the house three times over. Hugh made his entrance to a six-minute standing ovation. He shouted it down and said, "Okay, that's it! We're extending!" If only. Enforcing the no taping, no photo rules at that performance would have meant throwing out the entire audience.

In the space of a year, Hugh Jackman had become a great Broadway star. And once again, my life had been enriched by the privilege of talent.

CHAPTER 43

Finishing the Picture

Arthur Miller's *Finishing the Picture* was a witty and unsparing look at the making of *The Misfits*, a chaotic cinematic universe manipulated at whim by a drugged and drunken actress, nude and in bed except for an occasional screaming foray into the bathroom. Outside, her victims, characters representing John Huston, Lee and Paula Strasberg, and Miller, her beleaguered husband and author of *The Misfits* screenplay, waited, speculated, hoped, and perpetually readjusted their realities to her unreality. The play was honest to a fault, with one caveat. The author required that the actress be a brunette.

Finishing the Picture was to be the kickoff New York effort of Delphi Productions, a new company formed by David Richenthal and Anthony and Charlene Marshall. The group had provided enhancement money for a Robert Falls-directed production at Goodman with a starry cast featuring Harris Yulin, Stacy Keach, Linda Lavin, Stephen Lang, Matthew Modine, and Scott Glenn. Lang and Lavin rendered devastating portraits of Lee and Paula Strasberg, with Lee arriving on location in a shiny new pair of cowboy boots.

The producers invited me to the Chicago premiere in October and asked for my outspoken opinion. I was then seated directly behind Arthur Miller. Giving my opinion was no problem, as I absolutely loved the play. At intermission I circled around to Arthur and told him I thought it was great. "Yeah," he grinned, "I'm enjoying it myself."

As I headed to the opening night party with David and the Marshalls, I was looking forward to a continuation of my recent lucky streak with *Long Day's Journey* and *The Boy from Oz*. But we had barely sat down when Tony Marshall declared, "The play is injurious to the memory of Marilyn Monroe, and I want nothing to do with it." David had read the play, the Marshalls had not.

The next day, the critics had a similar response. Being used to hearing people tell their stories honestly in my recovery program, I found Miller's approach to be forthright and nonjudgmental. But Monroe is loved and revered by the public, and there is no doubt that those reviews would have kept them away. In my mind, *Finishing the Picture* is a great, valuable, and highly entertaining document, and I hope one day it will be given the production and the consideration it deserves.

Returning to New York, we launched into the London production of Delphi's revival of *Death of a Salesman*, which was to open at the Lyric on the West End in May of 2005. I dealt with contracts and arrangements for the Americans involved, including Brian Dennehy in his London debut repeating his Tony Award-winning Broadway performance as Willy Loman.

Things were all very straightforward until the price tag for building the complicated turntable set in the UK sent the production costs sky high. The producers were faced with the prospect of canceling unless the author, director, and other royalty participants joined them in dramatically reducing their weekly payments, making it possible to at least break even.

I was asked to ride in on the white horse and make that happen. On February 7, Arthur Miller, through his agent Sam Cohn, agreed to my proposal that the aggregate of the total weekly royalties be capped at 10 percent of the box office gross until recoupment. George Lane, on behalf of the director Robert Falls, would not agree. Four days later, Arthur Miller was dead. George Lane called me that morning and said, "It's a dark day; let's close this." I thought to myself, *I now know what it takes to close a deal with George Lane.*

In the meantime, work had begun on Jeffrey Richards' revival of David Mamet's *Glengarry Glen Ross* which would, indeed, continue my lucky streak. For openers, it was to be directed by Joe Mantello, assuredly among the top two or three directors on Broadway. It had a top-notch cast that included Alan Alda, Liev Schreiber, Gordon Clapp, Jeffrey Tambor, Frederick Weller, Jordan Lage, and Tom Wopat.

Early in rehearsal, Mantello and Mamet got into a tug of war over the issue of sound. Mantello wanted subtle micing and a spare use of incidental music. Mamet had boilerplate in his contracts prohibiting sound of any kind. Going on the Internet, Mantello discovered that the current London production of Mamet's *A Life in the Theatre* had a sound designer credit and immediately cited it to Mamet in an email. This was news to Mamet, and his lawyers notified the London production to remove the offending sound forthwith.

Things reached a critical stage at dress rehearsal as we sat there and heard actors clunking on and off the wagons (platforms on wheels which were used in the Chinese restaurant in Scene One) and the rolling sound as the wagons were moved on and off stage. Mantello got up out of his seat and said, "I don't want my name on this."

Jeffrey Richards and I had a quick conference, and the next day we called in Peter Fitzgerald, who provided what Joe Mantello called a "room tone" as the set and actors went on and off, and subtle micing that was a natural enhancement to the actors' presence without sounding amplified. Both effects were successful, but our greatest concern was opening night, when Mamet would see and hear it for the first time. There was no credit or bio for sound design in the playbill.

Remembering when Mamet heckled the critic John Simon at the opening night of *A Life in the Theatre*, I did have concern about what he might do. But what we had done was right and necessary for the production of his play. Worried that he might throw a temper tantrum or walk out, I sat him next to Steve Martin, which I hoped might provide some incentive for good behavior.

The opening night was as perfect an opening night performance as I have ever seen. David Mamet was elated. And there was no mention of sound. I was surrounded by dear friends at Sardi's when Steve Martin came over to our table and said, "I'm jealous. I want you back."

"Write a play," I said, "and I will be there in a flash."

Once again, the reviews were spectacular with the critics calling it a "high octane revival" with a "dream-team ensemble," "pitch perfect," "American theater at its finest," and "a land-office hit."

Two days later, I paid a very special visit to Betty Jacobs, to present her with a window card of *Glengarry Glen Ross*, the first commemorating the name change of the Royale Theatre on May 10 to the Bernard B. Jacobs Theatre in honor of her late and revered husband. This name change and renaming the Plymouth to the Gerald Schoenfeld were widely controversial. Many contended that Albee, Miller, Williams, and others should have been first in line for this honor.

As time goes by, history will show that the vision of these men and their ability to bring about change in the theater and in the Times Square area had not only saved Broadway but saved the city of New York, both of which were at the edge of the abyss when Schoenfeld and Jacobs came to power. I did, however, have a chuckle at the Frankie and Johnnie Broadway steakhouse after the ceremony. Morley Safer was at the next table with Ron and Isobel Robins Konecky. Across the street, the marquee lights for the Schoenfeld lit up for the first time, and Safer quipped, "Shoulda' called it 'The Jerry.' Woulda saved electricity."

Glengarry was nominated for six Tony Awards and took home Best Play Revival and Best Featured Actor for Liev's portrayal of Richard Roma. I had been thanked by my producers when *The Grapes of Wrath* and *The Last Night of Ballyhoo* won awards. Irene Gandy, Jeffrey's inimitable associate, came to me prior to the ceremony and whispered, "Jeffrey told me to tell you that if we win, he's not going to thank you. He's going to say things that he hopes will sell tickets." What a nice detail, I thought, of the new style of producing.

Jeffrey arranged for a real estate broker from Long Island to conduct an audience seminar onstage with some of the actors after one of the Wednesday matinees. I shuddered and sadistically suggested to Jeffrey that if we were putting the actors out there, he should take stage with them. He did and afterward made a point of telling me it was the most excruciating afternoon of his life.

When it came time for Liev Schreiber to leave the show, there was a movement afoot among the eleven producers to replace him with Donald Trump. It took me about four days to talk them out of it. Hope Schneider, who was my house guest at the time, listened in disbelief. "Is this what you *do*?" she said . . .

CHAPTER 44

Home Stretch

Jeffrey Richards had intended to produce Pinter's *The Homecoming* in the fall of 2005, but when Todd Haimes, for whom he had great regard, announced he was contemplating doing Pinter's *Old Times* at the Roundabout, Jeffrey put *The Homecoming* on hold, leaving me without a job. I took a loan to keep my office afloat. Jeffrey was now the only one hiring me. In an earlier, flusher time, I had opted out of two of his productions, establishing a precedent that we wouldn't work together on every show.

I was feeling diminished in any number of ways. For all its rewards, *The Boy from Oz* was also a year of constant stress, and I had never quite recouped my strength after my illness. In Jeffrey's productions, my role as general manager was evolving in a way I did not enjoy. I was now a voice on a committee, all of whom had to be heard from in the tiresome democratic process that producing had become. I was a born autocrat who liked vigorous collaboration with one or two real producers. I hated committees.

The rewarding of investment with billing and input combined with a newly relaxed approach to negotiating deals made it possible for things to move faster. As Jeffrey's output increased, it had the feeling of assembly-line producing. The checkbook producers didn't know what things should cost and did not care. And the new theater market was a worldwide moneyed group willing to pay any price for their tickets. The once-cherished theater audience had been priced out and was long gone.

All of this was against my grain, and Jeffrey noted it. "You seem angry," he said. "The business has changed, Albert."

The business had indeed changed, and I found myself innately resisting it. I liked the investors to be investors, and I prided myself on delivering tight deals for my producers. During my long career, I had reinvented myself several times. I had no interest in reinventing myself as an adding machine.

I told Jerry Schoenfeld I was contemplating leaving the business. "Why?" he asked. "I'm opinionated and outspoken, and I think that kind of management has gone out of style."

"Well, why don't you just stop it and shut up?" he suggested. I told him I didn't think that was very possible, and he responded, "You can't tell producers what you think in public."

"Do you consider production meetings to be public?" I asked. "I do now," he replied.

Jeffrey's next production, for the spring of 2006, was a revival of *The Caine Mutiny Court-Martial* directed by Jerry Zaks. One critic called it "eye glazing." It closed after seventeen performances.

It was nearly a year before I had my next two shows. *Bill W. and Dr. Bob*, an Off Broadway play about the founding of Alcoholics Anonymous, and *Talk Radio*, a Robert Falls-directed Broadway revival of the Eric Bogosian piece as a tour de force for Liev Schreiber.

Bill W. had earlier occasioned my last memorable exchange with Lucille Lortel. We did a reading in her Sherry Netherland suite that landed with a dull thud. Undaunted, I knelt down beside her and said, "Lucille, this play means a great deal to me." "Well," she said, "it means absolutely nothing to me, dear."

She died two weeks later. She was ninety-eight years old and an indelible part of the history of Off Broadway and of my own life in the theater.

When I began preparing the budgets for *Bill W.*, I realized I hadn't done an Off Broadway show for six years. Wanting to be current, I called the young producer/general manager of the newest Off Broadway hit and asked if he would share his budgets with me. He would. For $500. I was accustomed to a community where this would have been a gesture of goodwill. But feeling it necessary, I paid for it out of my own pocket. When the fax arrived, there were sections that were illegible. "I'm not sending it again," he told me when I called to complain.

No longer enjoying what the process had become and disdaining its participants, I decided that *The Homecoming* would be my swansong. It was, at last, on the docket for the fall of 2007. I liked the idea of my last show being called *The Homecoming*. Harold Pinter had, two years earlier, won the Nobel Prize for his body of work. It would be a prestigious end to my forty-three years.

Daniel Sullivan would direct a first-rate cast that included Ian McShane, Raul Esparza, Eve Best, James Frain, and Michael McKean. Eugene Lee, one of the reigning geniuses of Broadway, not to mention *Saturday Night Live*, would design the set. As we began rehearsals, Neil Mazzella, who now had a hand in nearly every show on Broadway and had become my resident technical supervisor, was presented a special Tony Honor for Excellence. When he presented the award to Neil, his good friend and veteran producer Emmanuel Azenberg spoke for all of us when he said, "Neil was always there . . ."

The checkbook producers considered "marketing" to be their area of expertise. They could talk about it for hours, and this group of eighteen believed that *The Homecoming* would be best served by a graphic that sold sex. A rendering of a woman lying on her back, knees up and crossed, a sheet draped around her naked thighs, was selected. A disgusting way to sell Pinter, I thought, but knowing I didn't stand a chance against the will of the group, I tried another tack.

"Pinter doesn't have contractual approval," I said, "but I think we would be well served to FedEx the artwork to him so he doesn't see it for the first time in the paper." The producers agreed. Pinter responded with a scathing email, and the artwork was modified.

Harold Pinter wanted desperately to attend the opening, but his health precluded it. As he was with all of his authors, Jeffrey was very caring of him and in constant touch throughout the production.

Our director Dan Sullivan delivered a stellar production, and Ben Brantley in the *Times* gave us the review of our dreams. "First of all," Brantley began, "it really is that good. You would expect it to have shrunk over the years, the way buildings that loomed large in your childhood seem smaller when you revisit them. But as the first-rate revival that opened Sunday night at the Cort Theater makes electrifyingly clear, 'The Homecoming' is every bit as big as its reputation."[13]

There was little audience interest in *The Homecoming*, and it closed on April 13 after 137 performances.

Jeffrey Richards went on to produce nearly forty shows in the decade that followed, including the spectacularly successful Steppenwolf production of *August: Osage County,* a Tony-winning revival of *The Gershwins' Porgy and Bess,* and a handful of David Mamet originals and revivals—to mixed results.

As for me, I kicked open the exit door and got out.

My career had given me the most exciting and meaningful life I could imagine, and I felt like leaving was as natural as any other part of it. It wasn't the best or the worst career, but it was mine. I knew the people I wanted to know. I did the shows I wanted to do. I now accepted that the theater and I had changed.

Perhaps as a result of my twenty years of sobriety, arguing and negotiation, once the core of my management style, were no longer a desired part of my daily menu. And the banality of marketing-related nonsense like whether or not we should pass out buttons that said, "Did she or didn't she?" didn't hold the same fascination as vigorous debates over the set budget or impassioned discussions of the first quote ad. It was time to move on.

The hits had contained their own small failures and disappointments, and the failures their small successes. At the end of the day, it was the joy of the process with its collaborative, combative camaraderie that had so vigorously engaged my passion for forty-three years. The process and the people of the process.

To those of you who are considering a career in the theater, I would offer the simple words that were first said to me so many years ago.

It's a tough business, darling. But it can be good to you.

Acknowledgments

I must start by gratefully acknowledging the formative influence that my first two friends—Dennis Leibowitz and Victor Rosenbaum—have had on my life. We have been friends since the age of six, and they were with me on this book—seventy-two years later.

A special thank you to my distinguished colleague, Patrick Herold, who was the first champion of the book. Patrick is revered and respected in our industry, and he is the first person I gave it to. His response and support have been very sustaining throughout.

Thanks to Victoria Traube for first suggesting that if I struck out with publishers, I should consider self-publishing (which I have done) and do a fundraising effort on Kickstarter. Thanks to all who supported me in that successful endeavor.

A special shout out to the inimitable Michael Riedel for his invaluable wisdom and assistance in preparing this book and for his splendid Foreword—much appreciated.

Thanks for help along the way from dear friends and colleagues Dessie Moyihan, Peter Schneider, Jane Harmon, Max and Helen Jacobs, Bill Evans, Joseph P. Benincasa, Tom Viola, Heather Hitchens, Arthur Makar, Buzz Stephens, Kyle Renick, Neil J. Rosini, Daniel M. Wasser,

Matt Goldman, Milton Justice, Susan Haskins-Doloff, Tom Langdon, Robert LoBiondo, Susan Dalsimer, Edward G. Carmines for the Estate of Al Carmines, Martha Wade Steketee, Stephen Eich, Malcolm Ewen, Judi Davidson, Earl Wilson, Jr., John Glines, Stevie Phillips, Angelina Fiordellisi, Valentina Fratti, and Jennifer Conn-Bonnar. And special thanks to my to my beloved cousin Maynard Poland, whose editing help took the book further than it could have ever been without him.

Thanks to all of the splendid theatre photographers for their permissions in helping to document *STAGES* with glorious photos: Anita and Steve Shevett, Peter Cunningham, Joan Marcus, Carol Rosegg, Cathy Blaivas, Michael McKenzie, Estate of Doug McKenzie, NY Public Library for Martha Swope, Actors Fund, BC/EFA, Lou Manna, Neil Stern for the Estate of Hale Haberman, Jean Dalric, Eileen F. Haggerty, Barbara Y.E. Pyle, Lee Salem, Kyle Renick, Robyn Taylor Barbon. Daniel Nicoletta, Everett Quinton for the Estate of Charles Ludlam, William Lauch. Brian Abel, Estate of Avital D'Lugoff, Lael Jacobs, Rebecca Schneider, Anthony Reyes, and David "Squid" Quinn.

Special thanks and gratitude to Barbara Hogenson, my friend and agent, whom I first encountered when she represented Uta Hagen on *Mrs. Klein*. Her belief in the book and her savvy, grace, and class are exactly what I wanted.

Lastly, a huge heartfelt thank you and hug to all the people of my career. You were people of real character, and I couldn't have loved it more.

Endnotes

1. From *The New York Times*. © 1968, *The New York Times*. All rights reserved. Used under license. Visit https://www.nytimes.com/.
2. From *The New York Times*. © 1981, *The New York Times*. All rights reserved. Used under license.
3. From *The New York Times*. © 1985, *The New York Times*. All rights reserved. Used under license.
4. From *The New York Times*. © 1990, *The New York Times*. All rights reserved. Used under license.
5. From *The New York Times*. © 1990, *The New York Times*. All rights reserved. Used under license.
6. From *The New York Times*. © 1993, *The New York Times*. All rights reserved. Used under license.
7. From *The New York Times*. © 1995, *The New York Times*. All rights reserved. Used under license.
8. From *The New York Times*. © 1996, *The New York Times*. All rights reserved. Used under license.
9. From *The New York Times*. © 1997, *The New York Times*. All rights reserved. Used under license.
10. From *The New York Times*. © 1998, *The New York Times*. All rights reserved. Used under license.
11. From *The New York Times*. © 2001, *The New York Times*. All rights reserved. Used under license.
12. From *The New York Times*. © 2003, *The New York Times*. All rights reserved. Used under license.
13. From *The New York Times*. © 2007, *The New York Times*. All rights reserved. Used under license.

Index

About the Author

*L*egendary Producer and
General Manager Albert
Poland's work has spanned the
dawn of Off Broadway to the
Broadway blockbusters of the
1980s and 1990s and beyond.
He worked with them all, from
an unknown Sam Shepard and
David Mamet to Edward Albee
and Arthur Miller. He was also
the founder of the Judy Garland

Jackie Rudin

Fan Club as a young teen. *STAGES—a theater memoir* is more than
an insider's view of his many major productions, although there
is plenty of that, from *The Fantasticks* and *Little Shop of Horrors*
to *Long Day's Journey into Night* and from *The Grapes of Wrath* to
The Boy from Oz. Witty, colorful, unconventional, and wickedly
insightful, Poland has had a career that comprises a fascinating
portrait of the social and cultural landscape of New York, from the
60s to the present, seen through the lens of a life in the theater (and
yes, he managed the play with that title). You will get intimate and

personal views of such stars as Judy Garland, Bette Davis, Hugh Jackman, Vanessa Redgrave, Truman Capote, and Liza Minnelli, as well as such theatrical titans as Cameron Mackintosh, Bernard B. Jacobs, Gerald Schoenfeld, and Ellen Stewart. Poland is the co-author/editor of *The Off Off Broadway Book*, and is a principal player in Michael Riedel's best-seller *Razzle Dazzle: The Battle for Broadway*. In June of 2019, The Off Broadway Alliance presented Albert Poland with a Legend of Off Broadway Award.

Made in the
USA
Middletown, DE